Science Fiction
from Québec

CRITICAL EXPLORATIONS IN SCIENCE FICTION AND FANTASY
(a series edited by Donald E. Palumbo and C.W. Sullivan III)

1. *Worlds Apart? Dualism and Transgression in Contemporary Female Dystopias* (Dunja M. Mohr, 2005)

2. *Tolkien and Shakespeare: Essays on Shared Themes and Language* (edited by Janet Brennan Croft, 2007)

3. *Culture, Identities and Technology in the Star Wars Films: Essays on the Two Trilogies* (edited by Carl Silvio and Tony M. Vinci, 2007)

4. *The Influence of Star Trek on Television, Film and Culture* (edited by Lincoln Geraghty, 2008)

5. *Hugo Gernsback and the Century of Science Fiction* (Gary Westfahl, 2007)

6. *One Earth, One People: The Mythopoeic Fantasy Series of Ursula K. Le Guin, Lloyd Alexander, Madeleine L'Engle and Orson Scott Card* (Marek Oziewicz, 2008)

7. *The Evolution of Tolkien's Mythology: A Study of the History of Middle-earth* (Elizabeth A. Whittingham, 2008)

8. *H. Beam Piper: A Biography* (John F. Carr, 2008)

9. *Dreams and Nightmares: Science and Technology in Myth and Fiction* (Mordecai Roshwald, 2008)

10. *Lilith in a New Light: Essays on the George MacDonald Fantasy Novel* (edited by Lucas H. Harriman, 2008)

11. *Feminist Narrative and the Supernatural: The Function of Fantastic Devices in Seven Recent Novels* (Katherine J. Weese, 2008)

12. *The Science of Fiction and the Fiction of Science: Collected Essays on SF Storytelling and the Gnostic Imagination* (Frank McConnell, edited by Gary Westfahl, 2009)

13. *Kim Stanley Robinson Maps the Unimaginable: Critical Essays* (edited by William J. Burling, 2009)

14. *The Inter-Galactic Playground: A Critical Study of Children's and Teens' Science Fiction* (Farah Mendlesohn, 2009)

15. *Science Fiction from Québec: A Postcolonial Study* (Amy J. Ransom, 2009)

16. *Science Fiction and the Two Cultures: Essays on Bridging the Gap Between the Sciences and the Humanities* (edited by Gary Westfahl and George Slusser, 2009)

17. *Stephen R. Donaldson and the Modern Epic Vision: A Critical Study of the "Chronicles of Thomas Covenant" Novels* (Christine Barkley, 2009)

Science Fiction from Québec

A Postcolonial Study

AMY J. RANSOM

CRITICAL EXPLORATIONS IN
SCIENCE FICTION AND FANTASY, 15
Donald E. Palumbo *and* C.W. Sullivan III, *series editors*

McFarland & Company, Inc., Publishers
Jefferson, North Carolina, and London

Excerpts from Jacques E. Brossard, *L'Oiseau de feu*, © 1989, 1990, 1993, 1995 and 1997 by Leméac Éditeur, Inc., are reprinted by permission.

Excerpts from *L'Aigle des profondeurs, Le Rêveur dans la Citadelle, L'Archipel noir, Aboli, Ouverture, Or, Secrets* and *Sorbier* by Esther Rochon are reprinted by permission of Éditions Alire.

Excerpts from *Tyranaël 1— Les Rêves de la mer, Tyranaël 2— Le Jeu de la perfection, Tyranaël 3 — Mon frère l'ombre, Tyranaël 4 — L'Autre ravage* and *Tyranaël 5 — La Mer allée avec le soleil* by Élisabeth Vonarburg are reprinted by permission of Éditions Alire.

LIBRARY OF CONGRESS CATALOGUING-IN-PUBLICATION DATA

Ransom, Amy J., 1964–
    Science fiction from Québec : a postcolonial study / Amy J. Ransom.
        p. cm. — (Critical explorations in science fiction and fantasy ; 15)
    Includes bibliographical references and index.

    ISBN 978-0-7864-3824-2
    softcover : 50# alkaline paper ∞

    1. Science fiction, French-Canadian — Québec (Province) — History and criticism.   2. Colonies in literature.   3. Postcolonialism in literature.   4. Utopias in literature.   5. Cultural fusion in literature.   6. Cultural pluralism in literature.   I. Title.
    PQ3912.R36   2009
    843'.08762099714 — dc22   2009009471

British Library cataloguing data are available

©2009 Amy J. Ransom. All rights reserved

No part of this book may be reproduced or transmitted in any form or by any means, electronic or mechanical, including photocopying or recording, or by any information storage and retrieval system, without permission in writing from the publisher.

Cover image ©2009 Shutterstock

Manufactured in the United States of America

McFarland & Company, Inc., Publishers
  Box 611, Jefferson, North Carolina 28640
    www.mcfarlandpub.com

For Dana and Richard

Contents

Preface and Acknowledgments 1

INTRODUCTION. Articulations: Québec, Science Fiction, and the Postcolonial 5
ONE. SFQ: History and Themes 33
TWO. Alien Nations: Dominance and Oppression in the SFQ Saga 60
THREE. Utopia and New World Myth in Québec's Science-Fiction Sagas 118
FOUR. *Logiques métisses*: Hybridity and Transculturalism 182
CONCLUSION 210

Appendix: A Selected Bibliography of French-Canadian Science Fiction and Fantasy in English 213
Chapter Notes 223
Works Cited — Primary Sources 235
Works Cited — Secondary Sources 243
Index 257

Preface and Acknowledgments

A growing number of writers from minority communities in the West and from the so-called Third World have begun to experiment with the tropes of science fiction (SF), exploring their usefulness for expressing postcolonial concerns. Similarly, while it has been somewhat slow in growing, a critical mass of analysis has come to form a body of work which applies postcolonial theories to science fiction from both the center of the SF empire (the U.S. and U.K.), as well as its periphery. This book examines how one doubly peripheral group, the French-speaking writers of SF in Canada, has begun to articulate this nascent entity that is postcolonial science fiction. For, Québec's dynamic, yet little-known science fiction (SFQ) provides a corpus of literature that fits into, yet stretches, the molds of both science fiction and the postcolonial.

The discourse of decolonization articulated by Frantz Fanon became the foundation for critics like Homi K. Bhabha and Gayatri Chakravorty Spivak who propose strategies for reading literature as either underpinning the ideology of Western imperialist civilization or as resisting it. Such "postcolonial" criticism typically focuses on either exposing the discourse of imperialism within works of the Western literary canon (as does Edward Said's seminal study for the field, *Orientalism* [1978]) or identifying aspects of Third World or minority literatures outside the canon that respond to or resist it.

This study steps somewhat outside the bounds set by orthodox postcolonial criticism, applying its terms and concepts to a literary form that remains at the margins of the Western canon — namely, science fiction — produced in a territory at the edges of what might rightly be termed postcolonial — that is, Québec. My goal is to reveal how SF from Québec depicts the colonial saga, from the moment of first contact through exploration, conquest, resistance, and liberation, as well as the postcolonial crises of nationhood and identity, in a manner that resists the hegemony of Western ideologies. Rather, SFQ opts to participate in a reconstruction of the world that recognizes difference and rejects hierarchical binaries such as center and periphery, reason and imagination, alien and native, savage and civilized, self and other.

The works discussed in this book implement the trope of the alien nation, obviously derived from the conventions of science fiction. This image also points to key concepts in theories of decolonization and postcolonialism: alienation, foreignness and the idea of a lost or new home territory. It recalls the application of works like Fanon's *Black Skin, White Masks* (1952) to the Québec-in-development by the province's own writers and intellectuals who argued that French-Canadian society evidenced at that time an alienation similar to that observed in other colonized and decolonizing nations and regions like Algeria and the Antilles. Significantly, to enhance his explication of the condition of alienation that occurs when one has black skin, but is forced to wear a white mask in order to fit into the social order, Fanon himself evokes an SF trope by asking readers to imagine their response if Martians came to colonize Earth (*Black* 95). He also argues that hope for decolonization comes from looking no longer to a past and present as determinant of the black subject's alien or other status in the system of the colonized world, but in looking to the future (*Black* 226). This intersection between decolonizing the mind and looking toward a postcolonial future demonstrates precisely the usefulness and pertinence of SF to postcolonial theory. Québec's own view of itself as an "alien nation" during the period immediately prior to its development of an active SF movement appears most clearly in Pierre Vallières's nod to Fanon's influence in the title of his manifesto for Québec's "decolonization," *White Niggers of America* (1968).

This book contributes not only to the discipline of Québec studies but also to the fields of SF theory and postcolonial criticism. As we shall see, while many have argued that SF is an imperialist-colonialist discourse — one of the reasons why it has taken so long for scholars to recognize the relationships between SF and postcolonial theory — the ability of SF to create subversive, resistant discourses will become apparent through readings of SFQ texts. At the same time, critics have resisted, for a number of reasons, applying the label SF to postcolonial writing that expresses one or more of its generic traits or exploits its tropes. Indeed, while Spivak's more recent landmark, *A Critique of Postcolonial Reason* (1999), reads Mary Shelley's *Frankenstein* (1818) in tandem with Mahasweta Devi's "Pterodactyl, Puran Sahay, and Pirtha" (1994) it skirts the question of genre for the former and outright denies its applicability to the latter. Spivak's analysis implies that Shelley's romance — a work often cited as the first modern SF novel — represents a proto-postcolonial work in its resistance to the reinscription of the Other in support of an image of England inseparable from its Empire (the project of much of nineteenth- and early twentieth-century British literature according to critics like Spivak, Said and Bhabha). Then, she posits Devi's novella, a non–English text by a Bengali writer, as a prime example of postcolonial discourse, making sure to qualify its depiction of an aboriginal Indian boy's discovery of a pterodactyl as "not science fiction" (*Critique* 145).

Spivak's assertion arises from the context of arguments that postcolonial literatures seek to escape the potential boundaries imposed by the generic labels of Western criticism. From this context, one might also object that Québec's literature should not be properly called postcolonial since it comes from the First-World, fully Westernized nation of Canada. Foreseeing these objections, the book's introduction examines critically the "Articulations" between the poles of science fiction, Québec and the postcolonial. Those readers less concerned with theoretical background and more interested in an overview of SF in Québec may wish to turn directly to chapter one, "SFQ: History and Themes." In addition to a brief history of SFQ and a discussion of its own sense of self-definition, I include an overview of a significant number of texts, including those available in English, to demonstrate the prevalence of themes typical of postcolonial literatures in the SFQ corpus. Subsequent chapters focus more specifically on how several multi-volume sagas published from the 1980s into the first years of the new millenium develop those themes. These texts have been chosen both for their significance within the SFQ canon and for their depiction of the colonial saga and its aftermath. Chapters two through four each introduce a specific issue (alienation, utopia/dystopia, hybridity/multiculturalism, respectively), discussing its conception in the work of one or more postcolonial critics, and then offer a close analysis of the issue as it appears in landmark works of SFQ: Esther Rochon's *Le Cycle de Vrénalik* and *Les Chroniques infernales*, Jacques Brossard's *L'Oiseau de feu*, and Élisabeth Vonarburg's two pentalogies, *Tyranaël* and *Reine de Mémoire*. Because of the breadth of their scope — they depict the entire epic of colonialism, from points of discovery and encounter, to colonization, to resistance of the colonized against colonial oppression, and, finally, how those liberated intend to create their utopian new worlds — these works demonstrate clearly SFQ's potential as a resistant, postcolonial discourse.

The second chapter, "Alien Nations: Dominance and Oppression in the SFQ Saga," examines the images of oppressed, alienated peoples and nations found in three of the SFQ epics mentioned above. Chapter three, "Utopia and New World Myth in Québec's Science-Fiction Sagas," discusses how all five of these works bring to bear the tools of the literary utopia in their depictions of new world colonies, working toward what Ralph Pordzik terms the "postcolonial utopia." The fourth and concluding chapter, "*Logiques métisses*: Hybridity and Transculturalism" focuses on how these texts by Brossard, Rochon and Vonarburg propose to resolve the tensions that result when multiple groups occupy the same territory, bringing together the strands of the close analyses of the thematics of the SFQ saga to examine its status as a truly postcolonial discourse.

This project would not have been possible without the assistance of numerous individuals who have contributed to my knowledge of the fields of

Québec's history, culture and, more specifically, science fiction and fantasy literature. First and foremost, I would like to thank the writers and publishers of SFQ whose accessibility allowed me to clarify numerous points and, really, inspired me to undertake this project. Some dozen years ago I contacted Francine Pelletier about my entry on her for the *Dictionary of Literary Biography* volume on *Canadian Science Fiction and Fantasy Writers*, thus embarking on this journey in space and time. An invitation from Jean-Louis Trudel to attend the annual Congrès Boréal, offered to help me find books by René Beaulieu, Élisabeth Vonarburg's translation of my first article on SFQ, interviews with Joël Champetier and Patrick Senécal, a request from Claude Janelle to serve on the jury for the Grand Prix de la science-fiction et du fantastique québécois, and the kind assistance of Pierre Filion at Éditions Leméac and Jean Pettigrew and Louise Alain with Éditions Alire, all advanced me along on its trajectory. In addition, I want to thank the sympathetic yet critical colleagues who read versions of this manuscript along the way: Neal Baker, Sophie Beaulé, Caroline-Isabelle Caron, Veronica Hollinger, and Nicholas Serruys. Besides people, I had two institutions behind me, providing support. I would like to acknowledge the assistance of Anna Maria College for a sabbatical leave and the College of Behavioral and Social Sciences at Central Michigan University for a summer stipend grant. Both schools also supported frequent conference trips where I could network and get feedback on some of the ideas expressed here, as well as excellent library staff to help me obtain materials. Alice Baron and Ruth Pyne deserve special kudos for bringing the interlibrary loan system at Mondor Eagan Library out of the dark ages of carbon-copy typed forms and into the twenty-first century. Finally, I wish to thank my family. My parents' and sister's unconditional love and support carried me through a long educational process. My son Richard's patience while "mommy just finishes working on this" has been inspiring; I hope his fascination with the cover illustrations of my collection of *Solaris* and Éditions Alire novels marks a sign of future interest in genre literatures. I offer thanks also to Dana Aspinall, for his long-suffering support and for setting this whole process in motion by showing me a call for papers over a decade ago. Since then, it's been a trip!

Introduction

Articulations: Québec, Science Fiction and the Postcolonial

> *I think thirty years ago if you wanted to discuss a general theme you would go to the historical novel; now you would go to what I might describe in a prejudiced way as science fiction. In science fiction you can isolate the factors you want to examine. If you wanted to deal with the theme of colonialism ... you don't do it by writing a novel about Ghana or Pakistan.... You set up worlds in space which incorporate the characteristics you need.*
> — Kingsley Amis to C. S. Lewis and
> Brian W. Aldiss [Lewis 92]

The significance of science fiction as a privileged form of discourse for social observation and criticism has become a commonplace since Kingsley Amis' conversation, cited in epigraph, with C. S. Lewis and Brian W. Aldiss some decades ago. Although its relationship with colonialism-imperialism[1] would appear obvious to even the most superficial consumer of the genre, Amis' example of colonialism as a theme pertinent to just such a socially aware SF, on the other hand, has gone surprisingly unnoticed by critics and theorists. One reason may be that while the exploration of space and the colonization of other worlds remain two of its most popular and perhaps most definitive themes, there is a perception that SF explores those themes from an uncritical, even pro-colonial political position. Even if that were the case, as it has been argued, analysis and deconstruction of SF's colonialist paradigms would represent nonetheless an appropriate task for postcolonial criticism.

In this study, however, I take a step further and shift the focus of inquiry from the identification of colonialist discourse to the qualification of certain types of discourse within SF as postcolonial. That is, rather than reading SF in order to identify its tendencies as imperialist-colonialist fantasy, tendencies still clearly found in its less sophisticated film, television and pulp fiction manifestations, which often draw upon somewhat outdated models,[2] I look at the potential for reading contemporary iterations of the genre as postcolonial discourse. That Bill Ashcroft, Gareth Griffiths and Helen Tiffin took inspiration from a well-known science-fictional film for the title of their pathbreaking study, *The Empire Writes Back* (1989), is not insignificant. For science fiction began reinventing itself in the 1960s precisely when the breakdown of the former empires and the dawn of the era of independence redrew the world map. At the same time, Canada's majority French-speaking province of Québec discovered science fiction's potential as a vehicle for the investigation of contemporary issues. Although more closely linked to the dominant Anglo-American SF than to other writers more commonly identified as postcolonial, Québec's francophone writers nonetheless view their position as that of a minority. Jean Pettigrew, head of the province's most successful publisher of genre literature, Éditions Alire, expresses this stance clearly:

> la SFQ ... est écrite par des hommes et des femmes issus de cultures nettement minoritaires (québécoise, mais aussi acadienne, franco-ontarienne/manitobaine, etc.) tant au Canada que dans la très anglosaxonne Amérique du Nord. Or, tant la science-fiction européenne qu'étatsunienne est, au contraire, écrite soit par des gens issus de peuple souverain, aussi petit soit-il, soit par les représentants de la culture qui domine pour l'instant la planète. Évidemment, cette "condition précaire" teinte particulièrement l'imaginaire [Dupuis 166].
>
> SFQ is written by men and women issuing from cultures (Québécois, but also Acadian, Franco-Ontarian/Manitoban, etc.) clearly in minority as much in Canada as in the very Anglo-Saxon North America. European or U.S. science fiction is, on the contrary, written either by individuals deriving from sovereign groups, however small they may be, or by the representatives of the culture that for the moment dominates the planet. Evidently, this "precarious condition" particularly taints the imagination.[3]

Pettigrew clearly stakes a claim to a minority position, one easily aligned with that of postcolonial writers.

Conversely, critics, like Homi K. Bhabha, speak of postcolonial literatures using terms that resonate clearly for those familiar with theories of SF and related genres of fantasy/the fantastic[4]:

> Being in the "beyond," then, is to inhabit an intervening space.... But to dwell "in the beyond" is also ... to be part of a revisionary time, a return to the present to redescribe our cultural contemporaneity; to reinscribe our human, historic commonality; *to touch the future on its hither side.* In that sense, then, the intervening space "beyond," becomes a space of intervention in the here and now.... The negating activity is, indeed, the intervention of the "beyond" that establishes a boundary: a bridge, where "presencing" begins because it captures something of the estranging sense of the relocation of the home and the world — the unhomeliness — that is the condition of extra-territorial and cross-cultural initiations [7 and 9; original emphasis].

This space "beyond" linked by Bhabha to the postcolonial, with its aim of touching the future, parallels the project of SF, in its creation of other spaces, the *ailleurs* (elsewhere) so frequently found in the science fiction of Québec, and in its projection of what the future might hold in the interest of intervening in the here and now. Bhabha invokes not only Freud's *The Uncanny* (1919), translating *das Unheimliche* literally as "the unhomely," to describe the estrangement of humanity in the colonial condition (42), but also Bertolt Brecht's Marxist-derived *Verfremdungseffekt* (strangeness effect) which provided the basis for SF theories like that outlined in Darko Suvin's *Metamorphoses of Science Fiction* (1979).

Significantly two critics from Québec, Marc Angenot ("Absent") and Jean-Marc Gouanvic ("Figures"), each in their own way, theorize SF as a literature of alterity. Postcolonial criticism shares a central preoccupation with representations of the other and otherness, along with the other's articulation of itself. When Edward Said speaks of the colonizer's often drastic effect on territory (*Culture* 225), the SF reader immediately thinks of its extrapolated equivalent, terraforming. The linguistic strategies identified by Ashcroft, Griffiths and Tiffin in *The Empire Writes Back* as typical of writers who must describe a culture often foreign to readers parallel those used by writers of SF as they describe alien and/or future cultures constructed in their own imaginations: untranslated words (52), neologism (72), glossing (56–57) and cultural allusion (58–59). Despite these obvious resonances, while several critics, most notably Stephen Slemon ("Magic"), have examined elements of magic realism in postcolonial literature, few have been willing to see the evident connections between the postcolonial and the science fictional.

A survey of the literature, undertaken in the second section of this introduction, reveals the newly budding relationship between SF and postcolonial theory in the new millenium. Patricia Kerslake's *Science Fiction and Empire* (2007), which claims to be the first book-length study of that interface, "explores experiments in the practice of power and empire in SF as it connects the imperial project from our past with the potential neo-empires of our future" (3). It focuses, however, on the Anglo-American canon and on the imperialist perspective. Ralph Pordzik's *Quest for Postcolonial Utopia* (2001), an excursion into a territory that closely intersects with that of SF, looks at English-language texts from outside the U.S. and the U.K., reflecting a goal much closer to my own project.

One of the difficulties in reading even the most sophisticated contemporary Anglo-American science fiction as postcolonial discourse lies in the ineluctable fact that although they are not, or no longer are, official political empires, the United States and Great Britain continue to stand in hegemonic, neo-imperial relationships with the rest of the world because of the dominance of the English language in commercial exchange and cultural production. In contrast, Québec offers something closer to a corpus of "authentically"—in scare quotes to signal the problematic nature of this term—postcolonial SF because of its unique colonial and post-colonial history, including its explicit self-alignment with decolonizing nations during the 1960s. Furthermore, although a growing body of French-Canadian SF has been made available through translation to the English-speaking public, no existing study has presented the case for the significance of the science-fiction of Québec (SFQ)[5] to the extent that this one does. Ultimately, it argues, echoing Jean Pettigrew's sentiment, that much of SFQ (like many postcolonial literatures) views its project as that of articulating the position of the Other, of asserting its difference from its own Others, which Richard Handler identifies as "[t]hese incarnations of 'not-Quebec'": France, Great Britain, English Canada and the United States (47).

This introduction articulates the relationships between the three poles of inquiry that concern us: Québec, science fiction and the postcolonial.[6] Targeting an audience from three areas typically viewed as unrelated, this study provides background material which will appear obvious for some, as well as analysis that may seem esoteric to others. I organize this introductory discussion as follows: first, I provide a summary of postcolonial theory's main concepts. I share the view of Patrick Williams and Laura Chrisman, editors of *Colonial Discourse and Post-colonial Theory* (1994), that literary texts stand in "a dialectical relationship with their social and historical context—produced by, but also productive of, particular forms of knowledge, ideologies, power relations, institutions and practices" (4). For that reason, I next outline aspects of the socio-political and literary history of Québec essential to an understanding of how Canada's majority French-speaking province can be seen as postcolonial. Admitting that the application of the term postcolonial to so-called white settler nations like Canada has been questioned by a number of critics, this section recalls how many of Québec's intellectuals and writers adopted theories of decolonization to describe their own situation in the 1960s as that of the *colonisé* (colonized). Finally, I conclude this introduction with an examination of the intersections between SF and postcolonial theory. For precisely at the moment when a major scholar like Istvan Csicsery-Ronay, Jr., argues that SF definitively represents a discourse of Empire, a small group of critics begins to write about a phenomenon they call "postcolonial science fiction."

Québec[7] and the Postcolonial

While those familiar with the history of Québec will be acutely aware of a certain historical vision that comprehends the province's past as a cycle of colonization and resistance, there remains in the United States a significant unawareness of this francophone enclave just across the New England border. Therefore, a survey of the geopolitical entity known today as Québec would appear useful at this point. Situated in the far northeast portion of the North American continent, covering nearly 595,391 square miles (1.5 million square kilometers) of territory bound by the Gulf of Saint Lawrence on the east, the Arctic Circle and Hudson's Bay on the north and west, and the United States boundary beyond the Saint Lawrence river plain to the south and Maritime Canada (New Brunswick, Nova Scotia and Newfoundland/Labrador) to the east, it represents the largest of Canada's provinces in size (only the recently created Arctic territory of Nunavut exceeds it). Québec nearly doubles France (or the state of Texas) in surface area; Alaska surpasses it in size by only a small margin (some 50,000 square miles). Its citizens include approximately 85 percent of the French-speaking population of Canada, while 82 percent of the population of Québec uses French as its primary language (Allaire 21, 76).[8] While its provincial capital resides in the city of Québec, Montréal is a world-class metropolis, the second-largest French-speaking city in the world after Paris. Québec's status as an isolated enclave of a unique French-language culture surrounded by a sea of English-speakers has remained a point of pride, a source of tradition and national identity, as well as a font of deep anxiety over the threat of that heritage being enfulged (Louder 4). The imagery of the archipelago better expresses the reality that deep-rooted, but at times threatened francophone communities exist elsewhere in Canada, including the Acadians in New Brunswick and Nova Scotia among others. Tensions over linguistic and cultural rights have been the focus of serious political battles between Québec and Ottawa over provincial and federal jurisdiction. Those tensions ran particularly high after Federal Premier Pierre Trudeau repatriated (from Great Britain) the Canadian constitution in 1982 in response to Québec's failed referendum on sovereignty-association in 1980. Subsequent talks to obtain Québec's approval of the constitution, coupled with resentment from the other provinces at what they perceived as special treatment, ended in yet another failed referendum for Québec's independence in 1995. This antagonism between the province of Québec and federal Canada originated in the colonial past, with the European conquest and settlement of what came to be called North America.

    The distinct French-speaking culture of Québec's majority population developed as a result of its unique history within the context of European imperialism and colonialism. That history has been represented as a cycle of colonial, or pseudo-colonial, oppression and resistance, finally broken with the Quiet Revolution. This apparent oxymoron refers to the period of massive reforms undertaken from 1960 to 1966, which ultimately gave control of education and social services to the provincial state (as opposed to the Catholic Church where they had been located) and included the nationalization of various natural resources, including the formation of Hydro-Québec. With these measures, as well as with the creation of a provincial Ministry of Culture (to reinforce the position of French language and culture and to strengthen Québec's international presence in the francophone world), Québec entered a stage of empowered self-determination, which paralleled — even though it did not reproduce per se — the independence indicative of a post-colonial status (Vautier, "Révision" 4). And yet, like many post-colonial nations in the developing world, Québec suffered an economic crisis so severe that 40 percent of Canada's unemployed in 1970 resided in that province alone (Provencher 22). This alignment of Québec with other post-colonial nations rests upon a definition of the term (often indicated, as here, by use of its hyphenated form) as meaning "after" a colonial period. Unfortunately, the application and definition of the term in either of its forms — post-colonial or postcolonial — is not so simple.

The present study, examining the relationship between the postcolonial, science fiction and Québec, cannot pretend to engage in the extensive debates over defining all of those terms. Science fiction, although often viewed as a marginal "paraliterature," has generated as extensive polemics over its definition as any canonical genre, including discussions of the adequacy of its name to the wide practices of writing that fall under its scope, including questions as to whether it is even a genre. The "postcolonial," in scare quotes here to signal its resistance to a totalizing definition, faces a similar situation. Significantly, for a domain arising directly from the conquest, colonization and ultimate liberation of territories, the appropriate territory for the term has been the source of heated debates. Postcolonial studies, postcolonial theory, postcolonial criticism — various groups have adopted a range of terms for this interdisciplinary field/phenomenon, which has been applied most actively in literary studies, but also in areas such as history, philosophy, economics, and other overlapping social sciences. Ironically, a field whose very goal has been defined as "dismantling the Centre/Margin binarism of imperial discourse" (Ashcroft et al., *Post-colonial* 117) has dedicated a considerable amount of energy to debating who is central to and who is at the margins of the term's legitimate application. While critics like Ashcroft, Griffiths and Tiffin would expand the scope of the postcolonial to include *any* nation/region once a colony (including the so-called white settler cultures of Canada, Australia, New Zealand, and even the United States), critics like Arun Mukherjee resist what they see as yet another appropriation by the West of something proper to its Others (the Third World, the South, the developing world, black nations). Rather than reargue these questions which have been addressed widely elsewhere,[9] I will posit a few initial assumptions and provide a synthesis of the body of literature from which those assumptions are drawn.

In order to read Québec's science fiction as a postcolonial discourse I take as given a few initial premises. First, the interdisciplinary field of postcolonial studies provides a valid framework to help us understand the cultural production of societies founded or affected by European colonialism-imperialism. Second, taken in its most literal sense, the hyphenated form of the term (post-colonial) refers to a historico-political moment occurring *after* a period of colonialism, while the unhyphenated term may be applied to a host of cultural productions and institutions which exhibit a certain shared set of traits and exploit certain common strategies, most of which work somehow in dialogue with or opposition to those of the imperial, colonizing instance. Third, that works of literature represent a form of discourse. And finally, that Québec properly qualifies as a society to which these terms may be applied.

While the first premise stated above will appear self-evident by the end of this study (that is, if the reader leaves this work with an enhanced understanding of Québec's science fiction then its application of postcolonial theory *has* proven its effectiveness), the others bear further discussion. As the reader will often notice in the range of citations appearing here, even by the mid–1990s, not all critics have adopted the practice suggested in my second assumption that post-colonial means after and postcolonial means something else. Defining this something else has been highly problematic, even for the foremost critics in the field. Judith Merril's anecdote about insiders' all-night attempts at defining science fiction that conclude with the admission, "I may not know what it is, but I know it when I read it!" might equally apply to the postcolonial (2). The following paragraph's citations intend nonetheless to provide the reader with some sense of a definition, but it is not clear that they necessarily will succeed in doing so.

With *The Empire Writes Back* (1989) Ashcroft, Griffiths and Tiffin introduced the concept of the "postcolonial" to the English-speaking academy. In their introduction to *The Post-colonial Studies Reader* (1995), which includes excerpts from major texts which define the growing field, they provide the following descriptive statements:

> Post-colonial literatures are a result of ... interaction between imperial culture and the complex of indigenous cultural practices [1].
> post-colonialism is a continuing process of resistance and reconstruction....
> Post-colonial theory invites discussion about experience of various kinds: migration, slavery, difference, race, gender, place, and responses to the influential master discourses of imperial Europe such as history, philosophy and linguistics ... post-colonial studies are based in the "historical fact" of European colonialism, and the diverse material effects to which this phenomenon gave rise [2].
> We use the term "post-colonial" to represent the continuing process of imperial suppressions and exchanges throughout this diverse range of societies, in their institutions and their discursive practices [3].

Bhabha, perhaps its foremost theorist, describes the field as follows in *The Location of Culture* (1994):

> Postcolonial criticism bears witness to the unequal and uneven forces of cultural representation involved in the contest for political and social authority within the modern world order. Postcolonial perspectives emerge from the colonial testimony of Third World countries and the discourses of "minorities" within the geopolitical divisions of East and West, North and South. They intervene in those ideological discourses of modernity that attempt to give a hegemonic "normality" to the uneven development and the differential, often disadvantaged, histories of nations, races, communities, peoples. They formulate their critical revisions around issues of cultural difference, social authority, and political discrimination in order to reveal the antagonistic and ambivalent moments within the "rationalizations" of modernity [171].

Bart Moore-Gilbert provides in his *Postcolonial Theory* (1997) a useful analytical survey of theorists and critics, noting that all express "a shared concern to decentre the cultural authority historically enjoyed by the West through a critique of its dominant ideology, humanism" (172).

Ultimately, most scholars working in the field agree that the term no longer indicates a simple, chronological relationship with an earlier colonial period as its original, hyphenated form (post-colonial) suggested. In current practice, the term refers (without apparent controversy) to the cultural production and discursive practices of so-called Third World nations who have gained political independence from former colonizers and *may* include subversive (that is, anticolonial) practices during the earlier colonial period. *Both* forms of the term (hyphenated and unhyphenated), it would seem, express *resistance to* a colonial-imperial entity, while the latter also encompasses a cultural *dialogue between* those who are/have been colonized and that entity. Deriving from this dialogue which typically resists/opposes the hegemony of the colonizer and asserts the position of the (formerly) colonized, the postcolonial becomes, then, a hybrid, syncretic phenomenon as it blends elements from a pre-colonial world with elements appropriated from the colonial world, forming a new position.

Many postcolonial critics, trained as they were in French theories of semiotics, deconstruction and post-structuralism, conceptualize a politicized reading of literature as a form of discourse analysis. Anne Cranny-Francis, in the feminist context (also a theory which openly states its agenda for social change), paraphrases a definition of "discourse" outlined by Gunther Kress in *Linguistic Processes in Sociocultural Practice* (6–7):

> discourses (for example, sexist and feminist discourses) are essentially sets of statements which define, describe and delimit the possibilities of action and of thought, of representation and self-representation, of a particular institution or site of power: in other words, discourses are the textual realizations of ideology.... Sexist discourse, for example, defines, describes and delimits the possibilities of action and of thought, or representation and self-representation, for subjects of patriarchy, an institutionalization of gender relations whereby masculinity is located as the site of power, femininity as powerlessness [Cranny-Francis 207].

A colonialist discourse, then, would define and delimit reality in a manner reflective of the dominant Western perspective, in which prevails a binary system of Self and Other, with Self representing the white, empowered, colonizing instance and Other representing the black/brown/yellow/red, non–Western, disempowered, colonized/native. A postcolonial discourse would rewrite the definitions and limitations of reality and self as established by this Western, colonialist discourse.

Most critics associate with the postcolonial one or more of the following preoccupying concerns, which help illuminate the dense definitions cited above:

- **History/time:** the postcolonial challenges Western notions of linear time and history (Ashcroft et al., *Empire* 33) and seeks to recover history suppressed by the colonial instance (Bhabha 198; Said, *Culture* 210–12; Ashcroft et al., *Empire* 81–82);

- **Center/Periphery:** it problematizes the hierarchical relationship between center and periphery, expressing a concern for, even a valorization of, marginalization (Mishra and Hodge 276; Ashcroft et al., *Post-colonial* 117 and *Empire* 83; Hutcheon 153);

- **Hybridity/Syncretism/Synthesis/Métissage:**[10] a blended, heterogeneous culture/subject results from the colonial interaction and its aftermath affecting both the imperial culture and the colonized culture (Ashcroft et al., *Empire* 15, 33 and *Post-colonial* 1; Bhabha 2, 25–26, 112, 173; Dorsinville, *Caliban* 59; Emberley 14, 158; Fanon, "National" 42–43; Lionnet 329–31; Soyinka 121; Tiffin 95);

- **Nationalism:** the postcolonial explores nationalism, most often by problematizing it (Said, *Culture* 215–17; Bhabha 173; Spivak, *Critique* 62);

- **Resistant/Subversive/Oppositional:** it resists, subverts, opposes the imperial instance, desiring social change (Ashcroft et al., *Empire* 33, 138 and *Post-colonial* 2; Tiffin 96; Slemon, "Unsettling" 106–07 and "Modernism's" 7; Mishra and Hodge 276; Hutcheon 150; Soyinka 66–67, 110);

- **Difference/Other:** the postcolonial asserts *difference*, as opposed to accepting *unifying/universalist* (as reflective of dominant group) conceptions of identity and culture; it contests liberal humanism's universalist and totalizing tendencies; it seeks acceptance for Otherness (Ashcroft et al., *Empire* 55; Bhabha 173, 175; Hutcheon 150–52; Soyinka x; Spivak, "Subaltern" 76–81 and *Other* 202);

- **Binarisms:** it dismantles/subverts the often hierarchical binarisms of European/imperial discourse; that is, rather than perceiving the world in terms of black and white, it offers a vision in shades of gray (Bhabha 28, 179; Ashcroft et al., *Post-colonial* 117; Lionnet 325);

- **Reality:** the postcolonial subverts/exposes the Western/Empire's positivist system of the "real," undermining mimetic representation to reveal the invented/constructed nature of literary discourse and the world/reality itself (Ashcroft et al., *Empire* 41, 55).

While most critics agree that a preoccupation with these issues defines the postcolonial, they do not necessarily agree upon the term's geographical or temporal scope.

Controversy developed during what Stephen Slemon calls "The Scramble for Post-colonialism" as some critics, most particularly Ashcroft, Griffiths and Tiffin with *The Empire Writes Back*, sought to develop a definition that could potentially include *certain types* of discursive/cultural production from *any* nation formed out of a colonial situation. Effectively including not only Australia and Canada, but even the United States — seen by many in the realm of Third World studies as the source of a neo-imperialism — within the scope of the soon-to-be unhyphenated "postcolonial," this team faced immediate accusations of operating a form of cultural appropriation.[11] In particular, their critics express concern with the application of the term to so-called white settler cultures, colonies in which a population of European colonists and their descendants displaced an indigenous culture, maintained (and imposed on others) the language and many of the cultural norms of the metropolitan center and accessed sovereignty with little or no political struggle or violence. Proponents of their inclusion argue that the cultures developed by these white settlers often followed patterns similar to those in the so-called black nations (a term sometimes applied to sites where an indigenous population remained a majority and the colonists typically left at the time of decolonization) and that these literatures, too, reflect a preoccupation with the issues associated with postcolonial discourses listed above.[12]

Anticipating concerns over the designation of Québec, a colony founded by white settlers, as postcolonial, it would be quite simple to adopt the approach of *The Empire Writes Back* and apply the most inclusive definition to accommodate Québec's literary production within that category.[13] Doing so, however, would undermine a major aspect of the argument presented here: that Québec, while its experience clearly differs from that of India or Nigeria or Aboriginal Australia, presents a case distinct from that of most white settler nations because of its history of a double colonization, first French, then English. This study, then, like those of Slemon and others working on the cultural production of white settler colonies in the so-called Second World,[14] adopts a position somewhere in between the two extremes.

I agree that the term postcolonial becomes meaningless and trivialized if it is applied without discrimination and without reference to historical context. Nonetheless, I posit that the term can apply to cultural productions beyond those of the Third World when it arises from certain socio-historical conditions. This study differs, though, from those of Sylvia Söderlind, Marie Vautier and Graham Huggan (who also includes Australia in his comparative analysis) which acknowledge Canada's biculturalism; but, precisely because they argue that both Anglo-Canadian and French-Canadian literatures may be postcolonial, they fail to stress the specificity of Québec's position. While this study does not seek to place Québec in the same category as Canada's First Nations and Inuit populations (who unarguably represent its postcolonial elements, along with its various new immigrant communities), it does seek to assert Québec's difference not only from Canada, but from a range of poles, poles even internal to Québec itself. It situates Québec, following Immanuel Wallerstein's classifications (56), not in the core, nor quite in the periphery, but in the semi-periphery. As the historical overview which follows demonstrates, Québec stands ever as somewhere in-between[15]; between French (from France) and English, between the Canadian and the American (as the U.S. has appropriated for itself this marker that may apply to all of the Americas), between its imaginary South and the Great North.

I am less concerned, though, with identifying Québec, the geo-political entity, as postcolonial nation and more with identifying how certain cultural practices in Québec (specifically its science fiction) reflect the traits of the postcolonial listed above. Yet, such an analysis cannot ignore the socio-historical circumstances of the cultural productions in question. The argument that we justifiably can apply the term to Québec or to its cultural productions rests on establishing a distinct colonial history that sets it apart from the typical pattern of other white settler nations in which indigenous groups were pushed aside in order to make way for the arrival of European settlers who at times sought simply to reproduce the culture of the mother country in a new setting. At the same time, it involves a certain element of coming to terms with the reality that the French, too, pushed aside the autochthonous peoples living in the land they called New France.

For Québec certainly follows the typical pattern of the white settler nation in many ways: it was settled by Europeans (first French, then British, American Loyalists, the Irish and others) at the expense of an indigenous population. It is not part of the Third World, and, while Canada did go through a certain process to obtain its sovereignty from Great Britain, that process did not parallel or coincide in any way with the colonial independences of India or various African nations.[16] That Québec unilaterally refused to sign the Canadian constitution repatriated by Trudeau in 1982, the act which made Canada "now a postcolonial nation-state" (Emberley 101), reflects the province's concern to establish its unique position resulting from the specificity of its colonial history. This position has in part been built up over the centuries since 1763 by an institutionalized version of history, as Jocelyn Létourneau so vividly points out in *Passer à l'avenir* (Moving on to the Future, 2000). Citing real students' college entrance exams as illustrative of how this history has been internalized by the average Québécois, he summarizes it as:

un récit du Québec et des Québécois, à savoir celui d'un peuple dont le destin fut tragique, qui fut longtemps arriéré, soumis au joug du clergé et à la domination des Anglais, et qui a réussi en partie à conjurer le terrible sort qui pesait sur sa destinée en se refondant par la Révolution tranquille, moment de grand *aggiornamiento* collectif [33].

a story of Québec and the Québécois, that is of a people with a tragic fate, backward for a long time, in submission to the yoke of the clergy and English domination, and which partially succeeded in shaking off the terrible spell which weighted down its destiny by remaking itself through the Quiet Revolution, a moment of great collective *aggiornamiento* (updating).

This pattern, established as a history of colonial victimization, ultimately led a number of political activists, intellectuals and writers to identify Québec with decolonizing nations of the francophone world during the 1960s. (Malcolm Reid paints a colorful contemporary portrait of this phenomenon in *The Shouting Sign Painters* [1972].) Québec continues to grapple with the legacy of this alignment, the adoption of the position of the colonized, as Franco-Ontarian Daniel Poliquin points out in *Le Roman colonial* (The Colonial Novel/Romance, 2000), which observes a continued exploitation of this position by conservative nationalists. A condemnation of the hypocrisy, and or simple unproductiveness, of this position on the grounds that its use simply reinscribes an ideology of colonization appears in Marc Angenot's description of it as an example of *Les Idéologies du ressentiment* (Ideologies of Resentment, 1997).[17] Critiques of nationalist ideology like those of Létourneau, Poliquin and Angenot reflect a postcolonial sensibility currently found in contemporary Québec. The titles of more recent works on national identity and sovereignty, like *Le Pays de tous les Québécois* (The Land of all Quebeckers, Ed. Sarra-Bournet and Gendron 1998), demonstrate that the province's political mainstream has transcended a vision of itself as colonized. Government "White Papers" like *Let's Build Québec Together* (1990) offer a more inclusive national identity than that of French Canadian simply renamed as *Québécois*, particularly to the province's growing number of minority communities as well as its remaining anglophones.[18] Contemporary nationalism in Québec, let me be clear, turns to conceptions of civic nationalism as outlined by thinkers such as the late Fernand Dumont in *Raisons communes* (Common Ground, 1995), rather than the traditional ethnic nationalism critiqued by Poliquin and Angenot and most forcibly outlined by Lionel Groulx in the 1920s and maintained by such recent leaders of the Parti Québécois as Jacques Parizeau in the 1990s. Indeed, the most recent development in the provincial state's initiative for an inclusive society resulted in a report by Gérard Bouchard and Charles Taylor, *Fonder l'avenir: Le temps de la conciliation* (2008). Heading Québec's Consulting Commission on Practices of Accommodation Linked to Cultural Differences, they conclude that "ce que révèlent nos consultations, au-delà des fausses notes bien connues, c'est une ouverture à l'Autre" ("our consultations reveal, apart from some well-known false notes, an opening to the Other"; 8).

The forceful demonstrations of how a collective memory and an official history have been constructed and shaped to meet the needs of nationalist rhetoric, such as those outlined by Létourneau and Handler notwithstanding, the historical reality that has allowed Québec to adopt the stance of colonized began, as did that of any other post-colonial nation, with a conquest. While the other provinces and territories that comprise Canada were obtained by a gradual colonization of lands occupied by often nomadic indigenous peoples, the territory we now know as Québec was acquired by Great Britain through the military conquest of another European power.[19] While revisionist historians have argued that for the European colonists of New France everyday life changed very little as they exchanged one distant master for another, institutional history has long portrayed French-Canadian life as a never-ending struggle against imperial repression, a portrait painted in the manner of a connect-the-dots, which links a series of iconic dates and the events associated with them. The tragic injustice of the deportation of the Acadians in the *Grand Dérangement* of 1755–56, the sound defeat of Montcalm by Wolfe on the Plains of Abraham outside Québec city in 1759, and the heartless abandonment by France with one stroke of Louis XV's pen at the 1763 Treaty of Paris all symbolize the ill treatment of the original *Canadiens* by both France and England.[20] Preserving their language and religion in the face of harsh policies designed to privilege Protestant English speakers (although these were revised soon after British rule was established with the Quebec Act of 1774) became a point of pride. Real, armed resistance to the new regime did not arise until the Patriots' Rebellion of 1837–38, led by Louis Papineau (which included, although this is often elided, a significant number of anglophone republicans). That revolt, however, was violently quashed and insult was added to injury with Lord Durham's oft-cited report which stated that the French-Canadian people had no history or no literature and which argued for a policy of total assimilation of the French culture to the English. The subsequent Act of Union of 1840 was felt by many French Canadians in what was now called Eastern Canada to enact that policy. Resistance to this assimilation, though, occurred at many levels. Some French-Canadian leaders, like George-Étienne Cartier, felt that participation in the process for the formation of the new Confederation, which came about in 1867, would place them on an equal footing with the growing number of their English-speaking (English, Scotch and Irish[21]) counterparts.

While many felt betrayed by the conditions of the all too *British* North America Act, as the law that founded the Dominion of Canada in 1867 was called, others, led by the hierarchy of the Catholic Church, turned away from politics and gave unto Caesar what was Caesar's, seeking cultural preservation through its expansion in agricultural colonization of the northern lands, as well as the *revanche des berceaux*, the revenge of the cradle — the utopian belief that by sheer force of numbers, French-Canadian, Catholic society would preserve itself, even expand across North America. Indeed, the Catholic Church was often accused of preferring to collaborate with the British Empire, the representative of monarchy and tradition (as opposed to a post–Revolutionary France with its on-again-off-again liberal Republicanism demonized by the Church). For nearly a century (1850–1950) French-Canadian society (or, at least its petty bourgeoisie), led by the Church hierarchy, adhered to a traditionalist, agriculturalist ideology, empowered by a sense of manifest destiny (Monière 228); instead of being colonized, the *défricheurs*, French-Canadian pioneers, were colonists, fulfilling a God-given mission as it was expressed in the agricultural novel, the *roman du terroir*, as well as in some early utopias of Québec's proto-science fiction.

Violent acts of rebellion, along with hope for political equality, peppered this period at long intervals, one of which — like the *Grand Dérangement*—did not occur in Québec proper, although it has been annexed for its symbolic power as part of the ongoing saga of British repression of the French in Canada. In 1869–70 and 1884–85, Louis Riel led Amerindians and Métis (mixed-blood descendants of French explorers/trappers and their often Christianized Native American wives) in the western territories to form an independent republic rather than submit to the newly created federal government. While the first uprising led to the creation of Manitoba, which gave specific rights to Métis and French Canadians, his execution after the second rebellion made Riel a martyr for the French-Canadian cause against British/Anglo-Canadian oppression. While Québec sometimes provided strong leaders for the Federal government, like Premier Wilfrid Laurier, his accession to increasing British demands that Canada serve the Empire during the Boer War in 1899 and after, led nationalist leaders like Henri Bourassa to frame their campaigns in anti-imperialist terms (Brown 483–86). This resistance set the stage for more active and open conflicts during World War I, when rioting over the question of conscription occurred in 1917 and was quashed with a brutal hand (Berger).

Nationalist groups, like the *Ligue nationaliste canadienne* (Nationalist Canadian League), founded in 1903 by followers of Bourassa, first targeted the imperial power of Great Britain, looking toward a pan-Canadian autonomy. Disillusionment with the apparent inability of their English-speaking counterparts to cut the apron strings that tied them to the motherland, as well as anger over the injustices of 1917, led to the development of other pro-French societies in the 1920s. A new leader, cleric and historian Lionel Groulx, turned the nationalist movement away from the political sphere and toward the cultural and intellectual. Journals, like his *Action française,* and pro-French cultural societies, like that of Saint-Jean Baptiste, formed and flourished. While the world around it entered modernity — as the hindsight of a large number of historians would argue — Québec suffered from a *Grande Noirceur* (Great Blackness) under the tutelage of the conservative hierarchy of the Catholic Church, along with the traditionalist, nearly fascist Maurice Duplessis, provincial Prime Minister from 1936 to 1939 and again from 1944 until his death in 1959.[22] Referred to by André Laurendeau as a *roi nègre*, the scornful, racist French term for the phenomenon of the colonized chief who gains personal power at home by exploiting his people for an outside imperial power (in this case, often, capital investment from the U.S.), Duplessis was demonized by liberal nationalists (Bélanger). Today revisionist historians have begun to reexamine the Duplessis era, finding in it the beginnings of a modernizing economy, thus questioning the myth of the Quiet Revolution.[23] For some time, though, it was felt that recognizing Québec's status as colonized must come as much from within, as from without, represented the first move toward self-determination for French Canadians.

At the onset of the 1960s, a new group of leaders stepped into the vacuum of power to operate a sequence of reforms that would come to be called the Quiet Revolution, a term coined by Thomas Sloan of Toronto's *Globe and Mail* (Dorion 353). Calls to modernize Québec's society had begun much earlier, most notably in 1948 from a group of artists led by Paul Borduas; their *Refus global* manifesto represented a global refusal of the clerico-agriculturalist ideology predominant in Québec as well as a call to open the province's horizons to the world outside. In 1950 a group of young leaders which would eventually take Québec into the modern era, working within the framework of Canadian federalism and liberal humanism, founded the periodical *Cité libre* (Free City). The classical notion of the *cité*, the democratic *polis*, based in a secular, rational civic-minded spirit stood at the heart of the reform measures initiated by the Liberal government of provincial premier Jean Lesage (1960–66), which secularized the state and its services and laid the groundwork for the modern nationalist movement.

Using the discourse of decolonization articulated in the French colonies of the Caribbean and Africa, liberal leaders in Québec sought independence from English domination. Since the Act of Westminster had given Canada its sovereignty in 1931, this no longer necessarily meant political domination by the British Empire, but now referred to the economic domination by British, Anglo-Canadian and United States capital. Oppression began to be seen in economic, as well as political terms. French Canadians were called to see the glass ceiling that kept them, as the *nègres blancs d'Amérique*,[24] in lower level slots while management positions, even that of foreman, were reserved for English speakers. In particular, the group headquartered with the journal *Parti pris* (Position Taken, 1963–68) issued a special number in summer 1964 called "Portrait du colonisé québécois" (Portrait of the Québécois as colonized). Another short-lived journal of the period made its agenda clear through the title *Les Cahiers de la décolonisation* (The Decolonization Notebooks, 1968–69) (Robert 146). Independantist politicians and activists increasingly adopted this discourse of decolonization. Co-founder of the Parti Québécois René Lévesque argues in his proposal for independence, *Option Québec*, that "[n]ous sommes, économiquement, des colonisés" ("we are, economically, a colonized people"; 23). A more radical interpretation, that such colonialism exists on all levels — social, political, cultural, and economic — appears in *Le Colonialisme au Québec* (Colonialism in Québec, 1966) by *Rassemblement pour l'Indépendance Nationale* (Assembly for National Independence) leader André d'Allemagne. In addition to the political renaissance, the drive to self-determination led to a cultural renaissance in Québec, fostered in part by the expansion of and increased access to higher education with the resulting development of a class of intellectuals and artists. The latter, often schooled in Marxist theory, as well as being aware of postcolonial theory's precursors like Fanon and Aimé Césaire, proclaimed their affinity with the decolonizing world as had their counterparts in the political arena. Indeed, politics and art appear particularly intertwined in Québécois cultural production from the 1960s and 1970s.

The movement often blurred the lines between the literary and the political, as seen in the *Parti pris* group, which included (future) politicians, social scientists and writers, and which was associated with a press that published literary and non-fiction works. One need only read a few pages of Pierre Vallières' prison memoir/cultural analysis *White Niggers of America* (1968) or a few stanzas of Michèle Lalonde's poem "Speak White" (1970) to comprehend the affinity felt among Québec's radical literati and activists for other groups that had sought or were seeking independence from either French or British colonial dominion. To qualify this nascent national literature, the term *québécitude* (Québec-ness) was coined, inspired by Guadeloupean Césaire's and Senegalese Léopold Sédar Senghor's earlier concept of *négritude* (negro-ness), formulated to describe African and Afro-Caribbean writers' celebrations of the black experience. As early as 1970 Haitian-Québécois literary critics Maximilien Laroche and Max Dorsinville articulated parallels between the two in their comparative studies of Québécois and Antillean literature examined through the lens of anti-colonial theories like those of Fanon. The utopian nature of the project of decolonization became explicit in its conception by the nascent counter-culture in Québec. Between 1967 and 1970, the counter-culture's interest in social change beyond nationalism appeared in reviews like *Mainmise*, whose first issue editorial focuses on the conception of its goal as the creation of "UTOPIE" (rpt. in Robert 150).

The massive changes of the Quiet Revolution were not, however, revolutionary enough for a radical element of the developing society in Québec and, in light of the ultimate success of violent resistance to colonial rule witnessed in France's Algerian War, a handful of extremists were inspired to form their own version of the FLN (Algeria's Nationalist Liberation Front), the FLQ (Québec Liberation Front, c. 1963–70). Beginning with a few bombs in mailboxes, the FLQ's insurgence culminated in the botched kidnapping of British diplomat James Cross and Québec's Minister of Work and Immigration, Pierre Laporte in 1970. The resulting October Crisis represented a collective trauma for some. Laporte's murder allowed an immediate groundswell of reactionary sentiment which approved Canadian Premier Trudeau's declaration of a state of emergency (Provencher 75). And while only a tiny minority supported the FLQ's level of violent resistance, their articulation of long-nourished frustrations followed by the sight of tanks rolling through the streets of Montréal radicalized lukewarm nationalists. The continued imbrication of the literary with the political appears clearly in novelist Jacques Godbout's incarceration for arms' running, and the imprisonment of poet Gaston Miron for suspected collaboration with the FLQ. By mid-decade the independantist Parti Québécois and its leader René Lévesque parlayed this radicalization along with charges of the Liberal party's poor skills in managing the government to victory at the polls in November 1976.

For many, the forces of resistance appeared ready to deliver up Québec's liberation on the eve of May 20, 1980, as its citizens prepared to vote on a referendum for sovereignty-association, a concept engineered by Lévesque. This term, in which the province would wield the status of national sovereignty, but would remain in close association with its neighbor (on two sides, as Québec's independence would divide Canada, leaving its Maritime provinces on the Atlantic coast isolated), was felt to be a necessary compromise to achieve a victory for the "Yes" vote. Its narrow margin of defeat left many in shock, as expressed by literary critic André Belleau's essay "Après le Réferendum de 1980: On ne meurt pas de mourir" (After the Referendum of 1980: You don't die from dying). His reaction to Québec's failed call to its own citizens for independence reveals the depth of the imprint made by the discourse of decolonization on the nationalist movements and illustrates the cultural climate out of which Québec's science-fiction movement was distilled:

> La défaite du OUI, c'est simultanément la victoire, dans une Amérique du Nord homogène, du MÊME sur l'AUTRE, de l'uniformité sur la différence. Contrairement aux Noirs et aux Chicanos, les Francophones du Québec constituaient une minorité (ou plutôt une marginalité) nord-américaine en position de se doter d'un pouvoir politique distinct ... nous ne sommes pas ... à la périphérie de l'«Empire» ... nous logeons tout près de son coeur même [103–04].

> The defeat of YES is simultaneously a victory, in a homogeneous North America, of the SAME over the OTHER, of uniformity over difference. Contrary to the Blacks and the Chicanos, the Francophones of Québec constituted a North American minority (or rather a marginalized group) in the position of giving themselves a distinct political power.... We are not at the periphery of "Empire." ... we live right next to its very heart.

For Belleau and others of his generation, this defeat shattered the very marker of cultural identity that the term *Québécois* was meant to represent since 1960. The victory of "No" voided that term of its meaning, rendering it forever as a "non-identité, le *non identifiable* ... Je ne sais pas ce que je suis.... J'étais «X» qui n'a pas réussi à devenir Québécois" ("non-identity, a *non identifiable*. I don't know what I am.... I was 'X' who has not succeeded in becoming *Québécois*") (104; original emphasis). The evident identity crisis expressed by Belleau reveals a sense of alienation that we shall see mirrored in Québec's science fiction, which had just begun to develop a growing sense of its own identity in 1979.

Hoping to close the rift between French- and Anglo-Canada, Trudeau repatriated Canada's Constitution in 1982, a definitive act toward establishing Canada's sovereignty. The prior negotiations, however, became depicted in Québec's nationalist mythology as yet another act of treachery memorialized as "The Night of the Long Knives," a reference to Hitler's ordered assassination of Ernst Röhm and other SA officers. While accounts apparently conflict, René Lévesque recounts having reached an agreement with seven other provinces satisfactory to both his province's interest in securing control over education and language legislation, but this was undone by a secret accord reached between Jean Chrétien, Trudeau and all nine anglophone provinces during the night of 4–5 November 1981 (Cousture). Stories of this apparent betrayal fueled Québec's unilateral refusal to sign the act to repatriate the Constitution. Brian Mulroney fulfilled his promise to the Parti Québécois to reopen negotiations, but another set of talks at Lake Meech in 1987 led again to stalemate. An agreement finally appeared in the Charlottetown Accord of 1992, which a pan-Canadian referendum failed to ratify. Voters in the predominantly anglophone provinces feeling it went too far in granting Québec status as a "distinct society," and voters in Québec considering that it gave not enough. Québec had become just one of many minorities with Canada's new policy of multiculturalism, rather than one of two founding societies, the status it wished acknowledged. This Constitutional Crisis culminated in a second referendum for sovereignty-association in 1995, which also failed by an extremely close margin with 49.4 percent in favor of sovereignty (Baker, "Politics" 33). Although nothing has come of promises for a third referendum made after the Parti Québécois' victory in the 1998 elections, and Quebeckers of the third millennium seem to be preoccupied by other concerns, the issues of colonization and sovereignty are far from dead. As recently as October 2000 a bomb exploded in a Montréal Second-Cup Café, ostensibly in protest of the Canadian coffee shop chain's violation of provincial laws regulating the use of English in public signage. Current Canadian Premier Stephen Harper's November 2006 landmark recognition that "Quebecers form a nation within a united Canada" has failed to mark a major turning point in federal and provincial relations (qtd. in Hamilton).

In his literary study of Québec, *L'Écologie du réel* (Ecology of the Real, 1988), Pierre Nepveu refers to Belleau's essay cited above to underline a sense of non-identity occurring in the 1980s (182–83), which manifested itself both as a nostalgia for the "Québec that might have been" as well as in a disillusioned flight into individualist concerns for form and rhetoric. The literature since the 1960s, "un projet fondé sur une mémoire collective et une visée totalisante" ("a project founded on a collective memory and a totalizing vision"; 14), sought the creation of a truly "Québécois" literature. In contrast, according to Nepveu, "la pluralité, la diversité, la mouvance" ("plurality, diversity, movement"; 14) dominated the nascent "littérature post-québécoise" by the end of the 1980s. While recent critics like Söderlind and Vautier see the literature of the 1980s as still representing a continued working and reworking of what it means to be (or not to be) Québécois, they share Nepveu's notion of a period after, a "post," speaking rather of its postcolonial traits.

In my application of postcolonial theory to a particular form of Québec's literature since 1980, I depart somewhat from current trends in French-language Canadian literary studies. Since Nepveu's pioneering work, the latter have framed similar discussions in terms of *littératures migrantes* (migrant literatures) perhaps in order to distance themselves from the now criticized application of the term "colonisé" to Québec. This term applies most clearly to Québec's "other" literatures, works most often deriving from Montréal's multicultural communities, like Régine Robin's *La Québécoite* (1983; *The Wanderer*, 1989) or Dany Laferrière's best-selling *Comment faire l'amour avec un nègre sans se fatiguer* (1985; *How to Make Love to a Black Without Getting Tired*, 1987). However, a handful of critics also see the fruitfulness of examining writers with more traditional French-Canadian roots in terms of hybridity, alterity, and multivalent identity, as well. Indeed, Clément Moisan and Renate Hildebrand's study identifies four periods in Québec's literary history, all focused around the category of cultural diversity: "the monocultural (1937–1959), the pluricultural (1960–1974), the intercultural (1975–1985), and the transcultural (1986–present)" (Ireland and Proulx 3). Presenting this literature to an English-language audience, I felt that using the more familiar terms of postcolonial theory would make this study more accessible. My criticism itself represents a hybrid, cross-fertilized form which allows for a new optic; that is, viewing Québec's literature through the lens of Anglo-American theory sheds a different light than that of theory from France or Québec. Nonetheless, I take into account along the way francophone literary criticism and will return to the notion of the transcultural in my concluding chapter.

To summarize, then, in the French-Canadian/Québécois *imaginaire*, as it was constructed by a range of historians, politicians and writers, the Conquest of Canada was not that of France over the Amerindians, but that of the British over the French. The cession of New France to the English included a corollary sense of betrayal by France, resulting in a range of ambivalent attitudes toward the problems of colonialism, nationalism, and individual identity. While Québec has truly remained a "société distincte," in spite of Federal Canada's (or rather, the confederation's other provinces') refusal to admit this during the constitutional debates of the early 1990s, it has often done so through the nostalgic remembrance of its colonial past — its *French* colonial past. At the same time, particularly since the 1960s opened up worldwide criticism of colonialism with the massive decolonization of the Third World, certain Québec activists have argued that it, too, was an oppressed nation colonized by the British two hundred years before. Just as the concepts of conquest and colonization have been central to Québec's imagination, so, too, these concepts lie at the heart of our third pole of inquiry, science fiction.

The Postcolonial and Science Fiction

While we can trace observations about the prevalence of the themes of imperialism and colonialism in SF back to its "first full-scale academic study," J. O. Bailey's *Pilgrims Through Space and Time* (1947) (Clareson *viii*), science-fiction criticism has taken some time to embrace postcolonial theory. Landmark histories such as Brian W. Aldiss' *Billion...* (1973) and then *Trillion Year Spree* (1986) are riddled with references to SF's critiques of imperialism and colonialism (and/or the racism attendant upon these ideologies). Only as recently as 2002 do Nancy Batty and Robert Markley speculate that their publication of a special issue of *Ariel* (a Canadian "review of international English literature") devoted to SF as a site of exploration for postcolonial concerns marks a turning point, thus contradicting the conventional wisdom that SF is a colonialist genre. One year later, however, in a seemingly definitive article, "Science Fiction and Empire," Istvan Csicsery-Ronay, Jr., appears to establish once and for all that SF is, indeed, a discourse of Empire. What conclusions can we draw, then, from these conflicting stances?

A review of the literature reveals the development of three different types of articulation linking the postcolonial and SF, most published since the year 2000. The most conservative approach may reinforce, rather than contradict, the argument that SF represents a colonialist genre, as it simply applies postcolonial theory to works from the genre's canon in order to reveal their stances on imperialism and colonialism. The second strain, which directly contests arguments like those of Csicsery-Ronay, Jr., analyzes the use of SF (or its tropes and techniques) by mainstream writers typically identified as postcolonial in order to create discourses resistant to Western imperialism. Finally, the third application seeks to identify a corpus of "postcolonial SF," texts produced by writers coming from minority or immigrant communities living in former imperial centers, as well as those from unarguably postcolonial regions (often those of the so-called Third World). This last category does not necessarily contest the argument that Western SF is a discourse of colonialism; rather, it sets up a parallel non–Western/minority canon.

Only recently critics have begun to apply postcolonial theory to works from the traditional SF canon, drawing a range of conclusions about the potential relationship between these two domains. This application can either serve the argument that SF is indeed a discourse of imperialism or it can make the case that at least some (typically Anglo-American) SF possesses certain postcolonial traits. Overwhelmingly, though, rather than apply postcolonial theory to canonical SF, especially from the United States and Great Britain, to expose and identify blatantly imperialist-colonialist works (perhaps a task too obvious to be interesting), such critics seek out texts that at least approach a postcolonial sensibility. This appears in the respective analyses of James Tiptree, Jr. (Alice Sheldon) by Kevin Carollo and David Galef. Carollo, while identifying elements of an anti-colonialist critique in Tiptree's work, must ultimately conclude that it adopts "the colonial impulse in science fiction [which] seems inevitable" (221). Galef goes farther, asserting that her firsthand experience with colonialism in Africa informed Tiptree's "postcolonialist outlook" (202), which allows her to develop a more sophisticated, ambivalent approach to the depiction of the alien Other in her work. This sort of depiction, Galef implies, is absent from other SF of that era. Several studies assert that Kim Stanley Robinson's more recent Mars trilogy (*Red Mars*, 1993; *Green Mars*, 1994; *Blue Mars*, 1996) reflects a postcolonial approach to the colonization of the red planet. Robert Markley argues that "Robinson undoes the values and assumptions that have motivated previous imperialist enterprises" (781). Similarly, Walter Benn Michaels contrasts Ben Bova's unsuccessful attempt to transcend the problems of New World exploration by simply writing off the native in *Mars* (1992), with Robinson's valuation of the indigenous elements of Mars which extend beyond "the idea that it is only humans or persons who have cultures" (269). Elizabeth Leane, drawing on Fredric Jameson's analysis of Robinson's trilogy as utopia ("If"), identifies it as "self-consciously postcolonial" (86) in its synthesis of indigenous and colonizing elements. These and other recent essays expose the fallacy of a simplistic logic which argues that if a novel depicts the adventure of space colonization then it must, by definition, adhere to a colonialist ideology. They call attention to the fact that the question for analysis should be *how* colonization is depicted.

The first book-length project to undertake this study appears in Patricia Kerslake's *Science Fiction and Empire* (2007), which employs "a more elastic approach to postcolonialism [which] enables us better to understand SF's dealings with empire" (3). Kerslake draws to some degree upon the work of well-known theorists, like Said, Sara Suleri and Leela Ghandi, but not heavily. Her readings of canonical Anglo-American SF texts by Wells, Asimov, Wyndham, Heinlein, Dick, as well as by some Soviet and Eastern European writers, interrogate the very assumption that "SF is inherently imperialistic" (26). She argues for "the possibility that SF writers are simply incorporating imperialism into their works as a means of testing such inherency" (26), seeing these works as an expression of Anglo-Americans' ongoing fascination with and ambivalence about our imperial history and future. While she sees some evidence of a progressive, increasingly critical trend in the work of Le Guin and Robinson, Kerslake also observes the paradox that SF does not echo the current perceived political desire not to "repeat the political and cultural errors of our colonial history" (28). As thought experiments about "the function and manipulation of political power, of empire and its abuses" (1), the SF texts studied by Kerslake derive from the colonial power itself, and Kerslake applies a much greater body of theory that is non-postcolonial to understand how imperialism and colonialism occur, and how they impact such things as self-other relations, conceptions of culture, and notions of center and periphery.

The question *how* also lies at the core of the second type of articulation made between SF and postcolonial theory, which analyzes the use of SF and its tropes in texts which contest the dominance of Western imperialist ideology by writers usually aligned with the literary mainstream, albeit with its geographic peripheries. Doris Lessing's monumental *Canopus in Argos Archives* (1979–83) inspired a range of studies, some of which address its stunning indictment of European colonialism coupled with its strange potential apology for the possibility of a "good" form of colonialism as practiced by the Canopean Empire. Without explicitly drawing upon postcolonial theory, Eckhard Auberlen's description of Lessing's portrayal of conflicts between three stellar empires as subverting the traditional SF binary logic of good versus evil nonetheless implies its potential for an oppositional reading. Similarly, Cherry Clayton analyzes the phenomenon of the white settler depicted in the SF conclusion to Lessing's *The Four-Gated City* (1969), positing that it represents "a postmodern fiction that serves post-colonial ends" (61). As a white settler, raised in Southern Rhodesia (now Zimbabwe) who moved to the colonial metropolis (London) while still a young woman, Lessing's status as a postcolonial writer may be questioned. Few would argue with that of Mahasweta Devi (discussed in the Preface to this study) or of Salman Rushdie, whose use of SF tropes in *The Ground Beneath Her Feet* (1999) has been analyzed by Judith Leggatt. Yet several studies of Rushdie's *Grimus* (1975),[25] although it proclaims itself as SF on the Vintage edition of the text, do not necessarily address its relationship to the genre. On the other hand, the less well-known Amitav Ghosh's *Calcutta Chromosome* (1996) has been the object of two recent studies by Claire Chambers and Diane Nelson, both of which argue that this genre-blurring text undermines the notion of science as objective which serves as one of the underpinning ideologies of Western imperialism. This type of criticism clearly challenges the notion of SF as a discourse of imperialism because of its assertion that that writers are using SF and its tropes in literatures that undermine and resist the ideology of empire.[26]

Finally, critics have begun to identify an explicit corpus of "postcolonial SF," a term perhaps first employed in Somdatta Mandal's article on Bengali filmmaker Satyajit Ray's Professor Shonku series of juvenile SF novels. In some cases, writers themselves label their work as such, as seen in the recent anthology edited by Nalo Hopkinson and Uppinder Mehan, *So Long Been Dreaming: Postcolonial Science Fiction and Fantasy* (2004).[27] The collection explores themes traditionally associated with postcolonial literature, such as immigration and assimilation, hybridity and identity, exile and nationalism in texts by writers from unarguably postcolonial nations or from minority or immigrant communities in First World nations, such as Native American Celu Amberstone, Indian Vandana Singh, Indian-Canadian Ven Begamudré, African-Americans Sheree R. Thomas and Andrea Hairston, Caribbean writers Tobias S. Bucknell and Opal Palmer Adisa, Asian-Canadian Tamai Kobayashi and others. Although wary of the applicability of the term postcolonial because of the persistence of neocolonial relationships, Grace Dillon analyzes Hopkinson's SF from a similar perspective and advocates for Anishinaabe/First Nations science fiction and fantasy writers like Eden Robinson. Hopkinson's own SF has been the object of studies that use a postcolonial lens, including Bill Clemente's analysis of *Midnight Robber* (2000) and Ruby Ramraj's examination of *The Salt Roads* (2003). One of a tiny handful of critics currently applying the terms of postcolonial theory to SF from francophone Canada, Neal Baker describes Hopkinson's novel *Brown Girl in the Ring* (1998), along with Daniel Sernine's *Chronoreg* (1992) and Joël Champetier's *Dragon's Eye* (1991) as examples of "Syncretism: A Federalist Approach to Canadian Science Fiction" (2001). In a more recent article, Baker observes the concept of syncretism also at work in the use of language in stories by Jean-Louis Trudel, Charles Montpetit, Sion Hamou and Jean Dion ("Politics"). In Canada, Sophie Beaulé applies the language of migrant literature to SFQ texts and Nicholas Serruys reads them as national allegory and utopia/dystopia. Before moving on to my own analyses of specific works of SFQ as postcolonial discourse, several concerns about the broader question of SF's potential designation as such remain to be addressed.

This is not the place to reiterate the many assertions that SF is a discourse of imperialism which glorifies colonization. The success of pulp periodicals like *Amazing Stories* (founded in 1926 by Hugo Gernsback) and then *Astounding Science-Fiction* (1937–71) led the genre into its so-called Golden Age on the eve of World War II, just as the United States began to assert itself as a world power with a growing cultural and economic empire. Classic studies like Donald A. Wollheim's *Universe Makers* (1971) argues that the notion of developing a Galactic civilization, found in the SF of this era (and beyond), was based on the premise of colonization: "It implies colonizing where colonizing is possible" (30). He posits Asimov's *Foundation* trilogy as "the pivot of modern science fiction" as it involves "[n]othing less than the analysis and problems to be involved with the Decline and Fall of the Galactic Empire — and its reconstruction" (37). Yet even such an unquestioning acceptance of the reality of imperialism and colonialism as major themes of and/or ideologies supported by SF bears the seeds of later, more critical analysis. As Wollheim points out, even in such a culturally hegemonic system in which Terra Triumphant reduplicates a *pax romana*, the system implies cultural exchange between civilizations (30–31). Expressing the notion and finding examples of a relationship of two-way exchange (as opposed to a one-way hegemonic relationship) between colonizer and colonized figures clearly on the postcolonial critic's agenda.

Certainly, much of mainstream science fiction, particularly from the United States (and not only that written prior to the 1960s development of socially conscious genre writing), perpetuates imperialist fantasies of space exploration and colonization. Yet Christopher Palmer asserts that significant recent works which may appear to perpetuate Galactic Empire fantasies, such as Iain M. Banks' *Consider Phlebas* (1991) and Dan Simmons' *Hyperion* novels (1991–96), actually subvert the totalizing visions of earlier forms, tending toward a postmodern dynamic of "proliferation and inclusion" (75). In the same vein, David Hartwell and Kathryn Cramer identify "Banks and his brother-in-arms Ken MacLeod" as taking the "Marxist line" in the introduction to their anthology *The Space Opera Renaissance* (2006) (297). That line implies a stance critical of imperialism-colonialism. Even mainstream contemporary SF expresses a social conscience, attempting to resolve the obvious problems with imperialist-colonialist ideologies observed in recent real-world history. Yet, it often has difficulty escaping the simple reinscription of values it claims to contest. Ben Bova's *Mars* (1992), for example, tries earnestly to depict a politically correct version of the colonial narrative through the questions raised by its half-Native American protagonist. The potentially oppositional stance appears undermined by the assertion of a Russian character that space exploration can help solve the problems of poverty on earth: "We are changing the habitat of the human species. History has shown that every expansion of the human habitat has brought about an increase in wealth and a rise in living standards. That is objective fact" (235). This apology simply reinscribes the ideology of progress and economic growth associated with a capitalism driven by imperialism-colonialism.

The complexity of the relationship between SF and imperialism-colonialism cannot be denied. Istvan Csicsery-Ronay, Jr.'s "Science Fiction and Empire" provides an ostensible confirmation of the inextricable association of SF and imperialism.[28] The article, published in 2003, appears as a definitive response to the slowly rising tide of studies, like those in the special issue of *Ariel* of the previous year (Batty and Markley), which articulate a relationship between SF and postcolonialism and its resistance to Empire. Csicsery-Ronay, Jr.'s compelling development of the "homology" between Michael Hardt and Antonio Negri's concept of *Empire* (2000) and SF (240) might first appear quite discouraging for those of us seeking to create a homology between SF and the postcolonial. However, his identification of Empire and *a particular set of national* SFs, those of "Britain, France, Germany, Soviet Russia, Japan, and the U.S." (231), leaves open the door for contrasting readings and conceptions of genre literature. While the essay at times seems to imply that its argument covers *all of* SF, or rather, perhaps, that *all* SF comes from these nations, clearly, this reading simply elides or denies the existence of genre literature in non-imperial nations or non-sovereign regions. And, indeed, Csicsery-Ronay, Jr., himself appears almost disappointed with his own hypothesis "that the cognitive attraction of sf is closely linked to the imaginary world-model of Empire" (242), so that his conclusion sends out a call for projects that will reexamine it, expressing the hope for future studies and SF texts which will, "by showing us the extent to which we imagine the world in imperial terms, begin to challenge us also to see the world differently" (243). Clearly, it is my contention that there exists an entire corpus of SF that seeks to do precisely this.

Since Csicsery-Ronay, Jr.'s essay identifies certain national SFs as tools in the construction of the ideology of Empire, the potential remains for groups outside (or minorities within) those hegemonic states to use SF as a discourse of resistance. Furthermore, its restricted vision of SF (the text draws examples from a limited, albeit international, corpus that includes mostly Galactic Empire standards and cyberpunk) leaves a wide range of territory open for alternative analyses. Ralph Pordzik's *The Quest for Postcolonial Utopia* (2000) takes a step in this direction, representing the only full-length study of what can be identified as a corpus of postcolonial SF or SF-like texts (in English). His analysis follows the growing body of utopian theory (to be discussed at greater length in chapter three) which argues that in twentieth-century literature "the boundary lines between the different genres are no longer clear-cut" (4). Pordzik argues that a large number of utopian texts by English-speaking writers from both white settler and so-called black nations participate in the erasure of boundary lines in their creation of open-ended utopias which, like its classic form, imagine the world *other* than what it is.

The subversive potential in the creation of a space in which the world can be imagined as *other* has long been recognized as a trait of SF, as well, and is certainly central to the close relationship between these two forms.[29] Indeed, a significant flaw in Pordzik's analysis of a staggering number of texts resides in its conflation of utopian fiction and "speculative fiction" (13), which in some ways appears to be a means of avoiding the still-stigmatized label of SF. Many of the novels he analyzes could be referred to as science fictional just as well as utopian. And, Pordzik draws precisely on the work of a theorist of both SF *and* utopia, whose work essentially supports the notion of SF as a resistant, subversive discourse, namely, the internationally recognized Darko Suvin. Moreover, Suvin's move to historicize SF provides a theorization of the genre that takes into account the validity of both a reading like my own, which views SF as a potentially resistant, postcolonial literature, and that which views it as one that upholds a certain ideology of power. In the preface to his landmark work in SF theory, *Metamorphoses of Science Fiction* (1978), Suvin argues that "the history of SF is the result of two conflicting tendencies":

(1) the cognitive SF of Verne, Wells, Čapek, More, Lucien, Cyrano, Swift "allied to the rise of subversive social classes and their development of more sophisticated productive forces and cognitions" (ix), and;
(2) a "second-rate" form of SF dominated by a tendency toward "mystifying escapism ... steeped in the alienation of class society and in particular by the stagnation of a whilom subversive class," the bourgeoisie (ix).

While this division implies a political statement about literariness and non-literariness (that is, that the cognitive, thinking type of subversive SF is literary and that the popular evasive forms are not) to which I cannot quite subscribe, Suvin's division coincides with Csicsery-Ronay, Jr.'s historicization of SF's development coincidental to a period of national imperialist drives. The Western bourgeoisie changes position from a subversive class (at the moment when literatures of cognitive estrangement, as Suvin calls SF, were developing) to the dominant during the age of Empire, which produces Empire-SF. Csicsery-Ronay, Jr.'s analysis, which seems to rest upon a limited definition of SF, pertains then to forms that Suvin might place in the "second-rate" category. This reading now opens up the field for a new iteration, a new evolution in the genre. My argument that postcolonial SF reflects an oppositional discourse, a literature of cognitive estrangement (to which I apply the more universally accepted label of SF) produced by the subversive classes of minority, immigrant, Third World, even Québécois writers, demonstrates the continued applicability of Suvin's theory. More significantly, though, it seeks to recognize and affirm — as does Pordzik's analysis of utopia — that definitions of the genre are being stretched, are evolving and that the Galactic Empire fantasy of Earth's unquestioned domination and colonization of other worlds, so essential to what many see as the definitive, Golden Age of SF, has lost its relevance.

Using SF to critique the present world is clearly not a new phenomenon — writers have been using it since the 1960s, since the time of Mary Shelley's *Frankenstein*, since Swift's satires, depending on how far back you wish to trace its roots. A significant number of critics have examined how feminism employs

SF and its tropes to question patriarchal structures and to outline a discourse of resistance (e.g. Bammer, Barr, Hollinger, Lefanu, and Wolmark). A growing number of scholars have also explicated the relationship between SF and the postmodern (Broderick, Bukatman, Butler, Hollinger, Jameson), a form often viewed as exhibiting many of the same elements that the postcolonial uses to unravel the master narratives of Western discourse. This study's argument that contemporary SF presents a particularly fruitful format for postcolonial critiques of the present world is apparently a relatively new one. New, that is, for the genre's critics. For its writers, the idea is not so new after all, as we see in Québécois Esther Rochon's description of SF as "une littérature d'immigrants de seconde génération ou de déracinés" [a literature of second generation immigrants or of the uprooted] ("Présentation" 26)[30] or as Judith Merril realizes after putting together her first anthology of Canadian SF, *Tesseracts*, that the book is about "critical alienation" (274). It may be significant, though, too, that both of those citations come from *Canadian* writers and not Anglo-Americans.[31] Before we turn to detailed readings of the science fiction of Québec, a brief historical and thematic overview of the field will provide a foundation for the argument of the remaining chapters of this book: that SFQ indeed represents a form of postcolonial discourse.

CHAPTER ONE

SFQ: History and Themes*

> [L]a SFQ ... est écrite par des hommes et des femmes issus de cultures nettement minoritaires (québécoise, mais aussi acadienne, franco-ontarienne/manitobaine, etc.) tant au Canada que dans la très-anglosaxonne Amérique du Nord. Or tant la science-fiction européenne qu'étatsunienne est, au contraire, écrite soit par des gens issus de peuple souverain, aussi petit soit-il, soit par les représentants de la culture qui domine pour l'instant la planète. Évidemment, cette "condition précaire" teinte particulièrement l'imaginaire....
> — Jean Pettigrew, Literary Director, Éditions Alire[1]

Science Fiction in Québec: An Overview[2]

"Science fiction in Québec? You're kidding!" might be the initial response to this heading from the vast majority of the Anglo-American SF readership, a group often unusually well-read.[3] While a few authors, such as Élisabeth Vonarburg, Joël Champetier, Jean-Louis Trudel and Yves Meynard, have managed to publish in the English-language market, most readers of SF in the U.S., and indeed, many in anglophone Canada know little about the quality and quantity of SF produced in Québec. In spite of a firmly established community of writers, scholars and publishers, SF faces the same challenges and prejudices there that the genre receives elsewhere. Competition with its English-language (in the original and in translation) and metropolitan French counterparts for the same small market niche coupled with a lack of attention from an often dismissive literary establishment place it at a disadvantage. However, a handful of critics have slowly begun to recognize the significance of the French-language science fiction of Québec (SFQ) as a subgenre of, or a counterpoint to a form vastly dominated by English. In the year 2000, an Italian university dedicated an international colloquium to the topic of science fiction

---

*Works of French-Canadian science fiction available in English appear in the Works Cited marked by an asterisk.

in Québec,[4] and two more volumes of essays are in various stages of preparation.[5] This academic attention might be taken for a sign of the genre's maturity, but it (along with a handful of articles) represents only the first step in the development of an international reputation for the francophone writers of genre fiction in Canada. Many hope that the participation of francophone writers and fans in the organization of the World Science Fiction Convention in Montréal (Anticipation 2009) will also garner recognition.

Contemporary SFQ rose like a phoenix — one of its recurrent images — in the late 1960s and early 1970s out of the ashes of Québec's so-called Quiet Revolution burnt on the pyre of the October Crisis of 1970. The francophone province of Canada boasts, however, a long tradition of the fantastic, including a body of proto-science-fictional texts. Indeed, John Robert Colombo argues that SF came into its own in Québec before the rest of Canada (37). One of the tasks of SF communities everywhere has been to develop a canon that includes its precursors, and Québec has not been different in this respect.[6] The colony's very first novel, Philippe Aubert de Gaspé, fils' *L'Influence d'un livre* (1837; *The Influence of a Book*, 1993), deals with the theme of alchemy. Scholars trace its science fiction roots back to 1839, when Swiss immigrant Napoléon Aubin (1812–90) published a serial *Mon Voyage à la lune* (My Trip to the Moon) in his magazine *Le Fantasque*. Jean-Louis Trudel sees in Aubin's early work many characteristics still operative in today's SFQ: enriched by immigrant imports, published in a serial produced by a small private press, used to criticize the established order ("Science" 57). Like many later works, it also expresses the universal SF theme of space travel. More specific, nationalist debates, however, influenced the "rational speculations in French Canada" (to borrow Jean-Marc Gouanvic's term) at the end of the nineteenth and beginning of the twentieth centuries. The imaginative fiction of this period often rejects the universal, looking inward to rewrite Québec's past and project new potential histories for North America, reflecting the pro-French, ultramontane Catholic mission that dominated the province's ideology of that period. Franco-American Jules-Paul Tardivel's *Pour la patrie* (1895; *For My Country*, 1975) represents a rather paranoid, ultra-conservative Catholic fantasy which imagines Québec's struggle for independence from a Canada dominated by free-thinking, Satanic, Freemasons. Ulric Barthe's *Similia Similibus ou la Guerre au Canada* (Resemblances of the Same or War in Canada, 1916) presents an alternate history, which erases Prinzip's assassination of Archduke Franz-Ferdinand in order to begin World War I on Canadian soil with the German invasion of Québec city. The war provides Québec with a common enemy, allowing franco- and anglophones to work side-by-side. Ubald Paquin's *La Cité dans les fers* (The City in Chains, 1926) counters that federalist fantasy, depicting hero André Bertrand's independent Laurentian Republic brutally quashed by imperialists from Ottawa, the chained city of the title being Montréal.

Clear evidence of a growing knowledge of SF and its tropes, imported from a United States witnessing the genre's Golden Age, appears in several works, mostly utopian in nature, from the 1930s, 1940s and 1950s. The earliest, Emmanuel Desrosiers' *La Fin de la terre* (The End of the World, 1931) explores another major theme of later SFQ, the apocalyptic end of a civilization. Reflecting the "scientifiction" of its era, it includes extensive passages on the geo-climatic changes and future technologies of twenty-fourth century earth. A similar influence appears in the scientific extrapolations of Armand Grenier, publishing under the pseudonyms of Florent Laurin (*Erres boréales* [Northern Wanderings], 1944) and Guy René de Plour (*Défricheur de hammada* [Clearer of the Saharan Plateaus], 1953). Its title reflecting parallels with the traditional French-Canadian *roman du terroir* (novel of the land), *Défricheur* imagines French-Canadian journalist Louis Galliène exploiting agricultural and architectural technologies to build a domed paradise in the African desert. In this utopian fantasy, Grenier addresses the issue of multiculturalism; while respecting others and allowing them to participate in his community, the society is organized precisely to preserve unique cultural identities through settlement in homogeneous, family based villages. The nationalist, religious ideology that lies behind the utopian thrust appears more clearly in an earlier work. The self-proclaimed "rêve fantaisiste" *Eutopia* (1946), published under the pseudonym Jean Berthos by Thomas Bernier or Thomas Alfred Bernier (Trudel, "Science" 56–57), envisions the Order of Saint Michael rebuilding a French-Catholic North America (and beyond) out of the ruins of World War II. In spite of some similarities in theme, the sporadic science-fictional works from Québec and French Canada prior to 1960 did not develop out of any sense of interrelatedness on the part of their authors. It would take another fourteen years before what can rightly be called an SFQ "movement" began to develop.

During the 1960s and early 1970s, the experimentation occurring in Québec's mainstream literature, coupled with a budding literature for children and young adults, laid the foundations for contemporary SFQ. Indeed, the market for "jeunesse" (children and young adult) and the strong support of Éditions Paulines/Médiaspaul, among other more recent YA imprints, continue to provide a source of income and a creative outlet for several of SFQ's major players.[7] Now considered a classic, Suzanne Martel's *Quatre Montréalais en l'an 3000* (1963; rpt. as *Surréal 3000*, 1966; *The City Undergound*, 1964) pioneered not only in the province's science fiction, but also in Québec's, even Canada's, youth literature. Set in a post apocalyptic society built under Mont Royal, the novel explores possible outcomes for the future of Montréal as metonymy for Canada. Also targeting a young audience, Maurice Gagnon's *Unipax* (1965–72) and Yves Thériault's *Volpek* (1965–68) series blended James Bond-type adventure with SF tropes (Watson 38). These writers also produced adult SF and set the stage for those still practicing today. Gagnon's *Les Tours de Babylone*

(The Towers of Babylon, 1972), although derivative of the popular Anglo-American SF of the time, represents a seminal adult novel for the development of the genre in Québec, including as it does all of the features of an ambivalent, dystopian future society that controls individual behavior in the name of the collective good.

At this time, science fiction in general was stretching its legs, expanding definitions of what it could do, as seen in Michael Moorcock's New Wave in Great Britain and Harlan Ellison's *Dangerous Visions* (1967, 1972) anthologies in the United States.[8] These writers' focus on a leftist, socially conscious SF, coupled with contemporary Cold War fears about a nuclear holocaust, and stylish films like *Barbarella* (1968, dir. Roger Vadim) and Stanley Kubrick's *2001: A Space Odyssey* (1968) and *Dr. Strangelove* (1964) resulted in a general vogue for science fiction. This trend appears reflected in the nascent contemporary Québécois literature's experimentation with the fantastic and science fiction as part of a general tendency toward experimentation during this period of great political, intellectual and literary activity in Québec. Freeing themselves from the traditionalist conventions of the "French-Canadian" novel, writers sought new avenues of expression through avant-garde and marginal approaches. The former genre, which depicted in a realistic, but often idealized fashion (somewhat in the manner of George Sand's nineteenth-century social romanticism), the rural (as in Claude-Henri Grignon's *Un Homme et son péché* [*The Woman and the Miser*, 1933]) and, later, urban life of Québec (as in Gabrielle Roy's blockbuster *Bonheur d'occasion* [*The Tin Flute*, 1945]), no longer reflected their world or its aesthetics.

This confluence of influences, this context of textual experimentation led to the production of a body of unclassifiable works that are claimed as part of the SFQ canon by Gouanvic ("A Past" 72–75) and Janelle ("Au Québec" 7), while Sernine identifies them as marginal to the genre ("Historique").[9] These include such idiosyncratic texts as Emmanuel Cocke's *Va voir au ciel si j'y suis* (Go Look at the Sky to See if I'm There, 1971) and *L'Emmanuscrit de la mère morte* (The Emanuscript of the Dead Mother, 1972), self-referential novels influenced by the counter-culture and drug experimentation featuring Jésus Tanné who ultimately comes to see himself as Dieuble (Godevil), the central character in his manuscript, made into a film in the second novel. Cocke's hallucinatory work, which has more in common with that of André Breton and William S. Burroughs[10] than with those of Robert A. Heinlein or Philip K. Dick, demonstrates the truism that just because a book depicts a character flying around in a space ship it is not necessarily SF. Also included in this developmental, experimental period are the generically problematic works of Jacques Benoit (*Jos Carbone*, 1967; *Patience et Firlipon*, 1970; and *Les Princes*, 1973) and Jacques Brossard (*Le Métamorfaux*, 1974; "The Metamorfalsis"), whose later pentalogy, *L'Oiseau de feu* (The Firebird, 1989–97) will be treated in depth in subsequent chapters. Michel Tremblay, today a major force in mainstream Québec literature, began his literary career with a collection of fantastic stories influenced by H. P. Lovecraft and Belgian Jean Ray, *Contes pour buveurs attardés* (1966; *Stories for Late Night Drinkers*, 1977).[11] Janelle classifies Tremblay's *La Cité dans l'oeuf* (1969; *The City in the Egg*, 1999), a bizarre tale of a young man who inherits a glass egg which contains inside it a miniscule city of perhaps extraterrestrial origin, as SF ("Au Québec" 10). More correctly illustrative of the genre's budding development in Québec are speculations about a possible nuclear holocaust and potential human survival in mainstream Québec icon Yves Thériault's *Si la bombe m'était contée* (If the Bomb Was Told to Me, 1962) and philosopher Jean Tétreau's *Les Nomades* (The Nomads, 1967).

A significant gap occurs in the scholarship covering this period; while a number of articles (published in literary reviews, academic journals and the specialized reviews) focus on Québec's proto-SF and a growing number target the contemporary period as defined here (1974 to the present),[12] there appears to be little critical interest in this period from 1960 to 1974. In his early history, Janelle labels the handful of mainstream writers who strayed into the path of SF such as Tétreau, Thériault and Tremblay "dilettantes" ("Au Québec" 6). Sernine rightly points out that works from this period identified as SFQ typically represented isolated events in the author's career ("Historique" 41) with little influence on the writers who would soon come together as a group. Sophie Beaulé, in contrast, argues that experimental trends in mainstream literature did, indeed, influence certain writers involved in the nascent SFQ movement, citing texts that reflect the formal experimentation and the "éclatement" ("blowing-up") of genres ("Utilisation" 46).

Sernine, a core member since the group's inception, makes clear that SFQ formed not only a literary movement, but a *collective cultural project*: "On reconnaît couramment que la Science-fiction québécoise, en tant que mouvement littéraire, en tant que projet collectif, en tant que milieu culturel structuré, est née à Longueil en 1974" ("It is commonly recognized that Québec's science-fiction, as a literary movement, as a collective project, as a structured cultural milieu, was born in Longueil in 1974"; "Historique" 42). He refers to its commonly held starting point: the founding date of *Requiem*, a fanzine edited by Norbert Spehner and his students at the Cégep[13] Édouard Montpetit. Informal in tone, including a large number of brief reviews and news items, along with a small amount of fiction, it looked, at least in the eyes of the academic Gouanvic, to be relying on fandom to develop SF in Québec. In response, he turned to its writers and co-founded *imagine...* in 1979 with Esther Rochon and Clodomir Sauvé ("Réflexions" 5–6). The fact that many of the genre's writers began as its fans perhaps renders the question moot. Nonetheless, that year represents a major watershed in the movement's development. Not only did a third publishing venue for SF and fantastic appear (the fanzine *Pour ta belle gueule d'ahuri* [For Your Beautiful, Frightened Face], 1979–83), Spehner renamed his now professionalized magazine *Solaris*, hiring up-and-coming writer, the French immigrant and (then) professor at the Université du Québec-Chicoutimi, Élisabeth Vonarburg, as literary director.[14] That year she initiated another key institution for the group's development, the Congrès Boréal; this annual conference promoted personal contacts and provided a format for (often heated) debates over the genre. In addition, Vonarburg developed writing workshops to cultivate young writers' talents.

Instead of the isolated efforts of previous decades, Québec witnessed the development of an actual SFQ movement, quite conscious of its goals and its affiliation to genre literature. Janelle asserts that "depuis 1978, il existe une ... catégorie d'auteurs qui écrivent des œuvres de SF. Il s'agit, en fait, de la première génération d'écrivains québécois à pratiquer exclusivement ce genre littéraire" ("since 1978 there exists a category of authors who write works of SF. It represents, in fact, the first generation of Québec writers to practice exclusively this literary genre"; "Au Québec" 7). This first generation,[15] published short fiction and criticism in these three reviews, but also served on their editorial boards and in their physical administration. It included, in addition to Vonarburg (b. 1947), Rochon (b. 1948) and Sernine (b. Alain Lortie, 1955): Jean-Pierre April (b. 1948), René Beaulieu (b. 1957), Michel Bélil (b. 1951), Alain Bergeron (b. 1950), Denis Côté (b. 1954), Jean Dion (b. 1949), Agnès Guitard (b. 1954), Jean Pettigrew (b. 1955), Jean-François Somcynsky (publishing as Somain since 1989, b. [Paris] 1943) among others. The original core was very quickly joined by what Joël Champetier (b. 1957) calls a "second generation" which included (in addition to himself) Michel Lamontagne (b. 1954), Yves Meynard (b. 1964), Stanley Péan (b. 1966), Francine Pelletier (b. 1959), Claude-Michel Prévost (b. 1959), Marc Provencher (b. 1963) and Jean-Louis Trudel (b. 1967) ("*Solaris*" 214–15). Members of this group also founded or directed the other institutional structures necessary for the maintenance of a literary community, including conventions, conferences, literary prizes and regular columns on SF in mainstream literary reviews. They also took the essential next step and established relationships with existing publishers or founded their own presses to enable the publication of books: novels, anthologies and individual collections of short fiction.[16]

As early as 1974, Éditions Hélios had attempted an SF collection, Demain Aujourd'hui (Tomorrow Today), but it published only one novel, the Frenchman André-Jean Bonelli's *Loona; ou autrefois le ciel était bleu* (Loona, or, the Sky used to be Blue).[17] Le Préambule's "Chroniques du futur" (Chronicles of the Future), directed by Norbert Spehner, represents the first relatively successful collection, publishing eleven seminal works, including: Vonarburg's *L'Œil de la nuit* (The Eye of the Night, 1980), April's *La Machine à explorer la fiction* (The Machine for Exploring Fiction, 1980) and *Le Nord électrique* (The Electric North, 1985), Beaulieu's *Légendes de Virnie* (Legends of Virnie, 1981), Sernine's *Le Vieil homme et l'espace* (The Old Man and Space, 1981) and *Les*

Méandres du temps (The Meanderings of Time, 1983), Somcynsky's *La Planète amoureuse* (The Planet in Love, 1982), Rochon's *L'Épuisement du soleil* (The Exhaustion of the Sun, 1985) and Pelletier's *Le Temps des migrations* (The Time of Migrations, 1987). Janelle observes two developing tendencies in SFQ during this period, one universal and one distinctly North American ("Au Québec" 9). With the exception of April, whose works are almost exclusively set in some version of Québec, this first collection of SFQ, on the surface, reflects a strong tendency to look out beyond the provincial borders, creating future or interstellar settings that appear on the surface to have little to do with the contemporary issues of national sovereignty and a federal constitution. As we shall see in subsequent chapters, however, even the most universal work of SFQ reflects to some degree the concerns of the community producing it.

The rivalry between Spehner and Gouanvic continued through the 1980s;[18] just as the former's collection with Le Préambule fizzled out, the latter founded the Autres mers, autres mondes (Other seas, other worlds) imprint with Éditions Logiques in 1988. That firm began as a branch of Louis-Philippe Hébert's (*La Manufacture de machines*, 1977) software firm, Logidisque, which also sponsored the first major literary prize, the Grand Prix de la science-fiction et du fantastique québécois, renamed the Prix Jacques Brossard in 2007. This series published several anthologies edited by Gouanvic (*Dérives 5*, 1988; *SF: Dix années de science-fiction québécoise*, 1988; *C. I. N. Q.*, 1989; *Demain l'avenir*, 1990; *SOL*, 1991). In addition to novels by the veterans April, *Berlin-Bangkok* (1989), and Somain (formerly Somcynsky), *Vivre en beauté* (To Live in Beauty, 1989), it offered a forum for new writers appearing under its aegis: Guy Bouchard's *Gélules utopiques* (Utopian Gel-tabs, 1988), Michel Bélil's *La Ville oasis* (The Oasis City, 1990), Annick Perrot-Bishop's *Les Maisons de cristal* (Houses of Crystal, 1990), and André Montambault's *Étrangers!* (Foreigners! 1991). Like its predecessor, the imprint comprised less than a dozen volumes; however, the growing corpus of both science fiction and fantastic literature attracted, at least within Québec, an increasing amount of scholarly interest. To keep track of production, an annual handbook first appeared in 1984, *L'Année de la Science-fiction et du fantastique québécois* (The Year in Québécois Science Fiction and Fantasy/Fantastic); captained by Jean Pettigrew and Claude Janelle, a team of reviewers provides publication information, plot summaries and a critical assessment of literature of the imagination in all its forms. As a buyer's incentive, this invaluable resource also typically includes a few works of fiction. Further signs of legitimation appeared in 1986, when academics Aurélien Boivin, Marcel Émond and Michel Lord formed GRILFIQ (*Groupe de recherche interdisciplinaire sur les littératures fantastiques dans l'imaginaire québécois*) at the Université Laval.

Some recognition also came from their English-speaking counterparts in Canada, who were also seeking to establish an identity for themselves against the monolithic U.S.-SF. Judith Merril initiated the *Tesseracts* anthologies of

Canadian SF and included works from Québec in translation in each volume; other anthologists, like David Hartwell and Glenn Grant with their *Northern Stars* and *Northern Suns* collections, would later follow suit. At the close of the 1980s, it seemed that Janelle's assertion earlier in that decade, "La SF québécoise ne s'est jamais aussi bien portée que présentement et son avenir s'annonce prometteur" ("SFQ has never been in a better state than right now and its future holds promise"; "Au Québec" 9), held true, but this did not mean that genre literature in Québec did not face a number of challenges.

Through the 1980s and into the 1990s, many of the same core group of writers remained active in the creation and promotion of French-language SF in Canada and abroad, ensuring its survival, but this survival has often been a struggle: publishers abandoning SF collections only just begun, reviews folding, internal strife over issues of nomenclature, direction for the genre, the debate over publishing in France, concern over the development of a next generation of writers and not least of all the marginalization of SF by Québec's mainstream literary community. While in the 1960s and 1970s it was stylish for mainstream writers to dabble in SF, in the 1980s writers like Pierre Billon, whose highly successful novel *L'Enfant du cinquième nord* (1982; *The Children's Wing*, 1995) presents a tale in the vein of Stephen King's *Firestarter* (1982), involving a boy with special healing powers that government agents seek to exploit, outright refused to be associated with the perceived stigma of a genre label (Gouanvic, "Rational" 71). On the other hand, François Barcelo whose novel *Agénor, Agénor, Agénor et Agénor* (1980) depicts an extraterrestrial's visit to an allegorical Québec of the past, was spurned by critics because he refused to drop the association with SF, yet he no longer actively participates in the SFQ movement either (Gouanvic, "Rational" 71–72). Nando Michaud, whose title *Les Montres sont molles, mais les temps durs* (The Watches are Soft, But the Times Hard, 1988) reflects its surrealist bent, also remains at the margins of the movement. The cover illustration of his more recent collection *Virages dangereux et autres mauvais tournants* (Dangerous Curves and Other Bad Turns, 2003) pays direct homage to April's *Berlin-Bangkok*, whose genre-bending blend of SF, fantastic and postmodern pastiche/parody Michaud emulates. The struggle for survival is only too real for a group of writers which includes perhaps only a handful of individuals who live by their pen alone; most must hold down day jobs, some in other areas of the publication industry, quite a few in higher education and some in the civil service or technology. Competing for a share in a market slightly larger than the population of Massachusetts, a market largely occupied by editions from France and translations from English, while at the same time denied access to the larger English-speaking market because of U.S. publishers' reluctance to contract translations, Québec's science fiction community has had to rely on itself for support.

As the 1980s came to a close, Daniel Sernine asserted the importance of finding its market niche:

> Il reste encore pour la SFQ à atteindre son propre marché potentiel, les dizaines de milliers de véritables amateurs de SF, ceux pour qui les étagères de la moindre librairie sont constamment remplies de J'ai Lu, Fleuve Noir, Masque, Présence du Futur, sans parler de ce qui se publie en anglais et que nombre de francophones lisent en édition nord-américaine ["Historique" 47].
>
> SFQ still needs to reach its own potential market, tens of thousands of real SF lovers, those whose bookshelves are always full of J'ai lu, Fleuve Noir, Masque, Présence du Futur,[19] not to mention what is published in English and that a number of francophones read in North American editions.

The establishment of a reliable, brand-name identification for itself and its readers finally occurred in 1996 with the founding of Éditions Alire, which publishes not just science fiction, but also fantasy, fantastic/horror and *polar*, the French label for the detective/espionage novel. The success of Alire, celebrating its fifteen-year anniversary in 2009, can be attributed to several factors. First, in the area of science fiction, it draws upon an already established base of authors (Champetier, Meynard, Pelletier, Rochon, Sernine and Vonarburg) known to each other and Québec's fandom, something earlier collections could not necessarily do. Second, it publishes French translations of a few increasingly popular Anglo-Canadians like Guy-Gavriel Kay and Nancy Kilpatrick. Third, it spreads its net wide, yet not too wide, appealing to an audience whose interests may overlap from one genre to another. Therefore, many readers can simply look for the brand label and know that there will be something appealing inside. Still, it distinguishes clearly between its various lines so as not to disappoint readers of only one genre.[20] Finally, although Alire does not have a horror line per se (these are labeled either "Fantastique" or "Polar/Noir"), the film adaptations of five horror novels (Patrick Senécal's *Sur le seuil*; *5150, rue des ormes*; *Aliss* and *Les Sept jours du talion*, and Champetier's *La Peau blanche*), can only strengthen its reputation and financial situation.[21] It does not, however, hold a monopoly on the publication of SF and related genres as seen in the catalogues of Gatineau's Vents d'Ouest, as well as some micro-presses run by those in the milieu like Ashem in Roberval. Quite recently a handful of new presses, like Six Brumes, have sprouted up.

While Alire initially drew upon established authors, thus promoting its economic health, this meant that the same select few writers continued to dominate the 1990s into the first years of the new millennium. And dominate they did, as this decade witnessed the first monumental SFQ series on the order of Asimov's *Foundation* or Herbert's *Dune*. The first SF trilogy, Monique Corriveau's *Compagnon du soleil* had appeared in 1976, but Sernine speculates that its publisher Fides assumed the risk out of respect for an established children's author (and sister of Suzanne Martel) who died that year of cancer ("Historique" 41). The upscale mainstream publisher Leméac released SFQ's first pentalogy, Brossard's *L'Oiseau de feu* (1989–1997). Although its initial volume was critically well received, interest in the series had almost completely fizzled out by its completion in 1997 (Ransom, "Critical"). It was clearly overshadowed by Alire's release of several multi-volume works by SFQ's top three women writers, Vonarburg, Rochon and Pelletier. Francine Pelletier's *Sable et l'acier* (Sand and Steel, 1997–99) trilogy firmly established her reputation, begun with stories in periodicals and a number of adolescent novels, in the adult market (see Ransom "Distant"). She followed it up with *Les Jours de l'ombre* (Days of Shadow, 2004). In the 1990s, Esther Rochon, one of SFQ's most prolific and respected writers, published the last novel of her *Le Cycle de Vrénalik* (1974–2002) and began revisions of its earlier volumes, tying it in with her new series, the five-volume *Les Chroniques infernales* (The Infernal Chronicles; 1995–2000) (both analyzed in detail in subsequent chapters). A unique blend between fantasy and science fiction, her work lies closest to the more experimental types of mainstream literature and perhaps for that reason, as well as the feminist connection Rochon has received the most academic interest along with Vonarburg.

By this time, Vonarburg had already established her reputation as "la Première Dame de la SFQ" ("the First Lady of SFQ"; Péan); indeed, she is perhaps the group's only writer with a name recognition factor in the States. Following the success of Ursula K. Le Guin and other writers of "women's" or "feminist" SF, English translations of Vonarburg's early novels appeared not only in Canada, but in the U.K. and the U.S. (*The Silent City*, 1988/1992; *In the Mother's Land/ The Maërlande Chronicles*, 1992; and *Reluctant Voyagers*, 1995). Her *Tyranaël* (1996–97) pentalogy (discussed in detail in later chapters) bears favorable comparison, although it is in many ways quite different from, her near contemporary Kim Stanley Robinson's *Mars* trilogy. Like him, she also published free-standing stories centered upon the same setting and characters (*Contes de Tyranaël* [Tales of Tyranaël, 1994]). The first volumes of the English translation of the series, *Dreams of the Sea* (2003) and *A Game of Perfection* (2006) are now available. She has begun the new millennium exploring an increasingly popular subgenre of SF, the alternate history (or *uchronie* in French), with the five volume *Reine de Mémoire* (Queen of Memory, 2005–07), and Éditions Alire announces three more volumes set in the same universe (discussed briefly in chapter four).

As the publications for the 1990s and the first decade of the new millennium demonstrate, women have played an important role in the development of SFQ, often providing the genre-bending, experimental elements that, depending on how you look at it, lend this literature its unique flavor or steer it away from what can more easily be defined as SF. While men prove just as experimental in the short forms,[22] the novels by men that reach publication (with the clear exception of Brossard's *L'Oiseau de feu*) adhere more strictly to established forms. For purists, Daniel Sernine's SF exhibits all of the easily recognizable hallmarks of the genre, perhaps because he exorcized his fantastic impulses in separate works (*Contes de l'ombre* [Tales of Shadow, 1978]; *Légendes du vieux manoir* [Legends of the Old Manor, 1979]; *Quand vient la nuit* [When Night Falls, 1983]). His SF short stories, some of which explore the carnivalesque lifestyle of the minority who remain on Earth after a vast spatial emigration, appear in two quickly re-issued *Boulevard des étoiles* volumes (Stardust Boulevard, 1991 and 1998). Sernine's highly successful novel of drug-induced time travel, *Chronoreg* (1992, rpt.1999), was also republished at the end of the decade. He dusted off an earlier novel, already considered an SFQ classic, *Les Méandres du temps* (Time's Wanderings, 1983), revising it as the first volume of a trilogy (*La Suite du temps* [Time Suite, 2004–08]) which further develops a universe in which the Éryméens, a more fully evolved branch of humanity, watch over and intervene to ensure the survival of humans on Earth. During this period, Alain Bergeron, whose early novel *Un été de Jessica* (Jessica's Summer, 1978) had earned high praise, followed up with a collection of stories *Corps machines et rêves d'anges* (Machine Bodies and Angels' Dreams, 1997) and the closest thing to an SFQ cyberpunk novel, *Phaos* (2003). Its title refers to an artificial intelligence at the heart of a power struggle between ruling corporate interests and terrorist freedom fighters. Champetier's *La Taupe et le dragon* (1991), a tale of intrigue and espionage set in the future off-world colony New China, was picked up by Tor and translated by Jean-Louis Trudel as *Dragon's Eye* (1999). The latter published two of his own novels in France, *Pour des soleils froids* and *Le Ressuscité de l'Atlantide* (Toward Cold Suns and The Resuscitated Atlantan, both 1994), the former a blend of hard SF and cyberpunk with its identity shifting female anti-hero, the latter, as the title suggests, an exploration of the theme of Atlantis. Trudel's sometime collaborator (they write together as Laurent McAllister), Yves Meynard, produced a novel reminiscent of Tremblay's *City in the Egg*, *Un oeuf d'acier* (A Steel Egg, 1997) and a collection of stories, *La Rose du désert* (The Desert Rose, 1995). Meynard's SF reflects the finest of what might be called the Québec style, which blends motifs of national interest (loss of language, culture and identity, explorations of future dystopian societies) in settings that reach out to the universal reader.

On the eve of the third millennium, with the appearance of several English translations, publications in France, the production of several major series in Québec itself, and the re-edition of several SFQ classics, along with the hallmarks of a growing legitimacy, including an entire chapter devoted solely to SF and the fantastic in a major textbook on the contemporary literature of Québec (Lord, "Architectures"), it appeared that SFQ was healthier than ever. Yet, some argued that it faced a crisis crossing into the year 2000. Citing a decrease in production between 1990 and 1998, due in part to the folding of several fanzines as well as that of *imagine…* in 1997, which also meant a decreased presence in relation to fantastic works, Jean Pettigrew laments that, just as it had finally shaken off some of the prejudices faced by the genre, SFQ was in a state of crisis:

> Le constat, pour moi, est donc clair: la science-fiction québécoise vit actuellement une crise, et cette crise ne vient pas du manque d'intérêt du public, mais bien de la diversification de la production des auteurs traditionnels de SFQ, du manque flagrant de relève et de la raréfaction des supports de publication spécialisés [Dupuis 165].
>
> The facts are clear to me: Québec's science fiction is currently undergoing a crisis, and this crisis is not derived from a lack of audience interest, but from SFQ's traditional authors' diversification, a flagrant lack of a relay group and the reduction in supporting specialized publications.

Janelle expresses similar concerns in his state-of-the-field article also noting the loss of publishing venues, particularly for the short story, which he sees as essential to the development of a younger generation of writers who can hone their skills in short forms ("XXe siècle" 83).

Two of Pettigrew's major concerns involve the diversification of the established authors of SFQ into other genres and the lack of a new generation of writers, or at least a lack of new SF writers. The encroachment of related genres into the territory of SF cannot be denied, particularly among the younger generation of writers published by Alire and elsewhere. *Solaris*' publication of a special issue entitled "Pure Science-fiction" (151 [2004]) to celebrate its thirtieth anniversary implies that its regular issues throw the generic net a bit wider. Since it now labels itself "Science-fiction et fantastique" it cannot be blamed for featuring cover art and publishing works that code as other than SF. This departure from SFQ's SF origins can especially be seen in the growing presence of horror and heroic fantasy, both genres that were practically unpracticed in Québec as recently as 1990. Patrick Senécal (b. 1967) represents one of the milieu's hottest stars and he writes exclusively fantastic and psychological horror. He has been called the Québécois Stephen King, given the quality of writing and the skill with which he allows the fantastic element to enter the "real" world, as seen in *5,150 rue des Ormes* (5150 Elm Street, 1994, 2001). Claude Bolduc (b. 1950) honed his skills in the youth market, but his recent adult collections of tales of terror (Épouvante), *Les Yeux troubles* (Troubled Eyes, 1998) and *L'Histoire d'un soir* (Story of an Evening, 2006), demonstrate the growth of this subgenre in Québec. Relative newcomer Natasha Beaulieu (b. 1964) steeps her fantasy universe in a Goth atmosphere, developed in her trilogy, *L'Ange écarlate* (Scarlet Angel, 2000), *L'Eau noire* (Black Water, 2003) and *L'Ombre pourpre* (Purple Shadow, 2006). Experimenting in both fields, old hand Champetier's *La Mémoire du lac* (The Lake's Memory, 1994/2001) reflects a Kingian style horror, while *Les Sources de la magie* (The Sources of Magic, 2002) and *Le Voleur des steppes* (The Thief of the Steppes, 2007) provide fine examples of heroic fantasy.

Publications by Yves Meynard and Héloïse Côté illustrate the expansion of the latter sub-genre, which was argued non-existent in Québec in the 1980s (Janelle, "Fantasy" 22). The former's *The Book of Knights* (1998) appeared in English *before* he translated it into French and is acknowledged by Gene Wolfe in the dedication to *The Wizard Knight* (2004) bilogy. Meynard's forthcoming work of fantasy, *Chrysanthe*, was also written first for the English market. Côté (b. 1979) began her career with an ambitious trilogy, *Les Chroniques de l'Hudres* (The Hudres Chronicles, 2004–06). It is in the youth market, though, that heroic fantasy has boomed thanks to several successful series, including Anne Robillard's *Les Chevaliers d'Émeraude* (The Emerald Knights, beg. 2002) which has performed the rare feat of penetrating the market in France. Médiaspaul's staple fantasy (they use the term "fantastique épique") series include several figures central to the SFQ milieu, including Champetier, Trudel and Meynard (collaborating under the pseudonym Laurent McAllister), and, representative of a third generation of writers, Julie Martel.

Although Pettigrew's fears seem justified, particularly because of newcomers' interest in competing genres, this third generation of SF writers — whose style bears the imprint not only of Anglo-American SF, but of a now established SFQ — has appeared on the scene. Foremost among these stands Sylvie Bérard (b. 1965) whose prize-winning novel *Terre des Autres* (2004; *Of Wind and Sand*, 2008) represents a stunning exploration of racial relationships after Earth's colonization of the planet Sielxth. Michèle Laframboise (b. 1960) first entered the SFQ circle as an illustrator and young adult author; she published a novel in France, *Ithuriel* (2001), but her more recent adult-audience stories, like "Women are from Mars, Men are from Venus" and especially "Le Vol de l'abeille," mark a style finally coming of age. Other rising stars include Mario Tessier (b. 1959) whose "Du clonage considéré comme un des beaux arts" (Cloning Considered as One of the Fine Arts) won the 2003 Prix Solaris. Tessier's "Le Regard du trilobite" (2006) offers a suspenseful, suprise-ending treat and puts the science back into SFQ with its focus on paleontology. Mehdi Bouhalassa (b. 1974) represents the next generation of writers, and his contributions to *Solaris*, like "Anne de la Terre" (Anne of Earth, 2004) have been earmarked for upcoming translation projects. In his alternate history, "La Tentation d'Adam" (The Temptation of Adam, 2003), a historian from six hundred years in the future returns via Montréal to blow up the 1867 World Exposition in order to save his earth from dying. In addition, some founding members of the movement continue to contribute regularly to *Solaris*; since 2000, Vonarburg has published at least five texts in its pages, Trudel an amazing eight, Rochon three and Pettigrew five.

The historical overview above hints at some of the elements that characterize SFQ and set it apart from Anglo-Canadian or American SF: a somewhat incestuous relationship with its sister genre, the fantastic; a concern with style and literariness which, some argue, comes at the expense of plot; and, a dual-tendency in which it both looks beyond its own borders seeking the universal, while at the same time consistently looking back in on itself to interrogate the identity of Québec. From its conception, the science fiction of Québec has developed in tandem with the fantastic, in such a way that SFFQ (*science-fiction et fantastique du Québec*) frequently appears as an acronym and scholars often treat the two together. Rita Painchaud, author of one of a growing number of master's and doctoral theses that focus wholly or in part on SFQ and its writers, addresses the editorial approaches to the genre of works published in the early reviews, asserting: "Dès les premières années d'émergence du milieu de la SFFQ, SF et fantastique se trouvent liés, confondus même. Les deux genres forment ni plus ni moins un couple inséparable" ("From the first years of the emergence of the SFFQ milieu, SF and fantastic are linked, confused even. The two genres form no more and no less than an inseparable couple"; "Fantastique" 132). Michel Lord echoes that inseparability in his description for a French audience: "Les deux genres sont comme des frères siamois ou comme des cas de figures à la Janus" ("The two genres are like Siamese twins or like the case of Janus-faced figures"; "Feu roulant" 156). This development in conjunction with the fantastic has led to the creation of a corpus whose generic boundaries are often blurry; the works of Esther Rochon exemplify this element. The author self-identifies as a writer of SF, classifies her major works as SF, yet, in both theme and style they could be labeled heroic fantasy (*Le Cycle de Vrénalik*), philosophical allegory (*Les Chroniques infernales*), or feminist experimentation (*Coquillage*, 1985; *The Shell*, 1990).

The Janus metaphor applies not only to SFQ's development in tandem with the fantastic, but also its dual thematic approach, as it expresses both a universalist desire to present visions of human life in the future or in space that are accessible to any reader (and that could easily translate into any language) while at the same time participating—and this is key to this study— in the creation of "Québec." Even those writers whose works appear most universal in scope still appear compelled to produce at least one work that deals specifically with Québec, while others (namely April, Bélil, Barcelo) seem at times unable to escape provincial borders. For the writers of SFQ, SF may more rightly translate as "speculative fiction" or "structural fabulation" (Robert Scholes' construction) than as "science fiction," as they extrapolate alternate histories or futures for the French-speaking population of North America. The tendency toward genre-busting, particularly in Rochon and Vonarburg, in some ways reflects a similar disrespect or playfulness toward canonical Western genre found in postcolonial and postmodern writing. Whether we view them as straight science fiction or as some hybrid form (others can untangle these generic knots), these texts exploit the potential for a distanced commentary on and speculation about the current issues of debate in Québec and

Canada: issues of sovereignty, language, religion, immigration, and the cultural loss and hegemony involved in any type of colonialism. In spite of their unity in support of SFQ, these writers exhibit much diversity in both their lives and their works; it is not surprising, therefore, that each of these short stories or novels expresses its own uniquely inventive vision and transforms the form of science fiction in its own manner, to its own ends.

The extent of individual variation among a group of writers not content to follow (possibly stale) formulas demonstrates the clear self-consciousness of genre writing as *literature* in French-speaking Canada. Richard Saint-Gelais observes that "la science-fiction québécoise, au moment où elle est explicitement pensée, pratiquée et publiée comme telle, c'est-à-dire à partir des années 1970, apparaît dans un paysage littéraire fortement marquée par l'expérimentation formelle" ("Québécois science fiction, at the moment that it is explicitly thought, practiced, published as such, that is to say, from the 1970s onward, appears in a literary landscape strongly marked by formal experimentation"; "Science-fiction" 122). While, as the team of *L'Année de la science-fiction et du fantastique québécois* are not afraid to admit in their reviews, some really bad SF is regularly published in Québec, often at its author's expense, these are typically at the margins of the SFQ establishment. Those writers actively involved in the milieu maintain an extremely high standard of writing for each other; hallmarks of this literariness, as Saint-Gelais sees it, appear in the high level of intertextuality found in SFQ and its willingness to play with and defy the conventions of genre ("Science-fiction" 125–27). The inclusion of a small elite among them (April, Brossard, Carpentier, Rochon, Vonarburg) in general studies of Québec's literature, such as Laurent Mailhot's *La Littérature québécoise* (1997), confirms the literary quality of SFQ. While Robert Killheffer asserts that a certain resistance to "the siren call of plot for something more subtle and finally more rewarding" is a desirable trait, others bemoan experimentation, wishing that the science fiction of Québec was more interested in *science* (Pomerleau, "Science" 47). Given the generic ambiguity of some of the texts to be analyzed in later chapters, for clarity's sake it may be worth stating that the present study leaves questions of genre aside, accepting at face value that a text *is* SFQ if other critics or the author has labeled it as such.

In the face of this vast individual variation, how have critics identified traits common to all (or at least most) of SFQ, as well as traits that distinguish it from other SFs? In his response to this question (cited in epigraph to this chapter), Pettigrew's self-definition, which argues that one element that all writers of SFQ have in common, an element that sets them apart from Anglo-American, or even Russian or French SF, is their *difference*. Their status as minority implies a relationship between the writers of SFQ, members of a minority culture, and other writers of minority literatures, many of which make up what is commonly referred to today as postcolonial literature. Academic and noted writer of the fantastic, André Carpentier makes a parallel assertion in his discussion of SFQ's unique qualities in relationship to Québec literature as framed by one of the province's foremost literary critics, the late André Belleau. The latter argued that Québec's literature, like other "colonized" literatures, suffered from a conflict in codes, that "si l'Appareil est québécois, la Norme demeure française" ("if the Apparatus is Québec's, the Norm remains French"; 170). Carpentier argues similarly that for SFQ, the apparatus is Québec's, but the norms are imported from the Anglo-Saxon world, often translated into French and imported from France ("Science-fiction" 74). While, on the one hand, Carpentier seeks to expose a colonial-type relationship that for SFQ appears *even greater* than that of mainstream Québec literature, as he argues it suffers from a "double imposition institutionnelle, dont l'une en traduction" ("double institutional imposition, one of which is in translation"), on the other, he argues that "la SFQ a aussi développé, même si elle n'en est pas trop consciente, ses propres codes d'appropriation du genre" ("SFQ has also developed its own codes of generic appropriation, even if it is not so conscious of this"; "Science-fiction" 74). Belleau himself concludes his analysis with a description of Québec's literature that many critics would qualify as postcolonial:

> l'inscription de l'institution littéraire française dans la plupart des textes québécois ne les rend ni plus français, ni moins québécois ... le discours social québécois dans nos romans ... contredit, ou bien contourne ... les contraintes du code littéraire français [174].
>
> the inscription of the French literary institution in the majority of Québécois texts does not render them more French or less Québécois ... Québec's social discourse in our novels contradicts, or rather circumnavigates ... the constraints of the French literary code.

This argument, that Québec's literature may use French literary codes, while at the same time circumventing them, supports the thesis posited here: that SFQ represents a *post*colonial phenomenon standing in relation to, in dialogue with metropolitan powers, yet producing its own, unique, new forms. In an earlier essay, Carpentier notes SFQ's status on the periphery, but also its originality:

> il faut bien se l'avouer, nous participons encore peu à la définition et à l'évolution de la norme SF ... Qu'importe donc cette norme; ce n'est pas par elle que la SFQ trouvera sa qualité et son originalité, mais dans son imaginaire et dans son énonciation, dans son écriture ... une bonne connaissance de la SFQ passe non seulement par la compréhension des caractéristiques internes du genre, mais aussi par une juste lecture de l'action de l'histoire des idées et de la vie sociale du langage au Québec, ainsi que de notre culture et de notre société ["Aspects" 12].
>
> One has to admit that we participate very little in the definition and evolution of SF's norm.... How important is this norm anyway? It is not through it that SFQ

will find its quality and originality, but in its imagination and in its enunciation, in its writing ... a good knowledge of SFQ comes not only from an understanding of the internal characteristics of the genre, but also by a true reading of the action of intellectual and socio-linguistic history in Québec, as well as of our culture and society.

Here, Carpentier, like any postcolonial critic, removes literature from a position of text-immanence and argues for a reading that situates literature within a socio-historical, cultural and linguistic context.

This study makes explicit the connections between contemporary literature from Québec and the postcolonial context within which it has developed. The analyses of major critics like André Belleau and Pierre Nepveu do not necessarily apply explicitly "postcolonial" theories to the general literature of their province, in part simply because these developed out of the field of English-language Commonwealth literature and were not accessible to or exploited by the Academy in Québec, which typically turned to French theory. Nonetheless, their visions of Québec's contemporary mainstream literature resonate strongly with descriptions of other postcolonial literatures. This study bases its argument for reading the French-speaking province's science fiction and fantasy through the lens of postcolonial theory on the fact that it developed out of a similar socio-historical context. The inclusion of a round-table discussion of the topic, "Écrire dans une langue colonisée" (Writing in a colonized language), at the 2006 Congrès Boréal reveals the continued relevance of the socio-political climate surrounding SFQ's birth. As artifacts of cultural production works of SFQ reflect the socio-political climate in which they were produced. The following overview reveals the extent of French-Canadian science fiction and fantasy's exploration of themes also found in works of other literatures more commonly identified as postcolonial, such as alienation, oppression and resistance, the struggle for liberation, the utopian foundation of a new, post-colonial society, and the relationships developed between the various groups who now live in this society.

Alienation, Oppression and Colonialism in the SFQ Corpus

A central figure in the SFQ movement, Franco-Ontarian Jean-Louis Trudel asserts that "[a]lienation is of course a central theme" of French-Canadian SF prior to 1974 ("Science Fiction" 60). Academics Gouanvic ("Figures") and Beaulé ("Cauchemars") confirm its presence through the 1980s and after. The following overview samples contemporary SFQ since 1974, turning to the body of short stories translated into English, many for the *Tesseracts* anthology series. It also reviews the novels and anthologies published in the two initial SFQ imprints *Chroniques du futur* and *Autres mers, autres mondes*, finally turning to the publications of Éditions Alire. This representative sample reveals the extent of postcolonial themes in the contemporary science fiction of Québec and French Canada, looking explicitly at texts featuring alienation (in individuals who are strangers to themselves and in their societies, dispossessed of the world around them), oppression (by an authoritarian, hierarchically divided society), and colonialism itself. To illustrate this point, I survey a broad range of texts which depict alienated individuals or groups and/or two groups living in a dichotomous opposition which literally or metaphorically reproduces the power dynamic of the colonial situation of colonizer and colonized. Brief plot summaries follow without further analysis in the interest of space.

The title of Denis Côté's "1534" (1985) openly signals the colonial moment of Jacques Cartier's discovery of the mouth of the Saint Lawrence and aligns an imaginary Québec, frozen in time, with the totalitarian society of Orwell's *1984* (1949; also published as *Nineteen Eighty-Four*). Its alienated protagonist Winston lives in Nu-Franz, a society governed by dictator Duplex 6 (a reference to Maurice Duplessis) in a holy crusade (with its ally the Watican) against the Anglish. An internal division replicates this external division of society (French Catholic versus English Protestant) as the dominant Males harass and beat pariah class Redskins without sanction from the official peace-keeping force, the Blue Guards. The protagonist of Marc Sévigny's "The Train" (1983) shares this level of isolation in his quest to escape a self-contained society housed on an endlessly circling train. As he jumps from the safe and certain, albeit rigidly controlled, life on the carriage he leaps into a postapocalyptic desert of freedom in uncertainty. In the worlds of Sévigny's train and Côté's Nu-Franz, official control of sexual relations underscores the lack of personal freedom and self-possession wielded by the individuals in these societies. Bertrand Bergeron's "The Other" (1988) takes this element to its furthest logical step in the depiction of a future world in which men and women have become literally alienated from each other, living in total segregation through the construction of a massive wall. Joël Champetier's "The Winds of Time" (1987) imagines another totalitarian world, in which the winds blow from the future and the past, a trope which allows a moment of hope as the wind blows a fragment of a newspaper reporting on the regime's future overthrow. In "Geisha Blues" (1988) by Michel Martin (a pseudonym for collaborators Jean Dion and Guy Sirois) little girls raised in geisha boarding schools rebel against their controlled life, but when caught undergo personality modification — the ultimate estrangement from the self. An absolute alienation linked to dispossession from a home territory is marked by the very name, Nowher, of the protagonist in Jean Pettigrew's "Snoopymen All Die Like Bengal Goats" (1984), as he drifts alone through the universe, having lost all contact with others.

The decade of the 1980s also witnessed the publication of a significant number of SFQ texts that openly thematize the oppression of one group by another in a colonial or pseudo-colonial setting. René Beaulieu's "The Energy of Slaves" (1983) depicts the Planetary City's exploitation of political prisoners as labor in the mines of colony planets. Prisoner Gilbert Gilsen hopes that he can return to his family after fulfilling the Contract he has signed, not realizing that its fine print does not provide return transportation; the story's title suggests that such an interplanetary colonial system rests upon the energy of virtual slaves like Gilsen. "The Mother Migrator" (1985), along with the other stories of Francine Pelletier's collection *Le Temps des migrations* (1987), are set in a future world in which Earth has developed space colonies, in particular in the Asterman asteroid, but enforces strict control of immigration; as in Beaulieu's text, cheap labor is exploited to extract mineral resources. A number of Jean-Pierre April's works published in *La Machine à explorer la fiction* (1980) reveal protagonists alienated in a postmodern world, and a few openly thematize the real colonization of Canada by both French and English. His "Rêve canadien"[23] operates a total deterritorialization for its French-Canadian protagonist, an ethno-psychologist investigating reports of Jacques Cartier's discovery in 1534 not of Canada, but of Cameroon. When he refuses to believe the African story-teller's account of history, the latter takes his revenge by erasing Canada from the world map.

In spite of assertions like that of Jacques Pelletier that after 1980 Québec's writers move on from the intense nationalism of the previous decades ("October" 60), that Québec's literature no longer reflects an obsession with the idea of the province as "colonized," this thematic carries over into short forms of SFQ from the 1990s as well. In the postapocalyptic Montréal of Yves Meynard's "Equinox" (1992) Control City enforces order through a techno-Christian ideology which splits the world into black and white, limiting any effort at thought in shades of gray. The work implies a critique of Western philosophy's dichotomous approach to the comprehension of reality. His "Stolen Fires" (1991) depicts a man without a name fueling an endlessly circling train with no idea of why he continues; the Company provides all of his needs, but this material prosperity (as in Sévigny's "Train") comes at the price of a personal past and an identity. The "aphasia of the ego" suffered by the protagonist of Jean-Louis Trudel's "The Falafel is Better in Ottawa" (1992) signals clearly an identity crisis related to a situation of alienation (90). This bounty hunter who tracks down renegade artificial intelligences finds his own identity blurred in the sequence of aliases he has used and the machine interfaces employed in his trade so that, ultimately, distinguishing his own humanity from that of the artificial intelligences he hunts becomes impossible.

The omnipresence of the theme of alienation resulting from a dichotomous society comprised of oppressor and oppressed appears in the SFQ novel as well, including the precursors of works by contemporary writers. Unfortunately, few of these are available in translation. In Gagnon's *Les Tours de Babylone* (1972) two power blocks face off in the technologically advanced world of 2380 in which the State controls the individual by limiting knowledge. Jean Bonelli's *Loona; ou autrefois le ciel était bleu* (Loona, or, the sky used to be blue; 1974) depicts a devastated, postapocalyptic Earth divided between rival Cathars and Cytherians. Monique Corriveau's *Compagnon du soleil* (1976) sets up a dichotomy between the privileged, diurnal Companions of the Sun and the oppressed, nocturnal people of the Black Moon. The two groups are visibly distinguishable by the markings on their foreheads (sun or moon).

The two seminal SFQ collections, Le Préambule's Chroniques du futur, edited by Norbert Spehner and Éditions Logiques' Autres mers, autres mondes, directed by Gouanvic, provide another body of work to assert these themes' presence through the 1980s and into the early 1990s. In addition to several anthologies which include stories mentioned above or analyzed later (Pelletier's *Temps des migrations*, Vonarburg's *L'Oeil de la nuit* and April's *La Machine à explorer la fiction*), the former includes René Beaulieu's *Légendes de Virnie* (1981), whose setting in a post-apocalyptic Earth reflects in some ways the alienation, the dispossession from the world around them, of all humanity. Its inhabitants deal with problematized subjectivities and prejudice against new Others caused by the mutations resulting from exposure to radiation, as in the shape-shifting ability of the protagonist of "The Blue Jay." April's *Le Nord électrique* (1985) perpetuates the colonial-like exploitation of Québec's natural resources into the near future and features an alienated protagonist. A common trope of so-called soft SF, the development of extrasensory perception and telekinetic powers, seems to figure a dispossession of the self as those who discover such powers within themselves at first have no control over their own bodies and find themselves isolated from the mainstream by these powers. Such is the case of orphan Nicolas Dérec, the protagonist of Daniel Sernine's *Les Méandres du temps* (1983). The novel's successful reissue as the first part of a trilogy in 2004 demonstrates the continued relevance of and interest in these themes.

A number of short works collected by Gouanvic in the anthologies published in the series he edited (*Dérives 5*, *C. I. N. Q.*, *Demain l'avenir* and *SOL*) have been mentioned above. In addition, novels like Guy Bouchard's *Gélules utopiques* (1988) critiques the capitalist ideology typically connected to Western colonialism-imperialism and its use of science and technology to control individuals in the depiction of a megalomaniac scientist who has developed a pill to control aggression. He administers the drug to a group of androids who have been integrated into human society, adopted by families in Québec. Made aware that they are not human, the androids suffer from alienation themselves and also problematize the humanity of their adopters, since they integrate perfectly into that society. April's *Berlin-Bangkok* (1989, 1993) also explores the alienating effects of drug use on the individual, in a context that openly thematizes the postcolonial world. As a form of worker's compensation, a German drug company gives Axel Rovan, affected by "nowhere" syndrome, an ex-prostitute bride from Thailand; his disability's main symptoms include loss of memory (and its name recalls Pettigrew's "Snoopymen..."). Michel Bélil's *La Ville oasis* (1990) features the planet Razzlande, in which upper-class azures oppress the under-class turquoises. It only thinly disguises its allegory for Québec-Canada as reflected in the planet's historical periods, which include a reactionary repression called the "Grande Noirceur" (Great Blackness, the same name applied to Duplessis-era Québec) and the "Révolution paisible" (Peaceful revolution, mirroring, of course, Québec's Quiet Revolution). André Montambault, whose work is only marginally related to that of the SFQ movement, bears mention because his novel, *Étrangers!* (1991) addresses the issues of intercultural relations in an alternate- and future-history Québec. Narrated by an undocumented immigrant — an "illegal alien" — from Mexico, it tells of the near-future power struggles within the independence party against racist extremists within its ranks who wish to create a sovereign Québec that includes only the "Québécois de souche," of old French extraction. This fictionalization figures real conflicts internal to the *Parti Québécois*, divided between those adhering to a traditional, ethnic-based nationalism and progressives seeking to build an inclusive nationalist identity based on civism.

More recent novels also depict alienated protagonists living in societies reflective of a colonial-like repressive society. In an alternate future in which Québec has become an independent state, but in which Earth is under surveillance and manipulated by the, albeit benevolent, Éryméens, Daniel Sernine's *Chronoreg* (1992) carries forward current national politics within a broader context of colonialism. Yves Meynard's English-language fantasy novel *The Book of Knights* (1998) depicts a young orphan, Adelrune, raised by dour adoptive parents in an oppressive society, which he escapes by following instructions in a magic book found in his attic. Francine Pelletier focuses her trilogy, *Le Sable et l'acier* (1997–99), on three eponymous heroines, each of which faces some level of alienation and oppression. In its first volume (reminiscent of both Atwood's *Handmaid's Tale* and Vonarburg's *In the Mother's Land*), *Nelle de Vilvèq* (1997) leaves the privileged (but oppressive) realm of Vilvèq's *Hauteville* for the apparent freedom of its *Basse-ville*.[24] This ghetto establishes physical separation for the human oppressed class from its oppressor and also houses a subject mutant race, the *éfans*. The protagonist of its second volume, *Samiva de Frée* (1998) suffers a double oppression, as both a woman and an ethnic "islander" in Franchelande's military on the planet Sarion; her duty brings her to the planet of Vilvèq. Nelle and Samiva learn in the series' third volume of another group of outcasts, the survivors of an ecological holocaust, living in the *Désolation* which surrounds it. Most recently, Jean-Pierre Guillet's tribute to H. G. Wells, *La Cage de Londres* (London's Cage, 2003), depicts humans suffering from generations of slavery and oppression at the hands of Martian invaders who were not, after all, killed by a virus as in *The War of the Worlds*. Sylvie Bérard's *Terre des Autres* (2003; *Of Wind and Sand*, 2008), discussed briefly below, represents one of the most sophisticated explorations in all of SF of the topic of racial relations subsequent to Terran colonization of a planet inhabited by a sentient species, with direct references to French colonial history.

Even this small sample of texts demonstrates the frequency with which the themes of alienation, colonization, and colonial-like oppression occur in the SFQ corpus. Given the frequency of the alienated protagonist, the imaginary worlds depicted in French-Canadian science fiction and fantasy tend to be dystopian. As we shall see in the following survey, several directly utopian texts have nonetheless been penned by French Canadians.

Utopia and Dystopia in the SFQ Corpus

At least two Canadian scholars have undertaken extensive examinations of the literary utopia in Québec, Guy Bouchard and Nicholas Serruys. Bouchard's work, published largely in the 1980s and 1990s, focuses on Vonarburg's early novels, often in comparison with other feminist utopian/dystopian texts like Joanna Russ' *The Female Man* (1975) or Margaret Atwood's *The Handmaid's Tale* (1986). Serruys, whose works have just begun to appear in print, reads SFQ texts as utopian/dystopian national allegory, including Sévigny's "The Train" discussed above, Vonarburg's "Eon" (1980), and April's *Le Nord électrique* (1985) ("Véhicules"). Ceri Morgan interprets this last text as travel literature, a genre often identified as related to both science fiction and utopia. As the titles of *Eutopia*, *Les Gélules utopiques* and *La Ville oasis* suggest, a number of works mentioned above reveal SFQ's engagement with utopia. Similarly, alienation being a hallmark of dystopia, we observe overlap with the previous section's overview of that theme. An extended theoretical discussion of utopia and the related subgenres appears in chapter three, along with detailed readings of several major works. The following plot summaries simply serve to demonstrate the omnipresence of utopia/dystopia in SFQ.

Tardivel's *For My Country* (1895) represents the earliest utopian text from French Canada, according to Serruys ("Xénototalité") and demonstrates the truism that one man's heaven is another man's hell. Subtitled "a novel of the twentieth century," it projects a dystopian future in which liberal Freemasons in league with the devil control Canada, but offers a utopian horizon through its protagonist's struggles for a Catholic restoration. Alexandre Huot's *L'Impératrice d'Ungava* (The Empress of Ungava, 1927) represents a more traditional literary utopia as a Montagnais guide brings French-Canadian travellers to a hidden utopia in the Great North. Trudel describes the text as establishing a direct, although somewhat ironic, parallel between French-Canadian and Amerindian aspirations for self determination ("Science" 58; Serruys, "Xéno-totalité"). Indeed, Serruys' survey articulates a relationship between almost every known text of proto-science fiction from Québec and French Canada with the genres of utopia, dystopia and the related uchronia (alternate history), including several mentioned earlier in this chapter, such as *Eutopia* (1944), and two works published under different pseudonyms by Armand Grenier, *Erres boréales* (1944) and *Défricheur de Hammada* (1953).

Another precursor text to the contemporary SFQ movement, Suzanne Martel's *The City Underground* (1964), could be read as an ambiguous utopia. Its young hero violates the conventions by leaving his tightly controlled society under Mount Royal to explore the surface. He discovers a primitive society of anglophone survivors and must work collaboratively with them to return home, promising to bring them the wonders of underground francophone technology. Hélène Colas-Charpentier interprets it, along with Robert Gurik's play *Api 2967* (1966), Tétreau's *Les Nomades* (1967) and Gagnon's *Les Tours de Bablyone* (1972), as dystopian. She argues that these works reflect the climate of uncertainty faced during the Quiet Revolution's massive social changes. Sharon Taylor classifies Louky Bersianik's (pseud. of Lucile Durand) feminist novel *The Euguelion* (1976) as a "critical utopia" (vii). Although it uses the SF trope of the extraterrestrial to view Earth's patriarchal social systems as dystopian, it has more in common with Monique Wittig's well-known lesbian separatist utopia *Les Guérillères* (1971) than with the feminist-informed texts of utopian SF by Vonarburg.

Vonarburg's *The Silent City* (1981) deserves much more attention than it has received. By the time of its translation in 1988, the wave of feminist utopias had passed and its vision of the postapocalyptic future no longer offered to the Anglo-American audience the novelty necessary for an SF best-seller. Its female protagonist Elisa represents the last survivor in an underground, highly technological utopia, the City. She must ascend to the surface of Europe overrun by barbarian patriarchal societies which treat women, who far outnumber men due to the effects of a Trickster virus, as slaves. In order to do so, she uses her own ability — the result of genetic experimentations by her "father" Paul — as a metamorph to transform into a man. It remains a paradigmatic text for explorations of gender in SF. The French immigrant to Québec's second novel, *In the Mother's Land* (alt. trans. *The Maerlande Chronicles*, 1992), also plays with the tropes of utopia. Set in the same universe as *The Silent City*, but thousands of years later, it depicts women's domination of the social structure by keeping the tiny minority of men subordinate for sexual reproduction. Once again, the female protagonist Lisbeï confronts the rigidly codified gender relations of her society, calling them into question. I discuss Vonarburg's ambiguous utopian calling in the more recently translated *Tyranaël* novels, *Dreams of the*

Sea (1996, trans. 2003) and *A Game of Perfection* (1996, trans. 2005) in detail in chapter three.

Although I know of no other utopian/dystopian novels available in translation, a good number of the SFQ short stories translated into English for the *Tesseracts* and other Canadian anthologies take place in dystopian future settings. Esther Rochon's "Xils" (1983), "Memory Trap" (1985) and "Canadola" (1989), without describing full-fledged dystopias take place in future, often postapocalyptic societies that are clearly worse — in keeping with the definition of dystopia — than the reader's own. In the first story, New York has been taken over by the enormous flesh-eating beings of its title; in the second, a brother and sister leave their now glaciated homeland for the south, not realizing that their helpful guide is using them as guinea pigs in a study on the social disruption caused by relocation. Lorie Sauble-Otto describes the last, enigmatic story as a subversive feminist text in its depiction of an unnamed woman who agrees to work in the alienated conditions of the remote facility of Canadola (also a thinly disguised allegory for Canada) (49–55).

The entire universe of Louis-Philippe Hébert's collection of genre-bending stories in which machines seem to have the upper hand over humans, *La Manufacture des machines*, could easily be classified as dystopian. "The Hotel" (1976) provides a sample of its unsettling fictional universe. Fortunately, the inn of the title, which features staircases that lead nowhere and rats in stiletto heels who dance in a "daily folklorical demonstration" (166), "had not been conceived to entertain foreign visitors. To depend on tourism in a land like ours would certainly mean bankruptcy" (167). The welfare-state prison in which the K'rrs keep earthlings, in Roger Des Roches's "The Vertigo of Prisons" (1989), reproduces the type of controlled, authoritarian living space found in the classic dystopia. Claude-Michel Prévost's "Happy Days in Old Chernobyl" envisions Big Brother as the corporate entity McLOEDGER. Its Green Peace terrorist narrator describes resistance actions which allow for the "dream of your personal Utopia" to linger in a clearly dystopian future (190).

In addition to Denis Côté's homage to Orwell discussed above ("1534"), Anne Dandurand and Claire Dé's "Metamorphosis" presents a *1984*-style antiutopia. It allegorizes Canada through references to a four-hundred-year-old prophecy and "federast" government officials (397). Echoing the oppressive societies found in many feminist dystopias, its female protagonist lives in a world in which it is illegal for women to leave the house at night because crime is so common. Its title nod to Kafka (also apparent in Brossard's "Metamorfalsis"), refers to her transformation into a giant lobster after being scratched by a crustacean. This allows the heroine to avenge crimes against women as she rips her own rapist from crotch to head with her giant claws. During her rape, however, she has become impregnated and gives birth to one thousand hybrid lobster-humans, which she raises to become a new species with a positive influence on human society. As we shall see, the theme of hybridity, discussed in greater detail in chapter four, is also highly prevalent in SFQ.

Hybridity and Multiculturalism in the SFQ Corpus

Hybridity, syncretism, multiculturalism, *métissage*, assimilation — it is difficult to pin a name on the final major aspect of postcolonial criticism that will be explored in chapter four, with detailed analyses of several multi-volume novels. It is not surprising that a large number of SFQ texts deal with this theme, examining the question: What happens when two (or more) different cultures meet and occupy the same space? The following overview (again focusing when possible on texts available in English) leaves aside the topos of the cyborg, which Donna Haraway and others have described as a hybrid form of humanity, and looks only strictly at forms of hybridity, cultural adaptation, and multicultural approaches to depictions of societies of the future or on other planets.

Claude-Michel Prévost and Annick Perrot-Bishop, with ancestry from Haiti and Vietnam respectively, could be viewed as clear representatives of Québec's "postcolonial science fiction." Another Haitian-Québécois writer, Stanley Péan, has also participated in SFQ movement activities, but his fiction tends toward the fantastic. Prévost's fictions, like "Cappucino Buns" (1986) and "Happy Days in Old Chernobyl" (discussed above) take place in a not-so-distant future featuring corporate armies and a global multiculture. Hybridity figures more literally in Perrot-Bishop's "The Ourlandine" (1989), as its first person narrator is a literal half-breed. Her mother is an Ourlandine, a female-only race more highly evolved than the Mûriens, but forced to mate with their males to perpetuate their kind.

Bilingualism and language tensions, a central issue in Québec/Canada relations, appear central to a good number of SFQ texts. Neal Baker's examination of language politics in several stories targets this issue within the context of syncretism or hybridity. Charles Montpetit's story "Beyond the Barriers" (1992) extrapolates the development of a Babel syndrome in a Canadian future; its helpless victims uncontrollably switch from French to English in mid-sentence, producing a hybrid "Franglais." Montpetit's rendering of the societal response to this illness as a "sloganeering evocative of *Nineteen Eighty-Four*'s totalitarian Oceania" (Baker, "Politics" 41), rather than as a celebration of a ludic, multicultural code-switching reflects the tensions of the early 1990s. A similar tone appears in Jean-Louis Trudel's ""Report 323: A Quebecois [sic] Infiltration Attempt" (1994), in which a permit-bearing Franco-Ontarian worker is wrongly arrested and suffers from police brutality after Québec's independence (Baker "Politics"; Ransom "Oppositional").

Bilingual writers Trudel and Yves Meynard compose in both French and English; they are walking cultural hybrids themselves. A handful of their stories have been published *only* in English, others have been published in both languages, translated by the author. Including such texts in a survey of science fiction from Québec which otherwise ignores Anglo-Quebeckers might be viewed as problematic. And yet, the very existence of English-language science-fiction texts by individuals who are members of the francophone SFQ milieu demonstrates perhaps the very "postcoloniality," most certainly the cultural hybridity, in effect in this corpus. In particular, the Franco-Ontarian Trudel's work is typically politically engaged and takes great care to depict a relatively near-future, highly multicultural vision of the northeastern North America of the future. "Remember, The Dead Say" (1992) and "The Falafel is Always Better in Ottawa" (1992) depict a future in which particular cultures and languages confront dominant ones, struggling, sometimes successfully, to survive. His cosmopolitan cyberpunk tale, "The Paradigm Machine" (1996), even in a superficial way gives cultural and geographical nods to small-town Ontario, to a virtual Third Reich-era Nuremburg, to Havana, to North Africa. The multicultural world at the fingertips of the Net surfer, the VR hacker serves as an understood backdrop. "Proscripts of Gehenna" (1988), though, deals more directly with hybridity and creolization in a colonial setting. Francesco, one of the "imperial employees" on the "dangerous" colony planet of Gehenna (373), falls victim to the "wolfies" a pariah-group living outside the Pale. The literal mixing of blood that occurs during an attack will, however, ensure Francesco's longterm survival. The wolfies suffer not from an illness as the colonial administration qualifies their condition; rather the traits they have acquired on this planet actually represent a genetic adaptation to the new environment. These creole beings "are the ones who can survive and thrive ... the true Gehennites" (391). Like his literary collaborator, Meynard's work thematizes issues of adaptation and accommodation in multicultural, even multispecies, societies, as seen in the description of an immigrant's schizophrenic experience in "A Letter from My Mother" (1998). In "The Scalemen" the title race lives in symbiosis with Leviathan, a whale-like being that serves as their sea-going ship and which allows them to trade with other groups. Their benefactor-god Killin resembles a hybrid figure, "a Blue, a Black, a Scaleman, something of all the races" (18).

Two recent novels merit further discussion, although one remains unavailable in translation. Francine Pelletier's *Les Jours de l'ombre* (2004) explores issues of racial purity, impurity and mixing so pertinent to recent debates centered on the ethnically driven version of Québec nationalism. On O'gumbi, the humanoid (but non-mammalian, egg-bearing) race's religion recounts that an invasion by a race of metamorphs, the Akae, occurred long ago. The cult of racial purity now forces many descendants of supposed miscegenation with the Akae to either hide their true identity or to retreat to convents as penitents. Ema, the protagonist, embarks on a journey of self-discovery, as well as discovery of the truth about her culture, when she learns of her own "racial impurity." Working with a group of university researchers, she learns that the Akae are the indigenous people of O'gumbi and that the so-called "humans" who now dominate the planet are actually modified descendants of the Akae who adopted a human-style existence and culture based on the databanks of a ship that crash landed on their planet long ago. Pelletier's treatment of this theme leads the reader toward a sensibility we might label as "postcolonial," that of toleration of difference, the demonization of racism, and the acceptance of individuals and groups comprised of multiple poles of identity.

Sylvie Bérard's *Terre des Autres* (2003; *Of Wind and Sand*, 2008), like the multi-volume SFQ novels discussed at greater length in the remaining chapters of this study thematizes space colonization, intercultural relations, and eventual strategies of accommodation. Bérard explores every aspect of colonial relationships, with a complex speculation about the impact of colonialism on race and human identity as she makes sure that neither group comes off with flying colors. After an initial period during which the autocthonous darztls aid the humans in adapting to the hot, arid conditions of the planet Sielxth, racial and cultural biases soon lead to misunderstanding and outright war, including the enslavement of captive humans by darztls. In return, rogue bands of humans capture darztls and use their regenerating limbs as a renewable food source. Hope for a way out of the ugly cycle of violence and dehumanization of those involved in the colonial system appears in the Village, a secret town where escaped human slaves and renegade darztls live in harmony as equals. The Village represents an oasis-type space for those impacted by literal cases of hybridity that arose in part out of the hostile relationships between humans and darztls. A striking example appears in the case of Chloé Guilimpert who agrees to undergo genetic alteration to become a darztl in order to spy on the humans' enemies. Her experience with the sentient lizards so transforms her that, even though they never accept her fully, always suspecting a mole, when she returns to the human colony she sues to keep her darztl body. Bérard's stunning novel represents an important contribution not just to SFQ but to all SF (Ransom "Oppositional").

This catalogue-like list could go on and on. I believe the point has been made: Québec's science fiction reflects a significant preoccupation with the issues of individual alienation, hierarchical power-relations between social/ethnic groups, and colonialism (on Earth or extended into space), often setting tales dealing with these issues specifically within an estranged Québécois or North American setting. It is time now to leave behind this superficial analysis and look in-depth at how the SFQ saga deals with these issues in a manner reflective of a postcolonial discourse.

Chapter Two

Alien Nations: Dominance and Oppression in the SFQ Saga

It is engaged in what should be the simultaneous act of eliciting from history, mythology and literature, for the benefit of both genuine aliens and alienated Africans, a continuing process of self-apprehension whose temporary dislocation appears to have persuaded many of its non-existence or its irrelevance...
 — Wole Soyinka on his *Myth, Literature and the African World* [xi]

Nous avons beau déclarer que nous sommes des Nord-Américains, le regard de l'autre, hic et nunc, nous pose irrémédiablement comme alien, étrangers, comme FRENCH.
We can claim all we want to be North Americans, the gaze of the other, hic et nunc, irremediably poses us as alien, foreigners, as FRENCH.
 — André Belleau, *Surprendre les voix* [36]

J. G. Ballard's aphorism, "The only truly alien planet is Earth," as Colin Greenland observes, connects the Existentialist concept of alienation with SF's trope of the alien (qtd. in Greenland 51). The discourses of decolonization/the postcolonial and SF share this concern with alienation. The word play between the terms alienation and the alien nation signals the imbrication of the individual within the collective central to Québec's internal dialogue about nationalism and identity. This chapter argues that the science fiction of francophone Canada (SFQ), like the African literature described by Wole Soyinka above, participates in "a continuing process of self-apprehension" of what it means to be Québec or Québécois through its depictions of alienated characters living in literal alien nations that is, extraterrestrial worlds or estranged versions of Earth. Insofar as many of these alien worlds posit, albeit problematized, allegories of the French-speaking province or of French-speakers in Canada/North America, these texts also represent Québec as an alien nation estranged not only from itself but from its Others, and whose members, as a consequence, suffer from alienation. Increasingly, though, Québec and its citizens appear in these science-fictional visions as a postcolonial entity, a collectivity aware of the problematic nature of the nation, which itself can become alienating.

This chapter first outlines the concept of alienation in postcolonial theory and reveals its links to science fiction theory. The bulk of its analysis then targets a group of multi-volume novels, specifically Esther Rochon's *Le Cycle de Vrénalik* (Vrénalik Cycle, 1974–2002), Jacques Brossard's *L'Oiseau de feu* (The Firebird/The Phoenix, 1989–97) and Élisabeth Vonarburg's *Tyranaël* (1996–97). These works, examples of the "SFQ saga," explore the themes of alienation and the alien nation with particular force through the depiction of a power dynamic of domination and oppression. As we shall see, the SFQ saga represents, albeit in an estranged or distorted form, the saga of colonial history. Indeed, a striking number of SFQ texts tell all or part of a narrative that closely parallels the history of exploration, imperial conquest, colonization, resistance and, ultimately, liberation experienced by the majority of nations that comprise today's global community.

While references to colonialism-imperialism[1] may be explicit or present only metaphorically in the description of a power relation, time and again the reader of SFQ confronts threads of a common narrative that can be reduced to a few essential elements: an alienated people or individual struggles for liberation from an oppressive system, typically with the ultimate goal of founding a utopian society, often in a new world. This saga may require the erasure of the previous order through the staging of a cataclysmic event so that a phoenix-like rebirth from the ashes may occur. Many times, however, particularly in short works, only a fragment of this story is told and rarely does it end in a stable closure of utopia established. Rather, while a given text's ending may be equivocally hopeful, it may just as well dissolve into uncertainty. Because of the epic nature of this tale, works that recount it in full typically extend beyond the length of the novella or even the novel, hence my particular focus on multi-volume works. These SFQ sagas represent true cycles as Anne Besson distinguishes these from the SF or fantasy series. Rather than presenting episodic narratives that tend to stand alone within a single volume and that find unity in the presentation of recurring characters or settings, the cycle presents a narrative that develops across its several stories or volumes (22–23). Like the Icelandic family sagas, which recount the colonization of a rugged, northern land by men seeking greater personal freedom, these epic narratives depict "the struggle between man and environment, between man and himself" (Hoare 1–3). Although they focus on the individual character (Hoare 2), the "family sagas are a national literature with a definite, if not exclusive, focus on Icelandic affairs" (Andersson 197). Similarly, the SFQ saga recounts the exploits of a few central characters, and while set in a science-fictional setting, also addresses the affairs of Québec and Canada, participating in the development of a national Québécois or French-Canadian literature.

One of the difficulties in the application of postcolonial theory resides in the fluid boundaries between "the colonial" and what properly may be termed "the postcolonial" if the latter no longer refers to a precise historico-political moment, but rather, as suggested in the introduction, to a set of discursive practices. Thus, concepts initiated in the discourse of decolonization (identified with Fanon, Césaire and others contemporary to the anti-colonial movements which culminated in actual colonial independences in the post–World War II era), then employed in resistant analyses of colonial discourse (like Said's *Orientalism* or Bhabha's and Spivak's essays on nineteenth-century English literature) find themselves reapplied without distinction to the postcolonial literatures of the late twentieth century. This is true of several concepts used to organize this book's discussion of SFQ, including the notion of hybridity, but it is most particularly true of the Marxist concept of alienation. While the authors of *The Empire Writes Back* affirm that postcolonial literatures express "a condition of alienation" (Ashcroft et al. 10), alienation typically appears as the condition of the colonial subject. Such assertions, appearing in Fanon's *Black Skin, White Masks* (1952) and *The Wretched of the Earth* (1961), informed the work of later, highly influential critics like Homi K. Bhabha. They also informed the ideology of a generation of Québécois intellectuals and political activists in developing their conception of French Canada and French Canadians as colonized, which in turn influenced another generation, that of the writers of SFQ.

Obviously, the alien, the being from another planet, represents one of SF's best-known icons and its pages feature any number of alienated anti-heroes. But the concepts of alienation and its synonym, estrangement, also figure centrally in some theories of science fiction. One of the genre's foremost theorists, Darko Suvin,[2] relies upon this notion in the construction of a poetics of SF as a literature of "cognitive estrangement" in the now classic *Metamorphoses of Science Fiction* (1979). Positing that good SF, by definition, must effectuate a distancing from the "real" world of the reader that can, nonetheless, be apprehended by cognitive means, Suvin conceives the represented science-fictional world as strange, yet recognizable. This concept derives from Bertolt Brecht's theory for a Marxist theatre based on the *Verfremdungseffekt*, an effect of estrangement or alienation: "A representation that alienates is one which allows us to recognize its subject, but at the same time makes it seem unfamiliar" (192). This element of recognition, but also of *mis*recognition, is essential to both the postcolonial and the science-fictional concepts of alienation/estrangement and the critical discourses these literatures seek to establish.

Suvin indicates that Brecht adapted his term from formalist Viktor Chklovski's Russian *ostranenie*, a term which refers also to *foreignness*, itself a synonym for the alien (*Metamorphoses* 6). Then, in a footnote, Suvin reveals his own alteration of John Willett's translation of Brecht's *Short Organon for the Theatre*, which originally rendered *Verfremdungseffekt* as alienation, for his own term, estrangement. He provides the following reasoning: "estrangement was for Brecht an approach militating directly against social and cognitive alienation" (*Metamorphoses* 7n). What for Suvin appears as a matter of semantics, albeit a substantive one represents here a significant theoretical link between the postcolonial and SF. Just as Brecht sought to use his theatre to reveal and battle against class alienation, so, too, SF's estrangement can be used as a postcolonial discourse that reveals alienation in order to work against it.

In his essay on "Alienation, Estrangement," the utopian theorist Ernst Bloch reflects on Brecht's adoption of the *Verfremdungseffekt* technique and its intended goal of effectuating in the theatre spectator "a pulling back, displacing characters or occurences away from the habitual in order that they can be made to seem less self-evident. So that, if need be, the scales will fall from one's eyes" (240); "it leads away from the habitual ... allowing its object to be propped up and noticed" (243). This noticing that estrangement operates, then, should "become a supreme moment of discovery or realization. It offers insight into what lies nearest, drawn from astonishment at what lies farthest" (245). In addition to clarifying the critical function, Bloch also calls our attention to this paradoxically synonymous, yet converse relationship between the terms alienation and estrangement in Brecht's conception of them to Freud's *unheimlich* as outlined in the 1919 essay titled *The Uncanny* in English. Literally meaning "unhomely" and referring to that which is at once homely (familiar) and unhomely (strange), this concept applies directly to both the SFQ text and the colonial/postcolonial situation.

Bhabha asserts that "the 'unhomely' is a paradigmatic colonial and postcolonial condition" (9); both for colonizer and colonized, the notion of home becomes problematized. The colonizer attempts to establish a home that is familiar, which re-presents the metropolitan country of origin, but can never completely achieve this; for the colonized, the colonizer's imprint on their homeland renders the once familiar now strange. In science fiction, the alien nation, that is, the literal, extra-terrestrial or future-terrestrial community staged by the author reproduces this effect as it creates a world that is unfamiliar, yet, because the absolute Other remains unrepresentable and also because SF, as it has become a truism to assert, is often more about the here and now than about the future beyond, that world remains familiar. Here, the SFQ saga, then, is read as presenting an estranged version of Québec; the reader acquainted with the history of French-speakers in North America often faces elements of an uncanny familiarity, yet these have become unfamiliar, strange through the discourse of SF. In Suvin's theory, this estrangement operates through the effect of the *novum* (a concept borrowed from Ernst Bloch's utopian theory), the introduction of something new, and becomes the narrative strategy which ultimately defines a text as SF.

In addition to confronting the estranged, but not completely alien space or territory, we find the formerly familiar space populated with alienated individuals and collectives, that is, beings who are perhaps alien to the reader, who represent a non-human species or an estranged version of humankind, and who are often also alien to themselves. As Spivak interprets Marx for us, the condition of alienation is that of "the Being estranged from itself ... even as it seems to present Being coming home to itself through a process of necessary othering and sublating...: 'It is the confirmation of apparent being or *self-estranged* being in its negation and its transformation into the subject'" (*Early Writings* 393; qtd. in *Critique* 59). While we might initially read the "Being estranged from itself" as Québec, at first alienated, but then gaining consciousness of that state of alienation in order to attain a positive subject/national position — a process that proceeds through the othering and sublating of the forces that originally had suppressed and othered it — the deeper analysis of this chapter and the next, reveals a much more complex process at work.

Already in 1970, Haitian-Canadian academics Max Dorsinville and Maximilien Laroche observe the parallels between literatures of Québec and France's (not always) former colonies in the Antilles (Haiti, Guadeloupe and Martinique — the latter two islands remain political units of the French Republic). The best-known expression of the connection between French-Canadian literature and the alienated colonized subject, though, appears to be Maurice Arguin's *Le Roman québécois de 1944 à 1965: Symptômes du colonialisme et signes de libération* (The Québécois Novel from 1944–65: Symptoms of Colonialism and Signs of Liberation, 1985), which calls upon yet another influential volume from the era of decolonization, Albert Memmi's *The Colonizer and the Colonized* (1957). This latter work, which applies psychoanalytic theories of the subject to North Africans under the French régime, also influenced a generation of Québec's liberal and leftist sovereignists. Arguin uses its model of a colonized psyche to describe symptoms of cultural alienation, similar to those resulting from colonization, evident in literary representations of Québec. Although recently Pierre L'Hérault justifiably criticizes its totalizing approach (56), and the mainstream of Québécois literary studies has distanced itself from the discourse of decolonization, Arguin's work assists this study of contemporary SFQ in two ways. First, it establishes a pattern in Québec's earlier literary production as reflective of the cultural alienation typical of a colonized discourse. Using this as a baseline, we can then examine and argue how Québec's science fiction reflects a postcolonial discourse (this is not to say that its mainstream literature does not do so; it is simply outside the scope of this study). Second, in its definition of the *colonisé*, the colonized individual, it provides an organizing framework for our analysis of the alienated characters and societies portrayed in the SFQ saga.

Arguin identifies three phases in the development of the modern Québécois novel after World War II, which he distinguishes from the agricultural novel (*roman du terroir*) dominant in French-Canadian literature until then. First, the *roman de mœurs urbaines*, the urban novel practiced by Gabrielle Roy, Ringuet, Roger Lemelin and others between 1944 and 1961, portrays the urban space in terms of an ethnic conflict between anglophones and francophones, a conflict set up as a power relation that mirrors the colonial situation. Economic division (haves vs. have nots) and differences in value systems reinforce the conflictual relationship between the two ethnic groups, each presented as a coherent, essential whole. Geography reinforces this dichotomy as the texts represent a living space physically divided by a nearly insurmountable frontier separating the two groups (Arguin 31).

A second phase, according to Arguin, appears in the *roman psychologique*, the psychological novel of the 1950s and 1960s, which focuses on the personality of a type-figure, *le révolté* (101, 138, 143–44). Appearing in works like Françoise Loranger's *Mathieu* (1949), Anne Hébert's *Le Torrent* (1951), and Yves Thériault's *Cul-de-sac* (1961), this rebel typically remains personally alienated, finding himself (or herself, as in Marie-Claire Blais' *La Belle bête* [1959; *Mad Shadows*, 1960]) incapable of living within the colonized society that values religion, family and a mythic past (Arguin 139–50). The protagonist's rebellion against these oppressive *valeurs refuges* (refuge values) represents for Arguin early signs of liberation in Québec, as the psychological novel depicts its characters' realization of their oppression. Its dénouement varies, but typically the protagonist frees him- or herself from the cultural ties that bind or is destroyed by them. Self-awareness, then, represents a first stage toward a liberation that not all can achieve.

Finally, in a third phase, Arguin situates the much-analyzed protest novels published between 1960 and 1965 as *romans de contestation*, which reflect a more fully developed self-consciousness of Québec's francophone society as oppressed, not only by the anglophone grip on economic power, but also by its own conception of itself, its reliance on a national identity rooted in Catholicism, the family and a sacralized past history of victimization originating in the Conquest of 1760 (the same refuge values that bound the *révolté* of the psychological novel). These novels represent, for Arguin, "une véritable révolution culturelle" ("a veritable cultural revolution") as they engage in "la recherche d'une identité nouvelle qui seule peut permettre à l'individu et à la collectivité de prendre en main leur destin" ("the quest for a new identity, the only thing that can permit the individual and the collectivity to take control of their destiny"; 176). These novels, like Hubert Aquin's *Prochain épisode* (1965; *Next Episode*, 2001) or Claude Jasmin's *Ethel et le terroriste* (1964; *Ethel and the Terrorist*, 1965), depict a revolutionary aware of his alienation and its inextricable ties to collective history, but who choses violence as a (typically ineffective) means of overcoming it (220). Arguin does not, however, see a complete or a healthy liberation at work here, but rather "un projet collectif encore mal défini" ("a still poorly defined collective project"; 222). While he does not use the term, Arguin implies that Québec's literature does not yet reflect a fully decolonized, that is post-colonial, society.

This chapter argues that this next step in the "liberation" of Québec through its literature appears, at least in part, in the SFQ saga. Not only does SFQ develop precisely during the next temporal phase in Québec's literary development (from the early 1970s), the SFQ saga depicts characters in fictional societies which undergo an evolution from repression to liberation similar to that identified by Arguin in Québec's realist literature of the previous era. These later works, though, building on the foundations already laid, take this process a step further, staging collective projects that eventually come to define themselves much more clearly and depicting individuals who ultimately achieve a greater state of self-realization within those projects. The SFQ saga exploits elements of the realist urban novel, particularly in its depiction of two groups locked in a hierarchical opposition, which literally or metaphorically reproduces the colonial system. Typically, the identification group, the group from whose point of view the narrative is related and which attracts the reader's sympathy, stands in the position of the oppressed. As we shall see, however, the SFQ saga alters and manipulates this thematic in order to subvert or expose the binary logic of the colonial system which has often simply been reinscribed or repolarized in the novels from an earlier period. As forms of postcolonial discourse they typically seek to deconstruct the previously established site of power in order to redefine the limits of possibility for the imaginary groups and individuals they depict.

Arguin also describes the "colonized" stage of the French-Canadian novel as reflecting an "ideology of survival" and that signs of liberation appear in later works which outline an "ideology of rebirth." This pattern appears in SFQ, particularly in the subgenre's fascination with the image of the phoenix. Somewhat mirroring the model Arguin observes in the earlier realist novel, the postcolonial SFQ saga first posits a situation of an oppressed people living in survival mode, but it then develops the saga of liberation as an ideology of rebirth arises and is then acted out in the foundation of a utopian new world colony (the topic of chapter three). This chapter begins with a brief description of the works in question, their conception and publication, as well as a discussion of their authors' place within the SFQ movement. It and the following chapters then deal in detail with how the SFQ saga — a corpus comprised of the multi-volume novels of Jacques Brossard, Esther Rochon and Élisabeth Vonarburg — reflects the themes and discursive strategies of postcolonialism or, at times, how it simply reinscribes colonial fantasy.

The Asven Nation of Rochon's *Le Cycle de Vrénalik*

Esther Rochon's *Le Cycle de Vrénalik* (1974–2002) provides a classic example of the SFQ saga in the full development of its narrative. Tracing the evolution of a people, the Asven, from their foundation as a nation on the Archipelago of Vrénalik through prosperity, disaster, stagnation, renaissance and, finally, mass migration to a new homeland on another continent, Rochon explores the form's key themes of oppression, liberation and the founding of a new world utopia. She does so from what I identify as a "postcolonial sensibility," a sense of self and/in the world that includes an awareness of her own positionality,[3] an openness to the Other/difference, and a world view critical of Western, imperialist thought. This sensibility's influence can perhaps explain her genre-bending form of SF.

Raised in a cosmopolitan, yet nationalistic, literary and artistic milieu, Rochon admits that her fiction's privileging of marginal figures reflects her own "sentiment d'aliénation" when young (Beaulieu 14). Her peripatetic childhood reflects this sense of homelessness:

> Immigrante, je ne l'étais pas, mais déracinée, en un certain sens, oui.... Parmi cette multitude d'accents, de coutumes, de milieux déjà établis où j'étais demeurée quelques mois ou quelques années, qu'est-ce qui représentait la norme à suivre? ... Mon vrai pays était à l'intérieur de moi-même [Rochon, "Présentation" 26]
>
> Immigrant, I wasn't, but uprooted, yes, in a certain sense.... Amidst this multitude of accents, customs, pre-established settings where I had stayed a few months or a few years, what represented the norm to follow? ... My real country was inside myself.

Actively choosing to write under her (French-coded) married name so as *not* to elicit confusion as to her Québécois identity (she was born Blackburn[4]), later in adulthood, she came to question Québec's nationalism and the colonization of North America, admitting:

> En effet, depuis que j'étais enfant, j'avais mes doutes: qu'est-ce que nous étions venus faire sur ce continent-ci? Pourquoi vouloir le peupler de Blancs, alors qu'il y avait déjà des Indiens, qui ne nous avaient pas invités? ... En quoi le monde technologique était-il supérieur à ce qu'il y avait avant? ... Et puis toute cette rivalité entre Anglais et Français, ça rimait à quoi? [Rochon, "Présentation" 52].
>
> In effect, since I had been a child, I had my doubts: what had we come to do on this continent? Why desire to populate it with Whites, while there were Indians already here who had not invited us? ... And how exactly was the technological world superior to what was here before? ... And then this rivalry between English and French, what was that about?

Also an ardent Buddhist, Rochon effectively translates this sensibility in her works, as we shall see in *Le Cycle de Vrénalik* and *Les Chroniques infernales* (The Infernal Chronicles, 1995–2000; discussed in chapter three).

A central figure in Québec's science-fiction and fantasy community, Rochon published her first novel in 1974, a date coinciding with the commonly cited founding date of SFQ as a conscious movement. Reviewers have identified several of her works as major achievements in Québec letters of any genre, "tous genres confondus" (Pettigrew 168). Proud of her affiliation, Rochon asserts, "[c]e que j'écris, en mon for intérieur, ce n'est pas de la littérature. C'est de la science-fiction" ("what I write, deep down inside, is not literature. It is science fiction"; "Esther" 88). She nonetheless laments the ghetto Québec's mainstream press often reserves for genre literature. While her *œuvre* has received the most critical attention outside of Québec after that of Vonarburg, in part because her works — particularly her novel *Coquillage* (1985; *The Shell,* 1990) — reflect a strong feminist bent, its importance exceeds the modest body of criticism dedicated to it. As French critic Roger Bozzetto points out, her reputation in Europe has failed to grow because of the limited diffusion of her works (33), furthermore, the rarity of English translations and her own lack of self-promotion have kept her North American audience limited. Yet, in 2000 Rochon was the invited author at an international conference on SFQ in Italy (Novelli).

Although the label has yet to be applied to Rochon's opus, its themes and strategies blatantly reflect those identified as definitive of or appropriate to the postcolonial. Particularly striking is Bozzetto's view of her work's relationship to science, which neatly mirrors that attributed to Amitav Ghosh's *The Calcutta Chromosome* (Chambers, Nelson), as well as certain postcolonial critiques of Western science:

> Ce savoir de la science est impérialiste et totalitaire, car unidimensionnel: il tend à s'imposer comme seule référence de la réalité. Au point de se confondre, abusivement, avec "la nature des choses." Les fictions d'Esther Rochon, appuyées sur une quête personnelle, sur la fréquentation d'autres points d'attaque de la réalité, se présentent comme une ironisation détachée de ces prétensions [143].

> This knowledge that is science is imperialist and totalitarian, because unidimensional; it tends to impose itself as the sole reference to reality to the point of blurring itself, improperly, with "the nature of things." Esther Rochon's fictions, supported by a personal quest, by association with other points of attack on reality, present themselves as detached ironizations of these pretensions.

Rochon's undermining of science as the defining discourse of reality, reflecting Buddhist philosophy's focus on the relativity and illusiveness of the "real," contests a Western imperialist model. Gabrielle Pascal's analysis of her use of magic as transgressive also suggests Rochon's defiance of science and, consequently, the rules of logic to which it adheres. Furthermore, her works break down the traditional hierarchized dichotomies which Western philosophy and ideology employ to understand the world, as Annick Chapdelaine has observed of her feminist treatment of male and female characters (128–30).

Several critics (Bozzetto 138; Chapdelaine 129–30; Nepveu 216) have identified the "center" as a major theme in Rochon's work, notably in the stories referred to as the Labyrinth cycle in *Le Traversier* (The Ferry, 1987) and *Le Piège à souvenirs* (The Memory Trap, 1991). Center and periphery are focal terms in postcolonial theory which identifies the center as the mainstream, the metropole, the colonial power, while the periphery obviously includes those outside an identified Pale. While Rochon's characters are in search of a "center," her conception is anything but that of the site of power. In her conception, informed by the Eastern philosophy of Buddhism, this almost undefinable element appears as a center surrounded by a void, an image of divinity, but also an interface between the world and being, as well as "l'infinie potentialité de ses significations" ("the infinite potential of its meanings"; Vonarburg, "Notes" 19).

The genesis of the fictional universe of Vrénalik can be traced back to Rochon's teenage years in the early 1960s, during Québec's Quiet Revolution, whose changes its author witnessed first hand (Beaulieu 13; Lord "Esther" 38). Indeed, Rochon, along with the other original members of the SFQ group, belongs to the first generation of French Canadians to call itself *Québécois*. Acknowledging that, taking for granted this national identity, she did not feel it necessary to fight the same battles that her parents had fought (Rochon, "Présentation" 36); Rochon nonetheless read the literature engaged in defining that identity as a young adult. She read writers analyzed in Arguin, including Gérard Bessette, André Langevin (Lord, "Esther" 37), Jean-Guy Pilon and Fernand Ouellette (Hannan 229), as well as Gaston Miron and the Hexagone group (Beaulieu 13). The initial publication of the first volume of the Vrénalik Cycle, *En Hommage aux araignées* (In Praise of Spiders; later republished as *L'Aigle des profondeurs* [The Eagle of the Depths, 2002]),[5] occurred only four years after the traumatic events of October 1970.

The second and third novels of the series as reissued by Alire, *Le Rêveur dans la Citadelle* (The Dreamer in the Citadel, 1998) and *L'Archipel noir* (The Black Archipelago, 1999), first appeared as a single volume *L'Épuisement du soleil* (The Exhaustion of the Sun, 1985). Reflective of the peripatetic nature of the saga's publication history, *Le Rêveur dans la Citadelle* was published in German as *Der Träumer in der Zitadelle* (1977) nearly ten years before its inclusion in *L'Épuisement du soleil*. The novel's conception and composition precedes its publication in Québec by a considerable length of time. This time lapse holds significance in the context of my argument that the SFQ saga reflects a developmental stage in Québécois literature that directly follows Arguin's description of the novels of the 1960s. All three works discussed here, although not published (or republished) until the 1980s and even the late 1990s, were conceived and initially drafted during the 1960s and 1970s. Rochon comments on the atmosphere in Québec during the final stages of editing:

> C'était en 76–78, vers la fin de la contre-culture, mais il y avait une sorte de questionnement très aigu, de type philosophique. Le Québec se rendait compte des limites de son mythe du pays, mais aussi ne pouvait pas prendre inconditionnellement tout l'apport culturel, économique et politique sans faire une synthèse. C'est alors qu'il y a eu un hiatus, une crise économique aussi [Lord, "Esther" 38].
>
> It was in 76–78, near the end of the counter-culture, but there was a sort of intense, philosophical questioning. Québec was realizing the limits of its national myth, but still could not accept unconditionally any cultural, economic and political contribution without making a synthesis. At that time there was also a hiatus, an economic crisis.

This chapter's analysis will focus in particular on this atmosphere of questioning a national myth, which appears reflected not only in Rochon's depiction of the oppression of Vrénalik's Asven people, but also in her portrait of the more "civilized" land to the south, whose inhabitants also face alienation and economic oppression.

Composed, revised and edited over nearly forty years (c. 1963–2002), Rochon's *Cycle de Vrénalik* reflects an embeddedness in the literature and culture of Québec developing throughout that period. Anyone familiar with Québec's history and its nationalist debates will immediately see parallels with the universe of the Asven, as have nearly all of Rochon's reviewers and interviewers. And when Michel Lord refers to her work as "une vaste métaphore de l'histoire du Québec" ("a vast metaphor for the history of Québec"; "Esther" 37), the author does not deny the connection. In her review of *L'Aigle des profondeurs*, Élisabeth Vonarburg argues "l'on ne manquera pas d'établir des parallèles avec la situation du Québec depuis trente ans, mais heureusement la fiction de Rochon ne se prête pas à ce genre de réductionnisme facile" ("one will not fail to establish parallels with the situation in Québec of the last thirty years, but happily Rochon's fiction does not lend itself to this type of facile reductionism"; "Notes" 128). The following analysis, while it does make some reductive comments, concludes with Vonarburg that the sophistication of Rochon's narrative transcends a simplistic "a = b" allegorical reading.

The very multi-valence of Rochon's work, resulting in the difficulty of pinning neat allegorical labels upon its actors, aligns it with the postcolonial. For the moment, though, precisely in order to demonstrate how her work surpasses colonial models that preceded it, we will return to Arguin's description of earlier depictions of French-Canadian society as alienated and colonized through the establishment of two groups, oppressor and oppressed, set in opposition along ethnic lines. Arguin identifies the following traits in the *roman de mœurs urbaines*' (the novel of urban mores') depiction of French-Canadian society:

(1) an oppressed group with a *clear consciousness of its identity* expressed as a pre-existing, essential quality (45–47);

(2) that group is sustained by an *ideology of survival* which closely guards cultural traditions (versus an ideology of development or progress) (61);

(3) the status quo of cultural survival is no longer viable because of changing conditions, drastic decline, or an *impending cataclysm* (61);

(4) related to its non-viability is the group's *dispossession*, its lack of material possessions, including property and material sustenance which may alone result in the group's disappearance (37–38);

(5) related to its dispossession and its identity, the group is both protected and isolated by a nearly *uncrossable frontier* (42–45);

(6) that frontier separates it from a *dominating Other* (50);

(7) the group's oppression by that Other can be traced back to a *key date in the historical past*, namely, the Conquest of 1760 (51–52);

(8) the difference between the group and its dominator is not only ethnic, but constitutes a *difference in value systems*. (53)

Rochon's description of the Asven as an oppressed, alienated people in *L'Aigle des profondeurs* and *L'Archipel noir* reflects precisely these traits.

The narrative emphasizes Vrénalik's isolation, subjection, and the apathy of its inhabitants. It is clear, though, that the Asven possess a distinct sense of their identity as a group, even as a nation, albeit not a sovereign one. Held together by an ideology of survival, they seek to preserve the status quo, to maintain the society as it has always been, refusing change: "Les Asven[6] n'avaient pas envie de changer d'attitude" ("The Asven did not want to change their attitude"; AP18). This ideology becomes increasingly untenable as the "superstition nationale" ("national superstition"; AP129), a four-hundred-year-old curse, holds the Asven prisoner on their islands preventing them from leaving or developing. In their efforts to hold things together, neither have they been able to find a way to seek help from beyond their borders: "Ils avaient l'impression que le monde avait évolué au loin, en les abandonnant derrière" ("They had the impression that the world had evolved far away, leaving them behind"; AP24). Yet, in spite of their abjection and the threat of "l'anéantissement de notre peuple" (the extinction of our people; AP134), sorcerer's apprentice Anar Vranengal makes it clear that "nous formons une collectivité malgré tout" ("we make up a collectivity nonetheless"; AP49). This group has reached, however, a crisis point, fearing not only the loss of their language and culture, but also physical extinction:

> On ne parlera peut-être plus asven; peu importe si nous avons des descendants, ils ne connaîtront pas nos traditions.... Ils ne sauront plus d'où ils viennent. Et même si ce n'était pas le cas, le monde que nous connaissons est condamné [AP199].

Asven will no longer be spoken; it matters little if we have descendants, since they won't know our traditions.... They won't know anymore where they come from. And even if this is not the case, the world that we know is condemned.

It is clear that the status quo will soon lead to annihilation: "leur monde lentement s'immobilisait, tendait vers un moment ultime où plus rien ne bougerait dans l'Archipel" ("their world was slowly immobilizing, tending toward an ultimate moment where nothing else would move on the Archipelago"; AP20).

This extinction will arise directly from the clear state of dispossession in which the Asven live. The disrepair of once flourishing cities reflects the precariousness of their physical existence:

> Les pierres voulaient que les hommes s'en aillent; ceux-ci s'acharnaient à rester, et leurs maisons s'écroulaient les unes après les autres.... Les frises, les bas-reliefs qui avaient orné les édifices ne subsistaient qu'à l'état de fragments si subtilement défigurés.... Restait-il un seul balcon intact? Un jardin qui ne fût encombré des ruines de sa maison? Une rue qui ne fût pas défoncé? Tout tombait en morceaux, plus rien ne tenait [AP23].
>
> The stones wanted the men to leave; the latter dug in to stay, and their houses caved in one after the other.... The frescoes and bas-reliefs that had adorned these buildings remained only in a state of subtly disfigured fragments.... Was there even one balcony left intact? A garden that was not encumbered with the ruins of its house? A street that was not uprooted? Everything was falling to pieces, nothing held together anymore.

The capital city is so delapidated that animals have begun to inhabit unoccupied sections of the ruins (AP117). The declining population, resulting from a decreased natality, stands as a clear sign of impending extinction. The sister islands of the Archipelago lie almost completely depopulated, their inhabitants having come to the capital "sans doute pour se sentir moins isolés" ("no doubt to feel less isolated"; AN53). The concern over food and other resources occupies them, as well as the threat posed by the elements.

In Arguin's schema, the division of space reinforces the notion of dispossession and separates the oppressed group from its Other(s), while preventing it from transcending its ideology of survival to develop a viable philosophy of growth. The Asven perceive themselves as imprisoned because of the Ocean-god Haztlén's curse, which has raised an uncrossable barrier between their Archipelago and the world outside. Indeed, this space continues to recede, the island closes in on them even further, especially in winter when the entire community finds shelter and companionship in the Citadel of Frulken. Ostensible proof of the curse's efficacy appears when a minor character, Iskiad, fails in his attempt to leave the Archipelago and visit his daughter, Chann, on the mainland.

That another group exerts dominance over the "gens de l'Archipel" ("people of the Archipelago") appears clearly from the start as the early pages of the first volume depict their submission to the violence of outsiders (AP13, 232). Once a year trade ships visit and:

> Dans la ville, les marins couraient après les femmes Asven: ils aimaient leur faire violence et, de retour au pays, se vanter de leurs prouesses, tandis qu'elles avaient profité de l'occasion pour mettre en train un enfant. Les courses, les cris, les gifles et le reste se déroulaient sous les yeux de quelques Asven fumant leur pipe; d'autres s'enfermaient chez eux pour ne rien entendre. Aucun d'entre eux ne manifestait d'hostilité: si les marins décidaient de ne plus revenir! [AP22].
>
> In the city, sailors would run after the Asven women: they loved to do them violence and, once home, brag about their prowess, while the women had profited from the occasion by getting a child underway. The running, the cries, the slaps and the rest went on under the eyes of a few Asven smoking their pipes; others shut themselves up at home so as not to hear anything. None of them showed any hostility: what if the sailors decided not to come back!

This relationship reveals the Asven's subject status, as well as the Other's pleasure in exerting dominance. Already, though, Rochon seems to be subverting the binary logic of oppressor/oppressed as the raped women benefit if they conceive a child, as the literal seeds are sown for a métissage that will contribute to survival. Not an independent nation, the Archipelago belongs by international law to the land of Ister-Inga (AP222). The official Other that exerts dominance over the Asven appears as "le Sud," the continent to the South. As Christian Morissonneau explains the "Cardinal Directions of the Québécois," this geography codes the dominant culture in the United States, as "[p]opular consensus places the South beyond Québec's territory, in Miami and the rest of Florida" (31). The Archipelago, then, may represent not only Québec, but also other islands of French-speaking cultures scattered throughout the sea of anglophone North America. However, the multivalence of Rochon's allegory also allows a reading of the Asven as Amerindian, which changes the coding of the South in Morissonneau's schema, since "from a Native (Inuit and Cree) perspective, the South is the Montreal-Quebec City corridor, the seat of government and economic institutions, which milks the resources and pillages the cultures of the North" (31). The pillaging of Frulken described in the first pages of *L'Archipel noir* supports this interpretation.

Realist novels dating from the period of Vrénalik's conception in Rochon's *imaginaire* depict French Canadians as a colonized, oppressed group since the Conquest of 1760. Similarly the moment of Asven subjection can be identified clearly with a precise moment in the collective history. Through its repetition, the refrain "quatre siècles de malheur tombés sur le pays" ("four centuries of unhappiness fallen on the land"; AP11), marking the date of the fatal curse, seems to echo and even parody a nationalist discourse that harps back to the French defeat on the Plains of Abraham. The length of time appears particularly significant as Québec city celebrated the 400th anniversary of its foundation in 2008.

Finally, two values systems, that of the Asven and that of the continent to its south, clearly stand in conflict. Anar Vranengal contrasts these: "Nous utilisons souvent symboles et légendes pour nous exprimer, tandis que les gens du Sud se contentent de décrire ce que leurs sens et leur intelligence leur transmettent" ("We often use symbols and legends to express ourselves, while the people of the south are content to describe what their senses and their intelligence transmits to them"; AP28). While the Asven believe in the efficacy of magic, Southerners rely on empirical, materialist thought systems in their "civilisation fondée sur le rationnel" ("civilization founded on the rational"; ED266). The two societies also differ in the degree to which they value individual humanity; while the small community of Vrénalik validates interpersonal relations and practices mutual aid, the large city of Ister-Inga, for example, reduces individuals to anonymity. Its impersonal system requires identification cards and "une des premières règles de vie était de ne pas attirer l'attention" ("one of the first rules of life was to not call attention to oneself"; ED158).

While Rochon's depiction of the Asven, then, mirrors in many ways the French Canadian painted in the novels of the 1940s and 1950s, this image quickly becomes distorted. The contemporary writer of science fiction no longer fully accepts either the portrait her realist literary forebears painted or the totalizing critique which sees their world in such terms. Rochon takes the tropes of the discourse of decolonization and turns them on their head. Her sophisticated vision of the world transcends the black and white dichotomies established first by colonial discourses which seek to justify oppression, then by anti-colonial discourses which call attention to that dichotomous structure, but often simply reverse its poles. Rochon's postcolonial discourse seeks a synthesis that will transcend this situation; while the Asven appear to reflect the traits of a colonized society outlined by Arguin, their depiction also subverts and/or nuances those traits.

As opposed to Arguin's image of the colonized French Canadians depicted in the fiction of an earlier generation, the solid group identity of the Asven reveals itself not as an essentialist conception based on an ethnicity into which one must be born in order to belong. Rochon takes care to depict the Asven as accepting others who wish to join them, an element discussed in further detail in chapter four. This constructed, rather than essential, notion of collective identity appears most clearly reflected in the development of Taïm Sutherland traced through *L'Archipel noir* and into *L'Espace du diamant*. This outsider who liberates the Archipelago from its curse by recovering the ancient idol of Hatzlén gradually *becomes* Asven.

As critics have noted, aspects of the last two novels in the cycle resemble the *roman d'apprentissage* (Beaulieu 15; Le Brun, "Planète" 125) or *Bildungsro-*

man, as Sutherland (among other characters) searches for a meaningful life. His search ultimately becomes a quest for his place and identity within a group, which begins in his newly adopted home:

> Avec les jours qui passaient, sans changement, Sutherland avait l'impression de s'intégrer au monde de la Citadelle. Il avait appris quelques mots de la langue de l'Archipel, et il somnolait dans la grande salle avec les autres tandis que, dans son esprit, les souvenirs vivants d'Ister-Inga, d'Ougris, de sa famille et de Chann Iskiad, devenaient de simples images des pays du Sud, des gens qui y demeuraient, du passé [AN52].
>
> With the days that passed, without change, Sutherland had the impression of integrating into the world of the Citadel. He had learned a few words in the Archipelago's language, and he dozed in the great hall with the others while, in his mind, the fresh memories of Ister-Inga, Ougris, his family and Chann Iskiad became simple images of the South, of people who lived there, of the past.

Already asking himself "si ce pays-là n'était pas, de manière mystérieuse, sa véritable patrie" ("if this land was not, in some mysterious way, his true homeland"; AN60), Sutherland has begun the process of adapting to his new environment and his former existence takes on an unreality. Yet it seems that he must lose his past identity before he can undertake the quest that will lead him to a new one. Rochon describes this identity crisis in terms of alienation: he "avait l'impression d'être dépourvu de droits ou d'identité" ("had the impression of being deprived of rights or identity"), and he experiences "un sentiment de dépaysement ... vis-à-vis de lui-même" ("a sense of being outside of himself"; AN62–63).

Ultimately, the quest he has undertaken by leaving home will be transformatory. Ivendra, the Archipelago's sorcerer, and his apprentice Anar Vranengal, believe Sutherland destined to find the ancient temple of Haztlén, to restore his statue to the capital city Frulken, and thus to liberate the Asven from the Ocean-god's curse. He fulfills this mission, but as a result of his traumatic adventure, Sutherland loses his memory, crossing the Archipelago back to Frulken in a sort of fugue state. Temporarily stripped of his past, Sutherland becomes a national hero for the Asven, having recuperated theirs, but accepting this new identity within the collective, however, takes some time. Returning to his homeland of Ister-Inga simply leaves him still more alienated; there he remains silent about the land he now realizes is his home: "Sutherland ne parlait à personne de son pays, le Nord inavouable" ("Sutherland spoke to no one about his country, the inavowable North"; ED113). Recognized by the people of yet another region, Catadial, as "un homme de Vrénalik" ("a man from Vrénalik"; ED133), like Saint Peter, on three occasions, he denies this identification (ED133, 169, 172). Only at the end of the Cycle, having accomplished a second mission to further Vrénalik's independance, he accepts who he is, returning to "le pays selon son coeur" ("the land of his heart") for good (ED354).

His role as Vrénalik's national hero culminates and legitimates his gradual acceptance upon arrival in Frulken and the growing conception of his identity as somehow Asven, even though his name references its Other, S[o]uther[n]land. Sutherland's conversion, then, not only represents a healing of the alienation attendant upon a sense of homelessness, it subverts essentialist definitions of identity tied to race or ethnicity necessary in the creation of a world view as ethnic conflict, a notion at the heart of the colonial system of oppression, which uses it to justify one group's dominance over another. Rochon's postcolonial discourse works against such essentialization of identity through her depiction of Asven identity as a work in process, which may be adopted by others like Sutherland and Tchil (see page 146). As we shall see in chapter three, Rochon further outlines the notion of national identity as something to be imagined and developed in the Asven nation's eventual construction of a new, utopian homeland.

In addition to her critique of essentialist notions of collective identity, Rochon also subverts its conception as a monolithic phenomenon standing in diametric opposition to another collectivity, the pattern Arguin observed in the *roman de mœurs urbaines*. Not only does she paint individualized portraits of characters from both the oppressed group and the more privileged group, she upsets the oppositional dichotomy of haves and have nots, oppressor and oppressed, through the images of three major characters from the dominant lands to the South — Jouskilliant Green, Taïm Sutherland and Chann Iskiad — as dispossessed and alienated. Indeed, although they live at the brink of survival, the Asven, because of their sense of community and group identity, actually appear less alienated than those living in the South. Sutherland perceives this difference between the two societies and the individuals within them:

> Sutherland songea un peu à Chann avec laquelle, d'emblée, il s'était senti en accord. Il lui semblait plus difficile de communiquer avec Anar Vranengal, qui venait d'un pays si différent du sien, et qui semblait y remplir des fonctions assez bien définies, socialement utiles, tandis que Chann et Sutherland lui-même avaient constaté toute leur vie durant qu'ils n'étaient que tolérés dans leur patrie, qu'ils s'y trouvaient sans doute de trop [AN64].
>
> Sutherland thought a little about Chann, with whom, right away, he had felt a connection. It seemed more difficult to communicate with Anar Vranengal, who came from a land so different from his own, and who seemed to fill rather well-defined, socially useful functions, while Chann and Sutherland himself had noticed that throughout their entire lives they had merely been tolerated in their homelands, that they were really not necessary there.

While Asven leaders Anar Vranengal and Strénid do undergo an identity crisis, it appears much less acute than that of their Southern counterparts and at times they appear less as distinct individuals and more as serving their respective roles in the community (sorcerer as keeper of tradition and administrative leader). In contrast, the figures from the outside world stand out acutely as individuals precisely because they are alienated at home. Defying a totalizing depiction of the Asven's Other, Rochon's development of the stories of Sutherland and Chann Iskiad demonstrate alienation, oppression and dispossession as traits associated not with Vrénalik, but with life in the South.

The métisse Chann Iskiad, daughter of a rebellious Irquiz debutante and an Asven, is eternally excluded from her society, since no one will ever marry a half-breed. Her self-description speaks so strongly of the depth of her alienation that it bears citing at length:

> ma vie est une provocation quotidienne. Je n'ai aucun droit d'être ici, on me le fait clairement sentir. Malgré les conseils, j'ai insisté pour porter le nom de mon père, me dissociant ainsi de la famille Arkandanatt, d'où vient ma mère. Je m'appelle Chann Iskiad, mais je n'ai jamais vu mon père. J'ignore d'ailleurs si dans son pays les enfants portent le nom de l'un de leurs parents. En choisissant ce nom, je ne comprends pas ce que je fais, je revendique une part d'inconnu, je me décerne un titre dont je ne connais pas le sens. Dans une telle incertitude mes gestes quotidiens prennent la forme de démenti de mon origine et du nom que je me suis attribuée [AN17].
>
> my life is a daily provocation. I have no right to be here, and they make me feel it clearly. In spite of advice, I insisted on using my father's name to disassociate myself from my mother's family, the Arkandanatts. I call myself Chann Iskiad, but I have never seen my father. I don't even know if children in his country use one of their parents' names. By choosing this name, I don't understand what I am doing, I claim a stranger's lot, I give myself a title that I don't even know the meaning of. In such uncertainty, my daily gestures represent a denial of my origins and of the name I have given myself.

Feeling imprisoned, Chann was in fact born in prison where her mother died soon after giving birth.

The trope of parental loss and the resulting identity crisis signals alienation in these (and other SFQ) characters, for Taïm also has lost a parent. When he was still a boy, his unemployed father was killed during government repression of a labor rights demonstration (AN18). This event also signals the precarity of life for those in Ister-Inga; people from the South face the same economic struggles to survive, deal with the same forces of oppression as the Asven. Rochon's depiction of the dominant society's underclass thus subverts the traditional dichotomy of haves and have-nots, as well as the reader's ability to develop clear-cut allegorical identifications as to which groups "represent" Québec and its Other(s). Her description of Taïm's adolescence could just as well be a description of a Québécois youth in the realist novels of the 1970s:

> Comme ses amis, il avait quitté l'école tôt, et occupé de nombreux emplois subalternes, dénués d'intérêt. Cela l'aurait satisfait si sa vie n'avait pas été aussi

insignifiante. Les grands idéaux qui avaient animé la génération précédente s'étaient avérés désuets, l'enthousiasme n'était plus à la mode ... [AN18].

Like his friends, he had left school early and held a number of subaltern jobs of little interest to him. This would have satisfied him if his life had not been so insignificant. The grand ideals that had inspired the preceding generation were old hat; enthusiasm was out of style.

Sutherland's attitude reflects listlessness similar to that observed in Québec after the idealism and activity of the Quiet Revolution, followed by the violence and repression of the October Crisis of 1970. The same description, as Claude Janelle observes, can also be tailored to fit the 1970s as a decade of idealistic identity-building followed by an era of disillusionment after the failure of the 1980 Referendum. Yet, as Janelle recognizes, the novel's composition occurred prior to that event ("Rochon" 104).

Rochon's postcolonial discourse further undermines the dualistic world view of the colonial novel in the imaginary geography of the world of Vrénalik. While the Asven's Other appears at times as a monolithic unity, the South, this unified image becomes refracted not only through the depiction of several lands, Irquiz, Ister-Inga, Ourgane and Catadial, themselves different and divided, but also through the introduction of a third pole to the north. Through its problematization of a simplistic allegorical structure, the text subverts the dualistic opposition of French Canadian versus English Canadian (or Anglo-American) found by Arguin in the *roman de mœurs urbaines*, thus transcending the colonial model. On the one hand, we might identify Vrénalik and the Asven as allegories for Québec and French Canadians. Just as the stagnant Vrénalik stands paralyzed by its past as the direct result of a religious belief (that the Ocean-god's curse *literally* prevents the Asven from leaving the Archipelago) while the world around it has entered the postmodern era, so, too, Québec has been depicted as living through such stagnation during the premiership of Maurice Duplessis, a régime supported by the traditional, agricultural ideology of the Catholic hierarchy. Both nations stand not as sovereign powers, but as often-forgotten appendages to a larger nation, the Pays d'Irquiz/Canada, but both awaken from their stupor and seek a greater level of self-determination. On the other, as Claude Janelle warns: "une lecture politique de ce roman me paraît extrêmement hasardeux" ("a political reading of this novel seems extremely hazardous to me"; "Rochon" 104). The giants to the South, the Pays d'Irquiz and the Pays d'Ister-Inga could be the U.S. and Canada respectively, but Claire Le Brun ("Planète"123) and Jean Pettigrew (168) suggest that, instead, Irquiz reflects a contemporary, industrialized, urban society, which includes Québec, in opposition to an Amerindian-like Vrénalik. The northern land of the Hanrel further problematizes the issue of allegorical assignments. Assigning those to the North an Inuit symbolic identity perhaps bolsters a reading of the Asven as Amerindians since anthropology (and Canadian law) distinguishes those groups as distinct. Yet, if the Hanrel are interpreted as *all* autochthonous peoples, opposed to Anglo-Europeans to the South, then one can interpret the Asven as Québécois. Rather than representing a failed allegory, the multiple positions that various groups can hold in relation to the "real" world works in Rochon's SFQ saga as a postcolonial strategy, namely the refusal of a totalizing, unified interpretation.

This same subversion of expectations (of both Western canonical literature and of French-Canadian literary forebears) appears in Rochon's revised vision of the barrier that separates the oppressed group from the oppressor, as well as the historical events leading up to the moment of subjection. Rather than an outside force erecting this barrier as the result of an identifiable historical moment of conquest, the source of the Asven's current abjection is internal. That is, the four-hundred-year-old trauma was not an invasion, but the curse, inflicted by their own Ocean-god, which, as the second volume, *Le Rêveur dans la Citadelle*, recounts, appears to have been a just punishment. At that time their authoritarian leader Skern Strénid had brought the Asven to the height of their development; their civilization "était en plein essor" ("was in full flight"; RC33) and even had plans to exploit the then declining society to the South, Irquiz. However, claiming to work for the collective good, the State repeatedly imposes on individual rights (RC48–49), as seen in the manner in which Skern "recruits" the Rêveur Shaskath and treats his own wife, Inalga de Bérilis. It is she who points out the immorality of his utilitarian policies: "Vous détruisez les fondations de votre société; vous empêchez les gens d'honorer leurs traditions, vous les privez de leur héritage culturel pour leur donner à manger" ("You are destroying the foundations of your society; you prevent the people from honoring their traditions; you deprive them of their cultural heritage in order to give them bread"; RC112). Having abandoned his society's god, having eliminated its sorcerer class, Skern's *hubris* must be punished and with him the people of the Archipelago who have accepted the rule of an immoral State.

The uncrossable frontier that separates the Asven from the rest of the world differs, then, from that which isolates French Canadians from their dominating Other in the *roman de mœurs urbaines*. Contrary to various realist/experimental novels of this period, which, for Arguin, depict Anglo-Canada, Great Britian and/or the United States as the sources of oppression, all of the oppression suffered by the people of the Archipelago has really been brought on themselves. While a standard national allegory would depict the source of oppression as coming from outside the nation under duress, here, the postcolonial allegory rejects such a reading.

The play on sonorities in proper nouns further reflects this notion. Rochon establishes an apparent relationship between Vrénalik and Québec. In the separate short story "Canadola" (1989), Rochon clearly attributes totalitarian control and exploitation to the land of that name, whose resonances with Canada are obvious. The perhaps puzzling attribution of the same sounds in the Vrénalik Cycle reflects a greater ambivalence to Canada. At the series' conclusion the utopian land that *helps* Vrénalik realize its ideal of a sovereign, empowered existence, Catadial, resonates with Canada. In its first volume, however, this sonority appears in the name of Strénid's father, Fékril Candanad. While the latter first dreams of opening up the Archipelago to the outside world, the frustration of his efforts leads to madness, the abuse of power and violent atrocities.

Fékril's failure results in part from his inability to fully accept the measures prescribed by the rational positivist Jouskilliant Green, a professor from the South. In Rochon's postcolonial vision, a simple adoption of the apparently succesful Other's value system will not serve to found a healthy community. As already discussed, the materialist values of the South have caused as much oppression and alienation in its own territory as Haztlén's curse has for Vrénalik. Again, Rochon subverts the dualistic model of the colonized discourse. Rather than revealing the values of the oppressed group as "good" ones and those of the power group as inherently "bad" (a strategy Marc Angenot observes as typical of an ideology of resentment), she blurs these distinctions demonstrating that the respective values of both groups have led to their problems (Vrénalik's over-valuation of the past and the South's impersonal materialism). This blurring continues as the text asserts that, indeed, Vrénalik and Ister-Inga once shared the same values (ED25).

As we shall see in subsequent chapters, several elements will be necessary to rebuild the community, for Rochon's SFQ saga eventually operates a transcendance of the hopelessness of the ideology of survival that Arguin associated with the "colonized" French Canadians in the realist novel of an earlier generation. Signs of a new ideology of hope and rebirth for the Asven appear already in the first volume of the cycle; while the end of this civilization appears direly imminent, those same individuals announcing its death also hold up utopian hope for the future (matter for chapter three). Ivendra repeats a litany of doom to Anar Vranengal, referring repeatedly to: "notre mort imminente ... l'anéantissement de notre peuple" ("our impending death ... the destruction of our people"; AP134). However, a lingering hope that the condemned ideology of survival might give way to a new ideology of renaissance already appears in his prediction that "notre monde touche à sa fin, des changements se préparent" ("our world is coming to an end, change is in the works"; AP141). Out of its own ashes, phoenix-like, the Asven civilization will rise again. The seeds of change and rebirth are sown at the end of *L'Aigle des profondeurs* as Jouskilliant Green departs with manuscripts of Asven legends that he has copied from buried archives. As Anar Vranengal describes it: "Un peu de nous a traversé la mer. Un peu de nous a déjoué la malédiction de l'enfermement.... Nous ne sommes pas complètement en marche vers l'extinction. Quelque chose va se perpétuer" ("A little of us has crossed the sea. A little of us has foiled the curse of imprisonment.... We are not completely on the road to extinction. Something will continue"; AP287). Those seeds bear fruit as Taïm Sutherland, about to embark on his voyage to the Archipelago, reads Green's book, *Le Rêveur dans la Citadelle*.[7] This hybrid varietal's development will be discussed further in chaptres three and four; our focus continues here on alienation and oppression in a work I refer to as a "marginal monument" of SFQ, Jacques Brossard's *L'Oiseau de feu*.

Jacques Brossard's *L'Oiseau de feu*

While the genre's foremost critics, like Michel Lord ("Feu d'artifices") and Claude Janelle ("Totale"), consider Jacques Brossard's epic saga *L'Oiseau de feu* (1989–97) a monument not only of Québec's science fiction, but of the province's literature as a whole, others have rejected the work because of its complexity, its blurring of generic boundaries and its sheer length (Ransom "Critical"). Over 2500 pages, the work has been qualified as a "five volume trilogy" (1, 2.A, 2.B, 2.C, 3) (Trudel, Rev. 13), but it really represents one extended novel, given the continuous numbering of the chapters from book to book. Following the tradition of found literature, the author presents himself as the third translator of a diverse array of documents whose origin is ostensibly explained in a series of initial and concluding notes, prefaces, afterwords and more. Each volume of the narrative proper traces one or more stages in the *Bildungsroman* of an engaging central character, Adakhan Demuthsen, in three different worlds: the stagnant, pseudo-medieval society of the Périphériens of Manokhsor, the technologically advanced, underground Centrale and, finally, on a distant planet called Ashmev, which appears to be the reader's Earth.

In its depiction of the oppressed Périphériens, the dominant Centrale, and the utopian new world, *L'Oiseau de feu* reproduces the various stages of the SFQ epic. Like the other works discussed in this chapter, although published in the late 1980s and through the 1990s, it was conceived during a much earlier period. Brossard's SFQ saga reflects many of the traits Arguin observed in earlier realist novels, including the depiction of a dichotomous society divided by a nearly uncrossable barrier and a protagonist who typifies the alienated type-character of the *révolté*. Its author's background, however, stands somewhat in contrast to that of Rochon and Vonarburg; born into an earlier generation, Jacques Brossard actually participated in Québec's nationalist movement during the late 1960s and through the 1970s.[8] Perhaps in part for this reason, while it reflects the anti-colonial discourse of that era, *L'Oiseau de feu* remains at times ambiguous in respect to its reflection of a fully postcolonial discourse.

At first glance, Jacques Brossard appears as a true *Québécois de vieille souche* (old-stock Quebecker), the now politically charged euphemism for an ethnic French Canadian. He avoids the term while still signaling this identity on the back cover of his well-received collection of fantastic and science-fiction stories, *Le Métamorfaux* (1974): "D'origine franque et celte, Québécois de la crise, social-ambivalent: cela transparaît. En Amérique depuis trois siècles: le dirait-on?" ("Of Frankish and Celtic origin, a Québécois of the crisis, a social ambivalent: that is clear. In America for three hundred years: would you believe it?") These few phrases reveal his political position and the problematic nature of the Québécois identity which that position implies. The thinly veiled reference to the October 1970 Crisis can be read as a metonymy for the entire "conflit canado-québécois" mentioned just a few lines down in the same back-cover blurb. Brossard declares openly his adherence to a potentially problematic form of national identity, based on the one hand on the fiction of a unified "French" identity, which itself appears divided into two components (a Germanophile, Brossard embraces the Franks with the Celtic Gauls, a potentially blasphemous move during certain periods of French history), as well as an American element, which has been denied it (that term having been usurped by those of us to the south). In a much later interview, Brossard further problematizes the myth of the *Québécois de pure laine* (pure [100 percent, dyed-in-the] wool Quebecker). Citing his Mohawk ancestry (AE584),[9] he further calls into question the possibility of a unified Québécois identity based on French-Canadian ethnicity.

Marginally recognized today as a writer of idiosyncratic, genre-bending, postmodern fiction, some of which has been annexed into the SFQ canon, the jurist Brossard first made his mark in Québec as a participant in the movement for sovereignty. Among several individual and collective works commissioned by Québec's legislative assembly and produced under the aegis of the University of Montréal's Institute for Public Law Research, Brossard composed his classic study of the legal bases for the province's potential bid for sovereignty, *L'Accession à la souveraineté et le cas du Québec* (1976), during the period that, on vacation in Antibes, he outlined the entire *L'Oiseau de feu*.

Brossard at times adopts the discourse of decolonization in his juridico-political writings and his active participation in the movement for sovereignty-association, including membership in the Parti Québécois, might be seen as clear evidence of an anti-colonial, if not a postcolonial attitude. On the contrary, nationalism stands in a very ambivalent relationship to the postcolonial, as Spivak points out: "nationalism in many ways is a displaced or reversed legitimation of colonialism" (*Critique* 62). As is the case with alienation, nationalism represents another element that complicates such discussions because of the frequent conflation of postcolonialism with anti-colonialism. While theorists of the actual decolonizations gradually occurring after World War II, such as Amilcar Cabral and Fanon, asserted that the liberated colony needed to develop a national culture and identity — and nationalist movements did, indeed, serve as catalysts for expulsion of colonial powers in places like Algeria — later theorists, as postcolonialism developed in the 1980s, viewed nationalism rather as something to be transcended, as simply a reinscription of the Western values of the colonizer. Indeed, Edward Said sees it critiqued already in Rabindranath Tagore's 1917 lectures "On Nationalism" (*Culture* 215). Many of these critiques tend themselves to totalize "nationalism," failing to distinguish between its various forms. When considering contemporary Québec, it is important to note the historical dynamic between, among others, two types of nationalism: the traditional ethnically based nationalism versus a liberal, civic nationalism. Brossard's overt nationalism, which hovers somewhere between these two forms, although tending more toward the latter, places him, then, in an odd relationship with the postcolonial.

Calling attention to Brossard's non-fiction works, including their references to the Québécois as colonized, does not necessarily suggest that his fiction represents another forum for him to carry on a nationalist polemic. Indeed, the significance of Jacques Brossard as a literary figure appears in his ability to escape the traps of the *roman-à-clef* or the *roman d'idées*, in which the ideas often overtake the novelistic aspects of the work. Besides his own disavowal to Claude Grégoire of any link between his politics and his literary work ("Écriture" 61), the contrast between Brossard's literary works and the polemical "rational speculations" of earlier French-Canadian writers speaks volumes.[10] Brossard's fictional œuvre represents one of the most complex and enigmatic of any Québécois writer, yet it suffers from an almost total lack of critical, academic literary analysis. This corpus is both fascinating, yet sometimes maddeningly indecipherable, precisely because of its postmodern subversion of the linear, realist narrative. It includes an overt national allegory, "Retours" (Returns, 1973), similar in style, yet predating, the better known works of François Barcelo, (*Agénor, Agénor, Agénor et Agénor* [1980] and *La Tribu* [The Tribe, 1981]), which have been called postcolonial by Marie Vautier ("Révision"). A number of his texts ("Le Parc" [The Park], "La Grande Roue" [The Ferris Wheel], "L'Aller-Retour" [The Round Trip], "Le Cloison de verre" [The Glass Wall] all 1978) reflect an indeterminate relationship to the mimetic reality of the reader's world, similar in style to the magic realism of Dino Buzzati's "The Falling Girl" (1966). SFQ bibliographers appropriate his best known work, a collection of stories, *Le Métamorfaux* (1974, 1989), yet those texts employing SF tropes (time travel in "La Tentative" [The Trial Run], the future invention of a self-thought home in "Le Souffleur de bulles" [The Bubble Blower], and the rebellion of household appliances in "L'Objection") could just as easily be argued out of the genre. Its title story, translated as "The Metamorfalsis," depicts a Kafka-esque narrative of the increasingly divergent court testimony of twelve witnesses. His perhaps most overt SF stories, "Le Boulon d'Ernest" (Ernest's Knob) and "Le Mal de terre" (Earthsickness, both 1973), remain largely forgotten. A further element that has puzzled reviewers, the 2500-page saga, *L'Oiseau de feu* (The Firebird/The Phoenix), culminates a body of work previously comprised of short fiction, for even his surrealistic "novel," *Le Sang du souvenir* (The Blood of Memory, 1976), resembles a "fix up" in its assemblage of six linked episodes that could stand alone.

Although published between 1989 and 1997 the conception of *L'Oiseau de feu* dates as far back as 1975, as indicated in the final dates after the fictional thirtieth-century editor's afterword: "Antibes, printemps 1975/Montréal, 1983–1985/(décembre 1996)" (AE581). Brossard's editor Pierre Filion elucidates its development in "La Genèse de *l'Oiseau de feu* de J.-E. Brossard" indicating that the author returned from his 1975 trip to Antibes with a 475-page outline of the entire project (190). These dates are important because they situate the tone, thrust and themes of *L'Oiseau de feu* not with those of the late-1980s to mid–1990s, such as Élisabeth Vonarburg's *Tyranaël* pentalogy (although that, too, was composed in part much earlier), but rather with works like Jean Tétreau's *Nomades* (1967), or Monique Corriveau's *Compagnon du soleil* (1976),[11] the early portions of Esther Rochon's *Cycle de Vrénalik*, and other works directly following the Quiet Revolution. That period, in which Québec developed a secularized, more autonomous provincial state, and a nationalist movement which derived much of its rhetoric from the discourse of decolonization moved to the forefront, also witnessed the rise of a politicized counterculture, which, like the feminist movement, drew upon a utopian discourse in order to envision a changed world. These three trends — (1) a critique of a colonial-type relationship of power and oppression coupled with (2) the perceived need to decolonize and liberate the French-Canadian people and (3) the utopian ideal that the social changes which accompanied decolonization could lead to a new and better society — clearly influence Jacques Brossard's *L'Oiseau de feu*, conceived as it was in 1975.

A writer describes a society of people who are "endormis ... sclérosés, enfermés entre des balises morales étroites, encadrés par des tabous et des interdits édictés et entretenus par les dirigeants religieux et politiques" ("asleep, paralyzed, enclosed by narrow moral boundaries, hedged in by taboos and prohibitions dictated and maintained by political and religious leaders"; Dorion 352). While this image is reflective of the fictional dystopian societies envisioned by writers of SFQ, it is in fact a literary historian's description of Québec in the 1960s. Its similarity to Brossard's rendering of the Périphériens of Manokhsor, the setting for *L'Oiseau de feu: 1 Les Années d'apprentissage* (The Apprentice Years, 1989), suggests an allegorical reading. Just as Gilles Dorion's description of Québec might be that of an SFQ writer's dystopian future society, Adakhan Demuthsen's journaled description of his people in the first volume of Brossard's novel reflects the French-Canadian society in which its author grew up, as well as the desire for change expressed by him and other young intellectuals in the 1960s and 1970s:

> Loguth, le vieux tailleur de pierre ... me reproche de manquer de «réalisme». Je la vois bien, leur «réalité»: c'est précisément pour cela que je la refuse. Il y a ce qu'il faut accepter: ce Nuage qui nous écrase, le désert qui nous entoure,—mourir de maladie ou d'âge? Il y a, par contre, ce qu'on pourrait abolir, modifier, corriger, renverser, remplacer: les murs, les écroulements d'édifices, les incendies, les biscuits de merde, les sacrifices d'enfants, les disparitions, les dirigeants qui nous dominent, les jongleurs qui chantent leurs louanges et nous distraient, les professeurs qui nous bernent, nous bourrent de légendes et taisent la vérité, les prêtres, les bons prêtres qui nous offrent de si beaux spectacles sans rien expliquer,—bref, tous ceux qui encouragent notre ignorance, notre inertie, notre médiocrité et notre abêtissement docile de Périphériens [AA300–01].
>
> Loguth, the old stonecutter, reproaches me for my lack of "realism." I see their "reality" well enough: that's exactly why I refuse it. There are things that have to be accepted: this Cloud that crushes us, the desert that surrounds us, dying of sickness or old age? On the other hand, there are things that could be abolished, modified, corrected, reversed, replaced: the walls, the buildings caving in, the fires, the shitty biscuits, the sacrificing of children, the disappearances, the leaders who dominate us, the troubadours who sing their praises and divert us, the teachers who deceive us, fill us with legends and keep the truth shut up, the preachers, the good preachers who offer us such beautiful spectacles without explaining anything; in short, everybody who encourages our ignorance, our inertia, our mediocrity and our docile Périphérien stupidity.

In spite of several critics' observations of the possible political interpretation of this first volume (Basile; Filion 190; Gégoire, "Écriture" 61), Brossard tells his *Solaris* interviewers that any political connections, including the sonorities of Adakhan with Canada, "ce n'est pas absolument conscient" ("this is not absolutely conscious"; Pomerleau and Sernine 20). In that interview Brossard admits thinking in universal terms of oppression (20), but his readers cannot escape the similarities between this portrait and that of Québec painted in nationalist journals like *Parti pris* in the years preceding the SFQ saga's composition.

The Périphériens, "les victimes de leur aliénation" ("victims of their alienation"; GP120), also reflect many of the characteristics of the "colonized" French Canadians Arguin finds in the Québécois novel of the 1940s and 1950s (see page 71): they are clearly *dispossessed*, most of them living day-to-day, surviving on the free biscuits provided by the government; shelter is precarious as buildings seem to cave in regularly for no known reason. *Uncrossable frontiers* separate them not only from their own ruling class but also from each other, as walls separate each of Manokhsor's twelve quarters, as well as from what they are disingenuously told is a jungle surrounding them. Their height regulated so that one quarter's inhabitants cannot look over to see the others, even approaching these walls can lead to "disappearance." A subject people, *dominated* in this first volume by an upper class of leaders, the second volume reveals that, indeed, another socio-economic, if not ethnic, group exerts dominance over them and some elements of that group obtain great pleasure from the sheer exertion of power. The Périphériens abide by an *ideology of survival,* always acting conservatively, in the interest of tradition and self-preservation. Any novelty is seen as dangerous and even the knowledge necessary for the various trades is closely guarded by the secrecy of guild rituals. Difference is punished with beating by the law-enforcing Archers or disappearance. Finally, Brossard's depiction of the Périphériens introduces an element outlined in Arguin's description of the *roman de moeurs urbaine*'s establishment of a dichotomous society not present in Rochon's portrait of Vrénalik: the participation of the colonized group's leaders and educational system in its oppression (61–64). The heavily "edited" (AA297) facsimile of Adakhan's "journal" condemns the meaningless indoctrination of Manokhsor's youth through a curriculum of rote memorization meant to reinforce submission (AA301). Like its educators, the city's leaders play a major role in the oppression of its citizens; not only are they simply collaborating with the power group of the Centrale many of them are actually Centraliens in disguise.

Although Manokhsor remains ignorant of it, their domination traces back to a specific *moment of historical "conquest"* coded as a cataclysmic event. *L'Oiseau de feu: 2.A Le Recyclage d'Adakhan* (The Recycling of Adakhan, 1990) describes the city's foundation not long after the "Great Catastrophe of 2793 AC" (GP114). The Centraliens below drugged those who had gathered on the surface above, erased their memories and then built the city as it currently stands crumbling.[12] The 1760 Conquest of Québec appears doubly coded through the apocalyptic moment that affects *both* Manokhsor and the Centrale — founded by a group of surviving scientists who built an underground complex in preparation for an impending nuclear holocaust. The latter, fearing that the mob of survivors above ground might enter their safe enclave, literally conquered these future Périphériens.

Brossard's SFQ saga differs with that of Rochon in that rather than focusing on the struggle of the collective (although, of course, certain individuals stand out in that struggle), *L'Oiseau de feu* really targets the development of one central character. This emphasis reflects another French-Canadian novelistic form analyzed by Arguin, the *roman psychologique* of the 1950s and 1960s. The psychological novel works to demonstrate the cultural alienation "qui conditionne la vie des personnages" ("which conditions the life of its characters") within a system of colonial or colonial-like oppression (105), typically focusing on a main type-character identified by Arguin as *le révolté* (the rebel).

Arguin describes this figure as "celui qui, devant l'échec, prend conscience de son aliénation et revendique le droit d'exercer sa liberté individuelle dans l'accomplissment de sa destinée" ("he who, faced with failure, becomes conscious of his alienation and reclaims the right to exercize his individual freedom in the accomplishment of his destiny"; 139). The *révolté*, according to Arguin, typically exhibits five traits:

(1) his outside, physical appearance reflects his interior conflict/alienation (143);
(2) he is dispossessed not only of the world around him, but even of himself: "Le héros est essentiellement étranger, aliéné" ("The hero is essentially a stranger/foreign, alienated"; 144);
(3) isolation characterizes him, which
(4) leads to despair, and
(5) his conflicts occur at the level of conscience (144–45).

Overall the rebel looks for "un nouveau sens, sens de la vie et sens de la souffrance" ("a new meaning for life and for suffering"; 145). Alienation, then, represents the psychological key to the *révolté*, an individual who, although he has become conscious of his oppressed situation and rebels against it, does not necessarily possess the skills to lead his people through a positive, truly liberating change. In addition, Arguin describes the protagonist of the *roman psychologique* as suffering from "conditioning" (105), the very term chosen by Brossard to describe the individual's socialization as a form of indoctrination.

The central theme of *Les Années d'apprentisage* is, indeed, its hero's rebellion against the conditioning of the tightly controlled society of Manokhsor. From childhood, Adakhan rejects and questions the system of ignorance, wanting to know more; throughout his youth he refuses to adopt the self-preserving stance of submission and acceptance of misfortune. As he acts for himself and helps others, though, he suffers the consequences: beatings by the Archers, imprisonment, and, ultimately, disappearance. Throughout this *Bildungsroman* from this first volume until his his death at the end of volume three, Adakhan Demuthsen bears all the defining marks of Arguin's *révolté*.[13] In contrast with the external ugliness which reflects the rebel's inner turmoil in the realist novel, Adakhan appears extremly attractive. Yet, the signs of his alienation within the society of Manokhsor reveal themselves in his obvious physical difference as his darker skin ("le teint brun cuivré" ["the copper brown skin tone"; AA27]) and hidden "anomalie" (AA307) set him apart. This anomaly consists of Adakhan's possession of only one set of sexual organs rather than the two borne by most Périphériens because of the Centraliens' genetic manipulation, an element illustrating their level of control, marked directly on the body of the oppressed. Adakhan's escape from this abjection, although it signals his difference, appears actually to reinscribe him as a member of the elite. Brossard's narrative disrupts a colonial-type dichotomy, associating difference not with the oppressed Other, but with the, albeit displaced, member of the power group. Indeed, Adakhan begins to distance himself, referring to his own people as Others ("they"), thus reinforcing this alignment: "tous ces Périphériens qui ne s'interrogent *jamais*: *pourquoi* leur indifférence et leur abrutissement?" ("all these Périphériens who *never* ask themselves: *why* their indifference and their brutishness?"; AA313; original emphasis).

Like all Périphériens, Adakhan suffers from material dispossession, particularly as a child and youth. His mother struggles to feed the family because his father has "disappeared," in the manner of suspected dissidents in Latin American dictatorships like Pinochet's Chile (AA27–29). Adakhan's dispossession includes psychological and physiological aspects. In moments of conflict with the dominant order, he suffers from "maux de tête violents" ("violent headaches"; AA147). Although he does not know it, others cause these migraines to punish him or to stop his subversive questioning (AA103, RA48). Furthermore, he does not know the full story of his identity. His repeated inability to repress his desires to gain further knowledge and to act against the oppression of others, both in Manokhsor and in the Centrale attest to Adakhan's inadaptation to the world around him.

Isolation, another hallmark of Arguin's *révolté*, surrounds Adakhan; although he has a mother, a brother and a few friends, these relationships appear riddled with misunderstanding and superficiality. Indeed, everyone in Manokhsor seems to be isolated; expression of emotion is punishable (AA237, RA417), and fear of denunciation makes genuine, honest friendship seemingly impossible. Even after his marriage, although he loves his wife passionately, he never achieves a full communion with her and he is distanced from his son from the moment of the child's birth (AA223, 305; RA131). Although he rebounds from setbacks again and again (for repetition and overdetermination are hallmarks of Brossard's epic saga), Adakhan cannot help wallowing into despair from time to time, and while some of his conflicts occur in the physical realm, his journals reveal that his conflict over the untenable situation in which he lives has become a matter of conscience (AA423).

While *Les Années d'apprentissage* reflects the situation found in Arguin's *roman de mœurs urbaines* in its detailed depiction of the oppression of the Périphériens, and its portrait of the *révolté* Adakhan bears comparison with the *roman psychologique*, the subsequent volumes of the series reproduce the next stage in Arguin's description of the French-Canadian novel. Arguin describes works from the early 1960s, such as Yves Thériault's *Ashini* (1960) and Claude Jasmin's *Ethel et le terroriste* (1964), as *romans de contestation*, protest novels reflective of a new level of consciousness about French-Canadian society as "colonized":

Si le roman de moeurs urbaines a décrit la situation socio-économique en termes de domination, si le roman psychologique a assimilé les valeurs-refuges à des empêchements à vivre, le roman de contestation tente de définir un homme nouveau, le Québécois [183].

If the urban novel described the socio-economic system in terms of domination, if the psychological novel described the refuge values as obstacles to living, the novel of contestation tries to define a new man, the Québécois.

While the title of volume *2.A Le Recyclage d'Adakhan*, underscores this new sense of self-determination, Adakhan continues to resemble Arguin's *révolté* throughout volume two's remaining books (*2.B Le Grand projet* [The Great Project], *2.C Le Sauve-qui-peut* [Every Man for Himself]). It is tempting to attribute the length of Brossard's work to Adakhan's stubbornness, his difficulty in overcoming all that keeps him colonized, yet his resilience proves that he may develop beyond the rebel's "inaptitude à vivre" ("inaptitude for life"; Arguin 146). Indeed, like the first-person narrator of Arguin's *roman psychologique*, Adakhan's experiences appear as "journal" excerpts during the last third of *Les Années d'apprentissage*.

In order for the new man to develop, however, a *prise de conscience*, an epiphany-like new understanding of the system of oppression and domination must occur, often described explicitly in terms of a colonial power relation (Arguin 175–76). Like his realist forebears, Adakhan realizes the injustice of his people's social situation; a process already begun in *Les Années d'apprentissage* continues and deepens in subsequent volumes. This awareness grows through the process of "recyclage," through which Adakhan, along with a select group of peers, will be literally recycled, physically rejuvenated and mentally reformed in order to participate in the dominant society of the Centrale. Their curriculum (reproduced in the text as pseudo-excerpts) reveals with clarity how the relationship of dominance and oppression developed between Manokhsor and the Centrale. In this relationship, the Périphériens have three official uses — as a labor pool, as genetic variety for the Centrale (through the *récupérés* like Adakhan), and as an escape valve for the claustrophobia of the Centraliens (who may make excursions or go to live in Manokhsor). Fully subject, they also come to serve as guinea pigs in various experiments and, ultimately, as pawns in the internal power struggles of the Centrale.

As the answers to the how and why of the Périphériens' oppression — something he already knew, but just could not attribute/explain properly — are revealed, the hero undergoes a literal *prise de conscience* as the osmotic learning devices of the Centrale insert this knowledge into the heads of Adakhan and his fellow recyclees. At the same time, a more authentic level of consciousness occurs beyond the fabricated "truth" provided by the Curriculum, as much a form of conditioning as his education in Manokhsor had been. On one level, as a *révolté*, an *inadapté*, bound to question *any* system he lives in, Adakhan intuits a reality beyond that presented to him and he embarks upon an epistemological quest, although he is often thwarted, seeking further answers to his questions through means both legitimate (asking MO, the Master Computer, or his sponsor, Syrius) and illicit (snooping in the offices of Syrius and later Lokhfer). At another level, though, elements of the narrative conflict with the assessment that any authentic *prise de conscience* has taken place. For, while Syrius' intervention spares Adakhan the final, fourth level of a recyclee's indoctrination, which consists of a complete brainwashing (RA167), he nonetheless internalizes a great deal of his training, undergoing a programming in spite of himself. Not only does he begin to shift his (albeit already weak) self-identification as a Périphérien toward that of a Centralien-in-process, he begins to further develop his (already present) sense of superiority to the oppressed people of his origin. This pattern duplicates the mentality of the colonial subject outlined not only by Memmi (Arguin's source), but also by Fanon, as well as in works of recognizably postcolonial fiction.[14]

In *Black Skin, White Masks* (1952), Fanon observes the phenomenon of a desired assimilation to the dominant group and rejection of their own people among colonized individuals in both North Africa and the Antilles: "The colonized is elevated above his jungle status in proportion to his adoption of the mother country's (*de la métropole*) cultural standards. He becomes whiter as he renounces his blackness, his jungle" (18).[15] This situation, Fanon argues, results in racial alienation. On the one hand, a self-rejection occurs in the individual who seeks to replicate the powerful Other by donning the white mask. However, it is recognized that the mask will never be more than a façade for the black man can never become "white," because the colonizing power will never allow the full integration into the Pale of the native elite necessary for its rule. Adakhan and the incoming "récupérés" ("recovered ones") resemble this colonial elite educated and trained by imperial powers to serve in its military or administrative system. Just as this system provides access to education and material advances, yet ultimately denies full participation in the dominant society, so does the process of recycling in the Centrale.

Adakhan and his fellow recyclees learn that they represent the fortunate elite: "Quinze pour l'année sur quelques milliers de disparus et plus d'un million de Périphériens du nord-ouest! «Éléments d'élite»!" ("Fifteen for the year out of some thousands of disappearances and more than a million Périphériens in the northwest! 'Elements of the elite!'"; RA125). Yet they are repeatedly reminded of "[l]a supériorité des Centraliens" ("the superiority of the Centraliens"; RA125). After a successful recycling, Adakhan and those in his cohort (the "class" of 376 AC), will be assigned to a work group as interns. If they succeed, as he is told by a trainer: "ils peuvent gravir d'eux-mêmes les échélons de la hiérarchie. Au gré de nos besoins. Il faut dire que les vacances sont rares" ("they can rise on their own through the ranks of the hierarchy. As our needs dictate. It must be said that vacancies are rare"; RA98–99). So while there is opportunity for integration and advancement within the system, these opportunities are limited. Although Adakhan's patronage by Syrius places him at a great advantage, his doctor also indicates that there are no guarantees — candidates must pass all tests successfully: "C'est un candidat d'élite. Un futur Centralien de 1re classe!— Peut-être" ("He's an elite candidate. A future first-class Centralien!-Maybe"; RA111).

This system, which mirrors a colonial power dynamic, establishes the superiority of the Centraliens, the privileged status of the Recyclees, and the subject status of the Périphériens. As a trainer informs Adakhan: "Les Périphériens nous doivent tout: ils n'existeraient pas sans nous" ("The Périphériens owe us everything: without us they would not exist"; RA110). Brossard exploits a science-fictional trope to extrapolate the power relationship to the extreme, which eerily recalls Jeremy Bentham's nineteenth-century panopticon, a system of total surveillance and behavioral conditioning, carried out from Manokhsor's central Tower to ensure this subject status.[16] The *Encyclopedia Centralis* entry on "Neurologie/Cérébrologie" explains how conditioning occurs through the use of "*électrosionique*" transmitters placed in the identity medallions that Périphériens must wear at all times on penalty of death (RA149), thus "la Centrale peut contrôler les pensées et le comportement des Périphériens" ("the Centrale can control the thoughts and behavior of the Périphériens"; RA159). This policy for protecting the Centrale by ensuring the complete submission of the Périphériens described here recalls various measures historically taken to ensure the safety of white colonists and to guarantee the profitability of the colonial enterprise or of capital over the proletariat.

Realizing their precarious position as a controlling minority, the Centraliens adhere to the following policies:

> *Il faut donc 1° s'assurer le contrôle absolu et permanent des Périphériens; 2° limiter leur nombre, compte tenu des besoins de la Centrale.... Objectif fondamental: l'ignorance et l'abêtissement des Périphériens* [RA181–82].
> It is necessary to 1st ensure the absolute and permanent control of the Périphériens; 2nd limit their number, keeping in mind the needs of the Centrale.... Fundamental objective: ignorance and stupidity of the Périphériens.

They do so by limiting the quantity and nutritional value of food and water, employing electrosionic manipulation of their nervous system, limiting knowledge of the world through the educational and religious indoctrination, punishing all forms of curiosity (AA330), and staging regular holidays and ceremonies in order to awe and stupefy. The public holidays also serve as a means of population control since they involve bloody massacres and sacrifices, often including large numbers of women and children. In addition to the Bread and Circus of the Roman Empire, these measures reference practices found in more recent imperial and totalitarian governments. The limited nutrition recalls practices in Nazi concentration camps and Stalin's Gulag and the ongoing concern about the nutritional adequacy of some infant formulas marketed in Third World countries.[17]

While those in Syrius' team, which Adakhan joins, have a more humane attitude toward the Périphériens, most Centraliens have internalized a sense of their own superiority and the Others' inferiority. One group in particular holds a large amount of power over and a sadistic disdain for the Périphériens, that of the alternating President, Lokhfer (LC4–FR5). He refers to Manokhsor as that "Cité qui n'était qu'une tromperie, un ghetto, un zoo" ("City which was nothing more than a hoax, a ghetto, a zoo"; RA367), and eventually calls for a "solution finale" ("final solution"; SQP71) for its citizens. His underling, Rodrik, who poses as Archonte, the highest leader, of Adakhan's former West-North-West neighborhood expresses a similar disdain:

> —Plus abrutis que jamais, vous ne trouvez pas? Les Périphériens, j'entends.... Ça gueule de temps à autre, ça râle, ça rouspète, ça se plaint des pénuries d'eau, de la hausse des prix, du manque de variété de nos bons biscuits [RA448].
>
> "More brutish than ever, don't you think? The Périphériens, I mean.... It hollers from time to time, rails, bitches, complains of the water shortages, rising prices, lack of variety in our good biscuits."

Adakhan's growing ambivalence toward his own people appears on a recreational visit to Manokhsor with other Centraliens in disguise. Having been educated in the metropole, Adakhan returns home to the "colony" and can only criticize the backwardness of the "ONOfs" of the West-North-West quarter:

> Tout cela, ces gens, ce quartier, qui avait été pour lui la seule réalité pendant 38 ans-P, lui paraissait étrangement irréel et transparent. Reconstitution, réserve, parc d'amusement pour les Centraliens, zoo, simulacre, décor de cinéma et figurants.... Décor solide. «Pour eux, pensa-t-il, voilà la réalité. *Leur* seule réalité?» Du moins trouvait-il un certain plaisir à réentendre l'affreux patois des ONOfs [RA415; original emphasis].
>
> All of this, these people, this neighborhood, that had been his only reality for 38 P-years, appeared strangely unreal and transparent to him. Recreation, preserve, amusement park for the Centraliens, zoo, simulation, movie set with extras.... A solid set. "For them," he thought, "this is reality. *Their* only reality?" At least he found a certain pleasure in hearing the awful WNW patois again.

The pleasure at hearing his mother tongue appears tempered with its qualification as awful, although that may reflect the attitude of the omniscient narrator. Furthermore, the recyclee's distance from his former cohort increases through the time differential between Manokhsor and the Centrale; as one "P-year" equals 690 days on its current calendar, one "C-year" spans seven years on the surface (RA45). The longevity of the Centraliens allows them to observe the Périphériens much like the reader may watch a long-running television series. Like his companions, Adakhan laughs at the thought of the Périphériens' second set of genitals, yet he expresses scruples about this scornful attitude: "Adakhan se rappela qu'il s'agissait là d'un tripotage génétique, d'une manipulation de la Centrale, et se trouva gêné et vulgaire, d'avoir ri ainsi des Périphériens" ("Adakhan remembered that this was the result of genetic tampering, a manipulation by the Centrale, and found himself bothered and vulgar at having laughed thus at the Périphériens"; RA416). Yet, he also wonders at how much he has changed: "Centralien d'adoption mais Périphérien de naissance — avec quelquefois les réflexes de Périphérien malgré le recyclage et ses années à la Centrale?" ("Adopted Centralien, but Périphérien by birth — with sometimes still the reflexes of a Périphérien in spite of his years in the Centrale?"; RA416) Symbolic of the inability to return home unchanged after his experience in the metropole, Adakhan gets lost as he tries to guide his companions through his old quarter (RA417) and later wonders if he has lost his native patois as he tries to communicate with local metalsmiths (RA421).

Adakhan's compromised identity, his position as no longer Périphérien yet never fully Centralien, is made clear through his failed attempt to incite rebellion among "his people," and his subsequent punishment for this subversion, a period of time spent with the rival team of Lokhfer. The title *Le Grand projet* (1993), the second book of volume two, refers in part to Adakhan's cherished project of liberating the Périphériens from the yoke of their oppression. Adakhan himself realizes its impossibility as he returns to Manokhsor in a series of passages which also reveal how living and being educated in the metropole (the Centrale) has changed the "native" who attempts to return home. The discourse of science fiction allows their inferiority, previously figured as a subjective perception, to become a real, physical change in the Périphériens. As Adakhan sees his own people through other eyes, he documents an actual reduction in height occurring in the Périphériens, the result of a molecular breakdown they now suffer:

> Les plus grands, les plus «élancés» des ONOfs, y compris les moins conditionnés, les plus *récupérables*, n'arrivent plus qu'à l'estomac des Centraliens—et les moins grands, à leur ceinture! Ils n'ont jamais paru plus petits. Il[s] n'ont jamais *été* plus petits. On dirait des enfants précocement vieillis. Chétifs, maigres, plus recroquevillés que la dernière fois [GP323; original emphasis].
>
> The tallest, sveltest of the WNWers, including the least conditioned and most *recoverable*, don't even reach the chest of Centraliens — and the shortest, their belt! They have never appeared smaller. They have never *been* smaller. You would say precociously aged children. Puny, thin, more shriveled up than the last time.

Adakhan nonetheless makes several attempts to reveal the truth to a range of Périphérien audiences; all of which fail. They refuse to listen because their own conditioning has become so deeply ingrained; their physical stature simply externalizes their smallness of mind. The mark of a real inferiority now painfully obvious, Adakhan unconsciously expresses the racism he now shares with the Centraliens. While trying to identify possible cell-leaders among those who may be less conditioned, Adakhan hears various female voices in the marketplace complaining about prices — potential subversion in this controlled society. Wanting to identify the speakers, he nonetheless realizes the futility of his actions: "Pas moyen d'y reconnaître celle qui a parlé, elles se ressemblent toutes. Physiquement" ("No way of recognizing the one who spoke; they all resemble each other. Physically"; GP347). No longer able to distinguish individuals among the oppressed masses, Adakhan thus expresses the othering commonplace that "they all look alike."

Adakhan, too, has changed as demonstrated by the Périphériens' inverse response to him as differing from themselves as a representative of the ruling classes. Not yet willing to abandon his project, he goes to the central square where the Archers tolerate a certain number of soap-box speakers. Adakhan tries to convince his audience that he is one of them: "Privilégié, oui, mais je ne suis pas un dirigeant. Nous ne sommes pas *tous* des «dirigeants», là-dessous.... Je suis des vôtres" ("Yes, I am privileged, but I'm not a ruler. We are not *all* "rulers," down there ... I am one of yours"; GP351). Their challenges to his speech demonstrate both their inability to accept the truth and his own difference from them. Back in the Centrale, recuperating among his friends, he admits: "C'est raté. J'ai été grotesque" ("It's a failure. I was grotesque"; GP381).

Adakhan's punishment for this unauthorized foray could be death. His patron Syrius' influence, along with the machinations of his rival, Lokhfer, result in a sort of plea bargain, in which Adakhan must spend six months in the latter's service. In this unit of lockstep authoritarian rule, comprised — although the original scientists who founded the Centrale included members of the full range of ethnic groups (RA171) — fully of light-skinned European types, Adakhan clearly stands out (SQP21).

That the recycled Périphérien can never fully become a Centralien appears clearly during his stint in Lokhfer's unit; Adakhan nonetheless identifies with the society that has adopted him. To further bolster his identity as an "authentic" Centralien — something suggested much earlier by virtue of the fact that his genitals reflect the Centralien (and real human) norm rather than the Périphériens' forced mutation — the narrative reveals that his father was a Centralien descended from Syrius, thus Adakhan's godfather is really his great-great-grandfather (RA326). Adakhan's identity shifts from that of a Périphérien to that of a Centralien; this shift disrupts the allegorical reading implied in this analysis.

Thus far, the relationship established between *L'Oiseau de feu* and Arguin's analysis of realist French-Canadian novels has identified the oppressed, colonized Périphériens with the francophones in Québec. To reiterate, Brossard's description of the stagnant, conformist society of Manokhsor reflects precisely the portrait painted of French-Canadian society prior to the 1970s by a long stream of intellectuals, a portrait that, according to Jocelyn Létourneau still appears in the work of historian Gérard Bouchard (43–66) and philosopher Serge Cantin (30). We can read Adakhan as the increasingly enlightened Quiet Revolution nationalist hero who seeks to liberate his people and establish a new society. The irrecuperable level of dejection into which the Périphériens have sunk forces Adakhan (and Brossard) to abandon them to their fate of destruction, as their society and their physical beings reach a state of total breakdown by the end of *2.C Le Sauve-qui-peut* (1995).

Adakhan's integration into the Centrale increasingly reveals how the colonial relationship affects not only the obviously oppressed Périphériens, but also the Centraliens. Life in the Centrale, although much more physically comfortable and relatively freer, has its limits and restrictions just like that on the surface. Early in the recycling process, just as in Manokhsor, he is told that underground "[c]ertaines matières demeureront secrètes: c'est la règle NKB, «Nitouno»" ("certain matters will remain secret: it's the NKB rule, "Nitouno" ["Need to know"]"; RA125).[18] The longer he stays in the Centrale, the more he learns of its society, the more Adakhan realizes that the majority of Centraliens live under the same régime of behavioral conditioning as the Périphériens, including the "fourth stage" of recycling, equivalent to brainwashing (RA207), making those who undergo it virtual zombies. In a discussion of the Centrale's system of law with his friend and mentor, Lenardth (also recycled from Manokhsor) Adakhan accuses the Centrale of hypocrisy and describes its society as being identical to the Manokhsor he left behind: "Tu veux savoir nos vraies «lois»? Il y en a cinq: la peur, l'inertie, la lâcheté, la bêtise et l'intérêt" ("You want to know our real laws? There are five: fear, inertia, cowardice, stupidity and self-interest"; GP271).

Subject to control not only by their ancestors who, they presume, were the Programmers of MO, the *Maître Ordinateur* (Master Computer), that governs their lives as strictly as they govern the Périphériens, the Centraliens increasingly face domination by their own leaders, especially the evil Lokhfer who gathers power to exercize. One of the first illusions to fade is that of an egalitarian society, as Adakhan notes in his journal:

> L'égalité, mon œil! Ici: les Grands Patrons du Collège > les autres Grands Patrons > les autres Nobles >> les autres Centraliens >> les recyclés en Probation > les récus de 1ère classe >> les récus de 2e classe >>; et là-haut: les Archontes >> les privilégiés >> les autres Périphériens sans compter les archers ni les cyborgs. Ni MO. Est-il cet «On» qui décide de la tâche qui *nous* «convient le mieux»? [RA198; original emphasis].

> Equality, my ass! Here: Great Patrons of the College > other Great Patrons > other Nobles >> other Centraliens >> recyclees on Probation >> 1st class recoups

\>> 2nd class recoups >>; and above (in Manokhsor): Archontes >> privileged individuals >> other Périphériens not including archers or cyborgs. Or MO. Is he this "One" who decides which tasks "best suit" *us*?

Adakhan provides here, in abbreviated form, a complete hierarchy of the Centrale which permeates down (but literally up) into Périphérien society, each group standing in a hegemonic relationship to the next, effectively indicated by the sign, which in mathematics indicates "greater than." A deeply entrenched hierarchical system allows the colonizer to justify and maintain power over the colonized through the establishment of his own superiority, the allotment of privileges to a colonial and an indigenous client class, which in turn dominate an oppressed native group. This structure of the Centrale's socio-political organization reflects this order, although it appears hidden behind a veil of democratic meritocracy: run by a College of Patrons, composed of and alternately chaired by the team-leaders of various disciplines, its "Président" must in turn answer for all decisions to the body of "Nobles" (previously called *Nobels*, an ostensible clue to their earliest configuration). While various issues become the subject of a form of direct democratic approval, these referenda appear to be the type of pro forma stamps of approval found in real dictatorships whose direct or implied campaigns of pressure ensure the outcome will fall in their favor. Ultimately, all decisions are subject to approval by MO programmed with certain directives intended to preserve the established order and, presumably, to prevent a recurrence of the Catastrophe that destroyed the world once already.

Above in Manokhsor, a hierarchy integrated into that of the Centrale, also reigns. From the Chambanes of the secret societies, to the Archontes of each of the twelve sectors, the hierarchy rises to the King, who turns out to be an animatronic puppet installed by the Centraliens. The first pages of Césaire's *Discourse on Colonialism* (1955) outline the argument that colonization results not only in the brutalization of the oppressed, colonized people, but also in the brutalization of the colonizer in his exertion of power. Postcolonial critics take up this stance finding and analyzing instances of how not only the colonizer exported his culture to the new dominions, but also how the colony influenced metropolitan culture. That colonization becomes an integral system of oppression for all involved appears clearly in Adakhan's reflections about his world. Brossard's demonstration that the system of power relations in institutionalized colonialism is a closed, integrated system which affects all those it touches represents a sophisticated, postcolonial critique.

Like Rochon's, Brossard's SFQ saga reveals many parallels with earlier French-Canadian "colonial" or "colonized" novels like those described by Arguin. There is no question that the novel is anti-colonial both in its critique of the Centrale and in its depiction of the power structure as a comprehensive system ecompassing the oppressed and the ostensible oppressor. Yet it is unclear whether other elements of the process his protagonist undergoes seek to expose the nasty underside of the colonial project of assimilation or if the novel itself cannot escape the "colonized" mentality it sets out to critique. Does Adakhan shake off the state of alienation experienced by the Périphériens? Or does he simply trade it for a new one as an assimilated Centralien? Daniel Poliquin argues precisely in *Le Roman colonial* that nationalist discourse in Québec, which turned to the discourse of decolonization in the 1960s, simply cannot free itself of this heritage. Arguing that Memmi's work represents the most influential imported work of that era (137), Poliquin asserts that adopting the stance of the colonized simply allowed Québec's nationalists to repolarize the dichotomy, a move which, as Angenot points out in *Les Idéologies du ressentiment*, simply reproduces rather than transcends the system. Paradoxically, Poliquin observes (as do Angenot and Fanon before him) that the superiority of the Other has been so internalized that the so-called colonized individual's first desire is to take the place of the colonizer. Poliquin finds evidence of this in the continued over-valuation of things French-from-France or of things English; he cites the example of Radio-Canada newscasters using English pronunciations of English terms, an effort which simply renders those terms incomprehensible to the general Québécois public. Similarly, Adakhan's identification as a Centralien and the text's making real the Périphériens' inferiority appear in many ways to reinscribe a discourse of colonization, demonstrating that the way to power and subject status must come through assimilation to the dominant group. And yet, the ambivalence of Brossard's text makes such a final pronouncement difficult to make; throughout the work Adakhan continues to struggle *against* just such desires.

Furthermore, as with Rochon's *Le Cycle de Vrénalik*, Brossard's *L'Oiseau de feu* resists any simplistic a = b allegorical reading. Between volumes one and two, and then across the three books of volume two, a slippage in allegorical assignment occurs. *Les Années d'apprentissage* presents a dichotomous society split between the average Périphériens, a clear figure for French Canadians prior to the Quiet Revolution, and their ruling class. The Archontes and other Périphérien leaders, given their combined public and religious functions, could well present an allegory for the Catholic hierarchy in French Canada. As *Le Recyclage d'Adakhan* introduces the Centraliens, these dominators first appear aligned with Great Britain, Federal Canada and/or the United States. However, across that volume and into *Le Grand projet*, as Adakhan learns of the Centraliens' control over the Périphériens, their own oppression within the hierarchical system of conformity and surveillance, as well as the imposture of Centraliens as Périphérien leaders, the Centraliens increasingly figure not as the anglophone majority, but the as the francophone minority in North America. Bunkered down in their enclave province, the French Canadians face the traditional threat of takeover not only by the continent's anglophone majority, but increasingly — as conservative nationalist ideologues have depicted it — by the potential hordes of immigrants coming in from outside.

This issue reveals the ambivalence of Brossard's fictional saga; on the one hand, these elements reflect its ability to transcend the dualistic representation of reality (French Canadians versus English Canadians) found in the *roman de mœurs urbaines*. Furthermore, its multivalent approach to allegory appears to support a description of the work as postcolonial, as does its critique of régimes of power which foster ignorance, and which draw upon the demonization and inferiorization of the Other to maintain themselves. On the other, this potential shift in the poles of the anglophone/francophone allegory seems to invalidate the analysis of Brossard's novel as postcolonial discourse. That is, if the novel is read so that the identification of the Québécois of French heritage has shifted to the dominant minority (Centraliens in their world/francophones in North America) rather than an oppressed majority (Périphériens in their world/francophones in Québec), this shift in the power dynamic transforms the novel into a colonialist fantasy. (And as we shall see in the next chapter, there are major elements of colonial fantasy present in volume three of Brossard's work.) Indeed, this apparent conflict highlights the complexity of Québec's position, an element that Linda Hutcheon argues must be addressed in any postcolonial criticism that wishes to avoid the trap of the totalizating account it accuses the Western of commiting.

To be sure, the unique nature of Québec's status lies in the fact that, while francophones are a *minority* in North America, they are the now powerful *majority* in Québec, as Jocelyn Létourneau asserts:

> il est clair que les francophones du Québec ont à l'égard du Canada (anglais), recréé un rapport de force qui leur est plutôt favorable, quoi qu'on dise.... A l'aube du XXIe siècle, le Québec occupe en effet, à l'intérieur de la fédération canadienne, une place qui est et reste effectivement centrale, voire unique [156].
>
> it is clear that francophones of Québec in relation to (English) Canada, have created a relation of power that is rather favorable to them, whatever anyone says.... At the dawn of the twenty-first century, Québec occupies, in fact, within the Canadian federation, a place which is and remains effectively central, even unique.

Létourneau makes his argument based upon forty years of hard-won political and social advances, yet the argument that French Québec has moved from the (Canadian) periphery to its center suggests yet another reading of Brossard's SFQ saga as highly visionary national allegory. The catastrophic destruction of both Manokshor and the Centrale at the end of *Le Sauve-qui-peut* clearly demonstrate that an unequal relationship between groups sharing a common territory is untenable and doomed to failure through the destruction of both Manokhsor and the Centrale. It suggests that the only way to escape the system is to start anew elsewhere, a utopian solution discussed in the following chapter's analysis of the series' concluding volume, *Les Années d'errance* (The Wandering Years, 1997). First, we conclude this chapter with an examination of alienation and oppression in the work of SFQ's foremost writer, Élisabeth Vonarburg.

Élisabeth Vonarburg's *Tyranaël* Pentalogy

Élisabeth Vonarburg's epic pentalogy, *Tyranaël* (1996–97), literally thematizes the problematics of colonization and post-colonial realities in its depiction of Earth's settlement of the planet Alpha in the Altair star system, dubbed Virginia, ostensibly after the first child born there (DS48).[19] The name, however, has obvious resonances with the historical colonization of the Americas and Vonarburg exploits stereotypes of the pioneer spirit of that continent's European immigrants, while at the same time overturning many of them. Like Rochon's *Le Cycle de Vrénalik* and Brossard's *L'Oiseau de feu*, *Tyranaël* encompasses the entire SFQ saga, including the struggle for liberation from oppression, the problems arising from new-found freedom, and, finally, the desire to found a new utopian society. It does so, though, in a manner typical of Vonarburg's writing: through a highly complex, sophisticated narrative which convolutes the story so that the main threads of the common narrative of colonization and postcolonial dynamics analyzed here are multiplied, reordered and interwoven.

Like Rochon, Vonarburg's biography and attitudes toward identity reveal a postcolonial sensibility, but one which cuts two ways. On the one hand, Vonarburg *is* a migrant, having immigrated to Québec in 1973. On the other, she is the child of two European colonials (her parents met in what was then French Indochina) and as a person of French origin and upbringing, she represents the colonizer as well. That these autobiographical elements appear in Vonarburg's œuvre has been noted by academic and SFQ writer Sylvie Bérard ("Venues"). The relationship between her situation and that of other postcolonial writers appears clearly in several of Vonarburg's statements, in which she refers to herself as a "displaced person" (Lebeau 38):

> I've been living for twenty-four years in Québec; they do speak French here, and that is not, will never be, my culture either!
> After twenty-five years here, when I go to Europe, I know that I feel rather alien over there.... Each time I go outside Québec, to the rest of Canada, it is very easy to get the same feeling. And when I go to the States, I realize I will never be a North American either....
> Mind you, being an "alien" has its advantages. Helps you see some things more clearly, even while it blinds you to some others. It puts questions of "nationality," "belonging," "group," in an entirely different light....

> I feel my only place is French, the language. And writing in French. France has taken leave of me as much as I did her, Europe too. Québec, Canada, North America have all seeped in somehow to replace most of it. But still, basically, I am at home nowhere. Except in my language [van Belkom 219].

Although frequently labeled the "grande dame de la SFQ" (Lebeau), Vonarburg tells an interviewer: "some very vocal Québecois [sic] writers don't consider me a Québecois writer—and they're right. I'm a world unto myself" (*Locus*). No longer French after over thirty years in Québec, at the same time, Vonarburg notes that she is neither fully Québécois; a fact indicated by her French, spoken in "cet accent hybride qui n'est plus tout à fait français et qui ne sera jamais tout à fait québécois" ("this hybrid accent which is neither completely French and will never be altogether Québécois"; Godin 17). And, while most of the *Néo-Québécois*, as Québec's recent immigrants (usually of descent other than French) are called, gather in Montréal, Vonarburg immigrated to the small city of Chicoutimi; even among immigrants she seems displaced. Like Rochon, although to a lesser extent, Vonarburg is also attracted to Eastern philosophies, commenting: "I am rather a Taoist, a light-and-dark-need-one-another kind of person" (Vonarburg, "Cities" 74). The East-West relationship figures greatly in her most recent series, *Reine de Mémoire* (Queen of Memory, 2005–06), briefly discussed in chapter four.

A number of critical articles (Bérard, Borgomano, Bouchard, Vierne), as well as several masters and doctoral theses (Bérard, Bogstad, Sauble-Otto, S. Taylor) focus on the question of identity, particularly as it relates to gender, in Vonarburg's first two novels, *The Silent City* and *In the Mother's Land*. Vonarburg's third novel, *Les Voyageurs malgré eux* (1994; *Reluctant Voyagers*, 1995/1996) deals overtly with the issue of colonization and, as her most clearly autobiographical work, helps establish this notion of her "postcolonial sensibility." Its title, literally rendered "voyagers in spite of themselves" may refer to her own immigration, based not on her own will but rather the result of her then-husband's job posting. Its main character, Catherine Rhymer, as Bérard notes ("Venues" 125), presents us with a clear avatar of the author: a French immigrant to Québec who teaches literature at the college level. Her origins include a French colonial grandfather with a dominant, unified identity, and a mother whose identity appears blurred: "toute petite, toute mince, toute brune, on dirait une Hindoue plutôt qu'une Annamite" ("all little, all slim, all brown, you might say a Hindu rather than an Annamese"; 7). Indeed, Catherine's story highlights the complexity of the postcolonial world in its links to numerous waves of colonization: the first French arrival on the North American continent where she now lives, the second colonial empire of France in Indochina and Africa, the re-colonization of Francophone Québec by Anglo-Saxon forces, her own late twentieth-century immigration from France to Canada, and finally the colonization of Earth by beings from parallel universes.

Reluctant Voyagers also represents Vonarburg's most overtly Québec-centered novel, staging many elements of the political conflict between Québec and Canada (versions of which can be found in several short stories by other writers of SFQ),[20] set in an ever-shifting alternate timeline/parallel universe in which an independent French-speaking Enclave stands in opposition to an Orwellian anglophone Canada. To its north stands the mysterious Independent Realm of the Sags, a Métis people comprised of the descendants of indigenous Iroquois and Inuit, as well as French settlers. Vonarburg enunciates the imaginary nature of the Americas for herself, reiterating her sense of homelessness: "Distinctions blur — 'Québec,' 'Canada,' 'the States' ... 'the Americas,' 'the New World' — it's all an imaginary place for me, all of it, even as I live there" (van Belkom 219). Indeed, *Reluctant Voyagers* lends itself as much to a postcolonial analysis as *Tyranaël*, but the latter text more closely (as a multi-volume saga) fits the narrative pattern of the SFQ sagas of Rochon and Brossard.

The five-novel sequence that eventually developed around Earth's colonization and renaming of a planet known to its indigenous inhabitants as Tyranaël shares their concern about the politics of colonization. Indeed, Sophie Beaulé has inscribed Vonarburg's SFQ saga within a context of the present-day settler's coming-to-terms with the guilt surrounding past wrongs enacted upon the indigenous group ("Enfants"). Like its counterparts by Rochon and Brossard, Vonarburg's SFQ saga originated long before its publication as the author indicates in several interviews as well as its composition places and dates ("Sergines [France] 1965–Chicoutimi 1996," DS 291). The universe of the planet Tyranaël developed out of a dream of a great sea engulfing a civilization (D. Pelletier). Indeed, her first published SF story, "High Tide," includes references to the mysterious Sea of energy, unicorn-like fauna, and a city abandoned by earlier inhabitants, hallmarks of the universe of Tyranaël. Its child protagonist, Aarne, cannot understand the ethical reasoning behind colonization, more specifically the purpose of reproducing a distant, seemingly irrelevant and previously abandoned homeworld, particularly when this is done at the expense of indigenous species. This sympathy is rewarded as a collective life form warns him to seek higher ground, while the strange bluish Sea's high tide engulfs the colony's adults who have refused to heed the native.

Like Rochon's and Brossard's SFQ sagas, *Tyranaël*'s five volumes present the reader with portraits of societies divided along pseudo-ethnic lines inhabited by alienated individuals reminiscent of Arguin's *révolté*. While those previous works foregrounded one central nation or character, Vonarburg's series features perhaps a dozen *révoltés* living in seemingly endless iterations and reiterations of its divided worlds over a millennium or more. Because of the length and the large number of examples that could be drawn, this analysis focuses on a few select cases. Furthermore, having familiarized the reader well enough with the models taken from Arguin in the previous two sections of this chapter, the structure of our discussion will loosen up to focus more clearly on the primary text material's presentation of alienated individuals living in a divided world and Vonarburg's postcolonial approach to the possibilities of identity in the world(s).

The series' first book, *Dreams of the Sea*, recounts the arrival of Earth colonists on a planet cleared of its indigenous, sentient and clearly human peoples, which have, however, left intact all architectural structures. Significantly, this volume's "Strangers" are not extraterrestrials, but rather the Earth colonists presented through the perspective of one of these absent indigenes, Eïlai Liannon Klaidaru. Generations earlier, her premonitory Dreams warned her people, the Ranao, of the impending arrival of humans from another world. The colonists' story, then, appears as a reconstruction of fragments of her own and others' Dreams remembered and recorded on metal plates. This reconstruction does not follow a strictly linear pattern, and so the reader, like Eïlai, must stitch together "what happened."[21] Similarly, the reader must reassemble the diverse elements of the lives and identities of the characters that inhabit the alien nations of Virginia/Tyranaël. This narrative fragmentation, as well as the establishment of his dual identity, reflects the alienation of a central character in this first book of the series, Tige Carigan/John Carghill.

One of only a handful of characters explicitly coded as French and/or French Canadian, Carigan represents Virginia's third generation of Terrans (DS232), the child of the second wave of colonists, conscripts forced to leave an Earth thought to be in its death throes. "Tige" is a self-revision of the stereotypically French-Canadian diminutive "Ti-Jean" (*petit Jean*, little John). The son of a loving, but sterilized step-father who toils in the colony's mines (mineralogical exploitation has also played a part in Québec's colonial history) at Tarmount (a site which resonates with various Québécois place names), Ti-Jean rebels against his parents' difficult life, but does not know how to create a positive situation for himself in the world. Briefly imprisoned for having killed (in self-defense) the obnoxious son of the capital city's mayor, Tige tries to reinvent himself as a petty gambler. Only the assistance of a famous Old-Settler (as the first, shipwrecked colonists come to be called) archeologist Wang Shaandar, who forces Tige into contact with the planet's natives through the excavation of their artifacts, can bring him to a partial consciousness of his alienated state.

Like Adakhan Demuthsen, Tige Carigan/John Carghill reflects the traits of Arguin's *révolté*, the alienated, colonized individual who rejects his condition, but who does not know how to transcend it productively. Not only does his external appearance reflect this internal conflict, Tige is isolated and dispossessed not only of the world around him, but even of himself. As a young boy, his classmates call him a monster; not so much because he is physically ugly, but because he is the product of artificial insemination (DS135–37). As a teenager, apparently handsome since he attracts the attention of upper-class girls, others immediately recognize Tige as a yokel (DS147). This utter dispossession of himself appears in his very origins: his mother had no control over his conception and has no knowledge of his paternal identity. This lapse derives from the regulation that all fertile women leaving Earth for the colony were required to bear at least one child. In what might be Vonarburg's commentary on the *revanche des berceaux* ideology, Tige's mother was artificially inseminated from a sperm bank guaranteed free of the genetic anomalies plaguing the contaminated Earth.

Tige develops an awareness of his own alienation through his encounter with Ranao ruins that Wang Shandaar illegally hires him to excavate. As he leaves the archeological site, he sees the sun and "for a moment Tige thought he was looking at a great broken mirror" (DS161); this encounter provides him with a broken reflection of himself, a sign of his growing self-awareness. Face-to-face with the relics of a great civilization, he realizes that his planet is *theirs*: "We are the strangers. We are the aliens" (DS163). He is not yet ready, though, for such a radical reconfiguration of reality and in his internal dialogue, he shifts back to the ideology of self-preservation that his environment has inculcated in him:

> What did the "truth" about what had happened on Virginia a thousand, fifty thousand or a million seasons ago have to do with the life of Tige Carigan? Nothing. Once he returned to Bird, to Cristobal or somewhere else, Tige Carigan would still be Tige Carigan.... Five thousand berys and a chest of gold pieces, though, that could change something in the life of Tige Carigan. That was the real world, not the one where people like Shandaar ... lived [DS218].

Tige uses the money he earns to develop a new, mainstream identity, which cannot, however, represent a true coming-to-terms with himself. Indeed, Tige's efforts to become a member of the dominant society, through the persona of John Carghill, simply reflect the colonized individual's attempt to assimilate to the dominant group, as seen in our discussion of Brossard's Adakhan. Eventually, his past self returns to haunt him, when Wang Shandaar calls on him for help. At first, not willing to blow his cover, Carghill hides behind the mask he has created, refusing to acknowledge his link to the archeologist now institutionalized because colonial officials view his theories as subversive. He wants to reply: "Tige Carigan does not exist, no longer exists," but when confronted with the question, "And now, who are you?" John Carghill verbalizes "I don't know;" but his thoughts provide another response: "a ghost" (DS154).[22] Although he eventually provides the requested assistance, his acknowledgment of his past self remains only partial and his continued alienation appears in "the wall that John Carghill has learned to erect between himself and the world" (DS225). In spite of this, or perhaps because the system requires it, Carghill succeeds in his bids for office and his historical role in the early colony appears memorialized in a boulevard named in his honor and referred to in later volumes.

The transitional figure between *Dreams of the Sea* and the series' second volume, *A Game of Perfection*, Simon Rossem is the only major character to appear in all five books of *Tyranaël*. A genetic mutation related to the planet itself endows him with extreme longevity, along with the increasingly common gift of extrasensory perception, although his power far surpasses any other known Virginian's. Simon's alienation appears in his difference as a child (his failure to speak and his mental and physical wanderings resemble a form of autism), then as an adult, through both his isolation (because of his profound difference from the mortals around him) and the necessary practice he adopts of shifting identities and personalities to match. Since his family and companions age while he does not, Simon must disappear and recreate himself to maintain the secret of his power. Indeed, he poses as an understanding, well-intentioned "normal" among the mutants that he works to save from the increasingly powerful behind-the-scenes governmental agents known as the Grays.

As the central character of *A Game of Perfection* and a minor figure in the third and fourth books of the series, *Mon frère l'ombre* (My Brother the Shadow) and *L'Autre rivage* (The Other Shore), he appears as a seemingly endless series of well-intentioned elderly, but capable gentlemen. His avatars Simon Légaré, Antoine Fersen, Élias Navanad, Anton Schermmering, Arturo Jékel, Constantin Apatridès, Serje Pérégrino, Abram Viateur, Dutch Grangier and Simon Fergusson continue to play various roles in the mutant underground resistance to the Grays, their names referencing his eternal wandering.[23] In the final volume, *La Mer allée avec le soleil* (The Sea Left with the Sun), having experienced yet another element in his mutation — a miraculous rejuvenation resulting from his contact with the Sea — he returns to a central role as Samuel/Simon Fergus. This multiplication of identities clearly destabilizes the Western notion of the ego, which attributes the individual with an essential core personality. A consummate actor, Simon plays a new role with each name he assumes.

The one constant appears in his dedication to recuperating and assisting abused and cast-off children, who, as the planet's mutation of the human genome changes over time, possess a range of extrasensory and telekinetic powers. Evolving with the mutation is the Virginian sense of normality so that in the early books children who *have* powers represent anomaly, in the middle books those who appear *not* to have any powers become pariah, and, finally, those who display *new* powers (such as levitation) cause yet another shift in the limits of the acceptable. The children Simon recuperates typically suffer from varying degrees of alienation: dispossessed of themselves, both physically and mentally, profoundly isolated, disconnected from the society around them, lacking in knowledge about their own identity and origins, and harboring deep anger against both the oppressing other (the Grays) or their own families who have either betrayed and abandoned them or kept secrets from them. This pattern recurs in *A Game of Perfection*: Michaël, the apparently autistic child (like Simon earlier) of a member of Virginia's colonial elite who exhibits the power of perceiving hidden doors that allow him access to caches of recordings made by the Ancients about their world; Éric and Tess, both of whom were tortured as children, the boy by his father, the girl by Gray scientists who had captured her; and Martin, whose family has hidden his heritage of extrasensory abilities from him.

The most profoundly alienated individual of the series appears in Mathieu of volume three (the narrative's central peak), *Mon frère l'ombre*. The novel's opening pages reveal his complete disconnection from the world around him; the reader, sharing his ignorance, can only slowly weave the narrative threads of his story together as it progresses, eventually providing more detail about his past. Again fragmentation and achronology mark the narrative. As Mathieu first perceives his world, all is gray; all is the same, his every movement monitored and his behavior controlled, presumably by the orange pills taken with every meal (MF4–5). Although he doesn't recall how he learned to do it, he can write and so he keeps a journal. His state of alienation and isolation is so complete that he cannot immediately grasp the concept of different individuals, as revealed in his description of the only other person he sees, "Gardien:"

> C'est drôle aussi que Gardien change de figure. Il ne change pas seulement de figure, d'abord, il change aussi de taille, de voix, de couleurs. Il change aussi avec moi: des fois il me parle gentiment, des fois il ne dit rien du tout. Et des fois il est méchant [MF7].
>
> It's also funny how Guardian changes his face. He doesn't just change his face; besides, he also changes his size, voice, his color. He also changes with me: sometimes he speaks nicely to me, other times he doesn't say anything. And sometimes he is mean.

The disjointed diary reveals that Mathieu is a "tête-de-pierre," a blockhead. Some four hundred years after colonization (MF163) a certain level of extrasensory sensitivity has become dominant among humans on the planet — the vast majority of individuals perceive each other's presence within a certain distance and they can communicate without vocalization to a limited degree. Virginians now erroneously associate the apparent lack of extrasensory ability with descent from the last arrived Terrans, a forced colonization that accompanied Earth's final efforts to maintain its hegemony over Virginia. This irony, that the reader knows more about Mathieu and his world (that is, if he/she has read the previous volumes of the series) than he does, reveals the extent of his alienation. Others hold complete control over his destiny as he has spent most of his adolescence as a human guinea pig, imprisoned in a series of laboratories (disguised as schools) each of which becomes progressively worse as Mathieu's "blockheadedness" resists the Grays' efforts to "open him up."

The theme of the guinea pig, a fairly common one in SFQ,[24] problematizes the nature of the human subject. In a world where the individual is bombarded with stimuli and conditioned in any number of ways he/she cannot even begin to know about, the Western subject, the supposed master self, as a subject of study, subject to the mastery of others becomes nothing more than an object. This subjection to the mastery of others becomes transparent in Vonarburg's use of the French term for teacher: "maîtres," school*masters*. Indeed, that his so-called teacher Jordan, really a powerful member of the Grays, wields the power of a master-slave relationship over Mathieu appears through the terms of an abusive love relationship, as Jordan tells the boy: "Tu sais bien que tu es à moi, Mathieu. Pour toujours" ("You know you are mine, Mathieu. Forever"; MF14). Jordan's control obviously extends to Mathieu's physical body, through drugs, but also through the "gift" of a bracelet that conceals a tracking device (MF14, 35). Not only is his body subject to outside control, but so is Mathieu's mind, as Jordan (like his previous teachers) withholds nearly all knowledge about Virginia from him. Oddly, he allows Mathieu to learn *setlaod*, the language of the Ancient natives, and to read their stories, including, presumably, the tale of Oghim.

The novel's title, my brother the shadow, refers to the Ancients' legend of Oghim, narrated alternately with the story of Mathieu. Another *aliéné*— he is dispossessed of his own shadow — Oghim recovers it only after a series of tests, aided by an ostensible beggar, Galaas. At the end of these he tells the gods that he would rather give up all of the powers he has acquired (the same powers, of course, now observed to varying degrees in Virginians), than be separated from the love of his fellow man. Oghim's quest represents a process of humanization which allows him to leave behind the alienated state of his birth. Similarly, Mathieu escapes the prison of the Grays' so-called schools, aided in his escape by a computer-generated Galaas, apparently the last sentient relic of the Ranao. This represents only the first step, though, in a process that lasts the length of this novel and continues into the next. For, led by Galaas through the same series of tests and successfully passing them in new, completely unexpected ways, Mathieu *becomes*, in a sense, Oghim's shadow. At the end of the volume, Mathieu's "blockage" actually allows him to traverse the Sea — which has proven fatal to all other Virginians who have come into contact with it — from Virginia to Atyrkelsaō. In this parallel world where the Ranao have made a new home he is welcomed as Odatan, the Stranger, fulfilling the prophecy made by Oghim, also held by legend to have dreamed of a coming Stranger. This central volume extends a measure of hope, then, that there is a way out of the alienation that permeates this colonial situation and that, eventually, representatives of the two shadow worlds can meet each other as brothers.

Mirror and shadow images continue into volume four, *L'Autre rivage*, the first two sections of which are dedicated to the telling of one central character's life, that of *halatnim* (a hybrid born of a Ranao mother and a part-Virginian father, the descendant of Mathieu/Odatan) Lian Flaherty. The technique of intercalated narration — the text alternates between the telling of Lian's childhood and teenage years on Atyrkelsaō and his young adult life on Virginia — recreates an effect of doubling and splitting the ego, as the reader continually confronts two iterations of the same character. On Atyrkelsaō, Lian has been raised as a full-blooded Rani by his mother and what Virginians would call a step-father. When he discovers his biological father's identity, he is given a new name: transformed from Lian Dougallad Laraïnu (his Rani name including both metronymic and patronymic) to Lian Flaherty (his father's last name) when he encounters the community of Virginians, descendants of "Passeurs" (like Mathieu/Odatan of the previous volume) who have arrived via the Sea on Atyrkelsaō, he again is renamed as Liam when he becomes the first to arrive *from* Atyrkelsaō *to* Virginia. Lian's story now creates a beautiful, perfectly reversed mirror image of that of Mathieu from the previous volume, adding yet another layer to the references of "my brother the shadow."[25] However, as a passive recipient of the multiple identities attributed to him, but never clearly certain of his own "true" self, Lian bears the hallmarks of the *aliéné*.

The pattern of alienation recurs in Lian's biography. He has grown up on Atyrkelsaō, the parallel world to which the Ranao have emigrated in the Great Passage from Tyranaël when the Dreamers warned them of the Terrans' coming. Raised in isolation by his parents as a Rani youth, he knows he is different from other children for he has none of the extrasensory abilities innate to the majority of Ranao for hundreds of generations. His mother seeks to protect him from his difference, but he, of course, knows she hides the truth about his father's identity — for he sets out on a quest of discovery — as a veil of lies. Alienated from his own identity, Lian also appears alienated from the rest of his society in a most profound manner. Besides not possessing extrasensory faculties, during his childhood it is discovered that Lian figures among the extremely rare cases of a mutation that makes him "réfractaire à la Mer," that is, unlike the rest of the Ranao who join the Sea at the time of their death (and who, thus, it is believed, gain spiritual immortality), Lian's body completely resists the force of the Sea that destroys all other biological matter that comes into contact with it. For his deeply religious mother, her son's inability to reunite with her in the afterlife represents the most tragic of all forms of alienation.

In spite of these traits of alienation, Lian's level of mental "health"— even as a teenager — appears superior to that of the series' previous central characters and to that of a number of more profoundly alienated individuals whom he meets in *L'Autre rivage*. Unlike the mutant children on Virginia of volumes two and three — who are rejected by their families, demonized, used as guinea pigs, tortured, or even killed because of their difference — Lian has been loved and protected. He has known real friendship and possesses a deep sense of ethics, revealed when his quest for his father and for his own identity brings him into contact with the Krilliadni, outcasts from Ranao society. Among the latter, he refuses to participate in rape, torture and murder with the members of a secret society he has joined. His sense of self contrasts with that of his friend, the ethnic-Virginian youth Thomas Llewellyn who feels no sense of belonging on Atyrkelsaō, as well as with that of his own misfit father, whose alienation as a *halatnim* (a part-Virginian on the Ranao's new homeworld) leads him to kill twice in anger and consequently to suffer the punishments of blinding and exile.

In his grief over the loss of a father he just met, Liam calmly walks into the Sea, floats, and loses consciousness, waking up on the Other Shore of this volume's title. On Virginia, he is not so much alienated as simply disoriented; his attitude reflects that of the melancholy of mourning. Having learned Virginian on Atyrkelsaō, knowing something of the society (although not of its present configuration since it has been some time since the last of the Passers crossed over), he simply needs to remain silent, observe and adapt. His inner strength again contrasts with that of Grayson James, a young member of the Virginian elite he encounters when recruited into military service. This military service was instituted as a result of the continued division within Virginian society between the Grays and the forces of resistance (which still include a disguised Simon Rossem), two factions that have been locked in an ongoing Civil War for several decades. This Civil War illustrates Vonarburg's elaboration of the dichotomous society typical of the *roman de mœurs urbaines* of earlier Québécois literature. However, as in the works of Rochon and Brossard, Vonarburg's series sets up an apparent dichotomy, only to complicate it, thus subverting the dichotomous logic of Western, imperial thought.

Indeed, *Tyranaël*'s five volumes repeatedly appear to establish binary oppositions of worlds, races, ethnic groups, political parties, and abilities, while at the same time insistently and incessantly, as one would expect of a postcolonial narrative, disrupting the bipolar logic through the introduction of third (or more) poles. The obvious dichotomy that Vonarburg establishes from the beginning of the series is that of Terrans and Ranao. This apparently simple distinction, though, becomes increasingly complex as the series progresses. Throughout *Dreams of the Sea*, Terrans from Earth, although no scene of the novel ever takes place on the home planet, arrive on a planet they name Virginia, and over the generations, they increasingly become "Virginian," establishing the typical colonial dichotomy between metropolitans and colonials:

Earth versus Virginia. This dichotomy appears to culminate in Virginia's independence at the end of *A Game of Perfection*.

Eternal exiles, the Terrans of Virginia thus appear dispossessed of their homeworld; in contrast, the absent indigenes, the Ancient Ranao, first appear at home on Tyranaël. Eylaï and the others depicted in *Dreams* have not yet left it. Soon, though, a third planetary pole of Atyrkelsaō, the parallel world where the Ranao abide after the Great Passage, complements Earth and Virginia/Tyranaël. As Earth fades from the picture after independence, the dichotomy of Virginia/Atyrkelsaō establishes itself, only to be disrupted through the repeated "return" to Tyranaël effectuated by the telling of Ranao myths and legends, which occur there, as well as through Earth's reappearance in the inverted form of the hollowed-out Lagrange asteroid, motorized and colonized by Earth's last survivors. And, while Atyrkelsaō seems to be an identical reproduction of Tyranaël, there are some exceptions. The moatroani, the amphibian proto-hominids, have not experienced the evolutionary transformation into full sentience (as did their descendants the Ranao on their original home planet) and neither have certain animal forms. The parallel world's cognate of unicorn-like *tovker*, which on Tyranaël shares the Ranao's empathic powers, shows no such special ability.

A Game of Perfection pits the desire of the metropolis (Earth) to exploit the colony and its resources against those who truly seek to build a new home and a new identity on Virginia. This distinction develops more clearly in the second volume's depiction of the metropolitan presence on the colony world in the form of multi-national — indeed, inter-stellar — corporations like the BET: Bounderye (a wink to early Canadian explorer de la Vérendrye) Extra-solar Trading Co (GP50). Vonarburg's image of the capitalist exploitation of resources for simple monetary gain, coupled with the desire to master and tame the Other land and its resources, whatever the cost, nearly reaches the level of a demonization. As exploitable resources include the flora and fauna, the Centre for Exobiology Studies and Advanced Research (CEXSAR) attempts to capture a family of the native unicorn-like species, an attempt which ends in the mother *tovker*'s destruction of her own corralled foal coupled with her subsequent suicide. While the emotional impact of this scene demonstrates Vonarburg's power as a writer, it also reveals her political stance in relationship to the environment. That stance critiques the Western desire to control through knowledge, as well as science's annexation by capital; for CEXSAR, the ostensibly neutral scientific research organization, is sponsored by BET (GP50), which itself participates in a range of "incestuous relationships" (GP157) with government agencies. These organizations will soon turn from the native fauna and begin to examine the effects of the planet on Terrans, effectively seeking human guinea pigs for their experiments.

The power relationship typical of the colonial experience appears again through the disdain expressed by representatives of the metropolis for any real understanding of the colony, a theme explored throughout *A Game of Perfection*. The Virginians, at least some Virginians, continue to study in order to understand the native Ancients, including delegating the main building of the capital city's complex as a museum. In contrast, Terrans have little or no interest in it, as one character witnessing this indifference comments:

> But how would this data keep Earth from doling out its meagre funding to Virginia? Earth couldn't care less about Virginia's mysteries. All Earth is interested in is being repaid the huge debt incurred by the Virginians! [GP142].

While this depiction of the vicissitudes of the colonial system could apply to any colonial/post-colonial nation, the political parallels to the specific Québec situation reappears when Virginia requires Earth to enter negotiations between BET and SeCom. Earth's ungracious reaction, "Earth's displeasure towards us for having demanded negotiations" (GP242), recalls to the Canadian reader Québec's demand for negotiations over constitutional repatriation and its request for recognition as a unique culture during the (failed) conferences at Lake Meech and Charlottetown, a topic also referenced in Jean Dion's "Base de négotiation" (1992).

On Virginia, new dichotomies, besides that of colonizer/colonized soon appear because of the mutation caused by life on the new planet, namely, the split between mutants who possess powers and those who do not. Yet again, the dichotomy shifts in terms of which group is oppressor and which oppressed, and also multiplies, as various forms of telekinetic powers begin to appear. In *A Game of Perfection*, the "new" Virginians represent the mutants who must at first hide from government forces who will kidnap them in order to understand the powers, but who eventually turn tables and secretly come into power. But in *Mon frère l'ombre*, the mutation for extrasensory perception has become dominant in the Virginian population and now those, like Mathieu, who do not appear to possess such powers have taken on the role of the oppressed. Also stigmatized, however, are those who possess the wrong kind of powers; the Grays will murder or sterilize the new mutants who can levitate or use telekinesis. In the second and third volumes, too, the planet becomes more deeply divided.

A Game of Perfection opens over two hundred Earth years after the arrival of the first Terrans on Virginia (GP15) revealing that in urban areas a colonial-type society has indeed developed. A privileged group, which seeks to reproduce Earth's civilization and ignore or erase indications of the native Ancients, exists alongside a marginalized underclass. The notion of a Pale, the term identifying the inner circle of Anglo-Saxon Protestant territories during England's colonization of Ireland, is obvious in the peripherals' relegation to the unauthorized "Hors-le-mur" (literally Outside-the-wall, but translated as "Off-the-wall"). The marginalized immigrants, criminals, and other pariahs gather in sections outside the city's walls erected by the Ancients to protect them from the effects of the Sea. The narrative, whose point of view reflects that of the underclass, refers contemptuously to the privileged as "gadjes." This term can be read as a transformation of the word "gadgets," referring to their desire to reproduce Earth's technology even in the face of the Sea's disruptive effects, indicative of a Western desire for mastery over nature. But it also means "alien" in Romany, the language of Earth's oppressed migrant community more commonly referred to as gypsies, thus indicating their alien status on Virginia (DS72). The suggestion here is that the upper class, the center, represents the truly alienated group which, rather than living in harmony with its new environment, seeks to change and transform, to manipulate it into a shape that it cannot accept. Further volumes reveal that the gajes' colonial project of reproducing Earth on Virginia is doomed and that adaptation to the new world — that is to say, living according to its terms and conditions — will be necessary for humans to thrive there. The reader's sympathy, instead, lies with the oppressed classes living beyond the Pale, particularly as we follow Simon Rossem who, because of the oddity of his longevity, enters this clandestine world.

The underworld's fluidity contrasts with the colonial government's desire to impose order, a desire introduced through the control of information and knowledge (a phenomenon seen in *L'Oiseau de feu*) through censorship of publications. This clandestine world's unofficial resistance to state control gradually solidifies, in criticism of police brutality in an unlicensed newspaper (GP35), then in the organized armed force, the Rebs. The physical separation of the central Pale and its margins is made clear, as well as the increasing institutionalization of this formerly separate society:

> thirty Years[26] after systematic, massive colonization ended on Virginia, the population levels in the great ancient cities of the natives have risen to the point where their Off-the-Wall districts can stop being invisible ghettos and officially become slums. In any case they're no longer temporary hideouts for outlaws, crazies or people living on the margins of society either by choice or out of bad luck. Ordinary people do live there now with their families ... they work and run businesses. The reason for the wall's existence has disappeared: the whole city is now inhabited even though the gaselec doesn't reach everywhere. The municipal administration will have to start paying attention to the squatters who now aspire to full citizenship [GP35–36].

So long after colonization, the lines between the Pale and its periphery have become meaningless; yet, the government resists regularizing its status and giving the full rights of citizenship to those who live there.

Another two hundred years later the loose, unofficial division of Morgorod, which Mathieu enters after escaping the Grays in *Mon frère l'ombre*, has now become institutionalized. The area outside the city walls has now become an official ghetto, "Orlemur," its name reflecting an extrapolated linguistic corruption of "hors-le-mur" ("outside the wall"). Vonarburg complicates the simple dualistic pattern, however, for not only is the city proper divided between an upper- and lower-city (the upper city retains electricity even during the Sea's presence and so the most wealthy elite live there), even the Orlemur ghetto has its own classes of more and less privileged based on wealth and status. The fragility of that status, though, appears as hooligans threaten a ghetto-leader as soon as he steps into the streets of the city proper. Earlier, this same man had mistreated Mathieu when the latter sought him out to obtain papers immediately after passing through the Sea from Atyrkelsaō. With this incident the text underscores the irony of the status of a "colonial elite," a term which becomes an oxymoron the moment the colonial comes into contact with even the lowest members of the Pale's hierarchy. Party lines also divide the society between the privileged "Maîtres," the Grays, and the remaining legitimate classes. The social pariahs consist not only of the Terrans, whose status is clear in the corruption of the proper French *Terriens* (Earthlings/Terrans) into "tériens," "t'es rien" ("you're nothing"; MF173). However, even the non–Terrans have their pariah class of the "irrécupérables" ("unrecoverables") those who simply refuse to conform and become homeless, often victims of substance abuse both chosen and imposed. Indeed, the Grays succeed in passing off a drug that assists them in controlling the population as a widely consumed vitamin supplement.

This social dichotomy appears most clearly as Morgorod/Orlemur, or Virginians/Terrans, when set in the terms of a racial conflict, as Mathieu experiences it after he escapes above ground. Learning his way around Orlemur, he considers looking for work outside, which he can do if he wears the red triangle (MF142) required of "tériens." This obvious reference to Hitler's anti-Semitic policy, as well as references to feared lynchings (MF142) underscores the issue of race in power politics. The parallel made here between Virginia's Grays and Hitler and Southern whites in the United States extends further as the Federals (the now legitimized front for the Grays) maintain power by exploiting racial tension. It also signals tensions between (federal) Canada and (the province of) Québec, as political debate between two characters reveals:

> Chaque fois qu'on parle de renégocier les accords fédéraux-provinciaux, le fédéral s'arrange pour ressortir les Terriens de leur boîte: attention, les vilains Terriens peuvent se réveiller et tout reprendre en main, alors réélisez votre bon gouvernement fédéral qui vous protège des vilains Terriens! [MF176].
>
> Every time they talk about renegotiating the federal-provincial agreements, the federal government arranges to pull the Terrans out of their box: warning, the

evil Terrans could wake up and take over everything again, so reelect your good federal government to protect you from the evil Terrans!

This liberal's interlocutor raises another issue in his response: "Toujours radical, eh, Étienne? Le fédéral vient pourtant de passer une loi protégeant les Terriens hors-ghetto" ("Still radical, eh, Étienne? But the Feds just passed a law to protect the Terrans outside the ghetto"; MF176). This utterance signals both the hypocrisy of the federal government who will protect precisely those it has demonized if it serves their interests, for this protection targets Terrans working outside the ghetto as "main d'œuvre quasi gratuite" (MF176)—almost free labor. These passages clearly reflect the ambiguous nature of Vonarburg's political critique. On the one hand, the Terrans could be read as Native Americans (or other colonial "natives"), settlers' fear of whom could be exploited by an imperialist government to extend its control, or more specifically as a critique of Federal Canadian strategies to keep the provincial powers at bay through a strategy of division and conquest that employs the diversion of a common enemy. On the other hand, this strategy could actually reflect one used by the nationalist Parti Québécois, if we read the Terrans as they are positioned in the text as, although not illegal still socially undesirable, immigrants. Remarks made by that group's head, Jacques Parizeau, attributed the failure of the 1995 Referendum on Québec's sovereignty to the "ethnic vote" (Bauch).

Vonarburg's indictment of racist stereotypes operates by placing the reader's own group alignment (a non-extra-sensory human from Earth) in the situation of the oppressed group, creating sympathy with the character Mathieu and then addressing the stand-bys of racism to him. When he is helped by the Merril[27] household, Mathieu wonders: "Vont-ils tous mettre un point d'honneur à ne pas se montrer racistes, dans cette maison?" ("Are they all going to make a point of honor in not appearing racist in this house?"; MF147). His experience as a *térien* on Virginia, at least in Orlemur, has made him completely suspicious of anything but flagrant hatred and aggression, as he wonders about the motives of his adjuvant's surprise that Mathieu, who at times lets his temper flare, refusing to be servile, has survived thus far:

> pas de menace, ni la note tyrannique du propriétaire. Non, une constatation un peu triste, un peu amusée, un peu étonnée. Un conseil donnée de bonne foi. Sans doute Merril lui-même croit-il en son personnage d'homme vertueux. Chacun doit être traité selon son mérite. Les têtes-de-pierre sont des êtres humains, après tout. Ce n'est pas leur faute s'ils puent [MF144].
>
> no threat, nor the tyrannical note of the owner. No, just a somewhat sad, amused, astonished assertion of fact. A piece of advice given in good faith. Undoubtedly Merril even believes his role of the virtuous man. Everyone should be treated according to his merit. Blockheads are human beings, after all. It's not their fault if they stink.

The exposé of racist society continues in a minor character's remarks about sexual relations between *tériens* and Virginians: "je me suis toujours demandé comment c'est possible de faire ça avec des Terriens. Il y en a vraiment qui doivent avoir des goûts ... bizarres, eh?" ("I always wondered how it's possible do *that* with Terrans. Some people really have ... weird tastes, eh?"; MF176).[28] Mathieu's choice of name, Nat Galas, obviously refers to the Ranao Galaas who helped him escape the Grays, but it also recalls Nat Turner, the leader of a slave rebellion in the reader's world.

In addition to her condemnation of race in the development of colonial systems of oppression, the SF trope of genetic mutation, which Vonarburg exploits in a large number of her works, problematizes the very category of "race" itself. A major branch of postcolonial theory resists and denies the creation of essentialist concepts as the bases for identity, as race has been established as an innate, genetic category, used to support arguments positing one group's superiority over another's deployed, particularly in the colonial context, in support of exploitation. *Tyranaël*'s staging of a genetic mutation which forcefully alters a group's perception of race underscores the socially constructed nature of this category (as opposed to its presumption as "natural" or innate as found in colonial discourse). Indeed, modern genetics has demonstrated the falsity of "race" as an essential category, that "there is a fairly widespread consensus in the sciences of biology and anthropology that the word 'race,' at least as it is used in most unscientific discussions, refers to nothing that science should recognize as real" (Appiah, "Race" 277). Conversely, DNA-analysis can been used to trace ancestry and kinship, allowing for a more scientific conception of ethnicity or, at minimum, family clan allegiance than ever before, as in the case of the Lemba. These "Black Jews of Southern Africa" underwent genetic analysis which demonstrated that they share a gene with the *cohanim*, a hereditary caste of Jewish priests believed to descend from the Biblical clan of Aaron, thus substantiating their traditional claims to such a relationship (Parfitt).

The realities of migration, colonization and immigration which bring different human groups into contact appear in Vonarburg's SFQ saga as the human "race" divides itself on Virginia, first between colonial lines of self-identification (as Terran or as Virginian), but later along the lines of the new mutations that develop after several generations on a new world. While debates over the colony's continued allegiance to Earth rage, some invoke the argument of classic SF from the Galactic Empire era of "the necessary unity of the human race across space and time." This amuses proponents of independence who reply: "What unity of the human race? We're *different!*" (GP253; original emphasis). The irony of this argument of a united human race to readers living in an early twenty-first century still marked by ongoing genocidal ethnic conflicts cannot be missed. While Vonarburg obviously seeks to valorize difference, have it be recognized, her critical discourse depicts the humans of the future continuing to use difference as grounds for oppression, with the Grays' efforts at times reaching, if not outright genocide, then certainly a program of eugenics in their desire to eliminate perceived undesirable elements of the mutation (MF251). Furthermore, the discourse of science fiction allows the writer to parlay the genetic mutation of humans into something actually different, perhaps no longer human, and set in contrast to the Ranao, a humanoid race whose behaviors appear so utterly more "humane."

Additional examples of racism and oppression based on ethnic/racial lines litter the remaining volumes of the series, which replay time and again the cycle of alienation/repression and resistance/liberation, mirroring the seemingly endless cycle of violence that makes up the human past. While on the one hand, *Tyranaël* seems to naturalize the cycle of conquest and colonization, as it also inscribes this cycle on the history of the Ranao. On the other, its depiction of those who wield the power to oppress as themselves alienated represents a postcolonial critique which extends over a range of themes, and, as we shall see in the following chapters of this study, refuses to simply reduplicate a colonialist fantasy of starting over again in an empty new world. It might be argued that Vonarburg's SFQ saga elides the brutalization of autochthonous peoples found in most colonization. Its erasure of the Ranao allows for a problematic indigenization of the Virginian settlers as they become the "natives" of the planet, subject to the planet's forces of mutation, a move which would simply reinscribe a colonial ideology. Yet, while it certainly explores the reality of white settler colonization, *Tyranaël* also thematizes elements of the racialist character of the imperial exploitation of so-called black nation colonies.

The narrative's repeated establishment of binary oppositions (between Earth and Virginia, Virginia and Tyranaël, Tyranaël and Atyrkelsaō, to mention only those written along planetary lines) seemingly only for the purpose of then undermining them, ultimately problematizes any allegorical reading of the text. As we have seen in both Rochon's and Brossard's unstable allegories, in *Tyranaël*, too, the reader becomes increasingly unable to identify clear-cut allegorical equations between fictional groups and their supposed representations of those in the "real" world. Poles of identification shift constantly, thus subverting or disrupting a classical, Western allegory, aligning the text more with the postcolonial. While most often, one may position the Virginians with the Québécois (or any other white settler group, for that matter), Vonarburg's division of the inter-stellar colonial society disrupts such a totalizing alignment. This disruption, however, actually renders the text more true-to-life than other political allegory which presents a totalizing image that must needs simplify and stereotype.[29] In her postcolonial discourse, Vonarburg nuances depictions of any one group, including a full range of opinion, belief and status within it. This appears, for example, in instances of anti-*halatnim* (Virginian) racism among the Ranao on Atyrkelsaō (AR138), who are otherwise depicted as typically tolerant of difference. Repeated representations of those resisting the totalitarian Grays as also ethically compromised, because of their recourse to manipulation and violence, further represents this blurring of clear-cut lines (MF195–96, 227, 251, 292–93; AR56–57, 377).

The shifting of poles of identification occurs in *L'Autre rivage* as it develops a history for "the Passers." While in *A Game of Perfection* the Virginians' struggle against Earth's oppression mirrors Québec's desire for independence from Canada, the Ranao's Great Passage recalls the Acadians' forced departure from their homes in *Grand Dérangement* (Great Disruption; 1755–62). The Ranao, former natives of Tyranaël having emigrated to their new home of Atyrkelsaō, now face the same problems the Virginian immigrants faced. This element also reconfigures the poles of any binary opposition made, as it allows the reconstitution of the original dualistic pairing of Ranao versus Terrans, this time not on Virginia, but on the new homeworld of Atyrkelsaō. However, the Terrans have lost all contact and memory of Earth; they have evolved to become Virginians. This split becomes increasingly complex, too, as the narrative describes how those who have passed over since Mathieu/Odatan's first arrival have either integrated into Ranao society or segregated themselves from it. While *halatnim* is the general name for those who have some Virginian blood, there exists a community of *Keldarao*, Virginians who resist all integration into Ranao society and wish to reproduce their world now on Atyrkelsaō. While all Passers must, by nature, have possessed the mutation that protects them from the Sea's ability to disintegrate biological matter, now called *naïstaos*, not all of their descendants share this trait. Furthermore, along that line, Vonarburg makes it clear that just as the Virginians have been formed out of a range of Earth races and ethnicities, so, too, the Ranao have developed both a culture and a physical being that represents a blend of four original ethnic/regional groups. Ultimately, then, Vonarburg's postcolonial discourse undoes any binary opposition it appears to establish, either by adding a third (or fourth) pole of opposition, or by fragmenting those poles, transforming an apparent unity into a multi-faceted group. As the novel progresses, the original Earth/Virginia colonial dichotomy also shifts to become a dichotomy between Tyranaël/Atyrkelsaō. While return to Earth is fully impossible, movement between Tyranaël, the original home to the Ranao, but also now to Virginians—who truly are no longer Terran because of the mutational effects the planet has had on them as a "race"—becomes a two-way pattern. This back-and-forth of migration and immigration reflects the reality of the contemporary world.

This chapter's analysis has referred to various elements of the oppressed,

Two. Alien Nations: Dominance and Oppression in the SFQ Saga 117

alienated, colonized individuals and groups of the SFQ saga resisting those forces of oppression and seeking liberation, at both the individual and collective fronts. Chapter three will now systematically examine how that resistance is staged and whether or not liberation occurs in the utopian new world societies depicted in the SFQ sagas of Rochon, Brossard and Vonarburg.

CHAPTER THREE

Utopia and New World Myth in Québec's Science-Fiction Sagas[1]

> *Nor is Utopia the final point, the terminus of human evolution. On the contrary. It is only the point of departure, the beginning, the first stage of the new history which men will embark upon together once they are liberated from their present condition as niggers, as sub-men.*
> — Pierre Vallières, *White Niggers of America* [60]

In *Scraps of the Untainted Sky* (2000), Tom Moylan asserts that no matter how distanced, utopia "nevertheless is an exercize in imaginative intervention in historical reality" (72). Certainly, the literary utopia's critical function, its ability to confront the problems of the day, appears central since its definitive inception with Thomas More's *Utopia* (1516). While the best known utopias derive from the Anglo-American canon, French-Canadian writers also turn to the cognitive estrangement afforded by utopia as a tool to express disillusionment with the present system and hope for greater levels of individual and/or collective autonomy. Indeed, *la science-fiction québécoise* (SFQ) developed over the 1970s as a self-conscious cultural movement (Sernine, "Historique" 42) precisely in tandem with Québec's very active campaigns for greater self-determination, campaigns often couched in the rhetoric of utopia. The SFQ sagas examined here took shape in their authors' minds during this period. The first volume of Esther Rochon's *Le Cycle de Vrénalik* (Vrenalik Cycle, 1974–2002), *En hommage aux araignées* appeared in 1974. Jacques Brossard conceived a complete outline for *L'Oiseau de feu* (1989–97) in 1975. As early as 1978, Élisabeth Vonarburg published short fiction, such as "High Tide" (1978) and "Thalassa" (1982), featuring the universe of *Tyranaël* (1996–97), and she dates composition of its first volume, *Les Rêves de la Mer* (*Dreams of the Sea*), as far back as 1965 (360). These works' subsequent revisions, additions, publication and, in some cases, republication coincide with SFQ's coming of age and the aftermath of a second failed referendum on Québec's sovereignty in 1995. That same year, Rochon began a second SFQ saga, the six volume *Les Chroniques infernales* (The Infernal Chronicles, 1995–2000), which she would ultimately link to the universe of Vrénalik. Vonarburg, as well, with her *Reine de Mémoire* (Queen of Memory, 2005–07) series produced another pentalogy to add to a growing list of multi-volume works from writers of SFQ, which also includes Francine Pelletier's *Le Sable et l'acier* (Sand and Steel, 1997–98) trilogy and Daniel Sernine's *La Suite du temps* (Time Suite, 1983, 2004–08).

In this chapter, we will examine how the SFQ sagas of Brossard, Rochon and Vonarburg exploit the tropes of utopia and its sister form dystopia. Reflective of contemporary trends in the literary utopia, variously described as the open-ended or critical utopia (Somay, Suvin "SF Novel," Moylan *Demand*) and the critical dystopia (Moylan and Baccolini), they reach toward the "postcolonial utopia," recently defined by Ralph Pordzik. Tending to site utopia in a new world these works risk reinscribing a colonialist ideology of exploration, conquest and settlement. And yet, they largely succeed in establishing what Marie Vautier calls a "New World Myth,"[2] an oppositional form that draws on the master narratives of the old world precisely in order to subvert them. In their engagement with the recuperation of originary myths, individual memory and collective history, the SFQ saga reflects the postcolonial practices of other Canadian novels read by Vautier and Sylvia Söderlind. Ultimately, they problematize the very form of utopia itself.

Once again, I turn to the work of Darko Suvin to provide a theoretical basis for the examination of science-fiction and fantasy literatures. His definition of the literary utopia draws upon the concept of cognitive estrangement (discussed in chapter two):

> The verbal construction of a particular quasi-human community where sociopolitical institutions, norms and individual relationships are organized according to a more perfect principle than in the author's community, this construction being based on estrangement arising out of an alternative historical hypothesis ["Defining" 132].

Stated more simply by A. L. Morton in *The English Utopia* (1952), "Utopia" is "an imaginary country described in a work of fiction with the object of criticising the existing society" (10). In its "verbal elaboration" of just such an "imaginary country" the literary utopia engages directly in a discourse of the exploration and colonization of new worlds; at its inception it explicitly referenced the particular New World of the Americas.[3] Let us recall that More's protagonist Raphael Hythloday discovered the kingdom of Utopos after being abandoned on the shores of South America by Amerigo Vespucci (More 12). In both the literary utopia and the real history of experimental utopian communities, the creation of a society "organized according to a more perfect principle" inevitably must occur through an act of colonial settlement. The first Puritan villages and later Quaker communities in New England represent the utopian hope for a better society as clearly as Étienne Cabet's New Icaria settlements in Texas and Nauvoo, which were based on his literary utopia, *Voyage en Icarie* (1840) (Richter 130).

Given the central role of the new world trope in utopia and in science fiction in general, the form appears inevitably linked to colonialist ideology. How can the utopian form and the new world trope function as an oppositional postcolonial literary discourse? According to Marie Vautier, a number of contemporary Canadian writers appropriate this trope, engaging in a "play with myth [which] constitutes a self-conscious effort to decolonize the mind and to undercut the influence of inherited, European-inspired myths" (32). Borrowing the term from Margery Fee, Vautier argues that the "New World Myths" found in works like François Barcelo's *La Tribu* (1981),[4] Rudy Wiebe's *Scorched-Wood People* (1977) and Joy Kogawa's *Obasan* (1981) modify the traditional function of myth, which is to "make unified sense of the world" (34). Fragmented and multiple in their narratives, these texts focus on the beginning itself (6), rewriting in order to appropriate the originary myth of colonial history as it has been handed down. Furthermore, their irreverent reevaluations of these received historical narratives of colonization represent "postcolonial questionings of the hegemony of eurocentric world views" (25). Of her corpus, Vautier argues that "[t]he six novels studied in detail here problematize issues traditionally accepted as givens — issues such as knowledge, history, certitude, truth or God" (35). As we shall see in the following analysis, these statements equally apply to the SFQ sagas of Jacques Brossard, Esther Rochon and Élisabeth Vonarburg.

Vautier's conception of the New World Myth clearly breaks with classical definitions of myth as a static form with a cyclical or eternal relationship to time. Indeed, her application of the term myth to the postmodern narratives she examines might be viewed as inaccurate. Rather, she argues that previous definitions of myth are overturned in the postcolonial context, that oppositional representations of an originary myth which revise official History upset the static and the eternal as they focus on change and relativity. In "The SF Novel as Epic Narration" (1988), Darko Suvin grapples with a similar apparent contradiction. Here and elsewhere Suvin defines utopia, often considered a static form akin to myth, as the "socio-political subgenre of science fiction" ("Science" 38). Utopia therefore shares with its parent genre the forward temporal momentum of epic, "the chronicling of a unique series of events" (77). Like Vautier for myth, Suvin argues for utopia that contemporary developments have altered the form's very nature and definition. Calling upon Bülent Somay's essay "Towards an Open-Ended Utopia" (1984) Suvin participates in a now generally accepted revisionist approach to literary theories of the utopia. Traditionally, "classic" utopias like those of More, Edward Bellamy (*Looking Back-*

ward; 1888),William Morris (*News from Nowhere*; 1890) and even B. F. Skinner (*Walden Two*; 1948) were read as static visions of insular, pre-formed, perfect (or at least better) societies. Inspired by the subtitle of Ursula K. Le Guin's *The Dispossessed: An Ambiguous Utopia* (1974) literary critics like Somay and Moylan identify a new approach to utopia in contemporary texts which, although they do not conform to the classic model, nonetheless present readers with a "utopian" vision. Their "verbal construction" of estranged, alternate "quasi-human" societies "with the object of criticising the existing society" (to draw from both Suvin's and Morton's definitions) present "ambiguous" or "critical" utopias which most often problematize the notion of a "more perfect" or "better" society central to the so-called "classic" definitions of utopia.

The renewed interest in the literary utopia mirrored a general "utopianism" found in social action movements and the counter-culture during the 1960s and 1970s. That the concept of utopia pertains both to literary and to socio-political thought appears clearly in Lyman Tower Sargent's seminal essay "The Three Faces of Utopianism" (1967; updated in 1994's "Three Faces of Utopianism Revisited"), which identifies those three faces as the literary utopia, utopian thought in philosophy and political philosophy, and the utopian experiments in communal living. This notion has congealed in the pages of the review *Utopian Studies* and in essays by political scientists and social philosophers like those found in the collection edited by Barbara Goodwin and Keith Taylor, *The Politics of Utopia* (1982). Although I aim primarily to deal with the SFQ saga as literary utopia, its critical discourse inevitably loops back to utopian political thought. According Susan Bruce, "the utopia [is] a reconstruction of its author's reality which displaces aspects of its own world onto the fictional world it represents, and in so doing foregrounds the social and economic contradictions lived by its writer and his contemporaries" (xv). Indeed, the works of Brossard and Rochon developed in a Québec fermenting with the utopian notions behind the Quiet Revolution and subsequent sovereignty movement. Vonarburg arrived in Québec in 1973, from a France recently upended by the events of May 1968, events analyzed through the lens of utopian thought by Alain Touraine and many others. In both Québec and France, Marxist thought was central to utopian hopes for social change.

As Ruth Levitas asserts, the relationship between utopia and Marxism has long been problematic (35). In spite of Marx and Engels' distancing of scientific socialism from the utopian socialisms of Fourier and others, certain Marxist philosophers, most particularly Karl Mannheim (*Ideology and Utopia: An Introduction to the Sociology of Knowledge*, 1929) and Ernst Bloch (*The Spirit of Utopia*, 1918; *The Principle of Hope*, 1954–1959) maintained that only a positively utopian attitude could effectuate the socialist revolution in society (Levitas 6, 96). Marxist philosophy also influenced both feminist and anti-colonial/postcolonial thought, as well as literary texts deriving from the feminist movement and other oppositional movements of personal and collective social liberation. Angelika Bammer (*Partial Visions: Feminism and Utopianism in the 1970s*, 1991) and Lucy Sargisson (*Contemporary Feminist Utopianism*, 1996) articulate the connections between feminist theory, literary production and the ambiguous, open-ended, critical utopia. Tobin Siebers and Fredric Jameson (*Archaeologies*) engage ongoing discussions about the possibility of a "postmodern" utopia. Finally, Ralph Pordzik in *The Quest for Postcolonial Utopia: A Comparative Introduction to the Utopian Novel in the New English Literatures* (2001), argues "[t]he active participation of postcolonial writers in the transformation of the utopian genre provokes the idea that for many of them the imaginative exploration of the future or their societies has a distinct meaning and value" (2).

In spite of the wealth of more recent articulations, the following analysis draws most explicitly upon Suvin's description of the "open-ended" or "critical" utopia prevalent since the 1970s:

> [U]topia as the idea of a radically more perfect life was understood as something to be achieved in a spiral and ongoing development rather than brought down once and for all from the heavens of dogma, as well as something to be accomplished by constant self-critical watchfulness against the temptation of the arrested moment ... [t]he best new utopian novels use an ongoing, complexly spatiotemporal voyage as analogue to the ongoing discoveries against a dynamically receding horizon.... Correspondingly, the ending will be open, but only ambiguously, not finally so. If in the dystopian works the closure can only be understood as non-openness, in the utopian works the revolutionary openness can only be understood as a permanent struggle against entropic closure ["SF Novel" 83–84].

This definition supports Suvin's identification of utopia as a subgenre of SF (a contention that remains open to discussion; Bouchard, *42,210* 151–62) with SF as a form of "epic narrative." The SFQ sagas take this generic function seriously; like the Icelandic sagas, they tell stories of "heroic achievement" and "marvellous adventure[s]" (*OED Online*), of individuals working within the framework of a collective. Brossard, Rochon and Vonarburg recount epic tales of the exploration of new worlds, encounters between civilizations, the establishment of (space) colonies and the vicissitudes of colonial history. Their multi-volume novels follow in the path of sophisticated models like Le Guin's *The Dispossessed*,[5] and yet they explore hopes for a better future and fears for the worse in a uniquely francophone manner, using Québec as a frame of reference. The SFQ saga reflects precisely Suvin's notion of a dynamic, epic utopia, in which development occurs in a spiral fashion and within which the persistent threat of the dystopian impulse to power and authority requires constant vigilance on the part of the utopians.

One more term in this theoretical introduction remains to be addressed, that of the "dystopian." Analogous to the utopia, the *ou-topos* (no place) commonly understood as the *eu-topos* (the good/happy place), dystopia refers to the bad place to live, its etymology being interpreted variously as deriving from the Greek prefix "*dys-*"bad or abnormal (as in dysfunctional) or from the name of the Greek hell, Dis. Just as eras of great social reform can be associated with revivals in utopian literary production (like those witnessed at the end of the nineteenth century and in the 1960s–70s), eras of great social concern can be associated with revivals of dystopian literature. In the period surrounding the two World Wars, and increasingly since the 1980s, a number of texts depict the utopian vision gone wrong. Yevgeny Zamiatin's *We* (1921), Aldous Huxley's *Brave New World* (1932), and George Orwell's *1984* (1949) typify the literary dystopia, which depicts a static, insular, society "worse" than that of the writer/reader. The reality of Nazi society in Germany illustrated clearly the idea that what represents a utopian paradise for some will very quickly become a dystopian hell for others.

Glenn Negley and J. Max Patrick first coined the term dystopia in their anthology *The Quest for Utopia* in 1952 (298; Negley *Utopian* xiii). Eugen Weber introduces a variant term a few years later in 1959 with "the anti–Utopian novel, which uses the familiar utopian convention to express a mood of dread and despair occasioned by the results or the implications of utopian dreams" (81). Moylan clarifies a persistent confusion of the two terms by adopting Weber's term — the anti-utopia — for those texts which clearly condemn utopia and utopianism, reserving the term dystopia for texts which, although they describe a worse society, do so with meliorative aims in mind, thus maintaining a utopian horizon of hope (*Scraps* 72, 155).[6] As with the utopia, more recent works, in particular the feminist dystopias of the late 1960s through the 1980s, problematize the notion of dystopia, as they at once depict bad places for women to live and promote feminist interventions expressing hope for positive change. Moylan and Raffaella Baccolini further nuance the discussion, then, with the concept of the critical dystopia, which allows:

> both readers and protagonists to hope by resisting closure; the ambiguous open endings of these novels maintain the utopian impulse *within* the work. In fact, by rejecting the traditional subjugation of the individual at the end of the novel, the critical dystopia opens a space of contestation and opposition for those collective "ex-centric" subjects whose class, gender, race, sexuality, and other positions are not empowered by hegemonic rule [6].

Just as they problematize utopian forms, the SFQ sagas examined here problematize the dystopia in a manner similar to the critical dystopia.

Now, a number of critics have already identified aspects of utopia/dystopia in the novels of the three writers examined here in various degrees of detail, commenting as well on their engagement of the issues of contemporary Québec and the history of French Canada. As in the previous chapter, I have organized the following analyses by author. After a brief review of previous links to utopia made for these several works, I will then engage in analyses of the three SFQ sagas already discussed, Brossard's *L'Oiseau de feu*, Rochon's *Le Cycle de Vrénalik* and Vonarburg's *Tyranaël*. In order to demonstrate how these writers contribute not only to evolving notions of utopian writing, but also to evolving notions of *québécitude* (Quebecness), I will also examine Rochon's *Les Chroniques infernales*, which takes the trope of hell and reverses it into a utopian construction. A very brief discussion of Vonarburg's latest cycle, the *Reine de Mémoire* pentalogy reveals how it, too, engages in the revision of the utopian New World Myth, offering perhaps a more pessimistic, post-nationalist view for the pluralistic society.

Paradise Lost on the Magic Island: Brossard's *L'Oiseau de feu. 3 — Les Années d'errance*

Although no extended academic analysis exists, I am not the first critic to comment on the ambiguous relationship between Jacques Brossard's SFQ saga and utopia. Several reviewers of *L'Oiseau de feu*'s various volumes mention its utopian elements; indeed, Patrick Imbert titles his combined review of *Les Années d'apprentissage* with Pierre Nepveu's *L'Écologie du réel* as "Utopias." He rightly asserts that Brossard's novel pushes the generic envelope as "une utopie ... débouchant sur une redéfinition progressive des paradigmes" ("a utopia opening onto a progressive redefinition of paradigms"; 225). Similarly, Claude Grégoire understands the meta-utopian commentary in Brossard's shifting text, calling *Le Grand projet* a "discours sur l'utopie" ("a discourse on utopia"; 20). This truly hybrid work reflects contemporary iterations of the form; like the postcolonial utopia, it blurs the boundaries between utopia and dystopia (Pordzik 4).

In a final afterword, Brossard remarks on the heterogeneous nature of *L'Oiseau de feu*: "le tome 3 diffère du tome 2 qui diffère du tome 1" ("volume 3 differs from volume 2 which differs from volume 1"; AE584). The differences between the three volumes (1, 2.A-2.B-2.C, 3) arguably reside in each book's relationship to the various forms of utopia. *Les Années d'apprentissage* (1989) stages a closed dystopia in the walled city of Manokhsor. As Claude Janelle asserts ("Brossard" 40), the depiction of the Centrale evolves over the course of *Le Recyclage d'Adakhan* (1990), *Le Grand projet* (1993), and *Le Sauve-qui-peut* (1995) from an apparently classic utopia into a critical utopia-dystopia. Finally, *Les Années d'errance* (1997) offers, at first view, a classic utopia set in an isolated new world. This utopian vision gradually blossoms, though, and ultimately shatters in its ambiguously open-ended conclusion. In this section, I examine more closely the relationship of *L'Oiseau de feu*'s various volumes to the diverse forms of utopia in order to determine whether or not its quest for a "postcolonial" utopia reflects a true New World Myth, as Vautier describes similar Canadian fictions, or if it simply reinscribes a colonialist vision in its protagonists' search for a habitable space. As the title of this section suggests, my analysis will focus most heavily on this last volume.

Chapter two of this study documents quite clearly the alienation not only of Adakhan Demuthsen and the walled society of Manokhsor in Brossard's work, but also of protagonists and societies depicted by Rochon and Vonarburg. This alienation represents the marker of dystopia. Levitas identifies "the transcendence of alienation" as the goal of Marxist utopian thought (7, 40, 91), a goal shared by the SFQ saga. I will not comment further on the dystopian aspects of *Les Années d'apprentissage* except to note that the walled city of Manokhsor represents a paradigmatic "simple dystopia," as Suvin labels the classic, "closed" dystopia ("Theses" 189). Isolated by a postapocalyptic desert (although its inhabitants are told that this is a jungle; RA486) this hierarchical society of surveillance and mass deprivation reflect the type of totalitarian society most often identified with the dystopia. The volume escapes, however, the despair of the anti-utopia, maintaining a horizon of hope not only through Adakhan's own determination to do right and to find truth and freedom, but also through the intervention of various adjuvants, both from within Manokhsor (various members of the secret society of the Diamant Noir) and from without (Selvah and Syrius in the Centrale). Their existence leads the reader to believe that change — or at the very least, escape — may be possible for Adakhan.

Our hero effectuates that escape in *Le Recyclage d'Adakhan* as he descends below the city to discover the ostensibly *eu*topian society of the undergound Centrale. As in the classic utopia, the protagonist receives a guided tour of "la Cité des dieux" ("the City of the gods"; RA 82), a realm isolated from the rest of the world for generations. The Centraliens have developed technologies which take care of their physical needs, including the elimination of illness (RA107) and increased longevity (RA112), and which allow for extended amounts of leisure. They have a rationalized, pseudo-democratic, theoretically egalitarian (RA197) governmental and economic system, and their social organization reflects a more communal model than that of the traditional patriarchal family. Utilitarian reason governs the Centrale's organization and daily life: "«tout a un sens et une raison d'être»" ("'everything has meaning and a reason for existence'"; RA143).

As the three books of volume two progress, the forces of dystopia — figured by the evil Lokhfer and his minions — gain an increasing hold upon the Centrale, so that its "organisation sclérosée" ("sclerotic organization"; RA 327) reveals itself as no less stagnant, oppressive and controlling than that of Manokhsor and its members no less alienated than the Périphériens. Lokhfer's nearly absolute power allows him to use captured Périphériens as slave labor and as subjects for various cruel and random pseudo-scientific "expériences illégales" ("illegal experiments"; GP31). He ultimately outlines a "final solution" for them, establishing a clear analogy with Hitler and his Third Reich (SQP71). Nonetheless, Syrius le Vieux maintains vigilance over his nemesis' activities and elaborates utopian plans for an alternative, should the situation in the Centrale become hopeless. The "principle of hope," as Ernst Bloch has called the utopian drive, provides the thrust for narrative development throughout the middle section of the saga.

Brossard's work plays, however, upon the original ambiguity of More's neologism which, as mentioned earlier, translates as either "no-place"[7] or as a "better place," often rendered for clarity's sake as eutopia. Just as in many a so-called classic utopia, the very elements that allow for a better life have become sclerotic, and a growing number of dystopian elements reveal themselves through the cracks in the Centrale's eutopian veneer. A number of critics, including Karl Popper (Sargisson, "Curious" 28), Ingrid Hantsch (Wiemer 180) and Ralf Dahrendorf (Sargent, "Three" 226), have perpetuated the notion of utopia's closed and static nature, at times linking this to a totalitarian impulse. The less severe simply assert that its frozen, perfected nature makes the utopia boring from both a narrative standpoint and from the perspective of characters living within such a society (Fitting 152–53). Utopia's proponents continue to assert the fallacy of this *a priori* assumption about utopian narratives. Suvin has long and repeatedly rejected the qualification that utopia necessarily implies perfection and the static ("State" 36; "Theses" 189, 193), more recently rejecting the position which denies utopia "*in toto* and *a limine* as static, dogmatic, and closed" as "the 'paradox of incoherent denial of utopia'" ("Locus" 126). As long ago as 1970, Robert Elliott cautioned against reading More's *Utopia* as a blueprint or literal assertion of his position (36). More recently theorists like Lucy Sargisson ("Curious"), Chris Ferns (2–3) and Philip Wegner (150) reaffirm utopia's fluidity and ambiguity.

While avoiding some of these narrative traps, it is precisely in volume two that Brossard's novel succumbs to others, particularly that of privileging exposition over action. Certainly, Brossard punctuates the entire cycle with action-filled sequences, like Adakhan's exciting sojourn within Lokhfer's laboratory, his discovery of the abominations carried out there, his struggle with his nemesis' "gorillas," and his liberation of a torture victim (SQP157–78). But in *Le Recyclage d'Adakhan* the hero undertakes the traditional "tour" of the ostensibly utopian Centrale, guided by a mentor, and in *Le Grand projet*, long discursive passages lay out Syrius' life-affirming philosophy of human development toward perfection (GP120). Nonetheless, both the text's narrative structure and Syrius' discourse contained within it clearly reflect aspects of contemporary open-ended or critical utopias as Suvin defines these. Syrius' philosophy directly invokes the metaphor of the spiral (GP173, 178): "d'un point à l'autre de la haute spirale ascendante ... *nous nous rapprochons un peu plus de ce que nous sommes*" ("from one point to another on the high ascending spiral ... *we arrive a bit closer to what we are*"; GP122; original emphasis). He appears utopian both in the current everyday sense of "impractically idealistic" (discouraged, he refers to himself as "un rêveur, un incorrigible utopiste!" ["a dreamer, an incorrigible utopian"; SQP259]), as well as in the more technical sense outlined by Ernst Bloch as hopeful for a better future (Moylan, "Bloch" 97). In order to transform his idealistic thought into revolutionary action, Syrius must, in a sense, *convert* Adakhan to his way of thinking. Through the extensive dialogue, which, as Luc Pomerleau notes, plays out almost in real time over the three books of volume two, Brossard seeks also to convert the reader ("Géométrie"). The process of conversion takes time, however, and Adakhan first rejects this new ideology of hope, scoffing in a passage revelatory of Brossard's self-reflexive style: "Je ne suis quand même pas dans un roman d'essef du Vieux!" ("Anyway, I'm not in one of the Old Man's essef [SF] novels!"; SQP106).

Eventually, as Lokhfer's hegemony solidifies, Syrius must abandon hope for improving life in the Centrale. His "Grand Projet," a two-pronged effort to explore and colonize the unknown other side of his own planet and to look beyond into space, marries utopian ideals with a potentially imperialistic ideology of new world settlement. Crucial to the success of his project is the idea of negotiating this marriage in such a way as to avoid the violence of conquest and the reinscription of dominance through power. As he conceives it, then, in the unexplored territory of "l'autre côté de la terre" ("the other side of earth"):

> il faudrait tenter de reconstruire là-bas, sur les terres préservées qu'on trouverait, une cité nouvelle qui ne fût pas divisée, celle-là entre des ghettos de surface pour Périphériens conditionnées et asservis et une Centrale souterraine et secrète pour «privilégiés» [GP30].
>
> we need to try to reconstruct there, on the preserved lands that we might find, a new city that is not divided into surface ghettos for conditioned and enslaved Périphériens and a secret, underground Central for the "privileged."

This rhetoric of the "new city" invokes utopian projects ranging from Campanella's *City of the Sun* (1623) to works as recent as Ernest Callenbach's *Ecotopia* (1975), as well as the discourse and projects for a sovereign francophone Québec employed by Brossard, Pierre Vallières (see epigraph), the editors of the counterculture journal *Mainmise*, sociologist Marcel Rioux (Duchastel 158) and others in the 1960s and 1970s. In this respect, Syrius' project reflects the classic utopia's desire to create (or to depict in literary form) an ideal state.

The association of the utopian space with a new world manifests itself through the SF trope of space colonization, and its centrality to Brossard's project appears clearly in its title, as the entire saga bears the name given to the second phase of Syrius' project: *L'Oiseau de feu* (the Firebird or Phoenix). Like the phoenix rising from the flames, the crew of a rocket captained by Adakhan abandons a collapsing Centrale to rebuild society on a new world. They express their utopian desire: "Jeter les bases d'une civilisation nouvelle.... Tout recommencer à neuf.... Magnifique aventure!" ("To throw out the basis for a new civilization.... To begin everything again.... A magnificent adventure!"; SQP107; GP32). They adopt Syrius' ideology of hope for this new world:

> Planète où la fraternité, la création et la liberté remplaceront la cupidité, la domination, la violence stérile et tous les dessèchements de l'âme. Planète fertile où l'affirmation et la vie remplaceront nos processus dégénérateurs ... [GP120].
>
> A planet where fraternity, creativity and liberty will replace greed, domination and sterile violence and everything that dries out the soul. A fertile planet where affirmation and life will replace our degenerative processes.

Yet, seeds of doubt about the feasability of this endeavor appear long before their departure: "Sommes-nous prêts à faire mieux qu'ici? Traîner là-bas tous nos conditionnements.... Ce n'était pas notre but quand nous avons élaboré le projet Phénix" ("Are we ready to do better than here? Dragging all of our conditioning there with us.... That wasn't our goal when we developed the Phoenix project"; GP33).

Indeed, large descriptive passages recounting this project pastiche a Golden Age, even an early Gernsback-style SF narrative of space exploration and colonization, and they appear to reinscribe the very imperialist discourse that SF has been criticized for reproducing (Csicsery-Ronay, Kerslake).[8] Early on, precisely these "space cowboy" elements of Syrius' project fascinate Adakhan:

> la découverte et l'exploration de Terra 2: oui. Les affrontements possibles avec les occupants de cette planète, s'il y en avait, et la domination éventuelle.... C'est-à-dire, plutôt, la collaboration avec eux, le développement de la planète sur de nouvelles bases ... [GP110].
>
> the discovery and exploration of Terra 2: yes. The possible confrontations with the occupants of this planet, if there are some, and the eventual domination.... That is to say, rather, the collaboration with them, the development of the planet on new foundations.

His reflections reveal the *Bildungsroman* elements of the saga, Adakhan's gradual enlightenment results in his shift in discourse from that of conquest to that of collaboration. Such collaboration rides upon, however, the perhaps naïve presumption that any native occupants would be willing to work collaboratively with newcomers.

And yet, Syrius' Great Project remains inevitably colored by a discourse reflective of the pioneer experiences of those who colonized New France and the rest of the Americas. These "pionniers d'Ashmev" (SQP213), as they call their future home, must prepare for the conditions of another planet, assisted in part by the Centrale's advanced medical technology. Their support team develops "un chronobiotique" ("a chronobiotics") to buffer the transition of their biorhythms from those of the Centrale to those adapted to Ashmev's day-night cycles (SQP210). Ultimately, "[i]l faudrait compter sur l'adaptation — et sur l'évolution" ("it will be necessary to count on adaptation — and on evolution"; SQP211). The effect of creolization (discussed in chapter four), that humans will adapt to a new world and be changed by it, represents a theme common to both colonial/postcolonial and science-fiction literatures. "Qui sait ce que nous serons là-bas — ou *qui* nous serons?" ("Who knows what we will be there — or *who* we will be?"; SQP360) they ask as departure becomes imminent.

Les Années d'errance concludes the series with ambivalence toward the possibility of the utopian project, a seeming expression of the author's own ambivalence toward colonialism and colonization. Leaving behind the dystopian world of the Centrale, the surviving crew of the Phoenix project arrives on the planet Ashmev to discover a full-blown island utopia, the paradisiacal *Zauberinsel*. Although they have lost most of their technology in the crash landing, resources offer themselves up to the survivors as fish jump from the water to their feet (AE142-43). On this literal Magic Island even communication becomes instantaneous and unmediated; endowed with telepathic abilities they no longer need the spoken word (AE127). In their landmark study of *Utopian Thought in the Western World* (1979) Frank and Fritzie Manuel locate its origins in the biblical Garden of Eden (33). In *New World Myth: Postmodernism and Postcolonialism in Canadian Fiction* (1998), Marie Vautier examines six novels which appropriate originary myths in order to remold and recast them in a critical manner meant "to undercut the influence of inherited, European-inspired myths" (32). In particular, the Québécois and Anglo-Canadian novels she examines reveal "a foregrounded awareness — and wariness — of biblical myths" (45). Brossard circles his tale of future space exploration back to this original utopia as the bulk of its final volume reworks the Biblical Genesis. With Adakhan cast in the role of Adam, his wife Selvah as Eve and their last surviving colleague Laïtha as Lilith, their children Sed, Abhül and Khan also represent humanity's first three offspring, Abel, Cain and Seth.

As in the original Eden, the unbridled desire for knowledge leads to its prohibition via human exile; in Brossard's revisionist saga, however, this departure is willed and not an explusion. Through Adakhan's persistent desire to know and to act, Brossard acknowledges the impossibility of happiness in a static utopia. Indeed, Adakhan's need for struggle appears almost as a primal human trait, or at least a primal male trait, as the women wish to stay on the island. The volume's title, *Les Années d'errance* (The Wandering Years), reflects the device of the ongoing voyage of discovery which Suvin associates with the contemporary, open-ended utopia. The years of wandering on Ashmev by Adakhan and his descendants also recall the mythicized French-Canadian figures of the *voyageur* (traveler) and the *défricheur* (pioneer, lit. clearer of the land). From novels like Frenchman Louis Hémon's classic novel of French Canada, *Maria Chapdelaine* (1916), to later, more ambiguous works like Germaine Guevremont's *Le Survenant* (*The Outlander*, 1945), the French-Canadian pioneer appears as a restless wanderer, rather than a settler. Following in the footsteps of his precursors, the travelling trappers and traders, the French-Canadian agriculturalist does not remain content to stay in one spot, as Christian Morissonneau asserts (21). Although its conclusion appears to reinforce settling, Hémon's novel establishes a tension between the sedentary and the nomadic (but also between urban/American and rural/French Canadian) life through its eponymous heroine's hesitation between two suitors. Furthermore, her father — who should represent the traditional settler — spends his life on the move, clearing one plot of land, rendering it cultivable, and then going further north to repeat the process, subsequently condemning his family to a life of poverty. Adakhan repeats this pattern and forces the serial pioneer's life upon his own offspring after leaving the *Zauberinsel*.

Just as for the first Europeans to arrive in the New World of the Americas, basic survival must precede any development of "civilization." Unlike on the Magic Island where all was provided, the colonists must adapt to new conditions on the continent in order to survive and physical adjustment to the environment becomes a major theme. Brossard's detailed accounts describe the daily struggles to find and use the resources of their new home to provide food, water and shelter. Several passages discuss their biological adaptation to the gravity and other aspects of their "nouvel habitat" ("new habitat"; AE140, 238, 245), including Earth's time cycles, for it appears that they are indeed on the reader's Earth. To enable such temporal adjustment, they must gradually accelerate the ageing process. The Centraliens, by lowering the body temperature and using a drug called aghératol, had slowed the human metabolism to a rate that allowed a life-span of even a thousand years-C. Gradually, this readjustment occurs: "le temps-T nous emporte avec lui, les années se précipitent. Elles n'ont déjà plus, pour nous, que la durée des *jours* d'autrefois.... Ce pays est devenu le nôtre" ("T-time carries us with it, the years roll along. They no longer seem to last only the length of *days* as they did before.... This land has become ours"; AE363; original emphasis). This detail fits into Brossard's biblical allegory as it "explains" the long pre-flood lifespans in Genesis (5:22–23). The greater length of the Centralien and Périphérien years than the Terran year, however, remains one of the deliberate contradictions in Brossard's text. This difference appears to foreclose on the supposition that the Centrale and Manokhsor themselves existed on a future, postapocalyptic earth sometime after the cataclysm of 2793.

In its staging of human society reduced to primitive conditions, Brossard's work follows patterns identified by Vautier in other Canadian novels like Gérard Bessette's *Les Anthropoïdes* (1977). Liberally classified as SFQ by Jean-Marc Gouanvic ("A Past" 73), that experimental novel speculates on the psychology of early hominid society. Vautier asserts that in such works "the notion of primitive myth is sometimes used to uncover and then to abuse inherited misconceptions" (53). Not only does he question the doctrine of original sin in his reappropriation of the myth of Eden and human ejection from paradise, Brossard disabuses his reader of essentialist notions of identity in his exploration of the truism that place shapes individuals. In postcolonial literatures, both white settlers recounting their arrival in the colony or, in reverse, immigrants moving to the metropole from colonized lands explore how their new home transforms them (Ashcroft et al., *Empire* 8). That their difference becomes more pronounced with subsequent generations reflects yet another trope of postcolonial literature: the difference between first generation immigrants and their children and grand-children who appropriate the new land as their own. Pregnant with the first child, Selvah wonders what will be "Son rythme naturel?... Celui d'Ashmev ou celui de la Terre?" ("Its natural rhythm? That of Ashmev or that of Earth?"; AE172). Ultimately, the colonists must take the mental step of changing their notion of home itself. Already on the space ship, Adakhan's log reflects this shift: "Sur Terra 1, quand nous disions «là-bas», c'était Ashmev; maintenant, c'est notre «ancienne» Terre" ("On Terra 1, when we said 'there,' it was Ashmev; now, it is our 'former' Earth"; AE35) To further this process, Selvah suggests that instead of referring to their new homeworld as Terra 2 or Ashmev, they now call it Earth, "[l]a vraie Terre...." ("the real Earth...."; AE134). This move, in addition to causing potential confusion for the forgetful reader (for from this point on in the text, the characters conversely refer to the world of the Centrale/Manokhsor as Ashmev), obviously plays into Brossard's myth-making process which casts humanity's ancestors as our own "extra-terrestrial" descendants returned from beyond the future Catastrophe of 2793.

The only child born on the magic island, Abhül has seen the ruins of the rocket, and ever remains halfway between his parents and his other siblings. His values reflect the old-world idealism of Syrius. It is Laïtha's first child who will be "la première vraie Terrienne" ("the first true Terran"; AE211), the first to claim "native" status. Born after their difficult crossing to the continent, they name her Sed — thirst in "l'ancien patois" (AE275) that we know as Spanish — another clue suggesting Earth as their ancestors' home. A generation gap appears, as Adakhan describes his progeny as "des enfants dont je ne connais presque rien" (AE413). An even greater difference appears between the idealistic parents and their firstborn Abhül, and their second, violent son Khan, who eventually fulfills his role as the biblical Cain.

The colonists desire to fully embrace their new home and to transmit Syrius' values to their children demonstrates that Adakhan and Selvah wish to build a new utopian society. The new Adam's reflections summarize their utopian colonial project:

> Il ne suffit cependant pas de semer, planter, cueillir ou récolter: encore faut-il que la moisson et le fruit soient bons. Il ne suffira pas de «peupler ce continent»: encore faut-il former nos héritiers, à commencer par Khan. Ils doivent non seulement s'adapter à cette Terre, à ce continent—ils le font mieux que nous—ils devront transmettre à *leurs* descendants la vision d'un monde à venir qui devra guider leur action vers l'amour et l'être ... [AE383].

> It is not enough to sow, plant, gather or harvest: the harvest and the fruit must still be good. It will not be enough to "populate the continent" [another element of the biblical allegory]: we must still educate our inheritors, starting with Khan. They must not only adapt to this Earth, to this continent — they do it better than we do — they must transmit to *their* descendants the vision of a world to come that should guide their action toward love and life.

The utopian ideology of Syrius, although passed on as one visionary perspective through Abhül, who plays the role of shaman, and Sed, the female pole which modulates violence, appears ultimately to be defeated as Khan's jealousy and ignorance inevitably drive him toward the expected fratricide. Ultimately, Brossard's biblical allegory sets up the new humans for their fall, condemning them to failure in their attempt for true, utopian change. For in the end they simply repeat the same patterns of behavior that they knew on the old Terra here on the new one reflecting the behavior of their "real" European models in the Americas.

The above passage reflects Adakhan's desire to transcend the tradition he has inherited. Brossard calques the specificity of Québec's colonial history and its postcolonial situation onto that of Genesis. In addition to the trope of the *défricheur*, his appropriation of past originary myths includes that of the French-Canadian strategy for continental hegemony through *la revanche des berceaux* (the revenge of the cradle). The ideology of reproduction to spread French Catholicism across North America, notably manifest in Jean Berthos' proto-science fiction novel *Eutopia* (1946), applies specifically God's command to Adam: "Be fruitful, and multiply" (Genesis 1:28 KJV). Brossard thus rewrites the myth of paradise lost by allegorizing the story of Genesis, blaming not woman's sin but man's curiosity, and suggesting that the seeds of humanity's future appear doomed to repeat the same mistakes. Khan embodies the perpetuation of the human drive for power through violence, and his existence presents a continual challenge to the establishment of a truly different world such as that dreamed by Syrius.

The novel's highly ambiguous, open-ended conclusion leaves hanging in the balance the question as to whether or not Syrius' vision has enabled the creation of a truly postcolonial utopia. That the *Oiseau de feu* project (both the novel and the colonization it stages) simply reinscribes colonial fantasy remains a possibility. The text and the characters that inhabit it, however, continually struggle to negotiate at least a kinder, gentler colonization, as we see in the central question of Ashmev's status as inhabited or uninhabited. Adakhan's team seems to feel that if Ashmev is uninhabited, then a politically just colonization can occur freed from the violent conflict that they know occurred in the "AC" (Avant Centrale/Avant Catastrophe) period, on ostensibly, though not certainly—Brossard privileges the ambiguity—the reader's Earth.

From early in their training period in *Le Grand projet* through their reproduction of several generations on their new world, Adakhan and Selvah speculate as to the presence of inhabitants on it. The team's early hopes for a virgin planet acknowledges the problematic nature of colonizing a space already populated. Even in initial discussions of the Verso project of sending a team to the other side of their own world, Terra 1, Adakhan asks Syrius: "Vous savez donc ce qu'il y a de l'autre côté de la Terre? Vous êtes sûrs que cette partie-là de la planète est habitable? Habitable ... et *inhabitée*?" ("You know, then, what there is on the other side of Earth? You're sure that part of the planet is habitable? Habitable ... and *uninhabited*?"; GP32; original emphasis). Syrius replies with uncertainty, speculating that either "les survivants de là-bas, s'il en fut, soient tous retournés à l'état sauvage, ou qu'ils aient tous disparus au cours des siècles" ("the survivors over there, if there were any, would all have returned to a savage state, or they would have all died over the course of the centuries"; GP32). His comment, of course, uncannily prefigures what happens to Adakhan and his landing party in the final volume—they themselves will return to a "savage" state and need to rebuild all over again. As they explore their new home, Adakhan and Selvah express ambivalence toward the possibility of meeting other humans: "[d]urant toutes ces années, d'errance en arrêt, ils n'avaient encore trouvé ... le moindre signe de vie humaine — ou apparentée. En souhaitaient-ils vraiment?... Ils ne savaient pas. Parfois oui, parfois non" ("during all these years of wandering and stopping, they had still not found the slightest sign of human, or humanoid, life. Did they really want to? They did not know. Sometimes yes, sometimes no"; AE305). The ostensible removal of the *indigène* allows the colonists to usurp this position, as seen in Selvah's comment that: «La Terre est-elle vraiment inhabitée?...— Ici, en tout cas, c'est *nous* qui l'habitons" ("Is Earth really inhabited?... Here, in any case, *we* inhabit it"; AE136; original emphasis). Both Kim Stanley Robinson's *Mars* trilogy and Elisabeth Vonarburg's *Tyranaël* pentalogy (discussed here later) demonstrate, however, that violence occurs even when one colonizes an apparently empty world. By allowing his colonists to become the natives, Brossard effectively erases any real indigenous presence. His erasure cannot, however, be complete. Even if they are not there, the natives of the new world effectively haunt Adakhan and his descendants — Khan, in particular — through their ability to obsess the colonists.

Repeatedly, often at times of internal tension, the colonists feel the presence of long-armed shadows watching them; they even develop a name for them, "les ombres-qui-se-glissent-dans-la-forêt" ("the shadows-that-slip-through-the-forest"; AE533). These ghostly figures could be read as primate species native to Africa or even as early hominids, the australopithecines. At one point, though, Adakhan discovers a clearly humanoid skeleton, but bizarrely, immediately represses the memory (AE409-10). Clearly, this repression is telling. The fantasy of the "clean" colonization appears untenable, a screen to hide the real violence enacted during any colonization. In *L'Oiseau de feu*'s colonial fantasy, the natives are the repressed element that returns. When two grandchildren are exiled because of their involvement in a violent crime, one fails to come home, his disappearance attributed to "«[l]a vengeance des ombres»" ("the revenge of the shadows"; AE533). After exploration of and migration through a large part of one continent (presumably Africa) and even after Adakhan's death, Khan still wonders in the last pages of the narrative: "cette Terre, après tout, serait-elle habitée par d'autres humains?" ("is this Earth, after all, inhabited by other humans?"; AE536). This erasure of the Other allows Brossard's characters to avoid replaying the colonial drama of dominance and exploitation of indigenous peoples like that which occurred in the history of the Americas.

This possible appropriation of indigenous status operated by the representation of Adakhan's descendants as the "real" Terrans reflects a problematic step in Québec's nationalist discourse and its desire to achieve full territorialization. As targets of discrimination and oppression, including sporadic policies of assimilation at the hands of the British/Anglo-Canada after the Conquest (1759–60) and the Treaty of Paris (1763) the argument can be made that French Canadians represented a colonized people. A highly questionable corollary, however, asserts that because they were on site prior to the British, and suffered the same imperial domination as other colonized peoples, they also hold a position analogous to that of an indigenous people. One can only make an ambivalent reading of the fantasy in play here — with ambivalence being a trait of postcolonial discourse, then I will use this element to shore up my argument.

Brossard's ambivalence appears nowhere more clearly than in his exit strategy for *L'Oiseau de feu*. The saga's conclusion could not be more open-ended or ambiguous, as the forces of utopia and dystopia come head-to-head, face-to-face in a series of conflicts played out in the final scenes of the novel's narrative, as well as in several paratextual "documents," which follow. Throughout this *Bildungsroman*, Adakhan's personal development has provided the central narrative motor. As he finally ages after years of wandering on the new world of Ashmev, a world increasingly coded as the reader's own Earth, he undertakes a last exploratory trip, during which he experiences a moment of epiphany just before dying (AE520-25). In spite of all his growth and development, Adakhan's utopian desires remain unrealized, defeated by "the most profound anti-utopia," death (Levitas 99). Meanwhile, somewhere across the continent, his sons play out the original human drama of Abel and Cain.

The novel proper concludes in a cliff-hanger with Khan's murderous stone hovering above Abhül's back. This open ending, while it seemingly condemns humanity to the eternal repetition of the act — now re-coded as the real original sin as this New World Myth succeeds in redeeming Eve —, leaves room for hope. And yet, an immediate series of paratexts both extends and undermines this hope. First, an "Annexe," presents the pseudo-transcription of a conversation between two "Programmeurs," identified as none other than Lokhfer ("LC4-FR5") and Syrius ("VH-JH"). Representing Lucifer and Yahweh they argue as to how this particular variant will end. Lokhfer, confident in the triumph of power through violence, asserts that: "De commencements en recommencements, de retours en spirales et en répétitions, de programmations en programmations, vous croyez vraiment finir par réussir?" ("From beginnings to beginning again, from spiral returns to repetitions, from programming to programming, do you really think you will end up succeeding?"; AE543). Their conversation implies an eternal return, a humanity doomed to an endless cycle of repeating the same actions with subtle variants, like figures programmed into a computer-generated simulation — a situation specifically staged during the training period for the *Oiseau de feu* mission. An "Epilogue" further reinforces this ambiguity, as it repeats in detail the opening sequences of the saga's first volume, *Les Années d'apprentissage*, substituting a little girl for the boy Adakhan and a "Desert" for the "Jungle" surrounding Manokhsor.

While in some ways this refusal of closure — which aligns precisely with the type of open-ended utopia that I am arguing the SFQ saga presents — constitutes a surprise ending, Brossard has patiently established reader expectations for the biblical allegory and even for the novel's final pages in previous volumes. In *Le Sauve-qui-peut* the team speculates on the means of propulsion for the craft they will soon board, including an option that later appears to be the most likely to the reader. Adakhan asks Syrius if his plan might not be to return to the past, to travel back in time, to "une Terre rajeunie: celle d'avant l'histoire?" ("a rejuvenated Earth, before history?"; SQP285). Syrius offers only an evasive reply: "Je crains ... que notre Oiseau de Feu ne vous conduise *ailleurs* que sur Ashmev. Nulle part ou ailleurs...." ("I fear that our Firebird will conduct you *elsewhere* than to Ashmev. Nowhere or elsewhere"; SQP285; original emphasis). Brossard's work plays with the tropes not only of utopia, the no-where that is elsewhere (Moylan, *Scraps* 5), but also with *uchronie*, the "alternative historical hypothesis" Suvin associates with utopia

("Defining" 132). In the end, his revision of the originary myth of Genesis proposes a grand alternate history for the origins of the human race on Earth, as we become the descendants of Adakhan, Selvah and Laïtha.

The circular nature of time in this text appears in the circular structure of the novel itself, which uncannily reflects the contention of Ernst Bloch that "*True genesis is not at the beginning but at the end*" (qtd. in Levitas 92; original emphasis). In Brossard's saga, a prediction made by a prophet during the decline of Manokhsor affirms that: "— *Le début dépend de la fin et la fin du début. Le début n'a de sens qu'à la fin, la fin n'a de sens qu'au début, mais il n'y a ni début ni fin*" ("*The beginning depends on the ending and the end on the beginning. The beginning has no meaning until the end, the end has no meaning but at the beginning, but there is no beginning or ending*"; SQP305; original emphasis). In order fully to understand the novel's beginning you need to read the paratext at the end of volume three and to understand the notes at the beginning of the first volume you must have read the work's concluding paratexts. In this fashion, *L'Oiseau de feu* reflects the contradictions that Darko Suvin sought to resolve when he proposed a specific relationship between SF as epic narration and utopia — a form usually related to myth — as a subgenre of SF ("SF Novel"). The question of closure is also conscientiously addressed. *L'Oiseau de feu* clearly represents a saga, an epic form as it presents the unusual and heroic deeds of Adakhan. It reflects the linear progression of the *Bildungsroman* in the trajectory of his personal development. And yet, it clings to the cyclical, eternal structure of myth in its presentation of these events as one version in an endless series of permutations. *L'Oiseau de feu* presents us with a paradigmatic text for Suvin's open-ended utopia as presenting "utopia as the idea of a radically more perfect life ... as something to be achieved in a spiral and ongoing development" ("SF Novel" 5). This figure of the spiral recurs incessantly across the five volumes, adorning architecture, in seashells found on the shore of the Magic Island, in philosophical discussions.

In *Utopics: Spatial Play* (1973, trans. 1984) Louis Marin coins the term "mythic narrative" to discuss how utopia engages the forms of both myth and narrative. While Marin focuses on More's *Utopia*, his discussion applies equally well to Brossard's SFQ saga:

> In their reciting and telling a world of oppositions, alienations, contradictions, and want symbolized by narrative is revealed.... It is precisely because mythic narrative symbolizes and, in this very symbolization, unfolds as a story that it can reformulate a society's story — as history — and origin in order to transform it through its telling [36].

Brossard's revisionist account of human origins through the biblical allegory of *Les Années d'errance* is precisely the type of appropriation and reformulation typical of Vautier's New World Myth novel.

Without a doubt, Jacques Brossard's *L'Oiseau de feu* reflects the characteristics of an open-ended utopia, a critical dystopia, and ultimately challenges the utopian form itself in its fluidity. Does it, though, represent what can rightly be termed a *postcolonial* utopia? Does it express an oppositional, postcolonial discourse or does it simply reinscribe a colonialist fantasy? My conclusion, like the text itself, remains ambivalent. On the one hand, even in his resemblance to the father in the archetypical French-Canadian novel, *Maria Chapdelaine,* Adakhan seems to be living out the new world pioneer fantasy of the *défricheur:* as soon as he has cleared a parcel of land and set up a comfortable camp for his family, something compels him to move on yet again. He never abandons his curiosity, his drive for power, or his desire for the freedom that he believes lies in the physical ability to move constantly. Yet, Brossard's concern that this colonial fantasy plays out without the indigenous victims that the real one did seems to exonerate it somehow; the author is clearly *striving for* a discourse that escapes the shackles of history. Unlike the classic utopia, *L'Oiseau de feu* describes a world of "fragmentation, discontinuity, and ambiguity," in which the protagonist and the reader must constantly adapt to new perspectives (3); it shares with Pordzik's postcolonial utopia the traits of open-endedness (16), resistance to SF classifications (31), and language play (36). This latter element which I have qualified as postmodern elsewhere ("Critical") appears in Brossard's extrapolated language of the Centrale. He lists titles of "vieux livres de essef" found in Syrius' library, disguising Asimov as "Asmoth" and Jules Verne as "Sol-Vherne" (RA305-06); elsewhere, Centraliens use English expressions modified according to a phonetic French spelling, for example: "Roger over" appears as "Rajeure. Oveure" (GP247) or "Need to know" as "Nitouno" (RA125). Although not as fully oppositional as a number of works examined by Pordzik, *L'Oiseau de feu* certainly works toward a coming to terms with a colonial past (20) and elaborates the possibility of a new discourse to frame human reality in terms of love, rather than power.

Elsewhere, I have argued the postmodern nature of *L'Oiseau de feu* citing in support the ludic use of the epigraphical citation, a strategy which also opens up the utopian text as it literally exceeds its own boundaries, pointing out to other fictional worlds as well as to the "real" world of the reader ("Critical"). Among the approximately one hundred writers cited in exergues found at the beginning of each major textual division of the work's five volumes appears the name of Esther Rochon. The extent to which Brossard read the work of other writers of SFQ remains unclear, and he cites fewer than a dozen writers from Québec.[9] Of Rochon, however, he asserts in an interview with *Solaris* that her novel *Coquillage* falls definitely into the category of "littérature" (Sernine and Pomerleau 20). Citing Brossard's epigraphical reference to Rochon's work serves as an apt transition into her utopian works: "Certains investissent tant dans la quête qu'ils se laissent prendre par toutes sortes de fausses pistes" ("Some invest so much in the quest that they allow themselves to be taken in by all kinds of false leads"; SQPvii)?[10]

Utopia in the Red City: Rochon's *Le Cycle de Vrénalik*

Like Brossard's *L'Oiseau de feu*, Esther Rochon's *Le Cycle de Vrénalik* follows a "puissant appel utopique" ("powerful utopian calling") (Lebrun, "Planète" 126). Claire Le Brun classifies its original first volumes, *En hommage aux araignées* (In Praise of Spiders; 1974) and *L'Épuisement du soleil* (The Exhaustion of the Sun; 1985), as "utopies modernes" ("Planète" 126). While her literary biographer Annika Hannan argues that the cycle's final, unrevised novel represents "the best of the series and possibly Rochon's best work" (232), the utopian aspects of *L'Espace du diamant* (The Space of the Diamond; 1990) received mixed reviews within the SFQ community (Ménard 27; Pettigrew 168). Sharon Taylor's incisive dissertation situates this novel within a tradition of open-ended feminist utopia from Québec, including studies of Élisabeth Vonarburg's two earlier novels, *The Silent City* (1981) and *In the Mother's Land* (1992), as well as Louky Bersianik's *The Eugelion* (1976) and *Le Pique-nique sur l'Acropole* (1979). Milena Santoro sees Rochon's staging of the Asven's opening up to the Other as an essential step in their development, linking this to Québec's nationalist debates, concluding that "la synthèse que Rochon propose dans sa trilogie est évidemment utopique" ("the synthesis Rochon proposes in her trilogy is obviously utopian"; 102).

Composed, revised and edited over nearly forty years (c. 1963–2002), Rochon's *Le Cycle de Vrénalik* reflects a publishing history almost as complex as its plot structure; it also reflects an imbededness in the literature and culture of Québec developing throughout that period. Belonging to the generation after that of Brossard, Rochon read periodicals with a nationalist bent during the gestational period of her saga. These included the counter-cultural, feminist and Marxist journals of the early 1970s, including *Mainmise* (Beaulieu 13), whose first issue serves as a manifesto for a utopian vision for Québécois society (rpt. in Hamel 151). The influence of these utopian tendencies, coupled with Rochon's adoption of Buddhist philosophy and practice appears clearly in *L'Espace du diamant*. Chapter two's discussion of alienation in the declining Asven civilization and in the urban societies of the Pays d'Irquiz and Ister-Inga adequately demonstrates the dystopian bent of the first volumes of Rochon's SFQ saga. Therefore, I turn directly to the cycle's final novel which offers a utopian horizon for the Asven nation to address the question of whether or not it constitutes a "postcolonial utopia."

In *L'Espace du diamant* Rochon depicts two clearly utopian societies: the altruistic land of Catadial and the Asven's Red City to be constructed in a new world territory ceded to them by Catadial. These collectivities' philosophy derives from Buddhist tenets, and Rochon's later work *Les Chroniques infernales* links both explicitly to the Tibetan utopia of Shambhala. Hannan describes Shambhala as "a secular spiritual path that is utopian in vision and socially (as opposed to personally) oriented" that shares with science fiction "a mutual interest in communicating values" (233). Rochon qualifies the book as an exercize in the presentation of Shambhalan Buddhism's social ideas "sous forme utopique" ("in utopian form"; Taylor 232, n. 79). This Eastern philosophical basis contributes to a postcolonial reading of *L'Espace du diamant* in that it proposes to balance a Western Enlightenment materialist rationalism with the recognition of the numinous and to approach binaries as complementary rather than in hierarchical opposition. Although it occasionally lapses into the traps of the classic utopia as action flags in descriptions of these utopian societies, the novel maintains narrative tension through their recognition of continued imperfection and their desire for further improvement, traits of the contemporary open-ended utopia as defined by Suvin ("SF Novel" 83–84).

L'Espace du diamant recounts how the Asven, liberated from the curse of the Ocean-god Haztlén and now fueled by an ideology of rebirth (see page 66 above), construct a new utopian homeland in which they can flourish. Strénid, the Asven's hereditary administrative leader, is the first to leave the Archipelago successfully after the curse has been lifted. He arrives on the mainland in order to bring his nation of some six hundred inhabitants back to life by restoring ties with its tutelary power Ister-Inga. On the island, he had created an Administrative Council, which includes a representative from the growing population of immigrants from Hanrel, the land to the north. Chance brings Strénid into contact with the utopian land of Catadial, hidden in the southwestern portion of the southern continent. In addition to Vrénalik's long-forgotten relationship with Ister-Inga (as the homeland of its founders), the Cathades reveal another relationship: they share a number of cultural elements, including a common language and a foundress, Suzanne Arkándanatt. The altruistic society of Catadial has held in trust the Asven's share of the ancestral queen's treasure and now offers to assist them in establishing a new homeland, a city on their southern coast in exchange for the services of their liberator Taïm Sutherland. *L'Espace du diamant* is as much about the Asven's opening up to the outside world as it is that of the isolated Catadial, which seeks Sutherland's assistance to realize fully its mission of altruism, by bringing its values of service, economic justice and full enjoyment of life to the alienated lands of Irquiz and Ister-Inga.

Although at least one critic has dismissed its "aspect gnan-gnan de l'utopie" ("inane utopian aspect"; Ménard 27), Rochon's description of Catadial resists the ho-hum character of the classic utopia through several strategies. In particular, the signal fact that the Cathades seek to develop beyond their current stasis aligns it with the open-ended rather than the classic utopia. For, although it appears as a model society far better than any in our own world or the others depicted in Rochon's fictional universe, Catadial has not fully embraced its altruistic mission. Indeed, falling into the trap of the classic utopia, it has become too isolated. As such, protected by magic and mountains — like the mystical Buddhist land of Shambhala upon which it is modeled —, it has not been able to help others actualize themselves as individuals or collectivities. It calls, then, upon Taïm Sutherland to help it achieve the "grand idéal" (ED138, 174). Rochon uses humor to defuse the over-earnest tendency of utopia, as seen in the text's first approach to Catadial from Sutherland's critical perspective.

Arriving in Catadial, having been sung its glories by Strénid, Sutherland remains skeptical, indeed suspicious that his friends the Asven will be exploited by a society that certainly appears to be too good to be true (ED120-21). Typical of the classic utopia, entrance to Catadial is restricted, its location isolated and kept secret, geographically by a mountain range and otherwise by magical spells that keep outsiders from becoming too curious (ED118, 123). In this land, everyone appears to be happy and courteous (ED119, 120-21), belongings are held in a communal fashion and there is a just distribution of goods and responsibilities (ED134-35). Unlike the dystopian worlds in so many narratives of SFQ and the Anglo-American tradition, in which manipulation and prejudice reign, the people of Catadial enjoy an almost complete lack of exploitation (ED136). Indeed, Taïm expresses the conditions of their existence as "un système social fait pour que les gens s'épanouissent" ("a social system made for people to blossom"; ED135); these words resonate heavily with utopian theorist Ernst Bloch's *Principle of Hope* (1959), which asserts that "'true being ... ends ... in questions of a life of fulfilling work, free of exploitation, but also of a life beyond work" (16). The common good serves no longer as a pretext for oppression, as it had under Skern Strénid in *Le Rêveur dans la Citadelle* (see page 79 above), but rather as a value according to which "tout le monde se souciait de tout le monde" ("everyone cared for everybody"; ED136).

At first, Taïm interprets the politeness of "cette société policée" ("this civilized/policed society"; ED135) as a façade possibly maintained by force. He is particularly suspicious of the fact that an emperor heads the state, seeing this office as antithetical to a free society (ED122). Eventually, however, he learns to take Catadial at face value and admit the utopian nature of "ce pays de cocagne" ("this land of Cockaygne"; ED312; a reference to a medieval sensual utopia [Morton 11-24]). Rochon's narrative reveals its open-ended nature to the reader in a number of ways, however, not the least of which in the fact that Taïm's very mission calls for the opening-up of this closed society (ED300). Although its citizens are happier than the average human, they remain nonetheless human (ED204). In spite of the "mentalité tolérante du pays" ("tolerant mentality of the land"; ED136) and its complete welfare system to care for the sick and the elderly, to educate children and to rehabilitate criminals, Taïm recognizes in some Cathades the same types of petty feelings of dissatisfaction and suspicion of foreigners which seem to be human universals (ED175–76). They deal with these tensions better than most because of the cultural practice of "laisser mourir" ("letting die"), a form of meditation modeled on Buddhist practice, in which the individual works on letting go of the envies, fears and desires inherent to the material world (Midal 67–68). In the end, he admits the superiority of its government (a hybrid form of democracy involving both direct and representative systems, notwithstanding that its head of state is an emperor) (ED136–37), of its economy "sur la base du bien commun" ("on the basis of the common good"; ED189 — its stores have four departments for merchandise: free, barter, new for purchase and special order), and of its employment system (there is 100 percent employment and jobs are remunerated based on the level of fulfillment they provide the individual; for example, a store clerk earns a lot of money because the position provides little personal fulfillment; ED154, 187–89). Furthermore, Catadial seeks a positive, balanced relationship with its environment, including a full recycling program (one source of the free merchandise in stores). Indeed, it reflects quite clearly what Fredric Jameson describes as "the grand Utopian idea or wish — the abolition of property, the complementarity of desires, non-alienated labor, the equality of the sexes" (*Archaeologies* 145).

However, as Catadial's emperor Othoum admits to Taïm, perfection has not been achieved in one key respect: "l'ouverture vers l'extérieur ... ce n'est pas encore notre fort" ("opening toward the outside has not yet been our forte"; ED141). Othoum describes the complacency and self-sufficiency of his people, qualities from which he wishes to liberate them. His goal, referred to as the "«grand idéal»" ("great ideal"; ED205) in a manner reminiscent of Syrius' Great Project in *L'Oiseau de feu*, is to open Catadial to the outside world, to offer their values with the aim of liberating their neighbors, not in a traditional political sense, but in a personal and collective sense. Just as Claude Grégoire described Brossard's SFQ saga as a discourse on utopia (Rev. 20), the same might be said for Rochon's underappreciated work. She introduces her metanarrative commentary on the genre in such a subtle, yet evident manner: the problem with the utopia is precisely that it is a closed society and to improve itself it must, in alignment with contemporary utopian theory like that prized by Suvin, become open-ended.

Rochon maintains this open-endedness in the narrative itself for, while plans for the Asven's utopian new world in the Red City are highly articulated before the novel's conclusion, and an epilogue provides the reader with a vision of what this society becomes, the novel reverses the basic structure of the classic utopia. In the latter, for example in Charlotte Gilman Perkins' *Herland*

(1915), the outside visitor arrives to observe a completed social plan; the society has already been made "better," a trope Rochon appropriates in Taïm's arrival and observations of Catadial. As Chris Ferns asserts, "the question of how utopia came about is often evaded" in the classic utopia (27). In contrast, *L'Espace du diamant* traces precisely the transition from the imperfect Archipelago to the more perfect Red City as the Asven discuss and design their utopia-in-process.

Rochon's Catadial reflects certain traits of the classic utopia, including those defining it as an outline for the ideal nation-state (Bouchard, "Utopies" 55). Through the establishment of the new Asven colony the Red City, however, she demonstrates how developing nations can create and preserve their own identity while living in harmony with their neighbors. Still on Vrénalik, the reviving nation takes several steps to assert itself, including designing and raising a flag (ED91–92), establishing government protocols (ED92), and reviving its founding myth (ED97–99). While it is clear that a new society will be formed that looks to "notre avenir collectif" ("our collective future"; ED278), the Asven express the need to maintain an identity that also cherishes their common past. As they develop "une société fondée sur des principes communautaires" ("a society based on communal principles"; ED134) — perhaps instinctively suspicious of the state — the Asven do not seek political sovereignty; all those who choose to leave Vrénalik for the new homeland will be granted citizenship of Catadial.

In *Margin/Alias: Language and Colonization in Canadian and Québécois Fiction* (1991), Sylvia Söderlind asserts that postcolonial fictions express the need to recuperate a lost past (6). Vautier, too, observes that Québécois writers like Noël Audet, François Barcelo, Madeleine Ouellette-Michalska and Jacques Poulin "re-disent l'Histoire dans une tentative de placer le peuple québécois *dans* l'Histoire et de *poser* ... une existence historique" ("retell History in an attempt to place the people of Québec *in* History and to *pose* an historical existence"; "Révision" 40). We see that the Asven predicate the foundation of a new society upon such historical recovery. First, Jouskilliant Green unearths and brings to light their lost history, buried in forgotten archives beneath the Frulken capital. Then, an archeological expedition (literally occupied with digging up the Asven past) brings to the Archipelago Taïm Sutherland who retrieves the statue of Haztlén. Later, the Cathades assist them in recuperating their lost patrimony, their share of Suzanne Arkándanatt's treasury and knowledge of her story, the founding myth of their people. Finally, Anar Vranengal joins with the spirit of the Dreamer Shaskath, the sorcerer involved in the utterance of the four-hundred-year-old curse, and even his wrath appears to be laid to rest. As Sophie Beaulé observes, drawing on the work of Gilles Bourque, until they recover the past and come to terms with it, the Asven cannot move forward to build a new society ("Mémoire" 12).

Nation building includes recognition by other states and control of one's own foreign policy in order to "sortir de son isolement, s'ouvrir au monde extérieur" (229), as Jacques Brossard asserts in one of his juridical essays, *L'Accession à la souveraineté et le cas du Québec* (Accessing Sovereignty and Québec's Case, 1976). The existence of the Asven must be acknowledged by the lands around them. Jouskilliant Green's translation and exportation of their stories begins this process, although it leads to a quaint image, *folklorisé*—a charge made at times about Québéc's cultural iconography (Major 123), as well as about its own superficial embracing of multicultural communities within it (Simon, *Hybridité* 19). The contemporary Asven must rejoin the flow of time, enter the modern world. As Santoro observes, their liberator Taïm's very name (roughly pronounced like "time") helps to reinsert the Asven back into the flow of time, back into a version of history that had been stopped by the four-hundred-year-old curse (99). While outsiders had helped the Asven recuperate their lost past, one of their own must lead the project for a new society. As Jack Zipes describes Ernst Bloch's conception of the utopian project, "the realization of individual autonomy was only possible if the 'we' came into its own as the collective agent of its own destiny" (xx). Strénid II represents the visionary leader who works to bring the Asven into the present and to seize control of their destiny: "Strénid voulait sortir de la pauvreté et en faire sortir son peuple" ("Strénid wanted to leave poverty behind and to bring his people out of it"; ED59). In order to escape the dispossession and poverty of life in the harsh climate of the Archipelago, Strénid leads the Asven to create a new homeland in the South.[11] Sutherland's initial reaction to Skern's project reveals its audacity: "Un nouveau pays! Mais ça ne se fait pas! Des gens qui émigrent, passe encore, mais tout un archipel qui déménage!" ("A new country! But that just isn't done! People emigrate, okay, but a whole archipelago moving!"; ED129)

Like the classic utopia, *L'Espace du diamant* spends a good deal of time discussing matters of the *res publica*; the novel makes clear that a new society is being built and its characters must attend to practical issues. Already in Vrénalik, Strénid has begun organizing services that will provide for the needs of the collectivity he leads (ED68). Liberation from the curse forces the Asven to retake responsibility for themselves and their land. They begin maintenance projects on buildings whose disrepair was foregrounded in earlier volumes (see page 71 above) (ED83). Strénid establishes a regular system of government, setting up an administrative council, an act that seeks perhaps to avoid the tragic, unsettling consequences of absolute power to which his own father fell victim (ED92). This system must be transparent, therefore its meetings are open and include financial reports (ED91–92). As part of their movement to re-enter the passage of time, to reclaim history as their own, the Asven must be recognized by the lands around them. This request plays into their favor, for, in his quest for recognition, Strénid obtains important information on the political status and the rights to finanical support and immigration that the Asven can claim from Ister-Inga (ED120–22). Finally, he seeks to develop an alliance with Catadial; to do so, he must sign accords (ED132). Both Strénid and the Emperor Othoum, however, must take care not to offend Ister-Inga, under whose political control the Archipelago officially falls.

Significantly, as the Asven build their new world homeland in the Red City within the territory of Catadial, they maintain Cathade citizenship. Having learned the lessons of the past — internalizing the punishment meted out to the hegemonic state of Skern Strénid — the Asven will build a utopian community based on the model of the city state. Its location within the space of the diamond recalls not only Québec City's site on Cape Diamond but also the Buddhist *vajradhatu*, an "indestructible or diamondlike space" (Midal 390). The color red may be a reference to the short-lived Cap Rouge settlement, where Roberval brought a group of convicts in 1542 (Lovecraft 117), or to Louis Riel's Red River Rebellion of the Métis in what would become the province of Manitoba. Red also recalls the liberal heritage of French-Canadian secular nationalists following the model of the Patriot Rebellion of 1837–38 and is, of course, the color of communism and, for Buddhism, the color of the life force. That liberal heritage based on the Enlightenment value of reason, notions of statehood and the nation as governed by the people appear clearly in this work. Like the nation of Québec — and my discussion must inevitably come to the possibility of a national allegory here — the Archipelago and the Asven's new Red City continue to hold a somewhat ambiguous political status. As Sutherland asks: "Le Catadial considère-t-il Vrénalik comme un pays?" His question is answered: "En termes de politique extérieure, non" ("Does Catadial consider Vrenalik as a country?... In terms of foreign policy, no"; ED133). Because "Vrénalik n'a aucune existence en tant qu'entité politique distincte" ("Vrenalik has no existence as a distinct political entity"; ED134), Sutherland fears its exploitation by the Cathades. Therefore "il voulait protéger l'archipel du ridicule: cette façon de le traiter comme un État ... sans toutefois rien reconnaître officiellement était une attitude suspecte" ("he wanted to protect the archipelago from ridicule: this way of treating it like a State without officially recognizing anything was suspicious;" ED134). As the actual diaspora occurs and the majority of the Asven *de souche* leave for the Red City, Strénid undertakes "la passation de pouvoirs," ceding governance of the Archipelago to the Emperor Othoum (ED231–32). The latter agrees to intervene should the colonialist exploitation of the Archipelago threaten its survival. This threat appears quite real, for since it has also opened up to the outside world, woodcutters, tourists, and others have invaded it. Although in theory Othoum recognizes "la souveraineté d'Ister-Inga" over the Archipelago, he vows not to let it become a clear-cut wasteland (ED246).

In the end the Asven have not obtained any form of full political sovereignty with the foundation of the Red City; rather they have transferred citizenship from a marginal status within Ister-Inga to become citizens of Catadial (ED128). On the one hand, their New World Myth is one of colonization, of a pioneering spirit, as revealed in the lengthy narrative of the Asven exodus including a perilous trip by boat from the Archipelago and then down the River Van. On the other hand, their treatment during this trip mirrors a sort of middle passage. Other possible allusions include recognition of the Acadian deportation known as the *Grand Dérangement* and even that of the Israelites from Egypt, as they are crowded onto a ship, placed into quarantine, and refused entrance by the officials of Irquiz until Catadial intervenes. Furthermore, they openly have purchased the land from a developed, industrialized civilization, not through ruse and artifice as our New World was obtained from its indigenous peoples. Like *L'Oiseau de feu*, *L'Espace du diamant* remains ambivalent about the project of colonization, seeking still to offer a redemptive vision of it, as seen in the idealistic, utopian vision that underlies the project for the Red City.

Again, this new society must be "fondée sur des principes communautaires" ("founded on communitarian principles"; ED134). Pride in Asven identity must return, "il fallait réapprendre à avoir fière allure" ("they had to relearn how to carry themselves with pride"; ED68), an element acted upon in the symbolic realm as they create a flag (ED83, 91–92, 170, 239, 257–58, 273). Furthermore, while attention has been paid to the practical elements of administration and politics, functional reason alone will not serve the establishment of a new home. The Asven must embrace not only elements of the logical materialism brought to them by Jouskilliant Green and their contacts with the outside world, but they must also implement their own religio-magical tradition in order to invoke the mythical beast, *la Dragonne de l'aurore* (the Dawn Dragon), who will guide their way. Strénid confirms: "La science a sa place, les légendes ont la leur" ("Science has its place, and legends theirs;" ED350). Sharon Taylor points out the relationship between Rochon's Buddhist concepts and their fictional reenactment:

> En créant cette nouvelle cité qui ressemble à une communauté shambhalienne, l'auteur introduit dans son texte une autre dimension spirituelle. La Ville Rouge fait partie de la même «structure» souterraine spirituelle, structure ancrée par des points d'énergie qui forment un «octaèdre» ou un «diamant» [233].
>
> In creating this new city which resembles a Shambhala community, the author introduces another spiritual dimension to her text. The Red City belongs to the same subterranean spiritual "structure," a structure anchored by the points of energy which form an "octahedron" or a "diamond."

The proper basis for a leader and a nation will be "[r]aison et amour du prochain" ("reason and love for one's neighbor"; ED56). The syncretic nature of the new ideology appears incorporated in the marriage of Strénid and Anar Vranengal; their union restores the past harmony of reasonable administration with respect for love and magic, a paradigm broken four hundred years previous by the tyrant Skern I's elimination of the *paradrouïm*, a recognized sorcerer caste, and his relationship with Inalga, in which possession replaced love.

While it is essential that they not forget the past, neither can the Asven remain its prisoners in this new land. This conflict between the impotent "historicité de l'oubli" ("historicism of forgetting") and a positive form of memory "centrée sur la modernité et l'américanité" described by Bourque ("centered on modernity and Americanness"; Beaulé, "Mémoire" 12), appears in the conflictual relationship between the Dreamer Shaskath and Anar Vranengal. The current Asven sorceress recovers the spirit of the original sorcerer who uttered the curse upon the Asven four hundred years earlier. Still consumed with anger and bitterness, he asks her: "Comment construire un nouveau pays si vos souvenirs sont détruits? Où sera son âme?" ("How do you build a new land if your memories are destroyed? Where will its soul be?"; ED274). The key to the Asven's "avenir collectif" ("collective future"; ED278) is learning how to balance the two. Anar tries to explain:

> Nous, nous allons construire une nouvelle ville, et avec les pieds sur terre, impossible autrement. Vous aurez votre place parmi nous, on vous honorera, n'ayez crainte.... Mais pas question que vous n'exerciez votre ascendant sur mes compagnons [ED277].
>
> We are going to construct a new city, with our feet on the ground — impossible any other way. You will have your place with us; we will honor you, don't worry. But it's out of the question for you to hold sway over my companions.

Anar's possession by Shaskath's spirit allows her to understand, and therefore reject, the epistemic violence of the system that allowed Shaskath to be turned into a drug-addicted pawn of a power that disingenuously claimed to represent the common good (see page 79 above). Anar perceives that nursing the anger it spawns becomes self-destructive rather than constructive (ED296).

L'Archipel noir and *L'Espace du diamant* increasingly reveal Vrénalik's diversity as a land comprised not only of the indigenous Asven, but also of immigrants like Taïm Sutherland who have settled there. These include refugees from the northern land of Hanrel and eventually from the Southern lands of Irquiz and Ister-Inga who integrate into Asven society, participating in rituals and even taking on leadership roles, exemplified by Strénid's appointment of Naffis Tchil, a homosexual Hanrel refugee, to his Administrative Council. In addition to these present-day contacts, after Vrénalik's liberation and opening up, the geographic flow of peoples reveals a common past heritage amongst a range of groups previously appearing in opposition to each other. The South (Irquiz and Ister-Inga) has completely forgotten that their land — to which Vrénalik now stands as a political dependency (ED24) — owes its foundation to Asven fleeing the catastrophe of four hundred years ago. When Sutherland leaves the civilized world of Ister-Inga, Anar Vranengal reminds him that "votre pays ... est issu du nôtre" ("your land came from ours"; AN102).

For the construction of this New World Myth, as Santoro observes, a syncretic vision is ultimately necessary. The new society must be founded upon a number of principles antithetical to a traditional Western imperial-colonial ideology. Eschewing the formula that good fences make good neighbors, Rochon's vision of a utopian society rejects a rigid sense of boundaries, and thus, a rigid conception of nationalism and national sovereignty. The opening of borders allows, of course, for the flow of people in and out, and in this sense, the Asven nation is to be built on a cultural syncretism as well as upon a relational attitude toward the lands around it in an implicit critique of immigration laws, closed and policed boundaries. Revealing the commonalities between cultures helps to build this relationality. Syncretism — an element discussed further chapter four — must also occur in the realm of logic and rationalism; unlike many classic utopias and classic dystopias, for that matter, Rochon's fictional universe demonstrates that utopia is not founded on reason alone. Instead, reason and mysticism must unite, as Sharon Taylor has observed (231). Finally, the recognition of the need for constant reevaluation and improvement, an essential element in Suvin's definition of the open-ended utopia — as well as in Moylan's and Sargent's developments, among others — appears in Rochon's depiction of the established utopia of Catadial and the plans for the Asven's utopian new society in the Red City.

L'Espace du diamant closes on a utopian harmony established between the two societies based upon altruism:

> le pays et même l'extérieur s'imprégnaient peu à peu d'une douceur de vivre inconnue jusqu'alors. Cela était dû à l'affection et à la confiance, soigneusement établies et maintenues, qui existaient entre ceux de Varagelle et les autres, Cathades et Asvens. Et, comme l'ouverture vers l'extérieur continuait à s'affectuer dans l'harmonie, cette atmosphère embaumée du Catadial rayonnait aux alentours. L'intimité de la Dragonne avec ceux qu'elle avait acceptés auprès d'elle devint parfaite [ED344].

> the land and even the outside gradually was impregnated with a sweetness of life previously unknown. It was due to the affection and confidence, carefully established and maintained which existed between those of Varagelle [the Red City's location] and the others, Cathade and Asven. And, as the opening to the outside continued to be effectuated in harmony, the sweetened atmosphere of Catadial spread forth to the lands around it. The intimacy of the Dragon with those she had accepted near her became perfect.

Seemingly in answer to her own concerns about the perfection of this utopian society, Rochon returns to the theme of the "Ouverture," the opening to the other, as the antepenultimate section of the final volume of the original *Cycle de Vrénalik* is entitled.

Rochon's Vrénalik Cycle ultimately participates in the spirit of the open-ended, postcolonial utopia in its resistance to the binary logic of the West, its integration of logic and magic, and its dissolution of strict national boundaries. As I argue elsewhere, it creates a truly imagined community in Benedict Anderson's sense (Ransom, "Imagined"). However, one puzzling contradiction remains: the vast majority of those who leave the Archipelago for the Red City are "Asven de souche" ("of Asven stock"; ED257), and the Red City's development is later limited because of fears that too many Cathades settling there will suffocate "la spécificité asven des lieux" ("the Asven specificity of the place"; ED348). This lingering conception of the community based upon the specificity of the Asven recalls perhaps too closely the exclusionism of an ethnically based nationalism. While fiction allows for the expression of such attitudes, behind which lie real concerns and anxieties, Québec understands that they cannot be tolerated in the official discourse. Indeed, their exposure through Parizeau's unfortunate attribution of the failure of the second referendum on Québec's sovereignty in 1995 to "le vote ethnique" (Bauch), further fueled the development of a discourse that conceptualized Québécois identity in pluralistic terms begun as early as the 1980s. Perhaps in direct response to the development of a more nuanced conception of Québécois identity, Rochon's subsequent SFQ saga presents a revision of her earlier work. This developing thought, increasingly influenced by Buddhism but also marked by the death of her son, led to a reassessment of the events surrounding the liberation of Vrénalik and the foundation of the Red City. She does this in her more recent epic, which chronicles the paradox of "life" in hell for two new heroic figures, Lame and Rel, as well as for Taïm Sutherland, who arrives in hell after his death on the Vrénalik Archipelago.

Paradise in Hell: Rochon's *Les Chroniques infernales*

Esther Rochon's *Les Chroniques Infernales* (The Infernal Chronicles, 1995–2000) identified by Claude Janelle as the first attempt in Québec's literary history to create an extended, systematic vision of hell (qtd. in Hannan 235), initially present the reader with an obvious dystopia. This generically hybrid work, which exploits a number of SF tropes within a narrative more comfortably labeled as fantasy,[12] opens with the first volume's eponymous heroine, *Lame* (Blade/The Soul, 1995), working as a secretary in "les enfers" ("the hells"). As one might expect, the hells and the world above them, which is eventually revealed as contemporary Montréal, appear clearly as dystopian sites. Yet, Rochon's astonishing goal for this cycle reflects Moylan's description of the utopian as "the sociopolitical drive that moves the human project for emancipation and fulfillment beyond the limits of the current system" (*Scraps* 65). How?

From the heart of the horror of the hot hells, the cold hells, the cutting hells, the poisonous hells, Rochon posits this utopian possibility: "Si chacun se conduisait avec droiture, les enfers disparaîtraient peut-être" ("If everyone conducted himself with rectitude, the hells would, perhaps, disappear"; L46).[13] In keeping with the classic utopia, a visionary, millenarian leader utters these words. Rel, the new prince of hell, seizes power and initiates a series of major reforms, transformative events which clearly follow the lines of the open-ended utopia, as development occurs in a progressive, often spiraling fashion, a form observed elsewhere in Rochon's *œuvre* by Linda Bonin. Rita Painchaud also comments on the instability of Rochon's approach to utopia ("*Sorbier*" 149). Through this transformation, Rochon's SFQ saga also reflects the preoccupations found in the New World Myth novels described by Vautier. In so doing, *Les Chroniques infernales* directly engage the issues of colonialism and the construction of a healthy postcolonial world, drawing analogically on the paradigm of heaven/hell, only to subvert this teleological system in order to promote the possibility of change.

Rel's father, Har, rules the intially dystopian hells with a Machiavellian idea of power based on violence that is patriarchal and homosocial in nature. The social structure is rigidly hierarchical; within it, everyone knows his (or her) place: the king leads, the *sbires* (henchmen) and the various *bourreaux* (executioners) torture and the damned suffer. Clearly subordinate, subaltern[14] even, Lame performs the task of registering the damned who arrive in the underworld ("les mondes d'en dessous [sic]"; O1) where justice is meted out by an array of torturers, ranging from monsters, the humanoid *sbires* (henchmen), robots, and even insects and birds trained for this purpose. As in Dante's *Inferno* (1308–21), the damned receive assignment to a specific hell with a punishment appropriate to their particular shortcomings during life in the external worlds above (the "mondes extérieurs" or "du dessus"; A112, 39). These may include sins of omission or excess, such as gluttony and self-centeredness, those which Lame atones in the *enfers mous* (the soft hells). Those who commit more violent crimes, including murder or engaging in warfare, expiate these in the *enfers chauds* (hot hells), the *enfers tranchants* (sharp hells), or the *enfers à pals* (hells of impalement). Their punishments include respectively being boiled in oil or grilled by the *bourreaux*, being torn apart (and then rehealed) by enormous, sharp-billed *oiseaux bourreaux* (torturer birds), or by being impaled on a post à la Vlad Tepes.[15]

This order prevails until the visionary prince Rel takes power and begins to implement his system of utopian reforms. In the spirit of the open-ended utopia, which must "be accomplished by constant self-critical watchfulness against the temptation of the arrested moment" (Suvin, "SF Novel" 83), dystopia continues to rear its ugly head at repeated intervals throughout the saga's six novels. This occurs partly through flashbacks in *Secrets* (1998), in which Rel describes the horror of his childhood, and in the series' conclusion, *Sorbier* (Mountain Ash/Rowan Tree, 2000). An exhausted Rel again recounts his life, "[r]écits de tortures, de sévices et d'états psychologiques pervers se succédaient. C'était abominable, parce qu'un certain niveau d'horreur devenait tangible" ("stories of torture, cruelty, and perverse psychological states followed one after the other. It was abominable because a certain level of horror became tangible"; So245). For him, the ultimate sign of dystopia is powerlessness: "l'impuissance face à l'abominable" ("impotence in the face of the abominable"; So246). Dystopian forces repeatedly threaten the progress toward betterment not only in the hells and the worlds around them, but also, as we shall see, in paradise.

Har's henchmen feel no compassion for the damned, as one asserts that "[c]e qui est bon, c'est de les forcer à faire ce que je veux avant de m'en débarasser.... Ce sont des damnés sans aucune valeur, sans aucun droit" ("what is good, is to force them to do what I want before I get rid of them. They're damned, with no value and no rights whatsoever"; L50). Rel's challenge to this power system recalls Stanley Aronowitz's description of the utopian function which, "[r]ather than follow rules of governance based on power or discursive hegemonies, [exhorts us] to create a new imaginary one that would recognize that a politics based on power endangers human survival" (Aronowitz 49). To break the cycle of violence, which brutalizes both victim and torturer, Rel announces the project of moving the punitive functions of his hells onto other worlds: "Plus un seul damné ici, fini les emplois de bourreau;" "Il y aura donc une nette amélioration du sort global de cette population" ("Not another damned soul here; no more jobs as executioner.... There will be a clear improvement of the global lot of this population"; L180, 177). As he renegotiates contracts with the worlds who send their damned to his realm to expiate their faults, he promulgates the notion of a "responsabilité globale" ("global responsibility"; L193) to rehabilitate the hells — a world destroyed by the violence of the activity of redemption carried out there — to some semblance of utility, to restore its damaged ecosystem and to operate a "reconstruction" (L231). This sense of shared responsibility recalls, of course, the philosophy of numerous non-governmental organizations working to rectify inequalities deriving from past colonial exploitation in the empirical world.

As the *Chroniques'* second volume *Aboli* (Abolished, 1996) opens, the majority of the newly created hells have improved upon the systems they inherited from the former hells. They, too, have initiated reforms in consultation with Rel which alleviate the suffering of the damned and now offer therapies which can result in a sort of fast-track to expiation:

Les autochtones ont pris goût au travail de bonne âme, ils consacrent du temps à soulager les damnés, et ça les rend joyeux d'avoir ainsi le cœur sur la main. Les damnés sont sensibles à ces efforts, donc les peines sont en moyenne plus courtes: succès sur toute la ligne [A72].

The natives took a liking to the work of good souls, they dedicate time to comforting the damned and that makes them happy to have their heart on their sleeve. The damned are sensitive to these efforts and therefore the penances are on average shorter: success across the board.

In one world only dystopia prevails. The land of Sargade, the homeland of Rel's mother and a haven of normalcy for Rel as he was growing up, has not adapted well to its new role. Previously a "limbe assez riche" ("rather wealthy limbo"; A7), this land of artists and technicians had contracted to become the *enfers froids* in exchange for remuneration and benefits. As a result, the Sargades have lost their sun, its warmth and light, as well as any plant life, and they now live now in a cloudy, freezing "cold hell." This society appears dystopian not because of its new physical conditions, though, but rather because the Sargades are not fulfilling their contract in good faith. As they imprison themselves inside their heated buildings all year round, they do so less to escape the weather and more to avoid the damned they have agreed to care for, outsourcing this task to robots and *sbires*. The new situation figures as a trope for the colonial/postcolonial reality, as Rochon depicts the interactions between the Sargades and the damned as reflective of those between "natives" and colonizers/immigrants.

In keeping with utopia's critical function, the worlds outside the hells also exist in a state of dystopia: "[p]lusieurs mondes sont en train de mourir. De pollution, de maladies. Des tyrans s'emparent du pouvoir. Le chaos règne" ("several worlds are dying. Pollution, sickness. Tyrants seizing power. Chaos reigns"; A103). This negatively normalized state of existence and death ultimately leads to a situation in which, across the universe, the majority of souls arrive in hell to expiate their sins (So123). Reborn again into another world, they will either attain some new level of enlightenment to progress, or they will repeat their mistakes and return to one of the hells, in keeping with the Buddhist vision of the afterlife adopted by Rochon here (So416). Simply stated, the hells reflect a distorted, mirror-image of the consensus reality world of the reader, the world of Lame before her death. She remembers life "en ville" (as the early volumes code Montréal) as full of horror and pain, as a dystopian existence that she escaped through suicide:

> Ville gonflée, polluée, où des factions s'affrontent sans que rien aboutisse. Volcan étouffé. Tensions qui perdurent, situations qui ne débouchent pas. On est sur une île ... serrant comme un étau. Sensations d'emprisonnement, d'arrogance, de congestion, de fragilité distendue. Dépendance de systèmes sur lesquels on n'a aucune prise [Or113].

A swollen, polluted city where factions clash without consequence. A smothered volcano. Tensions which linger, situations with no outlet. You're on an island, which squeezes like a vice. Sensations of emprisonment, arrogance, congestion, distended fragility. Dependance on systems over which you have no control.

Indeed, hell and the "monde des vivants" ("the world of the living") differ only to the extent that (L62): "en enfer tout est plus concret.... Ce qui est là-bas signe ou symbole acquiert ici une existence tangible" ("in hell, everything is more concrete.... What there is a sign or symbol acquires here a tangible existence"; S105). Conversely, the reformed hells, in which pain and suffering have been alleviated, now seem "trop apprivoisés: ils ressemblent dangereusement aux mondes extérieurs ... s'y joignent-ils carrément ou se replongent-ils dans le chaos ordinaire des régions infernales?" ("too tame: they perilously resemble the exterior worlds ... will they flat out join them or will they be plunged back into the ordinary chaos of infernal regions?"; S189).

Rochon's genius lies not in rendering the hells, or even contemporary Montréal, as dystopia, but rather in representing them as an open-ended utopia. In so doing, like Pordzik's postcolonial utopia, *Les Chroniques infernales* appropriate, in order to interrogate, the tropes of the "classic" literary utopia. As I argue in greater detail elsewhere (Ransom, "Maps"), Rel, "un visionnaire" ("a visionary"; S140), one of "ces réformateurs utopistes" ("these utopian reformers"; So266), institutes a better society in an isolated location, to which access appears limited. An outsider's arrival provides the narrative motivation for a descriptive tour of the utopia. Indeed, Fax arrives in the *anciens enfers* (former hells) not as one of the damned, but rather as a *juste*, a just person sent to claim his heavenly reward! Rochon ultimately problematizes the various elements of the classic literary utopia by compromising the boundaries of the insular, utopian space and by revealing that perfection can never be achieved, that development toward a better life occurs as a continual process. Over the middle volumes, the various new hells take on their role of meting out justice to the damned, but as they do so, they progress — but not without an array of hurdles and setbacks — toward making existence in hell bearable not only for the damned, but also for themselves. In the imaginary universe of the *Chroniques infernales*, the author problematizes the very notion of utopia, as hell (the former hells) becomes heaven (for Fax) and ultimately, paradise appears rather hellish.

Les Chroniques infernales' penultimate volume, *Or* (Gold/Yet, 1999), concludes with a didactic passage, which stylistically recalls the dialogic form of the Renaissance utopias such as Christine de Pisan's *The Book of the City of Ladies* (1405), which "could be considered ... one of the first utopias" (Bammer, *Partial* 26). Lame assumes the pose of an ignorant student seeking the wisdom of Rel, who, significantly, does not take the role of an all-knowing authority, but rather that of one who has "commencé à [se] documenter" ("begun [his] research"; Or257). She asks Rel if it would not have been better if the Europeans had stayed home rather than colonizing the Americas (Or256). His reply explains the short and long term effects of such events:

> —Une colonisation, c'est une grosse guerre. Ça engendre beaucoup de tragédies et de damnés, sur le coup et dans les siècles qui suivent—tu en es un exemple.
> —Je suis une victime de l'arrivée des Blancs en Amérique du Nord?
> —Une parmi d'autres, la plupart plus gravement touchées que toi [Or257].
>
> "A colonization is a huge war. It engenders many tragedies and damned souls, right away and in the centuries that follow — you're an example of it."
> "I'm a victim of the arrival of the Whites in North America?"
> "One among many, most of them affected more deeply than you were."

Here, Rochon's utopian novel openly raises the question alluded to throughout the series, that of colonialism, and of the place of contemporary Québec with regard to its history.

Montréal, as a site of colonization, immigration and now multicultural existence, comes into play as a template for the discussion of a postcolonial worldview. For, as the last volume's preface points out, the saga's central character Lame spent her previous life on "notre Terre, plus spécifiquement ... la ville de Montréal" ("our Earth, more specifically the city of Montreal"; So xvii). Inevitably, the transmigration of souls from "le monde des vivants" into the series' various hells, limbos, and paradises figures not only the processes of immigration and colonization but also, through Rel's utopian agenda, those of decolonization and liberation. Through Lame's developing understanding of this system in which one group maintains power over another through the threat of violence, the text condemns the model of European colonial imperialism. Indeed, the utopian impulses of Rel, Lame and Fax (who is later revealed to be Taïm Sutherland from the Vrénalik Cycle) — all hybrid figures, both migrant and exiled — operate in a manner consistent with the critical function of utopia as outlined by Moylan (*Demand* 10–11 and *Scraps* 5) and reiterated by Sargisson (*Contemporary* 98).

The first sentence of *Aboli* describes how Rel's kingdom of the former hells used to be "une colonie pénitentiaire" (A3) and that he has broken with this system by seizing power from his father and implementing a series of reforms, in which good will and mutual care and respect become the norms for relationships between groups. The choice of terms for the hells' various inhabitants and migrant groups reflects the codings of postcolonial discourse. The text refers to "autochtones" (the indigenous inhabitants of the former hells and the surrounding worlds to which their functions have been transferred) and "immigrants" (the condemned). Lame's entrance into the cold hells further reinforces the immigration motif as it resembles a bureaucratized border crossing (A100–03). In addition, in the *enfers mous* the larvae are "paralysés et colonisés par des myriads de fourmis" ("paralyzed and colonized by myriads of ants"; Or19), and the series' conclusion refers to the rigid entrance hearings at the gates of the paradise Anid as "ce processus d'immigration" ("this immigration process"; So349).

Rochon uses the vocabulary of the postcolonial, late capitalist world to indicate differences in ethnic origins, class and national status within the imagined community of the hells. While we can establish a certain hierarchy of positions, these change from world to world, as do their potential positions in a reading of this text as national allegory. Generally, the *damnés* lie at the bottom of the socio-political hierarchy of any world; they are the "damnés de la terre" referred to by Fanon in the title of his Marxist critique of colonialism, *The Wretched of the Earth*. This in turn refers to the first line of the *International*, the workers' anthem referred to by Rochon in the text (O142). Lame's impressions reveal the vast horror of the situation of the damned: "Des mondes sans issue et sans espoir, immensément majoritaires, peuplaient les souterrains de l'univers, le rongeant sourdement, naturellement" ("Beings without exit or hope, by far the majority, populated the basements of the universe, deafly, naturally eating away at them"; S137). Like the figure of the subaltern in postcolonial studies, the damned are denied agency, voice and subjectivity, particularly under the realm of Har and during the initial period of the *pays de Sargade*'s tenure as the cold hells.

As we saw in chapter two's discussion of Vrénalik, however, no simple allegorical assignment can be made for the various groups inhabiting the universe of the hells. The advantage of using science fiction and/or fantasy forms lies precisely in the technique of estrangement, which allows a distancing that renders the exploration of sensitive issues more comfortable. The ambivalence of fiction itself allows for a more thorough and meaningful, because more nuanced and authentic, working out of colonialist guilt and working through of postcolonial conflict in order to arrive at a position wherefrom new systems can be imagined, including "la possibilité du pardon" ("the possibility of forgiveness"; Beaulé, "Enfants" 136). Sargisson's observations about feminist works apply as well to the utopianism of Rochon and other writers from Québec: "through a new conceptual space that is not confined by binarism and dualistic oppositionality—a new 'no place' that is, in both positive and negative senses of the word, utopian" can be explored (*Contemporary* 75). Rochon's blurring of allegorical lines feeds into a larger pattern of undermining binary thought, which allows for the rethinking of difference so critical to a progressive redefinition of Québec identity.

The *damnés* may appear, then, as the abject immigrants described above or as parasitic colonizers, as in the new cold hells of the Sargades. Some come to obtain special status like Lame and Fax/Taïm Sutherland. No longer damned, the latter are nonetheless labeled as "immigrants" (A34, 38), but they possess a high level of agency and privilege within the system. Rel includes himself in this elite class, a minority within the majority: "Ici, nous sommes les privilégiés qui peuvent voir la situation.... La plupart des gens s'y refusent. Ce qui annule pratiquement leurs possibilités d'y échapper" ("Here, we are the privileged who can see the situation.... The majority refuses to do so. This essentially eliminates the possibility of their escape"; S157). Privilege bears the onus of guilt and shame, however, in the face of such abjection. Rel describes the bourgeois in his past life who became complicit in his torture of them because of "leur névrose collective de privilégiés" ("their collective neurosis as the privileged"; S201).[16] Lame describes the self-hate she felt before her suicide as similar: "[j]'étais comme le bourgeois dont tu parles" ("I was like the bourgeois you are talking about"; S203) feeling "[l]a honte d'être intelligent, riche ou en santé quand d'autres ne le sont pas" ("the shame of being intelligent, rich and healthy when others aren't"; S204).

The position of the *autochtones* varies from world to world. In the *anciens enfers*, the former *bourreaux* (torturers) have achieved self-determination and freedom as Rel's takeover resembles a national liberation. As the hells move onto other worlds, though, those who continue in the role of *bourreaux/sbires* assume a subordinate status to the *autochtones*. Overall, the text attributes to the *autochtones* a status of authenticity and agency; they have the most say in what happens in their worlds and they must operate change for the better. Indeed, in *Secrets* Rel refers to them as "les autochtones, ceux qui font le bien" ("the original people, those who do good"; S91).

The characters' discourse and their shifting allegorical positions reveal an ambivalence toward the colonial system and the various subject positions it initiates that is inevitable in postcolonial works issued from white settler colonies such as Québec. For example, Lame — an immigrant herself — expresses concern at Fax's unexpected arrival in the former hells: "Était-il le premier d'une série d'émigrants nouvelle vague?" ("Was he the first of a series of new wave emigrants?"; A18). Additional immigrants arrive and those "qui s'intégraient bien pouvaient demeurer" ("who integrated well could stay"; A53). While the text soundly condemns Har's regime of violence and power it treats immigration and colony formation as inevitable. If these are to be harmonious, however, they are predicated on certain comportments, an attitude which at times resembles the all too familiar assimilationist one.

The same ambivalence toward the discourses of colonialism and anti-colonialism appears in the treatment of the autochthonous peoples of the *anciens enfers*. Fantasy allows for a conflation within this one group of both colonizer and colonized, literalizing the metaphorical conflation of these groups found in Césaire's *Discourse on Colonialism*, which contends that colonization brutalizes the colonizer just as it does the colonized (13). Initially, the text reverses the roles of victim and torturer from their usual presentation in anti-colonial discourse, in which the indigenous suffer the tortures of the colonizer/immigrant. In the hells under Har, the indigenous torture the immigrants. Now, this may be read as an oppositional reflection of the xenophobia toward "Néo-Québécois" immigrants implicit in an ethnically based Québécois identity, a xenophobia described explicitly by Monique LaRue (7–15). Over time, though, as they live peacefully under Rel's reforms, isolated from the arrival of new immigrant *damnés* or from their own contact with the outside world, this "peuple de monstres" becomes "de moins en moins difformes à présent qu'ils n'étaient plus bourreaux" ("people of monsters" "less and less deformed now that they were no longer torturers"; A4). They evolve, giving birth to children less monstrous, "d'apparence de plus en plus humaine" ("more and more human in appearance"; A7). Now that the "indigènes" of the former hells have become "cette nation d'êtres autonomes, débrouillards et pleins de joie de vivre" ("this nation of autonomous, resourceful beings full of the joy of life"; A7), they reflect the positive image of post–Quiet Revolution Québec today. Relieved of the burden of an imbalanced, oppressive power relation with an Other (the *damnés* in Rochon's fiction or the economically dominant Anglo-Canadians in mid to late twentieth-century Québec), the group reaches a state of relative happiness and disalienation.

And yet, a problematic ambivalence remains in this description of the "ex-infernaux" (A12) represented as an indigenous people. This nearly evolutionary process which increasingly humanizes them also reflects racialist doctrines like France's civilizing mission, which sought to render those it colonized more like the French, and thus, it was supposed, more human. A similar ambivalence appears in the infantilization of the damned-as-immigrants in the new cold hells. There, the indigenous Sargades begin to treat the immigrant *damnés* just like their own children: "Les parents autochtones semblaient donner à leurs enfants et à leur suite de damnés une même attention incessante" ("The autochthonous parents seemed to give the same incessant attention they gave their children to their cluster of the damned"; O28). The paternalism inherent in this attitude undermines the growing altruism it is meant to reveal. Furthermore, the adoring damned who cluster around each Sargade develop a physical resemblance to their host, suggesting a form of assimilation (O23). The damned here recall the assimilated (and therefore alienated) colonized black man described in Fanon's *Black Skin, White Masks* who, having lived in France, returns "radically changed" (19). Ali A. Mazrui articulates a more recent discussion of this notion (342–44). Although the text again reverses the typical colonial situation, aligning privilege and power with the native Sargades while the colonizing damned represent subaltern immigrants, it accurately reflects the prevalent postcolonial reality. In the First World white settler colony like Canada/Québec, privileged citizens, who are themselves descendants of immigrants who colonized the land at the expense of actual autocthonous peoples, but who assume the position of "native" stand opposed to subaltern immigrants, the "natives" of former European colonies. The complexity of the situation appears in the complexity of the previous sentence, which further reflects the intricacies of Rochon's fictional representations of these various groups.

The case of the exiled "oiseau tortionnaire" ("torturer bird"; S159) Tryil recalls the situation of the Westernized African who cannot return home, who has become alienated from his culture of origin. Mazrui describes this situation as a case of "African *selves* [transformed] into semi-Western *others*" (351; original emphasis). Again, Rochon's text mirrors a blurred, reversed image of this trope also found in postcolonial fiction (see chapter two, note 14). Tryil belongs to a species of giant birds, exiled from their ancestral home and genetically altered to serve as executioners in the hells: "notre pays d'origine s'appelait Vrénalik ... le lieu interdit parce que nous sommes devenus trop horribles" ("our homeland was called Vrénalik, the place forbidden because we have become too horrible"; S159). In *Or* Tryil has been doubly exiled, punished with banishment from the hells for an attack on Fax/Taïm during Rel's audience in *Secrets*. Yet another alienated character typical of the SFQ saga, Tryil's behavior remains savage and petty until his rehabilitation, which occurs through a return to Vrénalik, a "retour au pays natal" in the vein of Aimé Césaire's *Notebook of a Return to the Native Land* (1939). But Tryil changes so much after this experience that when he returns to the hells after having his sentence commuted for an altruistic action, he no longer "fits in." He has been both physically transformed as a result of the first phase of his punishment, running through an abusive gauntlet of his brothers, and then mentally changed as a result of his experience in Vrénalik. Instead of the normal white, his feathers have grown back black and his formerly razor-sharp beak has been shortened as a result of injury. While he exhorts his brethren to rediscover their ancestral home of Vrénalik, they disappoint his hopes for a mass return: "Les oiseaux étaient adaptés à leur vie de tortionnaires" ("The birds were adapted to their life as torturers"; Or201). They quickly lose interest in his tales. Indeed, Tryil has worked so closely with the human Fax/Taïm that, like Mazrui's semi-Western postcolonial subject (351), he has become *métissé*, "une sorte d'hybride" ("a sort of hybrid"; 189); his difference appears both physically and emotionally as "Tryil, noir parmi ses congénères blancs rougis de sang ... ne se sentait plus chez lui" ("Tryil, black among his white brethren, now reddened with blood ... no longer felt at home"; Or201).

Later, though, a limited number of *oiseaux bourreaux*, inspired by Tryil's stories, decide to take advantage of Rel's new policy allowing them to return to their homeland. Their decision participates in a growing movement toward decolonization, reconciliation and integration developing across the hells as a result of the visionary leader's reforms. Referred to as the "oiseaux nostalgiques" ("nostalgic birds") they mirror in a different way the same trope reflected in Tryil's inability to return home unchanged after an experience of migration/immigration. In order to "réintégrer leur monde d'origine" ("return to the world of their origins") they must diminish in both size and intelligence, yet, they will be free: "c'est le prix de leur liberté" ("it's the price of their freedom"; So79). This coding of the "authentic" native as "less" than those who have come into contact with the forces of "civilization" may reinscribe racialist theories of native inferiority. However, since those very forces have transformed once seagull-like birds into enormous torturers it would be difficult to read this as anything other than a critique of Western colonialism's treatment of its Others. The logic of change through contact, though, remains inescapable: "Ils ne pouvaient pas avoir à la fois les vraies conditions du passé et les pouvoirs appartenant à la connaissance d'autre chose" ("They couldn't at once live according to the true conditions of the past and grasp the powers belonging to the knowledge of something else"; So185–86).

The text's apparent ambivalence appears clearly resolved in the assertions of Rochon's heroine, Lame. As she experiences a *prise de conscience* similar to that of protagonists Arguin finds in earlier, mainstream literature from Québec (see page 89 above). Lame explicitly accuses the whole system of European colonization:

> Les ancêtres avaient saccagé le continent au nom de Dieu et de la patrie. Comme cela se faisait beaucoup à leur époque, ils avaient tué, volé, accompli horreur après horreur en s'excitant de grands principes. Ils avaient connu la misère et avaient travaillé jusqu'à l'épuisement, pour transformer un beau paysage inhospitalier, qui ne leur appartenait même pas, en lieu hideux où leurs descendants pourraient proliférer [Or114].
>
> The ancestors had pillaged the continent in the name of God and the fatherland. As often occurred in their time, they had killed and stolen, they had accomplished horror after horror by working themselves up over grand principles. They had known misery and had worked until exhaustion in order to transform a beautiful, inhospitable land, which didn't even belong to them, into a hideous site where their descendants could proliferate.

With this statement, she condemns not only colonization in general, but the specifically French-Canadian phenomenon of the nationalist cult of the ancestors, early twentieth-century campaigns to clear and colonize the northern woods (Linteau 137–45), and the notion of the revenge of the cradle. *Les Chroniques infernales* represent, then, a major indictment of the violence of colonization, the cult of nationality and its icons, and the mistreatment of new immigrants arriving in a now prosperous colony. This occurs at a more general level of the novel as allegory, as well as through a very specific, explicit critique leveled directly at Québec itself.

Reading *Les Chroniques infernales* as yet another example of the SFQ text as national allegory necessarily proves to some degree reductionist, given the nuances and ambiguities of Rochon's work that we have already seen in the *Cycle de Vrénalik*. And yet, the development of the former hells outlined across the first section of *Aboli* reflects nothing so clearly as it does the development of French Canada/Québec. Not only does Rochon employ the term "nouveau monde" on several occasions (O 235; Or 124), the utopian rhetoric of a new society recurs. *Lame* ends upon "le commencement très discret d'une nouvelle époque" ("the very discreet beginning of a new era"; L242), as in this vast wasteland "un lichen commençait à pousser" ("a lichen began to grow"; L243). This description's suggestions of a parallel with Québec's ambiguous situation, claiming status as a nation without actual sovereignty, appears reinforced by Rel's rejection of inventing a new name for the budding world, saying: "Nous sommes l'ancien enfer et nous garderons ce nom tant que nous ne serons pas autonomes" ("We are the former hell and we will keep this name as long as we are not autonomous"; L241).

Participation in the discourse of colonization seems inevitable. In their project for the *anciens enfers*, the leaders of the hells must propose a vision for the new society in a remote land which addresses past violence, a tendency that reflects the traits of Vautier's New World Myth. In order to pave the way for the new society, the old hells are razed (literally "passé au bulldozer"; Axiii) so that as *Aboli* opens and, as its title suggests, they have been utterly abolished. Nothing physically remains but "une sorte de hangar" ("a sort of hangar"; Axiii): "Une fois vidé, l'ancien territoire des enfers devint un désert de pénombre" ("once empty, the former territory of the hells became a desert of shadow"; A3). Upon this tabula rasa, Rel and his people can write a new world. The therapeutic and redemptive power of work apparent in utopian texts comes into play as the former torturers, like the colonists of New France, become "cultivateurs." Reflecting the science-fictional trope of terraforming, their world is reshaped as they construct a desalination plant, canals for irrigation, a hydroelectric facility for power, and thus turn the desert green (A4). Indeed, not only have parts of the land have become near-Edenic gardens, the social revolution has been so successful that the place becomes a literal paradise for select souls.

This development, however, cannot be attributed to any real era as the text operates what Vautier calls a "slippage between historical periods" (*New* 226). Rochon's Infernal Chronicles conflate historical periods refusing any one version of history as Truth, allowing for the heterogeneity typical of the postcolonial. This ambiguity appears when Rel observes the progress of his people: "[l]es anciens enfers forment un territoire avec son autonomie, ses coutumes, sa joie de vivre" ("the former hells form a territory with its autonomy, customs, and lust for life"; A76). These qualities align somewhat with traditional visions of the pre–Conquest, pre–Confederation "anciens Canadiens," but they equally apply to the culture of contemporary, post–Quiet Revolution Québec. While Rochon's use of the term "territoire," instead of "nation," avoids reinscribing nationalist ideology, it nonetheless operates a reterritorialization. The infernals, at home in their own territory, finally know the joy of an authentic existence.

After the consolidation of its culture, the former hells manifest the desire to explore outside their own boundaries, as well as to admit influences from outside to enter. Now that their own customs have been strengthened, Rel allows Fax, Lame and some of her friends to explore the passages that lead to the "mondes extérieurs" ("exterior worlds"; O37). Again, the conflation of historical periods occurs as this moment invokes not only the 1940s Refus Global movement, which called for the modernization and the cosmopolitanization of Québec, but also the Quiet Revolution led by Liberal leaders Daniel Johnson, Jean Lesage and Robert Bourassa from 1960 onward, and finally the confident Québec of today. Sherry Simon notes the changed attitude toward outside influences in the province today in relation to language: "Where the presence of English in a French text was once an indication of infeodation, it is now the sign of a ludic indifference to language purity" (*Translating* 132). While the New World Myth text may conflate historical time in its explicit or allegorical references, it also operates a necessary recuperation of the past in order to reveal that rather than the one official History disseminated by the colonial power, there are many histories. This detotalization of history often results in a focus on personal, autobiographical narratives rather than on the grand collective narrative. We see this at work in the focus upon the three main characters of *Les Chroniques infernales*, but most particularly in Lame's journey to recover her past life in order to make sense of her present reality.

As Sharon Taylor asserts of the Vrénalik cycle, Rochon's works operate social change through the utopian transformation of individual characters (vii). The eponymous title of *Les Chroniques infernales*' first volume suggests the central role that Lame's transformation will play in this work which, like Brossard's *L'Oiseau de feu*, combines *Bildunsgroman* with utopia. Although the various characters' contributions to social change remain interconnected, subsequent volumes focus more or less respectively on an individual's subject development: *Aboli* for Fax/Taïm Sutherland, *Secrets* for Rel, *Or* again for Lame, *Sorbier* for all three, although its title refers to Fax/Taïm. Each character's development involves the recovery of memory, a reappropriation of the past and history identified by Marie Vautier as a trait of the New World Myth. It is made eminently clear that in order to move beyond its horrors ("pouvoir aller au-delà de l'horreur"; O143), the individuals and the societies in the hells must confront the past.

Lame must face the problematic elements of her identity both in her previous life and here in the hells. This identity appears clearly as a colonial/postcolonial one, but also reflects the specificity of Québec. An "immigrante" (L84) to the hells, Lame is a person of "the Borderlands," defined by Gloria Anzaldúa as "wherever two or more cultures edge each other, where people of different races occupy the same territory" (Preface; n.p.). Neither living nor dead, no longer human, yet distinct from the hells' autochthonous peoples: "Elle n'était qu'une ex-damnée, une créature de l'ombre, des limbes, qui n'avait plus vraiment de patrie mais qui survivrait sans doute très mal chez les vivants, dont elle se distinguait trop par l'apparence" ("She was nothing more than an ex-damned, a creature of shadow, of limbo, who really had no homeland but who would survive quite poorly with the living, from whom she stood out by her appearance"; L40). In her previous life in Montréal, Lame's lack of direction led to suicide and to her sentence in the *enfers mous*:

> son attitude défaitiste devant la vie lui avait valu sa sentence. Elle aurait pu se mettre au service d'un idéal; elle s'était complu dans l'inaction, passant son temps à ressasser de vieilles injustices au lieu de tourner la page [L92].
>
> her defeatist attitude toward life earned her her sentence. She could have been working toward some ideal; she remained content in inaction, passing her time by fanning the flames of old injustices rather than turning the page.

Arriving in this new place, with only vague recollections from her past life, Lame literally loses her sense of direction, becoming *déboussolée* (disoriented), as she admits to Vaste: "Je ne savais pas qu'il y avait un nord, ici" ("I didn't know there was a north here"; L20). So great is her disorientation, suffering from "un trou de mémoire" ("a lapse in memory"; L20), she forgets her name. Rochon invokes here a major text of post–Quiet Revolution nationalist literature, Hubert Aquin's *Trou de mémoire* (1968) to invoke the loss of memory attendant upon the alienated, colonized subject.

Söderlind and Régine Robin (21) examine the phenomenon of the memory lapse in the postmodern/postcolonial Canadian novel. In her reading of Aquin's novel, Söderlind likens this loss of memory to Albert Memmi's notion of the *carence* (deficiency, lack), a sort of "décalage d'avec soi" ("out of sync with oneself"; Memmi 125 qtd. in Söderlind 91). Robin posits the notion of a "roman mémoriel," an entire subgenre:

> par lequel un individu, un groupe ou une société pense son passé en le modifiant, le déplaçant, le déformamt [sic], s'inventant des souvenirs, un passé glorieux, des généalogies, ou, au contraire, luttant pour l'exactitude factuelle, pour la restitution de l'événement ou sa résurrection [48].
>
> by which an individual, a group or a society rethinks its past by modifying it, displacing it, deforming it, inventing memories, a glorious past, genealogies, or, on the contrary, fighting for factual accuracy, for the restitution of an event or its resurrection.

Robin expresses concern over the first type of *roman mémoriel* seeing it as implicated in the constitution of exclusive, essential notions of identity like that of *québécité* ("Quebecness"; 111). Through Lame's recuperation of the memory lost at the moment of her death we shall see that Rochon's work aligns more closely with Robin's second type of *roman mémoriel* in its search for *a*, and not necessarily *the*, truth. Contrary to Söderlind's conclusions about other Canadian postcolonial novels, in which a quest for identity becomes a loss of self (200), the identity of Rochon's heroine takes shape more clearly as her process allows her to assume, in the French sense of *assumer*, that is, to own, to accept, her own individual and cultural past, warts and all. By the prologue of the last volume, Lame's multicultural identity asserts itself as affirmative and multiple, as opposed to being presented as a deficiency, a *carence*, the void of the *trou de mémoire*: "métisse de Français, d'Anglais et d'Amérindien" ("mixed-blood of French, English and Native American"; Soxix). She comes to recognize herself as the person Rel invokes, "celle que tu dois être" ("the person you are meant to be"; Or59), thus resolving the "décalage d'avec soi."

As she transcends the state of alienation, the very goal of utopia for Karl Mannheim and Ernst Bloch (Levitas 6, 91), Lame understands the significance of the new name she chose for herself in hell. *Lame*, a word play on both "the soul" (*l'âme* in French) as well as "Blade" (the *lame* of a razor or a knife), identifies her essence not only as a larva in hell but also in her previous life in Montréal as "un tas de graisse avec une lame de rasoir à l'intérieur" ("a heap of fat with a razor blade inside"; Or164). Interestingly, this description resonates with the words of Rochon's Buddhist "master" (So416), Chögyam Trungpa Rinpoche, in his commentary on the *Bardo Thödol*, or the *Tibetan Book of the Dead*, a clear influence on Rochon's conception of the hells as sites of progress and redemption prior to return into the cycle of life and matter. One of the most influential, although also most unorthodox, emissaries of Tibetan Buddhism in the West, Trungpa refers to the teachings of Fan Chen:

> The spirit is the same as the body and the body is the same as the spirit. Therefore, when the body exists, the spirit exists, and when the body declines, the spirit is destroyed.... The spirit to the concrete stuff is like sharpness in the knife, and the body to the function is like the knife to the sharpness. The name of sharpness is not knife and the name of the knife is not sharpness. However, without sharpness, there will be no knife, and without knife, there will be no sharpness [qtd. in Trungpa 34].

In her self-analysis, and this choice of terms is not fortuitous because Trungpa couched Buddhist practice in the language of psychoanalysis in order to bring a secular practice to the West (Midal 99–100), Lame reconciles the inherent paradox of herself. While her physical body appears soft and mushy, her critical spirit lies unused inside until now. In the hells, as she uses her critical spirit, her exterior form also loses its abject softness, as she assumes a body that is outwardly lean and beautiful (Or171).

At a personal level, Lame must recover the events of her own personal life, work which begins in *Ouverture* during a stay in the now abandoned ruins of Har's capital city of Arxann (O195–208). While Lame admits her suicide in *Secrets* (205), the simple confession proves inadequate to the work of recovery necessary: "[l]a relation de Lame à son passé était pleine de trous, de souvenirs à l'accès interdit, de conflits non résolus" ("Lame's relationship to her past was full of holes, of memories whose access was forbidden, of unresolved conflicts"; Or33). Spanning several hundred years of hell time, crossing numerous worlds of the living and the dead, collected in five volumes equalling some 1600 pages published over five years, Lame's personal process of coming to terms with the past occurs over time and space, in both the fictional world of the character and the real world of the reader. This progress made (her departure from the *enfers mous* in *Lame*), lost (her return to the *enfers mous* in *Ouverture*), and regained, so that in *Sorbier* Lame can be described as fully "réhabilitée" (So270), reflects the open-ended utopia's use of a spiral form of development. While numerous examples could be drawn from the series' six volumes, I will focus my discussion upon one pivotal episode, Lame's apparent "fall from grace" (So171). This fall reveals not only the open-ended nature of Rochon's utopian vision in the idea that perfection is never attained, it also demonstrates the work's engagement with a critique of colonial/postcolonial relationships prevalent in the "real" world of the reader.

After Rel's revelations of his life story to representatives of the various worlds now functioning as hells in *Secrets*, Lame returns to her home in the *anciens enfers* traveling through the old *enfers mous*, the site of her initial condemnation. Just before her capture and colonization by the ants, Lame feels a premonitory anxiety as "trop de souvenirs, réprimés, voulaient soudain s'emparer d'elle" ("too many repressed memories suddenly wanted to take her over"; Or63) This unresolved past material surges forth in both literal and imaginary fashion as she submits to the ants' accusations and allows herself to be transformed into a larva in order to make atonement. In this state, Lame stages hearings reminiscent of those carried out by the Truth and Reconciliation Commissions in Chile (est. 1991) and South Africa (1995–2001) (Wilson 34, 13). Like those hearings, Lame's "Convocation" represents a "concerted attempt to come to terms with massive social disruption in the past so that there may be greater harmony in the future" (Daye 5).[17]

Although later revealed as part of a plot against Rel, this situation arises ostensibly because Lame has not fully atoned for her thoughtless destruction of ants as a child in Montréal. The view that killing insects represents a wrong act pertains, of course, to one of the five precepts of Buddhism, that no life shall be destroyed (Midal 160). This attitude contrasts with the accepted cruelties to "lesser" lifeforms carried out by Westerners on a daily basis, from the slaughter of animals we eat, to the "pests"—like ants and cockroaches—we systematically destroy, to the microbes we kill with our antibacterial soaps. It also represents, however, a larger pattern of behavior, that of the failure to respect all life, a tendancy that underpins imperialism. While she accepts personal responsibility, Lame also blames the society in which she was raised. Her larval state prevents her from moving (or even seeing the external world), but she retains the power of her imagination, which she uses now to enact a trial of her ancestors and their society in order to understand their role in her suicide. This episode which spans some three chapters of *Or* (83–94, 109–16, 123–32) stages a scathing condemnation of contemporary Western society, targeting in particular Canada/Québec and the city of Montréal, similar also to Doris Lessing's Trial of the White Race in the first of the Canopus in Argos Archives novels, *Shikasta* (1979).

Lame's "Convocation" seeks justice and not revenge. The legitimacy of the process must therefore be established. While she first imagines all of her ancestors standing naked before her, she quickly realizes that: "la justice ne s'administrait pas dans la colère. Il n'était pas question pour elle de se venger, même en imagination, mais de comprendre un mécanisme détraqué, celui qui lui avait fait tuer des fourmis comme passe-temps dans son jeune âge" ("justice was not administered in anger. There was no question that she should seek revenge, even in her imagination, but to understand the disorderly mechanism that allowed her to kill ants as a passtime while a child"; Or188). She then mentally dresses the vast array of individuals coming from various historical periods and ethnic groups before her. Her first attempt to confront them, however, ends in failure. While she asserts that "[j]e ne suis pas fière du pays où je suis née.... Je suis pourtant une représentante de ce que vous avez édifié. De mon temps, beaucoup de gens mettaient fin à leurs jours" ("I am not proud of the land where I was born. I am nonetheless a representative of what you made. In my time, many people put an end to their days"; Or89–90). While her case is individual, she links her fate to the collective. She accuses this society, coded as Quiet Revolution-era Québec society (O208), of creating conditions that led not only to her own suicide, but to that of many other young people.

Indeed, positive identification of Lame's former home as the city of Montréal occurs in *Or* (113). Lame describes Québec's most populous and most diverse city as "[c]e gros camp d'immigrants en région froide, vieux de quelques siècles à peine, qui n'avait pas envie de le quitter pour rentrer au pays ancestral" ("in a cold region only a few hundred years old, this camp of immigrants who didn't want to leave to return to their ancestral homeland"; Or165). Referred to as "la cité au temps figé" ("the city fixed in time"; Or2), a statement often applied to pre–Quiet Revolution Québec, Montréal appears as a closed, suffocating space of insular horror. Through Lame's transformation into a larva, a living ant colony, she becomes a synecdoche of Montreal and its inhabitants, the part standing in for the whole: "Je suis devenue Montréal pour les fourmis" ("I have become Montreal for the ants"; Or121).

A major breakthrough occurs as Lame remembers the precise location of her suicide at a monument erected on the site of the Patriots' execution after the 1837–38 uprising, which stands in Montréal at the Place des Patriotes, on Notre-Dame Street. This location explicitly ties Lame's individual destiny and malaise to that of the French Canadian/Québécois by invoking — and reinterpreting — the icons of the past. In this section, Rochon's SFQ saga clearly resembles Vautier's New World Myth novels, "historiographic metafictions" which reveal a "didactic urge ... to retell major historical events in a new light" (202). Lame rereads the story of the Patriots, typically viewed as glorious martyrs to the cause of nationalism, and compares their deaths to her own:

> sa mort honteuse et sans gloire avait par hasard eu lieu là où des hommes illustres, honorés à juste titre, avaient payé de leur vie leur amour de la liberté — d'une liberté proclamée sur des terres volées, liberté d'une faction au détriment des autres, mais liberté que tout le monde chante, comme l'amour [Or125].

> her shameful death, without glory, occurred by chance there where illustrious men, rightfully honored, had paid with their life for their love of liberty, a liberty proclaimed upon stolen lands, the freedom of one faction gained at the expense of others, but a liberty sung about by everyone, like love.

Lame's analysis reveals the contradictions inherent in a colonial society founded upon the Enlightenment principles of freedom, equality, and democracy, a society in which one group's freedom and prosperity occurs at the expense of another's. And yet, she rails to the imaginary ancestors assembled in her abdominal cavity, the system victimized as many of the colonists as it did the indigenous peoples. Transformed into pirates by the colonial propaganda machine, they, too, are victims:

> Ce n'était pas nécessaire, leur dit-elle, pour vous d'Europe, de venir sur ce continent-ci. On vous a vendu de la propagande et vous l'avez avalée. On vous a forcés à croire à des rêves d'expansion et de progrès; vous avez saccagé un continent. Votre génie de bâtisseurs ne m'impressionne pas. Vous auriez mieux fait de ne rien défricher [Or126].

> It wasn't necessary, she told them, for you Europeans to come here to this continent. You were sold propaganda and you swallowed it whole. You were forced to believe in dreams of expansion and progress; you pillaged a continent. Your genius as builders doesn't impress me. You would have done better to clear none of it.

In her anger, Lame questions all the founding myths of Québec and the nationalist cause. She not only reinterprets the Patriots' death for freedom as one tainted by the larger factionalism and colonialism within which it was implicated, she returns to the founding moment of the Conquest — the outcome of the European Seven Years' War (known in the U.S. as the French and Indian War)—as she asserts: "[m]a bataille des plaines d'Abraham s'est déroulée sous les roues d'un camion lancé à toute vitesse" ("my Battle of the Plains of Abraham played out under the wheels of a truck careening at top speed"; Or127). She carries within herself centuries of ancestral anger, a necessary result for a people whose identity was based more on its defeat than on its success, "[l]a force de votre rage ... s'est transmise jusqu'à moi" ("the force of your rage was transmitted down to me"; Or127). This rage, or rather, her suffocation of it through the creation of a dissembling, passive personality, ultimately led to her suicide. She is a product of her ancestors. They cannot renounce her. The moment of her death already existed with Wolfe's defeat of Montcalm on September 13, 1759. Finally, she cries: "[c]ombien de temps croyez-vous qu'il va durer, votre pays construit dans la violence?... L'Amérique aurait dû rester aux Indiens et tout ce déploiement n'a servi qu'à la détruire" ("how long do you think it will last, your country built on violence? America should have been left to the Indians and all this spectacle has done nothing but destroy her"; Or127).

Lame comes to terms with the past by understanding her personal oppression and alienation and by confronting her ancestors for their role in this and other wrongs that have been done in the name of the group, a group whose unity and ethnic uniformity are ultimately fictions. For during the invocation of her ancestors in the imaginary courtroom, she points out their ethnic diversity: "Il y avait des Normands, des Bretons, des Charentais, des Irlandais, des Écossais, des Montagnais, des Anglais et bien d'autres, rangés par clans qui se détestaient mutellement" ("there were Normans, Bretons, people from the Charente, Irish, Scotch, Montagnais, English and many others all grouped into clans who mutually detested one another"; Or126). She may disappoint them because she is "si métisse, si bâtarde" ("so half-breed, so bastardized"; Or127), but she represents the reality. The idea of the *Québécois pure laine* is itself a myth, as Monique LaRue asserts in her definition of "citoyen de «vieil établissement» ... quelqu'un dont les parents, les grands-parents et la plupart des ancêtres, quoique assurément pas tous, descendent des Français" ("citizen of 'old establishment' someone whose parents, grandparents and the majority of their ancestors, but surely not all of them, descend from the French"; 7).

Having sought the truth and confronted her ancestors for their part in the horrors of colonization, in order to progress further, her anger must be followed with something constructive. In the imaginary internal space of her abdominal cavity, now vastly enlarged by the ants, Lame begins to visualize herself helping the damned on their way to the *enfers mous*, harboring them inside her, caring for them and showing them the way to resistance, bringing out "leur dignité naturelle" ("their natural dignity"; Or163), a principle common to both the Roman Catholic heritage of Québec, as well as to Rochon's

Shambhalan Buddhism (Midal 226). Realizing what she had wanted when she was alive in Montréal, she acts in a way that "reflétaient le besoin qu'elle avait eu qu'on l'accepte comme elle était" ("reflected the need she had to be accepted for who she was"; Or148).

Ultimately, Lame must disconnect her hate from a specific object, reconciling with her community. Her new outlook must separate individuals from their actions and, while maintaining a sense of personal responsibility, it must also consider the environment around those she judges: "ce qui la mettait hors d'elle, c'était certains de leurs actes, certaines de leurs opinions.... Il était réducteur de ne voir en eux que les tueurs, les fanatiques religieux, les pillards loyaux" ("what set her off were particular acts they had done, particular opinions; it was reductionist to only see the killers, religious fanatics, the loyal robbers in them"; Or207). Able to look again from a new perspective, a perspective she has gained from living in symbiosis with the ants, Lame achieves "une nouvelle vision du monde" in which "[l]a richesse n'étaient plus étouffement, mais possibilité" ("a new vision of the world" in which "wealth was no longer suffocation, but possibility"; Or65). "Lame avait évolué" ("Lame had evolved"; Or206), and only now through this progress, can she refer to Montréal as "ma ville natale bien-aimée" ("the beloved city of my birth"; Or237).

In order to develop further, Lame cannot just renounce the past; she must recuperate and reappropriate it, formulating her own New World Myth in opposition to that sold to her by the ideology of her homeland. No longer associated with the dystopian space of an oppressive Montréal, she re-imagines her interior space as "forêts préhistoriques" peopled with "une faune légendaire de salamandres, d'araignées et de licornes" ("prehistoric forests" "legendary fauna like salamanders, spiders and unicorns;" Or205). This chivalric space recalls the peaceful harmony of late fifteenth-century tapestries, *The Lady and the Unicorn*, a work pre-dating her ancestors' first departure from France, invoking a sort of "once upon a time," distant, legendary past prior to the Fall of the colonial era of the seventeenth and eighteenth centuries. A symbol of purity, the unicorn also represents a utopian space in Vonarburg's *Tyranaël* saga (to be discussed shortly). Indeed, Lame's body now becomes a utopian site, a new world, as she explicitly states:

> Chaque jour de nouveaux ancêtres s'ajoutaient aux anciens, comme s'ils avaient découvert un curieux pays où immigrer, un Nouveau Monde.... Lame se sentait bien davantage la propriété des prédécesseurs que la terre d'Amérique ne l'avait jamais été [Or205].
>
> Each day new ancestors joined the old, as if they had discovered a curious land to immigrate to, a New World.... Lame felt herself to be the property of her predecessors more than the land of America had ever been.

After her rescue from this state, her enlarged abdomen severed from her body remains with the ants; they create in it "une société libérée d'elle-même, utopique à force de s'accepter" ("a society freed from itself, utopian by nature of its self-acceptance"; Or221).

Above all Rochon's postcolonial utopia seeks to rewrite the very myths it puts into play and invokes. Lame's own New World Myth specifically addresses not only the situation of French Canada, but also her personal afterlife as it appears in the series. In *Ouverture* the rapid and unquestioning modernization of the Quiet Revolution is reinterpreted as the "Enfers de plastique," the plastic hells in which everyone (except Lame) takes great pleasure in throwing out the old in order to bring in the new, ugly plastic of modernity (O195-214). Other cultural references include Jacques Brossard's novel, *Le Sang du souvenir* ("The Blood of Memory"; 1976; Or 238) — the title itself indicative of the importance of memory —, and the French-Canadian classic *Maria Chapdelaine* (1916). Rochon mimics the latter's description of Québec as a land where nothing ever changes: "Au pays du Québec, rien n'a changé" ("In the land of Québec, nothing has changed"; Or236). The fact that the novel was written by the Frenchman Louis Hémon perhaps indicates the "colonized" nature of the ideology it propagates. At one point, the mysterious "judges of destiny" seek to manipulate Lame precisely by invoking her nostalgia for and sense of patriotism toward her former home. When they try to force her to a quick decision, saying: "Oui ou non?," Lame thinks, "[d]iscours référendaire" ("Yes or no?... A referendum discourse"; Or239).

Through Lame's recuperation of the past Rochon engages directly with the language of the myth of the new world and its role in colonial ideology. Her critique works to overturn the received history, including the fundamental notion of the Americas as a "new" world, as Lame points out the fallacy behind that assertion. "On appelle mon continent le Nouveau Monde" ("they call my continent the New World"); her continent, its mountains and rivers, she asserts, is really old, geologically old (So229). At the same time, a lingering ambivalence to the fact of colonization remains. The redesign of the former hells reflects elements of the New World Myth. It, too, figures a very specific colony, that of Québec. Ultimately, Rochon undoes, only to rewrite the New World Myth.

Rochon's project in *Les Chroniques infernales* appropriates not only Québec-specific myths; its intertextual relationships to several major works of the European canon further support its reading as the type of New World Myth conceived by Vautier. While I am not prepared to offer a detailed comparison here, Rochon's work alludes to not only Dante's trilogy, *The Divine Comedy* (1308-21), but also Milton's *Paradise Lost* (1667) and Shakespeare's *The Tempest* (1611). In Rochon's appropriation and reworking of the central Western myth of Lucifer/Satan, Rel plays the central role of the "ange déchu" ("fallen angel"; S104). Ultimately reversing all poles in her postcolonial rewriting of *Paradise Lost*, Rochon places the fallen angel, the prince of Hell, in charge of heaven at the series' conclusion in *Sorbier*. Believing him to be near death, Rel's friends bring him to the home of his previous life, the paradise of Anid. In a confrontation between Rel and his former mentor, the shapeshifter, Vayinn — "un vieillard à barbe blanchie" ("an old man with a white beard"; So384) — the two assume respectively the roles of Lucifer and Yahweh. The narrator describes their confrontation as "une de ces étonnantes scènes de la littérature du XIXe siècle, Hugo ou Baudelaire, où Satan affronte Dieu" ("one of those astonishing scenes in nineteenth-century literature, in Hugo or Baudelaire, where Satan confronts God"; So386). The scene also resonates with the unresolved conclusion of Brossard's *L'Oiseau de feu* as a confrontation between Lokhfer and Syrius. After Rel prevails and Vayinn's house is revealed to be a sort of Bluebeard's castle with emprisoned victims and skeletons in the closet (again reminiscent of Lokhfer's laboratories whose human guinea pigs Adakhan liberates), "Un trou s'ouvrit sous les pieds de Vayinn, qui tomba dans le vide" ("A hole opened under Vayinn's feet and he fell into the void"; So387). Rel takes over to fulfill his destiny as it was predicted in an anterior life: "Libérer les enfers.... Vous êtes fait pour le mal qui se transmute en bien" ("To liberate the hells.... You are made for the evil that is transformed into good"; S19). For all of the SFQ sagas examined here, Shakespeare's *Tempest* serves as a prototype of a New World Myth. The figure of Caliban has been central to a number of postcolonial theorists' work including Roberto Fernández Retamar's early study of American culture, *Caliban and Other Essays* (1974), and Max Dorsinville's comparative analysis of Québécois and Caribbean literatures, *Caliban Without Prospero* (1974). As in the bard's play, the SFQ saga's "new worlds" are found by shipwrecked castaways, including the crew that crash-lands on Virginia in Vonarburg's *Tyranaël* and the crew of the Aigle d'Or in *L'Oiseau de Feu* by Brossard, who think they are on the planet of their destination but may not be. Rochon appropriates this canonical European myth and rewrites it with Rel as Prospero.

Perhaps Rochon's most remarkable move, though, is her rewriting of her *own* myth as she connects the *Chroniques infernales* to the *Cycle de Vrénalik* as Taïm Sutherland fully assumes his past. The series' final volume *Sorbier* refers to his totemic tree, the mountain ash or rowan. This metaleptic connection to her earlier SFQ saga violate the boundaries of the text, effectuating the type of open-ending typical of the contemporary utopia as it is described by Suvin, Moylan, Baccolini, and others. In this volume, Taïm reevaluates his actions as the Asven people's liberator, reinterprets the meaning of the curse and the role of the statue of the Ocean-god Haztlén. As he realizes that Rel is Haztlén, that the inhabitants of the Archipelago developed the legend of their Ocean god from the actual visit of Rel to the Archipelago as an adolescent, Taïm also realizes that the statue's destruction was not, after all, the key to Asven liberation. Instead, they should have loved and cared for it. With further news that the utopian civilization of Catadial has fallen victim to the dystopian forces outside it, Taïm embraces the principle of change as the only eternal force. With this resolution, Rochon herself appears to be reevaluating the problematic elements of the conclusion to *L'Espace du diamant* discussed above.

While the series' apparently apocalyptic vision brings it back to the millenarian aspects in Western utopian thought, outlined by Frank and Fritzie Manuel, it also reflects Rochon's Buddhist philosophy.[18] Apocalypse and catastrophe are major themes in Québécois and Canadian literature, both in the so-called mainstream and in the popular genres (Atwood *Survival*; Weiss "Canadian"). The connection between a cleansing, *tabula rasa* apocalypse and the foundation of a new world utopia for which it clears the way recurs in many texts, including Brossard's *L'Oiseau de feu* (AE17–19). While Brossard graphically stages the destruction of Manokhsor and the Centrale, Rochon denies such a spectacle to her readers. Instead, she closes peaceably, as Rel and Lame join the Asven in their new homeland, and the green door between the worlds, which had been sealed shut, reopens to allow "une oscillation," a back and forth movement to occur. Among the images she paints is that of a boat "arrivé de l'autre côté" ("arrived from the other shore"; So406).

Similar images conclude Vonarburg's *Tyranaël*, as the strange blue sea of energy that engulfs a large part of the planet for part of the year becomes a doorway between the parallel worlds of Virginia and Atyrkelsaō, to which Tyranaël's indigenous people, the Ranao, fled when premonitory dreams told them of the Terrans imminent arrival. The New World Myths staged in these works by a French immigrant to Québec (Vonarburg) and a Québécoise whose background includes French, English and Scotch ancestry (Rochon) seek precisely a sort of redemption and reconciliation for the violence inherent in the Old World myth, in which the New World appears as a virgin land for the foundation of utopia (by whatever means necessary). In their works, old worlds and new collide with catastrophic, apocalyptic results. However, understanding the mythic — as in fictional — nature of the Old World myth, these New World Myths imagine utopia not as a static, perfect society established from outside, but rather as an ongoing, processual movement of constant vigilance and development, including necessary setbacks and obstacles to overcome. This process allows for the narrative development of the epic saga that Suvin associates with SF.

Dreams of a New World: Élisabeth Vonarburg's *Tyranaël*

Élisabeth Vonarburg's two pentalogies, *Tyranaël* (1996–97) and *Reine de Mémoire* (2005–07), do not stage utopias or dystopias in the more obvious and structured ways found in the works by Brossard and Rochon discussed above. Vonarburg's engagement with utopian discourse remains undeniable in her first two novels *The Silent City* and *In the Mother's Land*, as Guy Bouchard, Sharon Taylor, Lorie Sauble-Otto and Janice M. Bogstad have observed. However, those early, strongly feminist works, set in an alternative future Europe, did not interrogate colonialist ideology in any overt fashion. In contrast, her more recent SFQ sagas participate clearly in the creation of New World Myths infused with a postcolonial sensibility. Like Vonarburg's earlier work, these multi-volume novels depict multiple imaginary spaces upon which the author projects a range of utopian and dystopian tropes. Most overtly, the not-so-virgin planet renamed Virginia by its Terran colonists in *Tyranaël* literally explores the tropes of colonization and the creation of New World Myths by its settlers. Its depiction of the indigenous Rani society also adheres to Suvin's definition of utopia as "a quasi-human community where sociopolitical institutions, norms and individual relationships are organized according to a more perfect principle than the author's community" (Suvin, "Definining" 132). That the Ranao, too, must emigrate to a new world allows for a duplication of the New World Myth and, ultimately, for colonizer and colonized to meet and exchange. Similarly, Vonarburg's recent cycle *Reine de Mémoire* multiplies and diffracts utopian tropes across European, American and Eastern societies within an "alternative historical hypothesis" (Suvin, "Definining" 132) depicting the era of exploration and colonization from about 1500 to 1800.

Of the three writers examined here, Vonarburg has the largest body of criticism devoted to her work, due in part to the interest by feminist scholars in her earlier novels which were translated into English and published in American mass market paperback editions, *The Silent City*, *In the Mother's Land*, and *Reluctant Voyagers*. At least three doctoral dissertations have devoted significant analyses to these novels. Janice Bogstad's pioneering thesis reads these novels with other feminist dystopias, as well as Samuel R. Delany's *Triton* as depicting a "heterotopian culture" (110), to examine the role of gender in identity formation. More recently, Lorie Sauble-Otto analyzes Vonarburg's work within the context of Anglo-American and French science fiction by women, without addressing the issue of utopia/dystopia. Sharon Taylor explores the role of language and gender in identity formation, seeing a transformation from a dystopian situation of the individual within society to a more eutopian state of development. Jenny Wolmark, for her part, reads *The Silent City* for its depiction of the cyborg (134–38).

In Québec as well, academics Guy Bouchard, Sylvie Bérard and Sophie Beaulé discuss utopian aspects of Vonarburg's novels. Bouchard asserts that *In the Mother's Land* "peut être considéré comme la quintessence des utopies féministes contemporaines" ("can be considered as the quintessence of contemporary feminist utopias"; "Vonarburg" 202). Vonarburg, on the other hand, defends herself against the apparent sin of having written a utopia, maintaining that "*Chroniques* n'est pas une utopie" ("*Mother's Land* is not a utopia") and that *Silence* in its critique of the male utopia "expose la dystopie totalitaire fondamentale à toute utopie classique" ("exposes the totalitarian dystopia fundamental to any classic utopia"; Bérard, "Dialogue" 100–01). These words reveal her desire to problematize the classic utopia. Proof of Vonarburg's thorough knowledge of the Anglo-American canon of utopian/dystopian feminist science fiction appears in her analytical essay, "L'Utopie ambiguë, érotisme et pouvoir dans quelques utopies féminines récentes" ("The ambiguous utopia, erotism and power in some recent feminine utopias," 1999), which engages directly Le Guin's concept of the "ambiguous utopia," a paradigmatic text for Suvin's open-ended utopia.

The length of Vonarburg's five-volume novel of off-world colonization, like that of Brossard's SFQ saga, allows her to explore the full range of utopian tropes from the perspective of both colonizer and colonized. The intercultural relationships between the various groups, as has been suggested in chapter two above, become so complex that it is difficult to differentiate the colonizer from the colonized. While it is less clearly a utopia/dystopia, *Tyranaël* distinctly exploits the trope of the New World Myth, erects a critique of colonialism as dystopian in nature, and ultimately proposes an ideology of acceptance and exchange within a pluralistic society. Rather than undertake a systematic analysis of the entire saga, I will focus on three of its utopian aspects: 1) the Rani dreamers as an example of Ernst Bloch's *Vor-Schein*; 2) Rani society as a "better" model than existing human society (in actuality or on the fictional future Earth/Virginia); 3) the interplay of utopian hope and dystopian power on Virginia. I will conclude this chapter with a brief discussion of how Vonarburg develops a Vautier-style New World Myth in her very recent SFQ saga, *Reine de Mémoire*.

One of the key concepts articulated by utopian philosopher Ernst Bloch is the idea of *Vor-Schein*. According to Jack Zipes's description of this "anticipatory illumination," it is a thought process, which Bloch likens to daydreaming, that becomes the source for envisioning the type of individual and collective agency necessary for a utopian society to develop. It represents "a type of consciousness, formed by the impulse of hope, in which inklings of what [humans] might become manifest themselves. For the individual, the not-yet-conscious is the psychical representation of what has not-yet-become in our time and its world" (Zipes xxxii). Just such a thought process, a sort of anticipatory dreaming, appears in the first volume of the *Tyranaël* saga. Its title, *Dreams of the Sea*, refers to the possibly premonitory dreams visited on gifted members of the indigenous Ranao of the planet Tyranaël, which Terran colonists will call Virginia. For Eïlai Liannon Klaïdaru, the first to dream of "the Strangers" (DS156),[19] her anticipatory illumination appears not utopian, but rather tragic. Like Bloch's concept, however, it does reveal the potential for revolutionary change: "as if everyone's lives had not been shattered because of me, as if the course of my own life had not been changed forever" (DS84). For her dreams, eventually joined by those of other Ranao, suggest the arrival of another group on Tyranaël.

Interpreted as signs of a millenarian catastrophe, the Dreams nonetheless allow the Ranao to act, to take control of their destiny. Rather than become passive victims to a massive influx of Strangers into their homeland (as had been the case of numerous colonizations in the history of the reader's/author's Earth), the Ranao use the information from the *Vor-Schein* to create a new destiny for themselves. Radical change occurs as they move onto the parallel world of Atyrkelsaō. Because of the Dream, not only do they avoid the inevitable conflict involved in the immigration of one group onto a territory already inhabited by another, they also develop their own New World experience in a land that mirrors their own. Through them, too, Vonarburg depicts a model of a better, eutopian society as the Ranao employ strategies to deal with conflict between groups which appear much more successful than those adopted by humans on Earth, Terrans on Virginia, and Virginians on Virginia.

Although Vonarburg eventually reveals the violence upon which the Ranao's presently peaceful and tolerant society was constructed, a utopian sensibility informs their history as a gradual evolution toward a better model. However, as Sophie Beaulé points out, the fact that the Ekelli, an extraterrestrial race that kept its presence on the planet secret, manipulated the Ranao in order to damper the violence of historical conflicts somewhat undermines the utopian thrust of the narrative (E-mail to the author 10 June 2008). For the most part, though, Vonarburg's SFQ saga tends to idealize Tyranaël's indigenous Ranao, and their culture appears "more perfect" than our own in its collective values (AR223), its ethics of choice and responsibility (AR193–281), its harmonious acceptance of the cycle of birth and death (AR4, 6, 19–20, 62–63), its respect for and stewardship of the natural world (AR21–22), and its acceptance of the multiplicity of being (AR136, 129–31, 180–81, 275). While it flirts with plastic shamanism[20] in its depiction of the utopian group of "Les Enfants d'Iptit" ("The Children of Iptit," a Kokopelli-like Rani trickster figure) which eventually develops on both Virginia and Atyrkelsaō, it also presents the Ranao with warts and all. Indeed, they have undergone patterns of imperialism and colonization similar to those on Earth and Rani history recalls that of India. There are racists (AR138), sexists (AR155, 171), outsiders and insiders among the Ranao. Ultimately, *L'Autre rivage* asserts the stagnance in the perfection of utopia (AR120–21).

Although their experience mirrors that of the Terrans (some of whom also see their own colonization of Virginia as a new start, abandoning a dying Earth to its fate), the Ranao are better equipped to deal with the arrival of the Strangers and less likely to transport their dystopian baggage with them as they move to a parallel world. So, although two factions evolve after their arrival on Atyrkelsaŏ— the *darnao* who propose adapting to the new world in a more radical fashion, and the *dânao*, who wish to duplicate the old in the new site (AR23, 120)— existing social structures allow the two groups to dialogue and negotiate solutions to conflict. Even their language appears more adequate to deal with and imagine change and contingency, as it has a particular verbal mode, "le mode han'maï, pour pouvoir parler des possibles" ("the han-maï mode, to be able to talk about the possible"; AR136), not available to the Virginians. Standing in metonymically for the collective of her people, Eïlai must overcome the alienation that occurs with First Encounter and deal with the reality of the situation: "it was not over, it was all just beginning. A new phase of history for my people, and for me...." (DS18). They will leave this planet for another, they will use the potentially catastrophic moment as a means of rebirth: "There is so much to do over there, everything can start again: a new life, a redemptive adventure" (DS268). For the Ranao, then, Encounter becomes a means of renewal as they start over on Atyrkelsaŏ, a move only possible because of the science-fictional trope of the parallel world. Similar dreams of a new start inform the development of a new Terran-based colonial society on the Ranao's former home.

In *Dreams of the Sea* members of the first colony of Terrans shipwrecked on what appears to be an uninhabited planet — although ruins from a past habitation remain — in the Alpha star system express the utopian impulse behind their project. Across this and the next two volumes, the text makes clear, though, that their inability to leave old ideologies behind condemns the self-named Virginians to repeat the mistakes of their ancestors on Earth, the home planet, which is ultimately destroyed. (A handful of survivors, though, perpetuate that branch of humanity on the asteroid Lagrange.) Vonarburg openly stages the type of new utopia described by Suvin as "something to be achieved by constant self-critical watchfulness against the temptation of the arrested moment" ("SF Novel" 83), allegorizing this watchfulness in the trope of an extrasensory perception that a mutation to the human genome develops in the descendants of the planet's colonists.

"How was it for the first colonists, the volunteers, seeing the lake after the long voyage? It must have seemed like the Promised Land" (DS269). The utopian nature of the first colonists' project is made evident through the perspective of Joris, a member of the first expedition stranded on Virginia after the effects of the planet's mysterious Sea of energy caused their space craft to crash, and thus forced them to settle there. When a fellow crew member Stoneheim describes how the Ranao had developed the land around that same lake, he expresses the hope that the settlers can reproduce what he perceives as the native's garden paradise. Joris reacts: "She did not expect him to entertain that kind of utopian fantasy" (DS43).

Many Virginians view the native Ancients' (as they call the Ranao) life on Tyranaël through an idealized myth of natives living in harmony with the land. David Barth knows that this and their own fantasies of creating a similar paradise are illusions, as he reflects on the fact that most of the indigenous fauna avoid contact with the new human arrivals. He likens this phenomenon to "[t]he fate of Adam driven from Paradise" (DS52), explicitly connecting this new world to Eden, considered the ur-utopian narrative by Frank and Fritzie Manuel (33). While the first colonists have dreams of creating a utopia (DS82), the reality principle of metropolitan interests from the colony soon rears its ugly head. Instead, Virginians repeat the errors made on Earth as they develop an authoritarian state, repress mutants, then non-mutant descendants of latecomer Terrans.

The impossibility of completely starting over appears in the irony of the settlers' choice of name for the colony. While Virginia invokes the notion of a virgin land, and the name ostensibly honors the first child born on the planet, past history soils this hopeful purity as it also references its original colonial application. Named after the "Virgin" queen Elizabeth I, a major player in the imperial conquest of the so-called New World of the Americas, the first Virginia built its wealth upon the backs of slaves, establishing a hierarchical society based on power and difference perfectly worthy of its European models. With this baggage, how could the new Virginia be anything but dystopian? As with the other works dealt with in this chapter, the discussion of alienation in chapter two reveals the dystopian nature of the societies depicted in the various volumes of Tyranaël: Earth has become such a dystopia that Terran society destroys itself and humans must leave the planet to survive; on Virginia, in its early days, Terrans sought to exploit and dominate the new colony; on an independent Virginia, the totalitarian régime of the Grays mirrors a classic *1984*-style dystopia of surveillance and control. At the same time, however, Vonarburg's SFQ saga maintains a utopian horizon, aligning itself more with the critical dystopia outlined by Moylan and Baccolini than with the straightforward, cautionary anti-utopia, which denounces the very notion of utopia.

The title of the second *Tyranaël* novel, *A Game of Perfection*, suggests the type of spiral development identified with the open-ended utopia, a development acted out in a game integral to and reflective of the values of the mysteriously vanished indigenous Rani culture. Somewhat like the Milton Bradley board game, The Game of Life, players assume various roles and professions found in the society: "The object of the game also seems simple enough. You try to finish first after having placed all your figurines on the map as you play each of the twenty-eight [traditional Rani] trades. You are then 'perfect'" (GP335). The game fascinates the central human character Simon Rossem as he likens it to "[t]he game of his own *lives*" (GP336). Like the Buddhist system seen in Rochon's work, rather than follow a linear route, in Vonarburg's

SFQ saga life represents a series of loops, repeated until perfection is achieved.[21] Each group featured in the text seems to raise a utopian hope for improvement of life for all, a hope that is temporarily shattered by dystopian power rising from an opposing sector (or even from within the utopian group), followed by a stage of further progress.

Resistance by the mutant children to their treatment as freaks leads to the formation of a new group based not upon the genetic relationship of the family (GP87, 91), but rather on self-acceptance and acceptance of difference. In the utopian construction of the communal living arrangements established by the underground resistance networks on Virginia, Vonarburg dismantles the legitimacy of the notion of a genetically based, ethnic community. In this utopian community, its members' similarities are not visible; "it's not stamped on their faces" (GP223). Indeed, the community or family based on genetic relationships appears heavily critiqued in this novel, as many of the mutant children come from abusive homes. Unfortunately, the father-figure of the group, the exceptionally long-lived mutant Simon, as he poses as a sympathetic "normal" for the children he rescues, perpetuates patterns of dishonesty and manipulation (GP77).

While some of the group's young mutant protagonists cherish a utopian dream of educating nonmutants to live with and accept them, others scorn this attitude as "complètement utopique" ("completely utopian"; JP237), using the pejorative sense that the term has come to take as an unrealistic fantasy reflected clearly in Howard Scott's translation of this exclamation as "pure fantasy" (GP253). The more cynical, and therefore ostensibly more realist, members of the mutant resistance group find alternate means to survive and become prone to abuse their special powers. The success of the Referendum for Virginian independence from Earth results, in part, from their infiltration of the "Union for Virginian Independence" (GP158) and their subtle manipulation of voter turn out (GP241). This potential for corruption not only makes clear the need for vigilance, it also propels the series forward as it reveals that postcolonial Virginia is *not* the utopia they had desired.

While the second volume makes clear that Earth's historical cycle of dominance and oppression has been imbedded in Virginia as well (see the story of Mama Dounya, GP89), the swing toward dystopia grows more evident. Indeed, subsequent generations of Virginians, as seen in the series' third and fourth novels (which have yet to be translated), depict an increasingly dystopian, estranged image of the colony planet. Its society becomes further divided by civil war, authoritarian control, and racist policies that create official ghettos, in which private property and economic development for profit exceed the value of individual human lives or stewardship of the environment. And yet, even in this highly dystopian society, utopian enclaves exist, as in the rebel province of "Licornia" in volume four (AR430–31).

In all of Vonarburg's writing, the utopian desire for an *ailleurs*, an elsewhere, comes through clearly. In *L'Autre rivage* (The Other Shore), Lian — the son of a Rani woman and a Virginian who has crossed via the Sea from the original Tyranaël over to Atyrkelsaō — himself crosses back to Virginia. As Liam Shaunessy, he assumes a new name and identity, feigning amnesia. He begins to write the stories of his youth in the Ranao culture and publishes these as *Légendes d'ailleurs* (Legends of Elsewhere; AR126). Although he was already an outsider as a halfbreed on Atyrkelsaō, Lian still perceives his life on his father's homeworld of Virginia as exile, and he longs repeatedly for the elsewhere that his original home represents (AR154, 216, 224).

Certainly, the Virginia on which he arrives continues to struggle for the establishment of a "more perfect principle" of social organization than that offered by the Grays in *Mon frère l'ombre*. Indeed, a civil war between the "Rebs" and the Grays rages periodically. The latter censor knowledge about the Ancients and misinform people about the various extrasensory and telekinetic mutations developing in the human population. In order for the society to heal, the various groups occupying this Borderlands territory (Anzaldúa) must come to terms with the inevitable presence of Others and accept them as co-occupiers. As the genetic mutation which facilitates crossing from Virginia to Atyrkelsaō via the Sea begins to occur more frequently in the populations of both worlds, a confusing array of Others appears, reflecting the complexity of the postcolonial situation on the shared consensus world of the reader. The series' last two volumes *L'Autre rivage* and *La Mer allée avec le soleil* focus increasingly upon blurring the lines between opposing groups through the process of *métissage*.

Through patterns of interracial mixing and cultural exchange with the Ranao on Atyrkelsaō (discussed in chapter four), by the series' final volume Vonarburg brings Virginian society to a space that is, if not fully eutopian, more perfect for all concerned. The planet has finally found peace, all eighteen to nineteen year olds perform a term of civil service, and tolerance of the planet's various groups is a dominant value (MA12). Yet the relatively happy ending for the Terran colony planet remains ambiguous, as Vonarburg throws in yet another group to be dealt with and understood, the Ékelli, a race superior to either Terrans or Ranao which appears to have been manipulating both groups for their own diversion all along. Their existence is discovered in a Shangri-la like space, reminiscent of the Buddhist Shambhala referenced in Rochon's SFQ sagas, hidden away in a secret cave in the mountains.

Rewriting the colonial myths: Vonarburg's *Reine de Mémoire*

In addition to all of the iterations of utopia that can be found in these SFQ sagas, elements of the uchronia, the narrative of another timeline, commonly called the alternate history can also be found here. Indeed Suvin's definition of utopia that I have relied on throughout this chapter seems to elide the utopia and the uchronia in its stipulation of the "alternative historical hypothesis" as utopia's basis. Clearly, Jacques Brossard's *L'Oiseau de feu* could be called a uchronia, as it offers an alternate version of the events of *Genesis* and describes human origins on Earth (Vial 7). It definitely plays with the trope of time with its circular ending which points back to its beginning. Élisabeth Vonarburg, though, openly engages with utopia's cousin in *Reluctant Voyagers* and most recently in her pentalogy *Reine de Mémoire* (Queen of Memory; 2005–07),[22] described as "historical fantasy" by its publisher. Vonarburg's second novelistic foray into the rising genre of alternate history, like all of her works, defies the standard tropes of the form in question, bending and twisting them to serve the needs of her story rather than using them to shape and outline the narrative. This complex story takes place in two interwoven timelines, both of which differ distinctly from and yet parallel to our own historical development. And both of them involve the creation of New World Myths in utopian spaces.

Reine de Mémoire's alternate vision of European society in the late seventeenth century and then at the end of the eighteenth and into the first years of the nineteenth centuries appears to be somewhat utopian, at least when compared to the Europe known to the reader through standard histories. Its utopia becomes ambiguous as the plot and the reader's vision of it develops, indeed, as its protagonist Gilles Garance flees from a society that to him has become dystopian and seeks refuge in a distant land. Vonarburg reconfigures history as he "discovers" the Eastern land of Mynmari, our former Burma. While for him the *comptoir*—the trading post, the first phase of a European colonial presence in any of its New Worlds—that he founds becomes an insulated utopian microcosm, his colonization of this space becomes cause for concern and its precepts are called into question. As we saw in *Tyranaël*, the problematic new world utopias are threatened by dystopian forces inherited from the old worlds of their founders. The hope established in the open ending of Vonarburg's earlier SFQ saga, which suggests the promise of transparency and equal exchange between the various societies sharing a common geographical space seems to evaporate in *Reine de Mémoire*, a work written perhaps in dialogue with a more somber post–9/11 world.

For Gilles Garance, the Géminite society's channeling and controlling of the magical gifts of its *talentés* (talented ones) represents a practice symptomatic of an oppressive, dystopian world. Just as it refuses to accept him for who he is, he rejects it, seeking an escape that, by chance, carries him to a new world in the East. Like many a classic utopia, the land of Mynmari has been isolated from the outside world, protected not only by geography but also by magic. The sole European, protected by powerful magical figures upon whom he has fatefully stumbled during a major ritual cycle, Gilles slowly takes advantage of his position and his accidental discovery of a combination of two magical elements which, as *ambercite*, produce large quantities of harnessable energy. Since no Westerners can follow him there, at least at first, the *comptoir* represents his own island paradise. However, following the classic pattern, the manipulations and deceptions (including self-deceptions) necessary to maintain a stasis of absolute control lead Gilles to abuse his power. Having fled Europe and its limited thought system, Gilles finds himself condemned to repeat and reproduce its errors, leading to precisely the same crimes in his domain, named (in a clear reference to Shakespeare's *Tempest*) La Miranda. Ultimately, his actions lead to the expulsion of Europeans from the colony and a renewed isolationism in Mynmari. This conclusion suggests the moral bankruptcy of even the economic colonization (as opposed to thick settlement) of the comptoir system, while it also reflects the growing rift between East and West in the current political situation worldwide. That is to say, the utopian horizon appears much more distant here than it did at the conclusion of *Tyranaël*.

The novel interweaves this overtly colonial plotline with the story of Gilles' descendants, three children who grow up at the end of the Enlightenment in an alternate France which has experienced no revolution because patriarchal Catholicism has not developed. Rather, the major religion in France (although not in all of Europe), is Geminism, a form of Christianity which recognizes Christ as having had a twin sister, Sophia. Read from a feminist perspective, this society appears eutopian since the religious model it proposes allows for the full integration of most French women into a range of public social roles. Structured somewhat like a Gothic novel, though, the narrative develops as the orphan children Pierrino, Senso and Jiliane uncover an array of clues which lead them to further knowledge about their parents' mysterious deaths and their identity which has been occulted. The utopian veil becomes transparent, revealing the tissue of past lies upon which the present has been constructed. Like today's postcolonial subject, these children discover that their heritage involves a mixture of Géminite French and Mynmari (for Gilles took a wife), as well as Native American and Northern European *christien*. As the two narrative threads unite, a third element develops: that of the colonization of our New World, called Atlandie. Although the children understand much more about their hybrid identities, they remain unable to reconcile the three solitudes from which they derive. As Vonarburg's publisher announces three prequels in progress that further develop this universe, for the present time, at least, Vonarburg's uchronia remains open-ended. It leaves the reader, though, with much less of a sense of understanding about its universe and the outcomes for its fictional inhabitants than did *Tyranaël*.

In keeping with the utopian thought of Ernst Bloch, who asserts that art and literature serve an important utopian function in their depiction of other realities, in their "anticipatory illumination" the SFQ sagas of Jacques Brossard, Esther Rochon and Élisabeth Vonarburg all privilege the power of the imagination in humanity's ability to reconfigure reality. If we accept Philip E. Wegner's assertion that the genre of utopia participates in the creation of the "imaginary community" of the modern nation (xvi), not only do the characters found in these postcolonial utopias create the spaces around them, their narratives participate in the creation of the idea of Québec. The New World Myth acknowledges precisely the notion that imagination makes the reality. In *L'Oiseau de feu* the space pioneers acknowledge that: "Aleph même n'était qu'un reflet, une image, un rêve, une belle illusion. Quels rôles leurs propres consciences jouaient-elles dans la création de ce monde? Qu'adviendrait-il, «là-bas», des pionniers d'Ashmev?" ("Aleph itself was no more than a reflection, an image, a dream, a beautiful illusion. What roles had their own consciences played in the creation of this world. What would happen to them 'there,' pioneers on Ashmev?"; SQP258). In *Secrets*, of Rochon's *Les Chroniques infernales*, Taïm Sutherland exhorts a despairing Tryil, asserting precisely that freedom (as well as emprisonment) lies in the imagination and that the imagination constructs reality:

> Vous avez accès à l'imagination, au rêve, à la licence poétique, que vous le vouliez ou non!... On a pu vous astreindre à une réalité consensuelle, où le consensus est dicté par les plus forts.... Mensonges! Les puits vers le haut existent toujours dans le mode du rêve. Les accès n'y sont pas bouchés. Il s'agit de ne plus s'occuper de ce que l'on croit être, de ne plus tenir compte du consensus. Il s'agit d'une réalité personnelle et non collective, donnant un plaisir au présent, sans attache, qui existe de concert avec le social, le collectif, le groupe et ses leaders [168–69].

> You have access to imagination, to dreams, to poetic licence, whether you want it or not! They were able to limit you to a consensus reality, where the consensus was dictated by the strongest. Lies! The pits reaching toward the heights still exist in the dream mode. It's a personal reality not a collective one, giving pleasure to the present, without attachments, which exists in concert with the social, the collective, the group and its leaders.

In a similar fashion the Dreamers of Tyranaël, like Eïlai, access a different reality, or rather infinite different realities, as it is uncertain that the parallel worlds onto which their Dreams open a window, exist or not. And yet, demonstrating what Moylan and Baccolini, following Bloch, call "The Use Value of Social Dreaming" (*Utopia*), they forge a collective reality based upon what is revealed in this unconscious realm.

As works of the imagination, the SFQ sagas of Jacques Brossard, Esther Rochon and Élisabeth Vonarburg, explore hybrid forms which blur the lines between allegory, fantasy and science fiction. This approach clearly estranges the reader from the shared consensus world dictated by the strong. As Sargisson has observed of feminist utopian writing, the estrangement of utopia serves:

various transformative and oppositional functions.... Utopian thought creates a space, previously non-existent and still "unreal," in which radically different speculation can take place, and in which totally new ways of being can be envisaged. In this space transformative thinking can take place, and paradigmatic shifts in approach can be undertaken [*Contemporary* 63].

The SFQ saga's utopian and its dystopian explorations participate in the elaboration of a postcolonial discourse, which condemns the former/existing colonial system of power and violence and envisions new relationships between various autochthonous, established and newly immigrant groups. It, therefore, remains engaged with "current events" (Jameson, *Archaeology* 146), commenting critically on the "real" world. Since these writers compose in French and publish in Québec, we assume then that shared consensus world of their readers would be that of contemporary francophone Québec. By privileging the imaginary, by imagining realities other than those to which we are currently constrained, the SFQ saga reimagines past realities of colonization and, in its most socially relevant form, offers possibilities for Québec's future in the futuristic visions it offers. In my concluding chapter, I will examine how these works appropriate and reconfigure the current templates for productive and peaceful coexistence of the various groups who comprise the pluralistic society of Québec today.

Chapter 4

Logiques métisses: Hybridity and Transculturalism

> *Il s'agit d'arriver au rivage opposé. Les hommes énergiques, les croyants, les fous se jettent à la nage. Les uns périssent, d'autres se fatiguent et retournent en arrière, d'autres enfin arrivent. Ils crient à la foule de les suivre, mais en vain. La foule attend qu'on lui construise un pont pour qu'elle puisse passer commodément, sans danger, sans fatigue. Mais en définitive, elle passe.*
>
> *It is a case of arriving at the other shore. Energetic men, believers, madmen throw themselves in swimming. Some perish, others tire and turn around, others still finally arrive. They shout at the crowd to follow them, but in vain. The crowd waits for someone to build a bridge so that it can cross properly, without danger or effort. But in the end, it crosses.*
> — Marie d'Agoult, *Mémoires, 1833–1854*
>
> *As the new century begins, Québec remains half-in and half-out. Its position is ambiguous, hybrid, and has remained so for at least fifty years.*
> — Guy Laforest [299]

In "Syncretism: A Federalist Approach to Canadian Science Fiction" (2001), Neal Baker argues effectively that a number of works of French- and Anglo-Canadian science fiction elect for a syncretic approach to cultural representations, including Nalo Hopkinson's *Brown Girl in the Ring* (1998), Joël Champetier's *The Dragon's Eye* (1991) and Daniel Sernine's *Chronoreg* (1992). "Syncretism," as Baker defines it, "entails the reconfiguration of various unified essences — be it the nation-state, ethnicity, race, language, the body, or time — and the fusion of radical differences" (220). Although difficult to distinguish from hybridity, Baker "purposefully" avoids this term "which in postcolonial theory has acquired connotations involving assymetries of power and is hotly contested" (229, n. 2). The negative valence long attributed to hybridity, however, has not prevented its appropriation by various critics and writers, most notably Homi K. Bhabha and, in Québec, Sherry Simon. As we shall see, the term opted for by Antillean francophone writers, *la créolité*, also has its applications in the wider postcolonial arena of the Americas. But Baker's essay also refers to "federalism." We should not forget the official Canadian policies of biculturalism/bilingualism and later multiculturalism, and Québec's own answer to these in the notion of *le transculturel*. The imagined communities of Jacques Brossard, Esther Rochon and Élisabeth Vonarburg figure a range of approaches to societal pluralism from apartheid and segregation (seen in the dystopian, alienated societies discussed in chapter two), to more utopian forms of mutual toleration, multicultural appreciation, physical and cultural hybridization, creolization, cultural exchange, and even the *braconnages*, the "poaching" recently discussed by Simon Harel. After a brief theoretical introduction to these various strategies, we will examine how each of the SFQ sagas solves the problem of pluralism inherent in any postcolonial society.

The SFQ sagas of Brossard, Rochon and Vonarburg offer a range of "stratégies ... d'accommodation" necessary when two or more groups occupy contiguous or the same space(s) (Beaulé, "Enfants" 124). Because of the omnipresence of similar situations in the "real" world, social and political theorists have offered a wide array of terms to describe (or prescribe) strategies for the development of peaceful pluralistic societies. It may be worth beginning a brief theoretical introduction here with a discussion of the term of "pluralism" itself, a paradigm offered in 1965 by M. G. Smith for the development of Trinidad. As Grant H. Cornwell and Eve Walsh Stoddard describe it, memory and history play important roles in definitions of identity for the present and future:

> On this view, Trinidad would be a composite of separate groups yoked together by history under a common constitution. This paradigm foregrounds the cultural distinctiveness and different histories, traditions, practices, and values of each group. It encourages the defining of present identities through origins, or "roots" [30].

As they also point out, if such pluralism incurs a process of "homogenization"—like that long prevalent in the U.S. notion of the melting pot, in which the diverse contributing immigrant cultures would ultimately be melted down and blended into one "American" culture—its strength "as a paradigm for multicultural nation-building" remains limited (Cornwell and Stoddard 30). The difficulty for postcolonial societies—both real and imagined as in the SFQ saga—lies in the problem of building frameworks within which the various groups making up the plurality are respected and acknowledged. Charles Taylor's essay "Politics of Recognition" (1992) provides a nuanced discussion of how to address the potential conflicts between the universalizing model of the liberal society and the need to recognize difference when that society decides to make accommodation for multicultural variation. Only in a situation of genuine mutual respect and recognition can intercultural relationships, and consequently law and public policies, be developed that treat the various groups in an equal or fair manner without forcing assimilation or homogenization upon them. The question here often hinges upon the definition of what is fair: is fair equal, in the sense of treating everyone the same and making everyone adopt the same behaviors and practices? Or, does fairness acknowledge — as do the now-challenged policies of Affirmative Action in the United States — that fair does not always mean exactly the same and that fairness may acknowledge or compensate for difference and different treatment, past or present?[1]

Although vastly different from Trinidad, Canada and Québec understand the need to address the situation of different cultural groups occupying contiguous or overlapping territories. From the time of Conquest, even in the colonial era, the British Crown had had to negotiate policies, such as the Québec Act of 1774, to ensure the respect for cultural difference between the two groups of colonists, French-speaking and English. While George III had originally "guaranteed certain rights to the indigenous population" (Kivisto 88), the First Nations/Anishinaabe and Inuit populations were left out of the concept of the two "founding nations" exploited by George-Étienne Cartier at the time of Confederation in 1867, as they would be later ignored when an increased presence of other groups developed after Canadian immigration opened up in the 1950s and was misidentified as a "third" cultural pole.

Discussions at the federal level took place against the backdrop of an increasingly self-aware nationalist movement in Québec, which sought to assert the predominance of French-speaking culture within the province, while at the same time guaranteeing the survival of the French language in the archipelago of francophone communities across Canada in other provinces. In 1961, the Royal Commission on Bilingualism and Biculturalism in Canada was formed and recommended that Canada should become an officially bilingual nation (Innis). In 1971 the notion of Canadian biculturalism was expanded to that of multiculturalism, and the Act for the Preservation and Enhancement of Multiculturalism in Canada was developed. It seeks to "promote the understanding and creativity that arise from the interaction between individuals and communities of different origins" (Canadian Multiculturalism Act, 3.1.g). With this effort, "Prime Minister Trudeau put in place a multicultural policy within a bilingual framework" (Dupont and Lemarchand 320). For understandable reasons, both Québec's nationalists and First Nations bands did not fully support the act, as they saw in it a move to undermine their own position (Dupont and Lemarchand 322). Rather than recognizing Québec as a "distinct society" (a status later offered, but not ratified during the constitutional accords at Meech Lake and Charlottetown), it seemed to place them in the same position as Ukrainians in Manitoba, Italians in Montréal, or Japanese in British Columbia, as simply one group among many other groups of non–English origin. A significant element that contributes to these tensions is the persistence of the erroneous equation outside Québec of nationalist aspirations in Québec with ethnic nationalism. Nonetheless, today the policy of "official multiculturalism" dominates the Canadian cultural landscape, which envisions itself through the metaphor of the mosaic, as opposed to the more integrative "melting pot" of the United States.

Just as the mosaic has its shortcomings as a metaphor for national identity, so does multiculturalism as policy for a pluralistic society in which mutual respect for difference is intended to exist. This policy is widely taken to reinforce the privileged status of English-language cultures versus all the rest, as Louis Dupont and Nathalie Lemarchand assert:

> The mosaic pretends that in (English) Canada there is no set culture into which to integrate; cultural diversity is Canada's identity. According to official multiculturalism, no individual is forced to retain his or her culture, but all cultures are granted a universal right to celebrate and even to develop their particularities. In principle and not without contradictions, the more cultural diversity there is, the more unity there should be. Immigrants are accepted for what they are and valorized for their differences. They decide themselves how to integrate into the (English) Canadian society [323].

Its critics like novelist Neil Bissoondath assert that official multiculturalism is just that — official, and that not enough has been done to truly embrace all aspects of the Canadian mosaic, from acknowledgment of the unique status of Québec's French-language common public culture, to the position of the First Nations as sovereign groups, to the range of Chinese, Haitian, East Indian and other immigrant populations. The cement of the English language nonetheless holds together the mosaic, in the official multiculturalist discourse of Canada, and these policies simply reaffirm the predominance of an anglophone culture in Canada. Long before the potential racism in a hardline, ethnically based nationality was revealed by Parizeau's comments after the defeat of the 1995 referendum cited several times in this work (Bauch), Québec offered its own vision of a francophone, yet pluralistic and multicultural society through the notions of civic nationalism and transculturalism. This society is envisioned without respect to the question of sovereignty.

Faced with the reality of an increasingly multicultural Québec, in particular an increasingly diverse Montréal, the nationalist movement had to acknowledge the impossibility of building consensus for sovereignty without acknowledging this "third pole," as well as acknowledging contributions and status of First Nations and Inuit peoples. Long before the failure of the 1995 referendum and its aftermath, the provincial government published at least two policy statements, *Autant de façons d'être Québécois* (1980) and *Let's Build Quebec Together* (1990), which sought to put to rest a prevalent notion that an independent Québec would be open only to the Québécois *de souche* (Ireland and Proulx 2). Before and after the 1995 defeat, nationalist rhetoric further emphasized civic nationalism in order to counter the divisive force of hard-line ethnic nationalism represented by Parizeau. The civic model, proferred for example by Fernand Dumont in *Raisons communes* (1995), offers a broader conceptualization for Québécois nationality as it "refers to a form of national identity based on shared citizenship within a state irrespective of the ancestry, race, ethnic origin, or religion of its inhabitants" (Resnick 282). Sociologists, political scientists and historians like Louis Balthazar and Dimitrios Karmis articulate new strategies for the creation of a pluralistic society in Québec. The inclusive titles of essay collections such as *Le Pays de tous les Québécois* (The Land of all Quebeckers, Sarra-Bournet and Gendron, 1998) and *L'Archipel identitaire* (The Archipelago of Identity, Ancelovici and Dupuis-Deri, 1997) reveal their engagement with this question. Most recently, Gérard Bouchard and Charles Taylor published *Fonder l'avenir: Le temps de la conciliation* (Founding the Future: The Time for Conciliation, 2008), the report of inquiries conducted by the provincial government of Québec's Consultation Commission on Accommodation Practices Related to Cultural Differences. They observe a clear "ouverture à l'Autre" ("opening up to the Other"; 7), particularly in Montréal, the area of greatest cultural diversity. Reasserting the legal requirements to provide reasonable accommodation for minority group differences, the report uses the term "interculturalisme," balancing a concern for the use of the French language in intercultural exchanges and the preservation of the "noyau francophone" ("French-speaking core") while stressing the need for Québec to cultivate "une orientation pluraliste et soucieuse de la protection des droits" ("a pluralistic orientation concerned with protecting rights"; 44).

Nationalist discourse sought to distinguish itself from the often criticized official multiculturalism of Canada by conceptualizing a similar, yet distinct form of pluralism for Québec with the notion of *le transculturalisme*. As Dupont and Lemarchand explain it:

> Québec's transcultural model is conceived as an exchange between the host society and the different cultural communities that have joined in and brought cultural diversity. In this, the Québec multicultural project (called "transcultural") is similar to Australia's which states that the English language is, with freedom, equality, and the rule of law, at the heart of Australia's value system. In Québec, the host society is composed historically of a French-speaking majority, an Amerindian population, and an English-speaking minority, the last being, however, part of the dominant majority group in Canada. In this society, the rule of law, individual rights, French as a common language, and a special status for English are the basic principles needed to preserve unity.... The idea of transculturalism is to keep an open dialogue between the different cultural components, while the Québec state provides protection and help to the immigrants in exchange for the acceptance of basic principles [327].

The notion of transculturalism reflects precisely the concerns of Frank Cunningham about the Canadian situation. As he observes, for civic nationalism to work, to be truly multi-ethnic in nature, the tolerance supposedly already implied in a liberal ethnic nationalism must exist, but like *le transculturalisme* as defined above: "[w]hat makes this tolerance substantial is not just that it is culturally internalized but that it opens up the pre-existing ethos to transformation by sympathetic contact with other cultures" (Cunningham 194).

This openness to multiculturalism could only occur in Québec at a point in time when the siege mentality prior to the Quiet Revolution and continuing into the 1980s after the defeat of the first Referendum on sovereignty-association had been transcended. During this period it was felt that French language and culture were in a state of imminent extinction (a situation reflected metaphorically for the Asven in Rochon's early Vrénalik novels or for the Périphériens of Brossard's Manokhsor), has been transcended. The newfound confidence in the status of French in Québec proper, even if it still appears threatened elsewhere in North America, resulted in part from legislation protecting and enforcing the use of French: "Bill 22 (1974) declared French the sole official language of Quebec, and Bill 101 made it the language of government and the workplace" (Ireland and Proulx 2). Francis Fukuyama asserts that Québécois nationalism should logically wither away "because Quebec [sic] is a subdivision within a prosperous and stable liberal democratic country" (28), and therefore appropriate political and socio-economic conditions for sovereignist nationalist movements do not exist.

For the time being, the political aspirations toward sovereignty seem to be at bay, with contemporary Québec often identified as in a "post-nationalist" phase. While some perceive that Canadian Prime Minister Stephen Harper's application of "nation" status to the province of Québec satisfied nationalist yearnings (Hamilton), others remain sceptical of its impact in the long or short term. In any case, in addition to various political efforts toward the recognition of the multicultural nature of contemporary society in Québec, a number of writers and scholars have begun to acknowledge the increasingly "postcolonial" elements of Québec's literary and cultural production. Working more often from the frameworks of French theory, however, the term "postcolonial" is rarely applied. Rather, we have seen, as Ireland and Proulx point out, discussions of the multicultural, transcultural Québec, as well as the rising *littérature migrante*, as the literary productions by and about non–French-Canadian Quebeckers has lately been termed. Monique LaRue asserts in *L'Arpenteur et le navigateur* (1996) that some *Québécois de souche* writers have questioned the inclusion (and growing prominence) of writers not born in Québec or not born of French-Canadian parents, such as Ying Chen, David Homel and Sergio Kokis (7–9). And yet, as Sherry Simon observes in *Translating Montréal* (2006), the growing acceptance of and desire to translate, particularly in the metropolis, the contributions to Québécois society by the so-called *Néo-Québécois*, or, as is the case with Pierre Anctil's translations of Yiddish works into French, of not-so-new immigrant groups.

Welcome to an extent as fellow francophones, Haitian exiles have been particularly present in Québec's literary and intellectual scenes; at least two writers of Haitian heritage have participated in the SFQ milieu, Claude-Michel Prévost and Stanley Péan. Indeed, the brief, but arguably transcultural, exchange between Haitian and Québécois poets at the Perchoir d'Haiti café in Montréal in 1964–65 may have contributed to the adoption of discourses of decolonization by certain nationalists, as Vincent Desroches observes (205). Writers like Émile Ollivier and Gérard Étienne[2] brought with them the Afro-Caribbean notion of *la négritude* formulated by Aimé Césaire — from which the corollary *la québécitude* derives — as well as those of hybridity and *la créolité*. The Martinican writers Jean Bernabé, Patrick Chamoiseau and Raphaël Confiant composed *In Praise of Creoleness* (1989) which "sets forth a concept of creoleness that espouses the simultaneous recognition and transcendence of multiple roots" (Cornwell and Stoddard 16). This term, however, has not been adopted widely by writers of science fiction and fantasy in Québec, or by the literary mainstream. Instead, one finds again and again references to a term more frequently used in postcolonial theory, that of hybridity, a term codified by the bilingual Montréal academic Sherry Simon in the reference work *Hybridité culturelle* (1999).

Hybridity has been both embraced (Bhabha) and eschewed (JanMohamed) for several reasons, including the long-held negative connotations of its relationship to the pejorative terms half-breed and mongrel (Simon, *Hybridité* 32–33). In contrast, the notion of *la créolité* focuses upon birth place and territory, rather than on genetic-ethnic origins. In various New World cultures, creoles have ranged from the children of pureblood Spanish colonists born in the New World, to the mulatto children of French colonists in Louisiana, to the mixed-blood French speakers of largely African descent in Martinique. Hybridity carries with it a potential reactionary taboo or stigma because of its relationship to miscegenation, interbreeding, including a threat of assimilation through "passing." There are also concerns that it retains the hegemonic dominance of white/Western culture over the so-called colored/African/indigenous cultures. But Bhabha and Gloria Anzaldúa see it as liberating, that its multiplicity offers choice and freedom for postcolonial identities, both individual and cultural. In his pathbreaking work, *Colonial Desire: Hybridity in Theory, Culture and Race* (1995), Robert J. C. Young asserts that Bhabha articulates hybridity as a "Third Space," in which "hybridity begins to become the form of cultural difference itself, the jarrings of a differentiated culture [which] challenge the centred, dominant cultural norms" (23).

Françoise Lionnet chooses the term *métissage*, from Jean-Loup Amselle's *Mestizo Logics* (1998) which argues that prior to colonial times cultural exchange was the norm and that notions of cultural and racial purity were introduced because of the colonizer's fears of miscegenation. As Lionnet asserts:

> The global mongrelization or métissage of cultural forms creates hybrid identities, and interrelated, if not overlapping, space. In those spaces, struggles for the control of means of representation and self-identification are mediated by a single and immensely powerful symbolic system: the colonial language and the variations to which it is subjected under the pen of ("francophone") writers who enrich, transform, and creolize it [322].

Yet, in the Canadian situation, the Métis has, of course, a specific historical value, which has, as Julia Emberley notes, been appropriated as "a figure for theories of cultural cross-over" (158).[3] More recent interventions from Québec, like those of Régine Robin, imagine a transcultural experience through the metaphor of the *brocante*, the second-hand shop that offers goods from the full range of cultural groups living in a particular neighborhood (Green 16). Somewhat contesting the notion of hybridity, Simon Harel counters with the latest in conceptions of postcolonial identity in *Braconnages identitaires* (2006), offering up the validity of poaching as a strategy for imagining oppositional forms of identity.

Patricia Kerslake has asserted of contemporary anglophone science fiction and fantasy that "many contemporary authors, such as Ken MacLeod and even Neil Gaiman, are already aware of and writing about those issues directly or indirectly bordering postcolonial criticism, possibly even to the point where fiction and academic writing converge" (127). Precisely the same can be said about writers from Québec, as we have seen and as we shall see in the following examination of the wide range of strategies of accomodation that they envision for the societies inhabiting the SFQ saga.

From the Mosaic to the Melting-Pot: Hybridity and Creolization in Brossard's *L'Oiseau de feu*

As I observe in the previous chapter, the space colonists sent to Ashmev in Jacques Brossard's *L'Oiseau de feu* repeatedly express their concern that the planet be uninhabited. The question remains, though, as to whether their expressed desire to avoid the violence of intercultural conflict during the colonial process equates with an oppositional attitude or if it simply reflects a desire to erase the native from the scene so that the fantasy of a kinder, gentler form of guilt-free colonization can be acted out. Although some ambivalence remains, I feel that the text adequately answers those concerns in several ways. While no irrefutable evidence of indigenous peoples presents itself, a shadowy hominid/humanoid presence nonetheless haunts the settlement. This haunting signals the real violence and genocide of actual colonial history; it denies the characters the full peace of mind that they seek in their colonial project. As in Vonarburg's *Tyranaël*, Brossard's SFQ saga refuses to allow a full erasure of the indigene. Further evidence of *L'Oiseau de feu*'s oppositional discourse appears in its treatment of race and ethnicity.

What is the racial makeup of Brossard's fictional colonists, and how has Brossard addressed the issue of ethnicity for characters who, as the novel proposes, will become humanity's ancestors? While Brossard's valorization of his own mixed ancestry has been observed (see page 82 above), let us deal now with his handling of race, both in Manokhsor /the Centrale and on Ashmev/Earth. As we shall see, from the Canadian metaphor of the multicultural mosaic, *L'Oiseau de feu* moves increasingly toward a hybridized model for humanity's future. In its embrace of this sometimes problematized concept, Brossard's work reflects concepts outlined as early as the 1920s in the Mexican philosopher José Vasconcelos' controversial *La Raza cósmica* (The Cosmic Race; 1948) and more recently in Bernabé, Chamoiseau and Confiant's *In Praise of Creoleness* (1989).

In *L'Oiseau de feu* Brossard depicts a representative sampling of ethnic groups or "races" on earth at the time of the Great Catastrophe of 2793, the event that inaugurates the creation of the Centrale and subsequently, the walled city of Manokhsor. Not only do the scientific elite who survive in the underground bunker include a wide range of human diversity (RA171), Manokhsor's twelve quarters reflect microcosmic images of human societies at various times in history and in various geographical regions (RA174). Within each quarter, however, ethnic and cultural homogeneity are strictly enforced. In this respect Manokhsor resembles the Canadian image of the mosaic: a unified picture made up of clearly circumscribed colored tiles, each of which, taken individually, however, contains within its bounds a single pigment. In Adakhan's quarter of ONO (West-North-West), his racial/ethnic difference (marked by darker skin and hair) sets him distinctly apart from those with the dominant traits of pale skin and red hair. While difference is coded as bad and disruptive in the fictional site of Manokhsor — indeed, Adakhan's refusal to conform either physically or mentally repeatedly results in conflict — it assumes a positive valence at the level of the text in the depiction of its hero. In *Les Années d'apprentissage* and the novels which take place in the Centrale, the protagonist reviles conformity, sameness, and others' failure to question and stand apart.

As opposed to Manokhsor, in which each quarter becomes a ghetto for the city's various historico-ethnic groups, the underground Centrale includes a wide variety of ethnicities. Adakhan expresses a range of emotions in his first reaction to this unaccustomed diversity: "ce qui l'avait d'abord ébahi, c'était les *couleurs* de certains *visages*: du jaune, de l'ambre ou du noir ... des chevelures dorées, cendrées, rouge feu...." ("what shocked him at first was the *color* of certain *faces*: yellow, amber or black ... golden, sandy, fiery red hair"; RA72; original emphasis). Indeed, he interprets the skin color of Chang-15, a nurse of Chinese descent, as a sign of illness. As he becomes accustomed to such variety, revealed in the phenotypical description for each new character encountered by Adakhan during *Le Recyclage d'Adakhan*, he delights in it. Its "plérômes" (a brilliant wordplay on the French verb *plaire* [to please] and the English "playroom") represent one of the potentially utopian aspects of the Centrale. Observing a group sex session he reflects that: "Le grouillement *multicolore* des chairs pendant ces ébats (blancs, noirs, jaunes, rouges) est assez réussi" ("The multicolored teeming of flesh during these frolics [white, black, yellow, red] was quite well-done"; RA152; original emphasis). However, the level of diversity varies from team to team within the Centrale as Adakhan reveals in his observations during an enforced term with the evil Lokhfer's group:

> il n'y a pratiquement que des blonds et des châtain clair ici, à commencer par le Chef. Seulement des visages pâles. On n'abuse pas de l'ultra-violet! On évite, devant moi, de parler des bruns, des noirs et des jaunes: soit par mépris, soit sur ordre du Chef à cause de moi et de notre équipe. (A commencer par Nyhrsangh et Mawa: 45% de «couleurs» chez nous; 30% à la Centrale; ici: 100% de blancs.) Il est cependant clair, si je peux dire, que ma seule présence, avec mon teint cuivré, leur est à charge sinon parfaitement odieuse [SQP21].
>
> There are practically nothing but blonds and light brown haired individuals here, beginning with the Boss. Only pale faces. They certainly don't abuse the ultra-violet lamps! They avoid talking about brown-, black- or yellow-skinned people in front of me, either out of contempt or under orders from their Boss because of our team. (Beginning with Nyhrsangh and Mawa: 45% people "of color" with us; 30% overall in the Centrale; here: 100% whites.) It's clear anyway, if I can say this, that my presence alone, with my copper skin, is a burden, if not absolutely odious, to them.

Through Adakhan's point of view, Brossard establishes the abhorrence of the racism displayed by Lokhfer and his team, particularly as Lokhfer takes on Hitler-like characteristics (with his sponsorship of human experimentation, use of slave labor in Manokhsor, and call for a final solution for the Périphériens [SQP71]) and the allegorical role of Lucifer. In this SFQ saga, the utopian society of the future does, however, theoretically embrace all races and ethnic groups, as seen in the harmonious functioning of Syrius' team within the Centrale.

Diversity as a positive trait appears further reinforced in the author's choice of a hero "of color" and in the composition of the six members of the *Oiseau de Feu* project's crew. In opposition to the majority of Québec's fiction, at least prior to the flowering of the *littérature migrante* in the 1980s,[4] the physical aspects of Brossard's hero specifically differ from the phenotype typical of the French Canadian/*Québécois de souche*. With the exception of his curly hair, Adakhan's appearance reflects more clearly that of the aboriginal inhabitants of the Americas: "Yeux noirs, Cheveux noir-bronze. Nez busqué. Teint brun/cuivré" ("Black eyes, Black-bronze hair. Hooked nose"; RA47). The remaining astronauts that join him on the mission to colonize Ashmev display a full variety of physio-ethnic features:

- Selvah: "blonde, de grands yeux pers, la peau pâle" ("blond with big hazel-green eyes, pale skin"; AA252);
- Laïtha: "la peau ambrée, les cheveux très noirs ... les yeux fendus en amandes" ("amber skin, very black hair ... and almond-shaped eyes"; RA80);
- Viviane: "Des cheveux bruns ... ce regard violet" ("brown hair ... a violet gaze"; RA58);
- Mawa: "jaune de peau" ("yellow skinned"; SQP141);
- Nyhrsangh: a "grand noir dégingandé," "dont la peau noire luit avec orgueil" ("tall lanky black," "whose black skin shines with pride"; SQP211, AE50).

One of the strangest moments of this epic occurs after the rocket's "traversée" ("crossing"), a sort of quantum leap in space or time that brings it into Alpha's solar system and within range of its target planet Ashmev. The crew awakens from stasis to find that the six ethnically diverse individuals described above have now become three. A literal hybridization has occurred and the genetic material and physical traits of all six will be carried on in the descendants of Adakhan-Nyhrsangh, Selvah-Mawa, Laïtha-Viviane. However, it should be mentioned that one identity remains dominant in each of the three survivors: those of Adakhan (the original native American with his copper skin), the very white Selvah (although her eyes are now "bridés," the French term for the epicanthic fold on the eyelid typical of Far East Asian groups) and the vaguely Eurasian Laïtha whose last name, Kabalevna, reflects a Slavic heritage. Throughout *Les Années d'errance*, as each child, grandchild and great-grandchild is born, Brossard lists — again echoing the "begats" chapters of the Biblical *Genesis*— eye, hair and skin color along with other carryons of various ethnic traits (AE387, 449). This openly nationalist, *Québécois de souche* author clearly envisions a future world that is ethnically diverse.

The notion of a postcolonial society based on hybridization, that is to say the genetic and cultural blending of the colonizing and indigenous peoples, arguably has been most widely accepted in the Latin American world, particularly in the case of Mexico where high degrees of true *mestizaje*, the union and offspring of European men and indigenous women, occurred. The prominent writer Carlos Fuentes presents the case for Latin American *mestizo* culture in his book *The Buried Mirror: Reflections on Spain and the New World* (1999) and the documentary series of the same name. Roots for Fuentes' work can be traced back much farther to one of the founding participants in the Mexican Republic, one of its most controversial figures, José Vasconcelos (Encinas). In *La Raza cósmica: misión de la raza Iberoamericana* (1925) the educational philosopher outlines the concept that through genetic hybridization the human race grows stronger, and that the mixture of peoples in the territory of Mexico and elsewhere in Latin America will lead to the development of a new level of humanity, the cosmic race (9, 53). The mystical aspects of Vasconcelos' work, including the adoption of the notion that the Inca and Maya represented decadent cultures derived from an Atlantan civilization that arrived in the New World (15–16), make it difficult to take seriously today and scholars like Nicandro Juárez admit that Vasconcelos did not always bother to anchor his ideas in the scientific method (75). Nonetheless, he influenced writers contemporary with Jacques Brossard, including Gloria Anzaldúa and proponents of the Aztlán/Chicano movement in the U.S. Southwest. The work resonates not only with Brossard's depiction of humanity developing precisely from the creation of a new man of the future derived from the hybridization of others, but also quite distinctly with the notion of *la créolité*, developed in Martinique, by francophone writers contemporary with Brossard, work he was much more likely to know directly.

In their *In Praise of Creoleness*, the Martinican writers Bernabé, Chamoiseau, and Confiant declare themselves "Créoles." They espouse a hybrid culture formed from European, African, and other backgrounds brought into the New World and informed by its development in the specific American space: "We declare ourselves Creoles. We declare that Creoleness is the cement of our culture and that it ought to rule the foundations of our Caribbeanness. Creoleness is the *interactional or transactional aggregate* of Caribbean, European, African, Asian, Levantine cultural elements, united on the same soil by the yoke of history" (87; original emphasis). These writers appropriate the inevitable hybridity that occurs when cultures come into contact, offering their own positive version of it to form the basis of an identity for Antilleans that would at once have certain elements in common with others in the Caribbean and the Americas and at the same time would remain distinct. The concept of *la créolité* combines the notion of inherited elements (both racio-ethnic traits through genetic mixing and cultural elements through importations from Europe and Africa) with that of place-developed elements, how those inherited things change and alter to become unique in a new space. These are concerns shared by Brossard's characters as they discuss how they will adapt to the new world they intend to settle. In its combination of nurture with nature, acquired with innate traits, *la créolité* seeks to escape the essentialism of classic racism, but also found in positive movements like *la négritude*. Both of these elements — assimilation to the European cultural model or submission to the estranged African one — bring their own forms of alienation, according to the authors of *In Praise of Creoleness*. The point of adopting creolity as a socio-cultural attitude and an artistic practice is the utopian goal of disalienation (77–78), the acceptance of the self in the fullness of its own existence lived in its own space through "authentic expression" (85).

At times, however, their language reflects the mysticism of Vasconcelos, invoking the concept of the new man, the cosmic race, also appropriate to Brossard's science-fictional discourse, as they assert that: "For three centuries the islands and parts of continents affected by this phenomenon proved to be the real forges of a new humanity" (87–88). Brossard uses precisely the imagery of the forge throughout *Les Années d'apprentissage* as Adakhan is a metal worker; this imagery recurs in the second volumes as he uses this knowledge of metallurgy to develop materials with which to build the *Aigle d'or* rocket. Indeed, Syrius expressly articulates the notion that those going to Ashmev will be "purifié" like metal in a forge ("purified"; GP120, 123). In addition to the melting pot of the forge — they use the image of molten rock, magma (89)—, Bernabé, Chamoiseau and Confiant invoke the metaphor of the mosaic, found in Canadian conceptions of national culture: "Interior vision defeats, first of all, the old French imagery we are covered with, and restores us to ourselves in a mosaic renewed by the autonomy of its components" (86).

Ultimately, their language seems to contradict itself, yet this very contradiction reflects the ambivalence of the postcolonial situation. It also points clearly to the idea of human origins being rewritten as a conglomerate, the igneous rock that combines the concept of the blended, molten lava and the mosaic of discrete pieces. This metaphor is paramount to Brossard's science-fictional colonization of Ashmev/Earth. As the Martinican writers proclaim: "We are at once Europe, Africa, and enriched by Asian contributions, we are also Levantine, Indians, as well as pre–Columbian Americans in some respects. Creoleness is *'the world diffracted but recomposed,'* a maelström of signifieds in a single signifier: a Totality" (88; original emphasis). Like the New World Myth stories, *L'Éloge de la créolité* calls for a reconstruction of history, or rather, of histories: "We conceived [*Nous nous sommes forgés* (lit. "We forged for ourselves"; 26)] our cultural character as a function of acceptance and denial, therefore permanently questioning, always familiar with the most complex ambiguities, outside all forms of reduction, all forms of purity, all forms of impoverishment. Our history is a braid of histories" (88). As opposed to a métissage, however, they reaffirm the notion of the mosaic, now calling upon the kaleidoscope: "Because of its constituent mosaic, Creoleness is an open specificity. It escapes, therefore, perceptions which are not themselves open. Expressing it is not expressing a synthesis, not just expressing a crossing or any other unicity. It is expressing a kaleidoscopic totality, that is to say: *the nontotalitarian consciousness of a preserved diversity*" (89; original emphasis).

Openness, *l'ouverture*, represents a key theme in the SFQ saga. Sophie Beaulé concludes her exploration of "l'expérience migrante dans la science-fiction québécoise" ("the migrant experience in SFQ") with the observation that "[l]'ouverture des personnages, l'accommodation entraînerait enfin un appel au pardon, à la prise en charge de soi à travers l'action" ("characters' opening up, accommodation would finally lead to a call for forgiveness, for taking responsibility for oneself through action"; "Enfants" 136). While the strategy of the melting pot in Brossard's *L'Oiseau de feu*— the literal hybridization of six ethnically diverse characters into three individuals — could be read as a hegemonic form of conquest through assimilation, in which the Other is simply bred out, I think the text's own ambiguity leaves room for an oppositional reading. For, we see in Adakhan, Selvah and their offspring the creolization praised by Bernabé, Chamoiseau and Confiant. Because the Other cannot be erased, he must be embraced. Both Brossard and Rochon proffer love as the foundation for social change. Before love, though, the pardon mentioned by Beaulé must be negotiated. Rochon's ethics of redemption relate directly to that sense of pardon. Openness and transformation remain central to her transcultural SFQ sagas.

Transcultural Synthesis in Rochon's *Le Cycle de Vrénalik* and *Les Chroniques infernales*

Milena Santoro applies the concept of "la synthèse" (102) to Rochon's *Le Cycle de Vrénalik*. This "synthesis" resembles Baker's syncretism, but goes further in its assertion of the need not only to accept, but to privilege the Other in the development of community: "Rochon s'applique non pas tant à retrouver une quelconque identité 'authentique' face à l'omniprésence de 'l'Autre' mais plutôt à réfléchir à ce que les autres peuvent nous apporter, par leur différence même" ("Rochon tries not so much to refind some kind of 'authentic' identity in the face of the Other's omnipresence, but rather to reflect on what others can bring to us by their very difference"; 98). The contacts between the Asven and the Hanrel, the people of Ister-Inga and Irquiz, and the Cathades clearly reflect "Québec's transcultural model" described by Dupont and Lemarchand "as an exchange between the host society and the different cultural communities that have joined in and brought cultural diversity" (327). For the Asven, this model is particularly important as they face extinction if they do not open themselves to the Other.

Nicholas Serruys observes that oppressed groups in other SFQ texts have reached a level of isolation and dispossession so critical that "l'élément salvateur ne peut être que l'intervention d'une perspective externe," ("the saving element can only come through the intervention of an outside perspective"; "Véhicules" 77). Similarly, the outsiders Jouskilliant Green and Taïm Sutherland play essential roles in the development and liberation of the Asven people from the prison of their Archipelago. Implicit in the privileging of the other, is, of course, the condemnation of the homogeneity that we have also seen in Brossard's demonization of Lokhfer. Santoro links Rochon's work directly to the situation of the province of Québec in relation to this issue in *L'Espace du diamant*:

> Malgré les différences entre un Vrénalik déchu et un Québec relativement prospère, on peut néanmoins constater un parallèle important: Rochon réussit à cerner ici les problèmes inhérents à tout projet social de type homogénéisant.... Dans ce roman, l'autre est donc l'instrument privilégié du destin: l'ouverture vers cet autre est ce qui permet l'émergence d'un nouvel avenir prometteur [ED99].

> In spite of the differences between a fallen Vrénalik and a relatively prosperous Québec, we can nonetheless observe an important parallel: Rochon succeeds in highlighting the inherent problems in any social project that is homogenizing in nature.... In this novel, the other is the privileged instrument of destiny: the opening to the other is that which permits the emergence of a new, promising future.

If it insists on its continued isolation the Asven nation will die out. Clearly, in order to survive, it must open itself up to the outside. It is precisely this opening that the SFQ saga recounts, an openness now observed as real, particularly in the Montréal area, at least by Gérard Bouchard and Charles Taylor in the inquiries of their Commission on Practices of Accommodation Linked to Cultural Differences (5). Already in its first volume, *L'Aigle des profondeurs*, the Asven nation embraces immigrants from outside, a step necessary to their very survival as they fear extinction and require injections of new genetic material (AP22).[5] In addition to this strictly physical need for diversity, the outsiders also provide new ideas. Jouskilliant Green's presence inspired Fékril Candanad and Ivendra to think of the world beyond the Archipelago, and in *L'Archipel noir* another outsider, Taïm Sutherlund, returns the statue of the Ocean-god at the origin of the four-hundred-year-old curse and thus becomes Vrénalik's national hero, its "libérateur" (ED41–42, 60).

Indeed, as the Asven recuperate their past mythology and history they come to understand that they, like the African ethnic identities described by Jean-Loup Amselle in *Mestizo Logics* (1990), formed as a result of a cultural syncretism. Their founding myth, the "Histoire de Suzanne Arkàndanatt," recounts their derivation from the marriage between the nameless original inhabitants of the Archipelago and outsiders from across the sea:

> *Avant, des gens habitaient l'archipel;*
> *Ils ne portaient pas de nom.*
> *Suzanne et ses compagnons vinrent de la mer;*
> *Ils n'avaient pas de patrie.*
> *Ils se marièrent ensemble*
> *Et s'appellèrent les Asvens* [ED98]

> *Before, people inhabited the archipelago;*
> *They didn't have a name.*
> *Suzanne and her companions came from the sea;*

Four. Logiques métisses: Hybridity and Transculturalism

> *They didn't have a homeland.*
> *They married each other*
> *And called themselves the Asvens.*

L'Espace du diamant further develops this notion of cultural links between nations through the revelation of the shared cultural heritage between the Asven and the Cathades. The ultimate message of the SFQ saga here is that change is eternal, that an isolationist form of ethnic nationalism inevitably atrophies, that transformation will eventually occur. In order to survive and prosper the postcolonial society must embrace change and open itself up to the other in order to achieve a harmonious blend of the various cultural elements that contribute to it.

These principles appear in Rochon's *Les Chroniques infernales* in a number of ways as well, notably in its creation of a syncretic form of fiction which blends Western fantasy and science fiction, as well as Western content, with an Eastern Buddhist form of religio-philisophical thought, the Shambhalan principles of Chögyam Trungpa. Most clearly, though, Lame's recollections of Montréal refer to the specificity of its situation:

> À Montréal, il y avait eu des tensions entre anglophones et francophones, plus ou moins envenimées, impossibles à resoudre.... On avait la fierté de vivre dans la lourdeur, de cultiver les rancœurs centenaires que tous connaissaient [Or114].

> In Montréal, there were more or less venemous, impossible to resolve tensions between Anglophones and Francophones.... We were proud of living under the weight of it, of cultivating the centenary rancors that we all knew.

Her memory of a building's frieze carved with (pre–Nazi) swastikas, coupled with the English rose, Scotch thistle and the French fleur-de-lys figures the city's plural origins. Lame observes that while the first settlers could *afficher leur identité* ("proudly reveal their identity") and feel a part of their surroundings, more recent immigrants were denied this engagement: "Rien de tel pour que les immigrants à teint sombre se sentent bien accueillis!" ("Nothing like that for the dark-skinned immigrants to feel like they were welcome!"; Or168).

Over time, though, Lame's memories of Montréal and Québec change from the bitter accusations of her "Convocations" discussed in the previous chapter to the bittersweet, reflecting the transformative process of the open-ended, critical utopia. Focusing on the swastika, Lame recalls similar symbols in Sargade carvings; Rochon seeks redemption of this Vedic symbol of good fortune (Geaves). As this redemptive process continues, Lame reclaims her hometown, describing it precisely as "Montréal la multiculturelle" ("the multicultural Montreal"; So269), a postcolonial city: "une ville où les marginaux de toutes acceptions, les minoritaires et les déracinés sont, en fait, majoritaires" ("a city where marginals of all sorts, minorities and the uprooted are, in fact, the majority"; So67). Lame's multiple descriptions of and trips through Montréal reflect the same sensibility found in Sherry Simon's portraits of her real-life neighborhood of Montréal's Mile End (*Hybridité* 11–17). Furthermore, her personal culture reflects a syncretic blend of Baudelaire, Lovecraft and Buddhism, the French tradition, the Anglo-Saxon and the Eastern, a viewpoint that also contains an Anishinaabe/First Nations respect for nature/stewardship prevails over Vayinn's exclusive attitude in the final showdown of *Sorbier*. "Montréal la multiculturelle ... devenait la métaphore d'une humanité en perpétuel changement" ("Multicultural Montréal ... became the metaphor for a humanity in perpetual change"; So269).

Syncretic blends occur not only on the surface, but in the hells as well. Indeed, the nation which has the most difficulty in adapting to Rel's reforms, which move the hells onto other worlds, is the *pays de Sargade*, a land that expresses particular nationalist pride (S60). And yet, the Sargades cannot be so different from the indigenous infernal beings that they despise, since Har was able to take a Sargade wife, Rel's mother. In fact, one of the *sbires* observes that all the infernals must share a common ancestry because intermarriage occurred and proved fertile (S32).

Since Rel's mother originated in the *pays de Sargade*, which, described as a land of technology and the arts appears coded as Northern European, almost Scandinavian in nature, the prince of hells proves to be a literal hybrid, a Métis. He further takes on the role of immigrant during his adolescent flight to Vrénalik, which he refers to as his "terre d'exil" ("land of exile"; S 97) but also as "son monde d'adoption" ("adoptive world"; S96–97). As an exile from "le pays natal" ("native land"; S110), he is also told that: "Tu as quelque chose à réaliser dans ton pays natal" ("You have something to do in your native land"; S163). He returns, then, to the hells where as a rebel he has no choice but to "dissimuler ses convictions et ses sentiments ... des détenteurs du pouvoir" ("dissimulate his beliefs and feelings from those who held power"; S134). As for Taïm and the other characters discussed above in chapter two, Rel's youth represents a time of alienation even in his own homeland.

Rel, the prince of the hells, represents the hybrid subject par excellence, *indigène* and exile at once, a half-breed, genetic synthesis of hellion and human. Like Adakhan Demuthsen, Rel's black hair and dark, copper-colored skin (A7; Or40) set him apart and align him with the Other, particularly for his two companions the formerly human, white-skinned immigrants of European-coded origin, Lame and Fax/Taïm. Lame wonders at one point how her ancestors would approve of her relationship with this "métèque dont les os mêmes étaient noirs" ("wog whose very bones were black"; Or168). Rel bears the pain of the mistreated victims of European conquest, including slavery and colonization. While unafraid to reveal his hermaphroditic genitals in public, Rel keeps his most intimate secret to himself: the scars on his back. Years of mistreatment (including sexual abuse) by his father leave him with a branched network of scars like those in the famous photograph "Scars of a whipped slave named Peter" (Louisiana, 1863). At its sight, Taïm recoils: "Il lui semblait se trouver devant une carte de la dévastation du monde" ("It seemed to him as if he stood before a map of the devastation of the world"; So253). The real shame, Rochon seems to be saying, lies not in an individual deviation from gender normativity, but in this history of hidden abuse.

As a visionary leader who will bring the people across to the other side, he is responsible for opening up the closed world. His very name is an anagram, referring to the *Roi à l'Esprit Libre* (the open-minded king). He embodies the defining traits of the transcultural as an opening of the self to the Other in order to effectuate a transformation. This type of transformation occurs at the individual level through the growth of Lame, Taïm and Rel discussed in previous chapters. But it also occurs at the level of the collectivity through the trope of the crossing over. In *Les Chroniques infernales* Rochon reworks the Tibetan Bardo, a text which precisely serves to assist the crossing of the dead soul into the next realm. The Comtesse d'Agoult, Liszt's lover and an author in her own right as Daniel Stern, refers to the notion of crossing as well in the passage from her memoirs cited in epigraph to this chapter. The notion of a crossing, a passage occurs not only in Brossard's *L'Oiseau de feu*— Adakhan's journey from Manokhsor to the Centrale and then from the Centrale to Ashmev — but also in Rochon's Vrénalik Cycle as the Asven cross the sea from the Archipelago to the continent to the south and then cross the continent to the location of the Red City. It equally plays a central role in Vonarburg's *Tyranaël* saga, where transcultural exchange eventually develops as a result of the passage from Virginia to Atyrkelsaō. In this respect, the exchanges presented in these texts reflect Cunningham's definition of meaningful transculturalism cited in the introduction to this chapter (194).

Vonarburg's Transcultural Communities on Virginia-Tyranaël/Atyrkelsaō

I have already asserted that the vast time spans covered in the SFQ saga allow for the exploration of a full range of thematics related to colonialism and postcolonialism. Élisabeth Vonarburg's *Tyranaël* saga is no exception, as it recounts the arrival of the first group of settlers, their various relationships with the metropolitan power and then through first encounter, contact, and eventually their relationship with the indigenous group on the colonized land. The sophistication of Vonarburg's science-fictional plot line allows her to develop these themes in a range of new and complex fashions, including the distanced and refracted contact between the descendants of the first Earth colonists and the native Ranao, as well as the Ranao's own status as colonizers/

pioneers as they move onto the parallel world of Atyrkelsaō to avoid contact with the Strangers from Earth. Eventually, however, the strange Sea of energy acts as a bridge between the two worlds, allowing travel and exchange between the Virginians on Tyranaël and the Ranao on Atyrkelsaō. As a work of postcolonial science fiction, Vonarburg's SFQ saga offers a wide range of oppositional positions to explore. These include the rejection of an ultimately racist, ethnically or genetically based communal foundation, the inevitable hybridization that occurs when two groups meet, and, in the final volumes of the saga, the development of two mature civilizations which can interact based on a model of exchange, reflective of the contemporary Québec values of civic nationalism and a transcultural model for the pluralistic society.

In her discussion of the *brocante*, the second-hand shop as a metaphor for the transcultural experience of contemporary identity in Montréal, Mary Jean Green asserts that in the novel *La Québécoite* (1983), Régine Robin's:

> second-hand shop points to a new Québécois "national text" that was finally being written in the 1980s. At the same time as Robin's immigrant narrator was protesting the imposition of an identity narrowly founded on the martyrdom of seventeenth-century Jesuit missionaries, the history of Quebec was being transformed from a single narrative thread, the heroic survival of a handful of French settlers, into a fabric woven from multiple migrations [17].

Vonarburg's *Tyranaël* series traces precisely the same historical transformation for the handful of shipwrecked Terrans who first arrive on Virginia in *Dreams of the Sea*, through to a complexly woven fabric of cultural exchange by the series' conclusion in *La Mer allée avec le soleil*. In doing so, the work explores a wide range of strategies of resistance and accommodation before the various groups in its imaginary territories can come to peaceful terms. The initial creolization of the Terrans — genetically transformed by their encounter with the spatial alterity of this place[6] — and the various forms of *braconnage* (poaching) and appropriation that they make of the remains of the Ancients' culture eventually lead to the experience of crossing to the other side via the Sea. They ultimately arrive at a sometimes uncomfortable individual and cultural hybridization across the two parallel worlds. The SFQ saga depicts the transformation of a monocultural society, the single narrative of a handful of Terran colonists, set in contact with a strange planet and its Sea of energy, into a complex transcultural society involving the Virginian descendants of Terrans, Ranao who cross back from Atyrkelsaō to their former home planet, a third race — the Ékelli — that has concealed its presence from the others, and even tourists from the Lagrange asteroid, the current home of the descendants of the last surviving humans on now-destroyed Earth.

As a first step in this transformational process, Vonarburg's work rejects ethnic nationalism as the model for a healthy communal society. Through the introduction of the science-fictional trope of the genetic mutation among first a few and then among the majority of the humans from Earth who settle on the planet Tyranaël, renamed Virginia, Vonarburg demonstrates how genetically based alliances typically lead to oppression of one group by another based on genetic difference. First non-mutated humans discriminate against mutants (in *A Game of Perfection*), then, as the mutation becomes generalized in the population, mutants discriminate against the "blockhead" humans who appear not to possess the extrasensory powers the mutation entails (in *Mon frère l'ombre*). As the range of genetic mutations grows, those with extrasensory perception discriminate against those with other, more telekinetic powers, and so on. As discussed in the previous chapter, by the second book of *Tyranaël*, a collectivity forms based not on the family or ethnic-genetic makeup, but rather on common interests and abilities in the group of circus performers brought together by Simon Rossem (Tobee, Max, Marc, Éric, Tess and Alyne).

A new notion of "home" develops around the common interests of those with the mutation. The notion of a community of choice carries forward into *Mon frère l'ombre* as the Civil War sides are represented as a choice, rather than as something one is born into (MF291, 344). Its resistance to essentialist genetic bases for identity appears clearly in the assertion by Lian "nous ne sommes pas que nos gènes" ("we are not only our genes"; AR162–163). The novel reaffirms that identity is a choice (AR202), that blood does not determine identity (AR225). At the same time, the mutation represents a literal creolization: the descendants of the colonists are physically changed by their new home planet.

As this group's interests evolve from basic acceptance and self-protection into a more hegemonic search for power, that is, as Tess and the others implicate themselves in the struggle for Virginian independence, their genetic relationship — a relationship that does not derive from their parents' ethnic background, but rather from their residence on the new planet colony — appears in a negative light. Vonarburg implicitly criticizes how a formerly marginalized group, as it unites and finds a common interest/trait — the genetic mutation — then seeks to gain greater power and status for itself. This process allegorizes both the nationalist movement in Québec and the darker, entitled side of the "politics of recognition" discussed by Charles Taylor. While on the one hand, the novels emit a positive message of resistance against a colonizing or oppressive force through the developmentt of the RVI, the Rassemblement pour une Virginia indépandante, which asserts that "it's downright intolerable for you to be colonized" (GP159), and while the Virginians must unite and develop an identity for themselves (GP198), at the same time, their reinscription of Terran power structures from the past in the new order problematizes these goals and desires (GP241, 285–86). This critique of genealogy (a widespread hobby in Québec, see Caron) is clear in *Mon frère l'ombre* in the fact that both the Grays and Simon's group keep genealogical records of the mutation. Both sides are implicated in the violence that results when communities are divided across genealogical lines (MF230–31, 248–50).

How the Virginians interact with the indigenous Ranao, first through their treatment of the artifacts found on the abandoned planet, and later through interactions allowed by the discovery of the ability to move from Virginia/Tyranaël to Atyrkelsaõ via the Sea, evolves over time, in a fashion reflective perhaps of colonial interactions found on the "real" world of the reader/writer, with the critical function of critiquing "bad" practices and proposing better, more productive practices for future communities. In their early encounters with artifacts of the Ranao, the Virginians reveal a distinct lack of respect for the "natives." When the body of an "Ancient" is found frozen in a block of ice, it is of course removed for study with no concern over the fact that this is a humanoid body, someone's ancestor who may be revered (GP101–03). A more totalitarian power comes to control the planet and represses the desire for knowledge of and respect for the indigenous "Ancients." Their historical revisionism attempts an erasure of the indigenous presence in the creation of a community, an erasure like that inherent in the concepts of the two founding nations, the two solitudes and other such metaphors for conceiving Canadian national identity without taking into account this crucial original pole. It is precisely the Virginians' forgetting not only of the Ancients but also of their own Terran roots (AR75–77) that compels them to repeat the mistakes of the past (AR123).

Notions of creolity pervade the *Tyranaël* saga. The genetic mutation that allows for the development of extrasensory and telekinetic powers proves to be the result of physiological changes that occur to the Terran immigrants once they arrive in their new homeland. Just as the team of astronauts from Brossard's *L'Oiseau de feu* must adjust physically to conditions on Ashmev, Vonarburg's Virginians are changed: "nous avons changé, nous nous sommes adaptés à la planète" (JP62), "une évolution est en cours" (JP76). The place forces the new immigrants to adapt to it, to create a new, creole identity, as the "nouveaux" Virginians are mutants (JP282; MF259–60). This adaptation occurs in more mundane ways as well. The longer day on Virginia forces humans to adopt a practice of a Meridien meal and nap, something the Ancients did not have to do because they were better adapted having evolved on the planet.

Again, ambivalence appears in how an oppositional postcolonialism plays out in the text and how various elements of Québec's "real" history are refigured in the SFQ saga. As in Brossard's work, the novel alludes to the *revanche des berceaux*: Alyne, the most placatory of the young mutants in *A Game of Perfection*, reasonably hopes that the solution to the societal rejection of her mutant kind will occur through just such a development. Her goal is to bear children, who will have their own children and so forth, so that eventually the mutation will generalize throughout the population, echoing the logic of the revenge of the cradle (GP109). Vonarburg allows this fantasy to play out over the volumes, but, as we have seen, the generalization of the mutation into the majority of the population simply leads to the creation of other factors through which to identify, and thus to discriminate upon the basis of, difference. This is seen in *Mon frère l'ombre* and even still in *L'Autre rivage*.

Another form of adaptation to place also occurs, as some Virginians opt to study the technology of the Ancients in order to adapt more effectively to the conditions of the planet. This movement clearly demonstrates a respect for the indigenous inhabitants of the planet and acknowledges the effectiveness of their technologies, in particular for adapting to the Sea's effects on electrical power sources when the tide is high. In Morgorod the Virginians have adopted the Ancients' practice of wearing bells while the Sea's fog blankets the city, an example of geography forcing cultural development as well as a cultural métissage (MF179). While a number of Virginians resist this, others appear almost ridiculous in their desire to imitate. Such is the case with the Immortals, a bizarrely "plastic shamanist" cult which adopts indigenous Ranao beliefs and practices, or at least the folklorized picture that has been developed of them through archeological and archival records accessed through the memory plaques. (Again memory plays an essential role in the development of collective identity in the postcolonial novel.) In the long run, the only constant is change: "Tout change.... Tout se transforme" ("Everything changes.... Everything is transformed"; AR32).

If change is the only constant, then multiplicity is valued and stressed. This is noted at the level of the individual and subjectivity, as exemplified by Simon Rossem, who in the final volume is understood to be a completely different form of mutant, a Hékellim. He has lived multiple lives and personalities because of his longevity (MA251). In addition, each main character contains within him- or herself multiple subject positions/origins from which to draw. These differ from those of mainstream society either through early development of the mutation for extrasensory perception or through hybridization between Ranao/humans, and so on. Vonarburg's universe resembles that of *la créolité* praised by Bernabé, Chamoiseau and Confiant, in which "complexity is the very principle of our identity" (90) and that "each culture is never a finished product but rather the constant dynamics ... interested in relating rather than dominating, in exchanging rather than looting ... the conscious harmonization of preserved diversities: DIVERSALITY" (114). Reality itself, of course, becomes multiple through the development of the parallel world theme as Sylvie Bérard has noted of Vonarburg's "arborescent" universe ("Fictional"). Perhaps echoing the title of a nationalist magazine (in which Jacques Brossard published), *Possibles*, the text refers to the multiplicity of potentials, using the term the "possibles" (MA46–47).

The issue of the "new" Virginians is reminiscent of the situation of the "new" Quebeckers, immigrants whom nationalist discourse has sought to include in the fold since at least 1990 and whose acceptance must be "sold" to more traditional ethnic nationalists. On Virginia, the "new" Virginians, that is, the mutants, must first "sell" their presence and acceptance to the majority population of "normals" in order to get out of the situation of persecution in which they find themselves for most of *A Game of Perfection* (GP253–54).

In addition to the notion of a creolization, which itself relates to hybridity, actual hybridization occurs among the various groups on both planets and eventually between the two populations on the separate, parallel worlds. Vonarburg underscores the notion that hybridization is ultimately the natural order of things, the inevitable result of extended interaction between cultures. As the backstory of the Ranao's history develops over the novels, the reader discovers that the present-day Ranao are, of course, the result of a blend of a number of different ethnicities, and that the Ancient races have blended to form one dominant type (GP124–27): Rani culture is made up of "quatre cultures et tous les hybrides" ("four cultures, all of them hybrid," AR188, 208). Indeed, their history and mythology privileges the story of Ktulhudar, an ancient chief who was a métis (GP148–49). A number of main characters are also hybrid figures like Liam/Lian whose mother was Ranao and his father a Virginian who crossed over via the Sea.

A cultural syncretism also occurs over time; first we see a desire to incorporate the Ancients in a new Virginian identity after the colony planet's independence from earth is established (GP280). Even in individual identity the text privileges the in-between as the best able to negotiate this hybrid reality. For example, Sandra Doven, the first Virginian President is elected perhaps because she "is neither a gaje [those who want full technological development, a serendipitous wordplay between the Romani word for foreigner and the English "gadget"] nor an Old Settler, but navigates between the two worlds with consummate skill" (GP246). Similarly, Virginian society is a syncretic society: its language is composed of several earth languages (MF202, 245; AR65), its immigrants, although all human, represent a wide range of ethnic varieties.

Allowed the free-play of ambivalence in the fictional form, Vonarburg's SFQ saga explores both the positive and negative aspects of hybridity. This appears in the identity crises of Taïriel, the central character of *La Mer allée avec le soleil*. As the ability, linked to the genetic mutation, to cross through the Sea from Virginia to Atyrkelsaõ and back has become more generalized in the populations of both worlds, increased contact between Virginians (of Terran descent) and Ranao occurs, including increased sexual contact. Taïriel, or Tiri for short, describes herself:

Hybride de troisième génération, moi. Mais ça ne se remarque pas à l'extérieur, au moins ou alors juste la peau brune et douce, dépourvue de pilosité ... yeux brun-vert, cheveux très noirs—longs, brillants, épais et lisses, vraiment rani, mais

Four. Logiques métisses: *Hybridity and Transculturalism*   205

> sinon un faciès à pommettes saillantes et nez court busqué, un peu asiatique, un peu africaine, un peu tout, une Virginienne moyenne [MA9].
>
> I'm a third generation hybrid. But you can't tell it from the outside, at least, except the soft brown, hairless skin ... greenish-brown eyes, very black hair — long, shiny, thick and smooth, really Rani, but otherwise a face with high cheekbones and a short, upturned nose, a bit Asian, a bit African, a bit of everything, an average Virginian.

She represents in a sense, Vasconcelos' cosmic race. Tiri lives on a Virginia that has developed a hybrid culture, with art, music and festivals that involve elements from a number of old Earth cultures, mixed with various Rani traditions. The text refers to the "croisement culturel" apparent in musical concerts which include a program of Mozart, Œniken (a Virginian) as well as "des compositeurs ranao" ("Ranao composers"; MA10). The Virginian language has also come to use a number of *setlâd* (the language of the Ranao) terms, particularly for the indigenous animals such as the cat-like *banki* (MA10). A major celebration occurs at the new year marked by the return of high tide for the enigmatic Sea of energy that covers the planet only part of the time:

> De nombreuses activités se déroulent à plusieurs endroits de Cristobal pour le Retour et la nouvelle Année, mais celles qui évoquent de près ou de loin les Ranao sont rassemblées au Parc de la Tête... Le Parc, aujourd'hui, c'est un lieu de rassemblement pour les hékellin, les halatnim et généralement les pro–Ranao [MA9].
>
> A number of activities are taking place at several sites in Cristobal for the Return of the new Year, but those that invoke the Ranao in any way are gathered at the Park of the Head... Today the Park is a gathering place for the hékellin [Ranao who have returned], the halatnim [descendants of Virginians who had passed over to Atyrkelsaō] and anyone generally pro–Ranao.

Tiri's description at the novel's opening of those present at these particular festivities (held in a town honoring the man who "discovered" the New World on Earth) reveals, however, her attitude of ambivalence as "an average Virginian." She only plans to attend these on the insistence of a boyfriend who "a toujours eu un faible pour l'exotisme" ("always had a weakness for the exotic"; MA9). Her rejection of her Rani roots figures the third-generation immigrant adolescent's desire to fit in and adapt to the culture in which he or she has grown up, seeing the "old country" of the grandparents as a foreign land. Across this volume, though, Tiri realizes that she must embrace both aspects of her identity to obtain a complete sense of herself—to become disalienated.

There is an uncanny relationship, really, between the two, between the self and the other, in which the same is not the same; it is familiar, yet unsettlingly different, or perhaps unsettling in its familiarity. Tyranaël and Atyrkelsaō are parallel worlds, virtually the same so that the Ranao can cross over and recreate their former home, and yet there are subtle differences (AR83, 137).

As in *L'Oiseau de feu*, when the colonists begin to call Ashmev Earth and vice versa, thus confusing the notion of home, a similar phenomenon occurs in *Tyranaël* with the question of the Other Side. First, in *L'Autre rivage*, the title of the fourth novel of the series, the other shore is Tyranaël, the former home of the Ranao, now on Atyrkelsaō (AR223). Lian/Liam crosses over to this other side. Later, though, in *La Mer allée avec le soleil*, Samuel (Simon Rossem's final avatar) refers to Atyrkelsaō as "l'Autre Côté" (MA42–45). The notion of home becomes confused, relativized and ambiguous for the migrant subject.

The series' final volume *La Mer allée avec le soleil* resolves a number of issues, without achieving a final closure — its ending is open in keeping with the ambiguous, or open-ended utopian novel discussed in the last chapter. Overall, the series works to undermine the situation of the dichotomous society that we saw in chapter two, a simplistic view of a colonial reality of oppressors and oppressed. Throughout, we have observed the multiple contributions of a wide range of groups toward the creation of both Virginian and Ranao societies. By this fifth novel, Virginia's population is seen somewhat in triune form. The majority comprises "Native" Virginians and "ethnic" Virginians returned (from Atyrkelsaō), called *halatnim* (MAS87). A small proportion of the population consists of Ranao *passeurs*, as those who who have returned to Tyranaël-Virginia from Atyrkelsaō are called. However, although certain telepathic and telekinetic abilities have become normalized, some three percent of the population reflects a distinct strain of the mutation, the exceptional longevity displayed by Simon Rossem (MA241). The vast majority (97 percent) is comprised of "nous autres simples mortels" ("we simple mortals"; MA3, 20), who include the "dormeurs," the new politically correct name for the bloqués also called Kerlïtai (MA36, 24). Then, of course, there remain those on Lagrange, who are all "normal" because no telepathic powers could have evolved in Terran stock off the planet Tyranaël-Virginia. On Atyrkelsaō, as well, while the Ranao have split into two sort of political/ideological parties, the dânao and the darnao, these groups actually work together rather than in opposition to one another to develop a negotiated vision for the future direction of societal development on the new planet. Again, the two poles are broken up by the presence of thirds. One is a proto-ranid species, analogous to australopithecines for humans on Earth, which on Atyrkelsaō did not develop into fully sentient beings. As well, there are, of course, the post–Terran human *passeurs* from Virginia. Even further, a species not fully humanoid called the Shipsha have nonetheless evolved into sentients: "Ces créatures se sont vraiment bien intégrées et cette planète leur réussit" ("These creatures integrated really well and this planet works for them"; MA 432). For their part, the Virginians, too, have grown in their ability to accept the Other: "pas très étonnant, cette acceptation aisée des Shipsha par les Virginiens: ils y étaient assez préparés" ("not surprising, this easy acceptance of the Shipsha by the Virginians: they were well enough prepared for it"; MA433). Harmonious societies can exist in the postcolonial world of Vonarburg's *Tyranaël*.

In this SFQ saga, humanity itself has been relativized and problematized in an oppositional discourse that denies the possibility of an essentialist identification of one sole group with "the Human" (MA252, 301). This has been done through the various mutations and hybridizations, as well as through cloning and artificially longevity (AR357, 436), all of which undermine the possibility of establishing one, unified definition for humanity. As they call into question notions of reality and linear time, the Dreams of the Ranao (MA247)—and of the Virginians who develop this skill as the novel's epilogue reveals (MA427)—render responses to ontological questions increasingly difficult to formulate. Never is it certain that the parallel worlds and beings seen through the Dreams are real or just possible (MA291–92, 298).

Overall, the *Tyranaël* novels privilege difference, multivalence and the heterogeneous. Consistently, reader sympathy is channelled toward the minority, those marginalized from society because of their difference. This occurs from the beginning with the narration through the eyes of Eïlai Liannon Klaidaru, the Ranao Dreamer who first dreams of the Strangers and who, because of this, is ostracized by some in her society as the bearer of bad news. It occurs again through the central characters of each volume, from Simon, who is different from everyone else in his family, to Liam, who as a half-breed Virginian-Ranao, is clearly ostracized both on his birth-planet of Atyrkelsaō and on Virginia when he crosses over.

The danger of over-valuing hybridization, however, is that it can also be put into practice as a form of eugenics, as Robert J. C. Young points out (*Colonial* 9). Simon briefly considers cross-breeding to specifically select for the mutation in order to speed up the *revanche des berceaux* process, but quickly rejects the idea (GP195–96). As mentioned earlier, the obsession with genealogy ultimately leads to attitudes of exclusion of the Other as seen in the Ranaos keeping of "lignées" ("bloodlines"; MA109). (Vonarburg also stages such an obsession in order to critique it in *In the Mother's Land*.) Indeed, the last volume of *Tyranaël* reveals the presence of individuals from a third race, indigenous neither to Earth nor to Tyranaël. They are shown to have been manipulating both humans and Ranao all along (MA346, 353, 364, 432), and they have in fact been practicing eugenics upon both groups, so that a great cloud appears over the utopian horizon of Vonarburg's SFQ saga. A sort of *deus ex machina* ending problematizes the entire series, in a fashion similar to that revealed at the end of his Brossard's work with the return to the notion that everything has been manipulated by beings more advanced, more powerful than either the humans or the Ranao. Like Prospero in Shakespeare's *Tempest* and like the first Terrans to arrive on Tyranaël, the manipulators (MA387, 397, 436) were shipwrecked on the planet and their manipulations of others simply serve to amuse themselves. Indeed, their obsession, revealed near the end of the series, with the various genetic variations produced by their experiments ("Quelles variantes?" ["Which variations"; MA365]), eerily recalls Brossard's "Annexe" at the end of *Les Années d'errance* in which Lokhfer and Syrius, in the guise of Lucifer and Yahweh discuss the "variante" of human history they have ostensibly just viewed.

There is the concern here that xenophobia and xenophilia become confused and that through hybridization the other can simply become absorbed into the same (Bammer "Xenophobia"). There is ambivalence in the text's distinctions between Terrans and Ranao: the two groups are the same, human, but also different. That they are different species and that they need surgical adaptations to interact for biological reproduction is made very clear (AR55, 182). Indeed, the possibility of interbreeding, of métissage allows the Ranao to accommodate the first *passeurs*, as Virginians who cross over, at first by accident, are called on Atyrkelsaō (AR137). That is, through interbreeding they can assimilate the Strangers. Eventually, though, enough Virginians have crossed over and a segregated, separatist *halatnim*, community form on Atyrkelsaō. In these, only Virginian is spoken, but they are populated by an essentially hybrid group: "des hybrides, les enfants que les passeurs ont créés avec les Ranao" ("hybrids, children that the passers made with the Ranao"; AR55). These hybrids are children of the borderzones, they don't really fit into either world (AR13–14), they are an "entre-deux" (AR150) — a term privileged throughout Vonarburg's series and in other SFQ works. (Vonarburg's stories of the Bridge Cycle and Rochon's Labyrinth Cycle stories also figure devices that allow communication between otherwise alien worlds.)

We might view these early *passeurs* as committing a form of *braconnage identitaire* in Simon Harel's sense; they are trespassing on the territory of the Other. This trespass represents, of course, the first step in what will eventually become a legitimized relationship. But the Sea as a means of passage, which both separates and connects the two worlds of Tyranaël-Virginia and Atyrkelsaō and which eventually becomes a means of communication between the groups who share these contiguous spaces, also represents this "entre-deux." In a similar vein, Homi K. Bhabha invokes the image of the stairwell in African-American artist Renée Green's work as a hybrid space that allows for difference to flourish unhindered:

> The stairwell as liminal space, in-between the designations of identity, becomes the process of symbolic interaction, the connective tissue that constructs the difference between upper and lower, black and white. The hither and thither of the stairwell, the temporal movement and passage that it allows, prevents identities at either end of it from settling into primordial polarities. This interstitial passage between fixed identifications opens up the possibility of a cultural hybridity that entertains difference without an assumed or imposed hierarchy [5].

The Sea itself represents just such a location. But it is not only a location. As in Stanislaw Lem's great intertext, the mysterious entity on the planet, Vonarburg suggests, is not only a means of communication for two separated worlds inhabited by species that are both human, but it is itself a sentient being: "pourtant, elle est curieuse de nous comme des autres. Est-ce cela qu'elle cherche, à travers les univers, des êtres capables de communiquer par son intermédiaire, ou avec elle?" ("nonetheless, she is curious just as we are. Is that what she seeks, across the universes, beings able to communicate using her as an intermediary, or with her?"; MA365)

Like the Sea, as Vonarburg asserts, we are curious about others. However problematic it may be, this is a primary goal of science fiction: to imagine the possibility of the existence of others in the universe and to work through, often in some symbolic or allegorical way, our relationships with the others that surround us here on Earth. Likewise, science fiction from Québec shares this aim. As in the emotionally charged assertion by the nationalist poet Michèle Lalonde in "Speak White," Québec's writers of SF assert: "We are not alone."

Conclusion

As we have seen, the alien nations depicted in the SFQ saga explore the possibility of disalienation through their utopian visions of the imagined community, the truly postcolonial society. Jacques Brossard, Élisabeth Vonarburg, and Esther Rochon offer a science fictional discourse that rightly can be termed postcolonial. Although not fully analyzed here, the survey of SFQ in chapter one suggests that a significant number of other writers of their generations, as well as younger writers of SFQ, like Sylvie Bérard and Mehdi Bouhalassa, do the same. To close the loop and return to Gunther Kress' definition of discourse cited in my introduction, we have seen that the SFQ saga fully represents a set "of statements which define, describe and delimit the possibilities of action and of thought, of representation and self-representation" (Cranny-Francis 207) that projects the need for not only Québec and Canada, but for all of humanity, to come to terms with the alienation caused by past and current systems of social, economic, and political relationships between individuals and groups in Western civilization(s) today, an alienation caused by a great number of factors, one of which is the singular legacy of the ideology of colonialism and imperialism. As a form of postcolonial discourse, the SFQ saga not only critiques the colonial system, it negotiates other possible social systems and relationships for individuals and groups, privileging the multiple, the hybrid, the transcultural, it allows for endless possibilities of action and thought. That, too, is the job of science fiction in general.

While my intention here has not been to offer a comparative study, I would like to make a few such remarks by way of conclusion, particularly as this seems to be a pressing question for those who express even marginal interest in SFQ to me: What makes SFQ different from the major canon of Anglo-American SF? Recent scholarship like that of Patricia Kerslake and Sharon De Graw on representations of empire and race in that SF canon demonstrates an evolutionary trend from quite distinctly colonialist-imperialist discourses for representations of the exploration, conquest and colonization of space in the language of Golden Age SF to forms more critical of that discourse, like those found in the work of Philip K. Dick, Ursula K. Le Guin or Kim Stanley Robinson. While this would be the object of another study, I can safely assert that, at least in its contemporary froms, Québec's SF avoids the language of conquest that has colored its Anglo-American counterpart for much of its history. As Nicholas Serruys asserts, SFQ developed during a period of "l'incertitude d'un peuple sur son identité et ses frontières" ("the uncertainty of a people about its identity and its borders"; "Véhicules" 76). As the Quiet Revolution blew Québec's self-image as a rural, agricultural, Catholic nation out of the water, what would fill that empty space was up for grabs. This ideological void allowed a number of writers and readers to explore, through the discourses of science fiction and fantasy, a vast array of possibilities, good and bad, utopian and dystopian, for filling that space.

One final comment on science-fiction studies in general that I am pleased to make. Over the course of this project's development (I drafted the first table of contents and outline in 2000), while the term "postcolonial science fiction" has yet to catch on as a major rising genre, science fiction scholars can no longer ignore postcolonial theory in their examinations of the Anglo-American canon. Not only have we seen monographs like Kerslake's devoted to *Science Fiction and Empire* (2007), single-author studies and reference works like Susan Bernardo and Graham Murphy's *Ursula K. Le Guin: A Critical Companion* (2006) include sections applying its concepts to their objects. John Rieder's *Colonialism and the Emergence of Science fiction* (2008) represents the most recent effort towards articulating "the connection between the early history of the genre of English-language science fiction and the history and discourses of colonialism" (1). A growing number of scholars have begun, as well, to look at "other" science fictions, evidenced by M. Elizabeth Ginway's elegant study of *Brazilian Science Fiction: Cultural Myths and Nationhood in the Land of the Future* (2004), or Grace Dillon's work on African American and Native American science fiction and fantasy. In the field of science fiction, both writers and critics have slowly come to acknowledge that the center cannot hold as the peripheries of the empire write back offering alternate visions not of a universe to conquer, but of the multiverse to explore.

APPENDIX

A Selected Bibliography of French-Canadian Science Fiction and Fantasy in English[1]

April, Jean-Pierre. "Rêve Canadien." Trans. Howard Scott. In *Tesseracts Q*. Ed. Élisabeth Vonarburg and Jane Brierley, 80–98. Edmonton: Tesseracts/The Books Collective, 1996. Rpt. *Northern Suns: The New Anthology of Canadian Science Fiction*. Ed. David G. Hartwell and Glenn Grant, 299–317. New York: Tor, 1999. Trans. of "Canadian Dream." *imagine...* 14 (1982): 8–25.

Beaulieu, Natasha. "Ève-Marie." Trans. Yves Meynard. In *Tesseracts[7]*. Ed. Paula Johanson and Jean-Louis Trudel, 98–108. Edmonton: The Books Collective, 1998. Trans. of "Ève-Marie." In *L'Année de la science-fiction et du fantastique québécois: 1992*. Ed. Claude Janelle, 243–52. Québec: Alire, 1997.

———. "Laika." In *Tesseracts[5]*. Ed. Robert Runté and Yves Meynard, 306–12. Edmonton: The Books Collective, 1996. Trans. of "Laika." *Solaris* 117 (1996): 15–17.

Beaulieu, René. "The Blue Jay." Trans. Jane Brierley. In *Tesseracts Q*. Ed. Élisabeth Vonarburg and Jane Brierley, 247–62. Edmonton: Tesseracts/The Books Collective, 1996. Trans. of "Le Jeai bleu." In *Légendes de Virnie*, 167–86. Longueil: Le Préambule, 1981.

———. "The Energy of Slaves." Trans. Yves Meynard. In *Tesseracts[8]*. Ed. John Clute and Candas Jane Dorsey, 275–90. Edmonton: The Books Collective, 1999. Trans. of "L'Énergie des esclaves." In *Un Fantôme d'amour*, 33–48. Roberval: Ashem, 1997.

———. "Mirrors." Trans. Sheryl Curtis. In *Tesseracts[9]*. Ed. Nalo Hopkinson and Geoff Ryman, 271–98. Calgary: Edge SF & F, 2005. Trans. of "Miroirs." In *Légendes de Virnie*, 19–42. Longueil: Le Préambule, 1981.

———. "Phantom Love." In *Tesseracts[10]*. Ed. Edo Van Belkom and Robert Charles Wilson, 249–64. Calgary: Edge SF & F, 2006. Trans. of "Un Fantôme d'amour." In *Un Fantôme d'amour*, 49–60. Roberval: Ashem, 1997.

Bérard, Sylvie. *Of Wind and Sand*. Trans. Sheryl Curtis. Edmonton: Edge SF & F, 2009. Trans. of *Terre des Autres*. Beauport: Alire, 2004.

———. "A Wall." In *Tesseracts[6]*. Ed. Robert J. Sawyer and Carolyn Clink. Edmonton: Tesseracts, 1997. Trans. of "Un mur." *XYZ* 40 (1994): 54–57.

———. "Wings to Fly." Trans. Sheryl Curtis. In *Tesseracts[9]*. Ed. Nalo Hopkinson and Geoff Ryman, 377–78. Calgary: Edge SF & F: 2005. Trans. of "Lettre à Brijjie." *Solaris* 133 (2000): 10.

Bergeron, Alain. "The Eighth Register." Trans. Howard Scott. In *Tesseracts Q.* Ed. Élisabeth Vonarburg and Jane Brierley, 150–79. Edmonton: Tesseracts/The Books Collective, 1996. Rpt. *Northern Suns: The New Anthology of Canadian Science Fiction.* Ed. David G. Hartwell and Glenn Grant, 46–76. New York: Tor, 1999. Trans. "Le Huitième registre." *Solaris* 107 (1993): 5–17.

———. "Happy Birthday Universe!" Trans. Mary G. Shelton. In *Tesseracts²*. Ed. Phyllis Gotlieb and Douglas Barbour, 139–64. Victoria: Porcépic, 1987. Trans. "Bonne Fête, univers!" *Solaris* 65 (1986): 12–21.

Bergeron, Bertrand. "The Other." Trans. Jane Brierley. In *Tesseracts Q.* Ed. Élisabeth Vonarburg and Jane Brierley, 330–35. Edmonton: Tesseracts/The Books Collective, 1996. Trans. "L'Autre." In *L'Année de la science-fiction et du fantastique québécois, 1987.* Ed. Claude Janelle and Jean Pettigrew, 239–43. Montréal: Le Passeur, 1988.

Bersianik, Louky. *The Eugelion.* Trans. Howard Scott. Montréal: Alter Ego, 1996. Trans. of *L'Euguélionne.* Montréal: La Presse, 1976.

Billon, Pierre. *The Children's Wing.* Trans. Sheila Fischman. Montréal: R. Davies, 1995. Trans. of *L'Enfant du cinquième Nord.* Montréal: Québec/Amérique, 1982; Paris: Seuil, 1982.

Boisvert, Claude. "A Slice of Nothingness." Trans. Michael Bullock. In *Invisible Fictions: Contemporary Stories from Québec.* Ed. Geoff Hancock, 257–60. Toronto: Anansi, 1987. Trans. of "Tranche de néant." In *Tranches de néant*, 143–47. Montréal: Biocreux, 1980.

Brossard, Jacques. "From a Nail in the Head." Trans. R. W. Stedingh. *The Canadian Fiction Magazine* 27 (1977): 81–85. Trans. "Le Clou dans le crâne." In *Le Métamorfaux*, 61–79. Montréal: Hurtubise HMH, 1974.

———. "The Metamorfalsis." Trans. Basil Kingstone. In *Invisible Fictions: Contemporary Stories from Québec.* Ed. Geoff Hancock, 121–48. Toronto: Anansi, 1987. Trans. of "Le Métamorfaux." In *Le Métamorfaux*, 25–60. Montréal: Hurtubise HMH, 1974.

Carpentier, André. "Bebe's Tears." Trans. Frances Morgan. *Canadian Fiction Magazine* 66 (1989): 124–37. Trans. of "Les Larmes de Bébé." In *Du pain des oiseaux*, 93–116. Montréal: VLB, 1982.

———. "Birdy's Flight." Trans. Michael Bullock. In *Invisible Fictions: Contemporary Stories from Québec.* Ed. Geoff Hancock, 63–82. Toronto: Anansi, 1987. Trans. of "Le Vol de Ti-Oiseau." In *Du pain des oiseaux*, 15–42. Montréal: VLB, 1982.

———. "Bygone Books." Trans. Frances Morgan. *Canadian Fiction Magazine* 47 (1983): 170–81. Trans. "La Bouquinerie d'Outre-Temps." In *Rue Saint Denis*, 123–44. Montréal: L'Arbre HMH, 1978.

———. "The Chest of Madame Corriveau." Trans. Patricia Clark. *Matrix* 17 (Winter 1982): 41–48. Trans. of "Le Coffret de la Corriveau." In *Rue Saint Denis*, 75–92. Montréal: L'Arbre HMH, 1978.

———. "Notes on the Possible End of a World." Trans. Michael Bullock. In *Tesseracts Q.* Ed. Élisabeth Vonarburg and Jane Brierley, 207–21. Edmonton: Tesseracts/The Books Collective, 1996. Trans. of "Carnet sur la fin possible d'un monde." In *L'Année de la science-fiction et du fantastique québécois, 1989.* Ed. Claude Janelle, 277–88. Québec: Le Passeur, 1990.

———. "The Seven Dreams and the Reality of Perrine Clark." Trans. Wayne Grady. In *Intimate Strangers: New Stories from Québec.* Ed. Matt Cohen and Wayne Grady, 53–47. New York: Penguin, 1986. Trans. of "Les Sept Rêves et la réalité de Perrine Blanc." In *Rue Saint Denis*, 9–32. Montréal: L'Arbre HMH, 1978.

Carrier, Roch. "The Bird." Trans. Sheila Fischman. In *Stories from Québec*. Ed. Philip Stratford, 111–13. Toronto: Van Nostrand Reinhold, 1974. Rpt. in *Invisible Fictions: Contemporary Stories from Québec*. Ed. Geoff Hancock, 149–50. Toronto: Anansi, 1987. Trans. of "L'Oiseau." In *Jolis Deuils: Petites tragédies (pour adultes)*, 9–13. Montréal: Du Jour, 1964.

———. "Creation." Trans. Sheila Fischman. In *Stories from Québec*. Ed. Philip Stratford, 116–17. Toronto: Van Nostrand Reinhold, 1974. Trans. of "La Création." In *Jolis Deuils: Petites tragédies (pour adultes)*, 63–67. Montréal: Du Jour, 1964.

———. *Floralie, Where Are You?* Trans. Sheila Fischman. Toronto: Anansi, 1971. Trans. of *Floralie, où es-tu?* Montréal: Du Jour, 1969.

———. "The Ink." Trans. Sheila Fischman. In *Stories from Québec*. Ed. Philip Stratford, 114–15. Toronto: Van Nostrand Reinhold, 1974. Rpt. *Invisible Fictions: Contemporary Stories from Québec*. Ed. Geoff Hancock, 157–58. Toronto: Anansi, 1987. Trans. of "L'Encre." In *Jolis Deuils: Petites tragédies (pour adultes)*, 39–43. Montréal: Du Jour, 1964.

———. "The Room." Trans. Sheila Fischman. In *Invisible Fictions: Contemporary Stories from Québec*. Ed. Geoff Hancock, 159–68. Toronto: Anansi, 1987. Trans. of "La Chambre 38." *Écrits du Canada français* 25 (1969): 155–60.

———. "Steps." Trans. Sheila Fischman. In *Invisible Fictions: Contemporary Stories from Québec*. Ed. Geoff Hancock, 151–52. Toronto: Anansi, 1987. Trans. of "Les Pas." In *Jolis Deuils: Petites tragédies (pour adultes)*, 75–79. Montréal: Du Jour, 1964.

———. "The Wedding." Trans. Sheila Fischman. In *Invisible Fictions: Contemporary Stories from Québec*. Ed. Geoff Hancock, 153–56. Toronto: Anansi, 1987. Trans. of "La Noce." *Études françaises* 5 (1969): 51–54.

Champetier, Joël. *The Dragon's Eye*. Trans. Jean-Louis Trudel. New York: Tor, 1999. Trans. of *La Taupe et le dragon*. Montréal: Québec/Amérique, 1991.

———. "Heart of Iron." Trans. Wendy Greene. In *Tesseracts Q*. Ed. Élisabeth Vonarburg and Jane Brierley, 222–46. Edmonton: Tesseracts/The Books Collective, 1996. Trans. of "Cœur de fer." *Solaris* 93 (1990): 34–42.

———. "Soluble-Fish." Trans. Louise Samson. In *Northern Stars: The Anthology of Canadian Science Fiction*. Eds. David G. Hartwell and Glenn Grant, 200–202. New York: Tor, 1994. Trans. of "Poisson-soluble." In *Aurores boréales 2*. Ed. Daniel Sernine, 209–214. Longueil: Le Préambule, 1985.

———. "The Winds of Time." Trans. Jane Brierley. In *Tesseracts³*. Ed. Candas Jane Dorsey and Gerry Truscott, 186–88. Victoria: Porcépic, 1993. Trans. of "Les Vents du temps." *Samizdat* 8 (1987): 7–8.

Charbonneau-Tissot, Claudette. "Compulsion." Trans. Michael Bullock. In *Invisible Fictions: Contemporary Stories from Québec*. Ed. Geoff Hancock, 315–28. Toronto: Anansi, 1987. Trans. of "La Contrainte." In *La Contrainte*, 11–32. Montréal: Pierre Tisseyre, 1976.

Châtillon, Pierre. "Ghost Island." Trans. Michael Bullock. In *Invisible Fictions: Contemporary Stories from Québec*. Ed. Geoff Hancock, 299–314. Toronto: Anansi, 1987. Trans. of "L'Île aux fantômes." In *L'Île aux fantômes*, 133–59. Montréal: Du Jour, 1977.

Côté, Denis. "1534." Trans. Howard Scott. In *Tesseracts Q*. Ed. Élisabeth Vonarburg and Jane Brierley, 111–21. Edmonton: Tesseracts/The Books Collective, 1996. Trans. of "1534." In *Dix nouvelles de science-fiction québécoise*. Ed. André Carpentier, 65–81. Montréal: Les Quinze, 1985.

———. *Shooting for the Stars*. Trans. Jane Brierley. Windsor: Black Moss, 1990. Trans. of *Les Hockeyeurs cybernétiques*. Montréal: Paulines, 1983.

Côté, Harold. "The Project." Trans. Marlene Hanson. *On Spec* 17 (1994): 18–31. Trans. of "Le Projet." *Solaris* 101 (1992): 51–58.

Dandurand, Anne. "Case Still Open." Trans. Basil Kingstone. In *Invisible Fictions: Contemporary Stories from Québec*. Ed. Geoff Hancock, 403–405. Toronto: Anansi, 1987. Trans. of "Dossier suspendu." In *La Louve garou*, 25–27. La Pleine Lune, 1982.

———. *The Cracks*. Trans. Luise von Flotow. Toronto: Mercury, 1992. Trans. of *Un cœur qui craque*. Montréal: VLB, 1990.

———. *Deathly Delights*. Trans. Luise von Flotow. Montréal: Véhicule, 1992. Trans. of *L'Assassin de l'intérieur/Diables d'espoir*. Montréal: XYZ, 1988.

———. *Small Souls Under Seige*. Trans. Robert Majzels. Dunvegan: Cormorant, 1994. Trans. of *Petites âmes sous ultimatum*. Montréal: XYZ, 1991.

———. "The Theft of Jacques Braise." Trans. Luise von Flotow. In *Three by Three*, 11–25. Montréal: Guernica, 1992. Trans. of "Le Vol de Jacques Braise." *NYX* 8 (1989): 36–44.

———. "To Console Myself I Imagine That the Bombs Have Fallen." Trans. Luise Von-Flotow-Evans. In *Celebrating Canadian Women*. Ed. Greta Hofmann Nemiroff, 354–55. Toronto: Fitzhenry and Whiteside, 1989. Trans. of "Pour me consoler, j'imagine que les bombes sont tombée." *La Vie en rose* 21 (1984): 40–41.

———. *The Waiting Room*. Trans. Robert Majzels. Toronto: Mercury, 1999. Trans. of *La Salle d'attente*. Montréal: XYZ, 1994.

Dé, Claire. "A Metamorphosis." Trans. Basil Kingstone. In *Invisible Fictions: Contemporary Stories from Québec*. Ed. Geoff Hancock, 397–401. Toronto: Anansi, 1987. Trans. of "Un cas de lycanthropie." In *La Louve garou*, 23–26. La Pleine Lune, 1982.

De Celles, Michel. "Recurrence." Trans. Basil Kingstone. In *Invisible Fictions: Contemporary Stories from Québec*. Ed. Geoff Hancock, 199–206. Toronto: Anansi, 1987. Trans. of "Récurrence." *Liberté* 146 (1983): 66–74.

Des Roches, Roger. "The Vertigo of Prisons." Trans. Donald McGrath. In *Tesseracts Q*. Ed. Élisabeth Vonarburg and Jane Brierley, 284–302. Edmonton: Tesseracts/The Books Collective, 1996. Trans. of "Le Vertige des prisons." *imagine...* 50 (1989): 117–37.

Dion, Jean. "Dead Season." Trans. Donald McGrath. In *Tesseracts Q*. Ed. Élisabeth Vonarburg and Jane Brierley, 336–51. Edmonton: Tesseracts/The Books Collective, 1996. Trans. of "Morte Saison." *Solaris* 50 (1983): 13–17.

Ferguson, Jean. "Ker, the God-Killer." Trans. Basil Kingstone. In *Invisible Fictions: Contemporary Stories from Québec*. Ed. Geoff Hancock, 229–40. Toronto: Anansi, 1987. Trans. of "Ker, le tueur de Dieu." In *Contes ardents du pays mauve*, 80–94. Montréal: Leméac, 1974.

Ferron, Jacques. *The Juneberry Tree*. Trans. Raymond Y. Chamberlain. Montréal: Harvest House, 1975. Trans. of *L'Amélanchier*. Montréal: Du Jour, 1970.

———. *Quince Jam*. Trans. Ray Ellenwood. Toronto: Coach House, 1977. Trans. of *La Confiture de coings et autres textes*. Montréal: Parti pris, 1972.

———. *Tales from the Uncertain Country*. Trans. Betty Bednarski. Toronto: Anansi, 1972. Trans. of *Contes du pays incertain*. Montréal: Orphée, 1962.

Guitard, Agnès. "Coineraine." Trans. Howard Scott. In *Tesseracts Q*. Ed. Élisabeth Vonarburg and Jane Brierley, 122–42. Edmonton: Tesseracts/The Books Collective, 1996. Trans. of "Coineraine." In *Espaces imaginaires I*, 7–27. Montréal: Les Imaginoïdes, 1983.

Hébert, Louis-Philippe. "The Hotel." Trans. Alberto Manguel. In *Invisible Fictions:*

Contemporary Stories from Québec. Ed. Geoff Hancock, 165–68. Toronto: Anansi, 1987. Trans. of "L'Hôtel." In *La Manufacture de machines*, 93–100. Montréal: Quinze, 1976.

Jasmin, Claude. "The Dragon." Trans. Patricia Sillers. In *The Dragon and Other Laurentian Tales*. Toronto: Oxford UP, 1987. Rpt. *Just Fantastic!* Ed. James Barry, Sharon Siamon, and Glen Huser, 56–72. Scarborough: Nelson, 1993.

Laframboise, Michèle. "Women are from Mars, Men are from Venus." Trans. Sheryl Curtis. In *Tesseracts[10]*. Ed. Edo Van Belkom and Robert Charles Wilson, 114–40. Calgary: Edge SF & F: 2006.

Lamontagne, Michel. "Hypercruise." Trans. Howard Scott. In *Tesseracts Q*. Ed. Élisabeth Vonarburg and Jane Brierley, 47–63. Edmonton: Tesseracts/The Books Collective, 1996. Trans. of "Hypercruise." *Solaris* 58 (1984): 17–24.

Lemaire, Marie-Claire. "A Patch of Garden Over Sarrapolis." Trans. Donald McGrath. In *Tesseracts Q*. Ed. Élisabeth Vonarburg and Jane Brierley, 180–90. Edmonton: Tesseracts/The Books Collective, 1996. Trans. of "Coin de jardin sur Sarrapolis." *Solaris* 77 (1988): 25–28.

Martel, Suzanne. *The City Underground*. Trans. Norah Smaridge. New York: Viking, 1964. Trans. of *Quatre Montréalais en l'an 3000*. Montréal: Le Jour, 1963.

Martin, Michel (pseud. Guy Sirois and Jean Dion). "Geisha Blues." Trans. Howard Scott. In *Tesseracts Q*. Ed. Élisabeth Vonarburg and Jane Brierley, 263–83. Edmonton: Tesseracts/The Books Collective, 1996. Trans. of "Geisha Blues." In *L'Année de la science-fiction et du fantastique québécois, 1987*. Ed. Claude Janelle and Jean Pettigrew, 245–61. Québec: Le Passeur, 1988.

———. "Tortoise on a Sidewalk." Trans. Laurent McAllister (pseud. Yves Meynard and Jean-Louis Trudel). In *Tesseracts[5]*. Ed. Robert Runté and Yves Meynard, 135–51. Edmonton: The Books Collective, 1996. Trans. of "La Tortue sur le trottoir." In *C. I. N. Q.* Ed. Jean-Marc Gouanvic, 123–49. Montréal: Éditions Logiques, 1989.

Massé, Johanne. *Beyond the Future*. Trans. Frances Morgan. Windsor: Black Moss, 1990. Trans. of *De l'autre côté de l'avenir*. Montréal: Paulines, 1985.

McAllister, Laurent (pseud. Yves Meynard and Jean-Louis Trudel). "The Case of the Serial 'De Québec à la Lune,' by Veritatus." In *Arrowdreams*. Ed. Mark Shainblum and John Dupuis, 173–91. Nuage, 1998. Trans. of "Le Cas du feuilleton *De Québec à la lune*, par Veritatus." *Solaris* 109 (1994): 35–41.

———. "Driftplast." *LC-39* 3 (2000): 65–105.

———. "Kapuzine and the Wolf." In *Witpunk*. Ed. Claude Lalumière and Marty Halpern, 317–35. New York: Four Walls Eight Windows, 2003.

Meynard, Yves. *The Book of Knights*. New York: Tor Books, 1998.

———. "Equinox." In *Tesseracts[4]*. Ed. Lorna Toolis and Michael Skeet, 89–107. Victoria: Beach Holme, 1992. Trans. of "Équinoxe." In *La Rose du desert*, 91–116. Québec: Le Passeur, 1995.

———. "In Yerusalom." In *Island Dreams: Montreal Writers of the Fantastic*. Ed. Claude Lalumière, 82–104. Montréal: Véhicule, 2003. Trans. of "À Yerusalom." *Solaris* 152 (2004): 19–42.

———. "Johan Havel's Marvelous Machine." *On Spec* 25 (1996): 8–30. Trans. of "La Merveilleuse Machine de Johan Havel." *Solaris* 107 (1993): 23–35.

———. "A Letter from My Mother." In *Tesseracts[7]*. Ed. Paula Johanson and Jean-Louis Trudel, 220–24. Edmonton: The Books Collective, 1998. Trans. of "Une lettre de ma mère." *Solaris* 121 (1997): 16–18.

———. "Principles of Animal Eugenetics." In *Tesseracts[9]*. Ed. Nalo Hopkinson and Geoff Ryman, 27–49. Calgary: Edge SF & F: 2005.

———. "The Scalemen." Trans. Jane Brierley. In *Tesseracts Q*. Ed. Élisabeth Vonarburg and Jane Brierley, 5–25. Edmonton: Tesseracts/The Books Collective, 1996. Trans. of "Les Hommes-Écailles." In *Sous des soleils étrangers*. Ed. Yves Meynard and Claude J. Pelletier, 183–203. Montréal: Ianus, 1989.

———. "Souvenirs." In *Tesseracts⁶*. Ed. Robert J. Sawyer and Carolyn Clink. Edmonton: Tesseracts, 1997.

———. "Stolen Fires." In *Northern Stars: The Anthology of Canadian Science Fiction*. Eds. David G. Hartwell and Glenn Grant, 286–95. New York: Tor, 1994.

———. "Tobacco Words." In *Year's Best SF 2*. Ed. David G. Hartwell, 137–73. New York: HarperPrism, 1997. Trans. of "Les Mots du tabac." *Solaris* 119 (1996): 24–35.

———. "Travels Through Torbay." *Prairie Fire* 15.2 (1994): 181–84.

———. "Within the Mechanism." In *Tesseracts⁸*. Ed. John Clute and Candas Jane Dorsey, 220–44. Edmonton: The Books Collective, 1999.

Montpetit, Charles. "Beyond the Barriers." In *Northern Suns: The New Anthology of Canadian Science Fiction*. Ed. David G. Hartwell and Glenn Grant, 207–13. New York: Tor, 1999. Trans. of "Dégénérer." *Solaris* 101 (1992): 21–24.

———. *Lost Time*. Trans. Frances Morgan. Windsor: Black Moss, 1990. Trans. of *Temps perdu*. Montréal: Paulines, 1984.

Pavel, Thomas. "The Persian Mirror." Trans. Michael Bullock. In *Invisible Fictions: Contemporary Stories from Québec*. Ed. Geoff Hancock, 107–20. Toronto: Anansi, 1987. Trans. of "Le Miroir persan." In *Le Miroir persan*, 121–45. Montréal: Quinze, 1977.

Pelletier, Francine. "Empty Ring." Trans. Howard Scott. In *Tesseracts⁵*. Ed. Robert Runté and Yves Meynard, 28–39. Edmonton: The Books Collective, 1996. Trans. of "Cloche vaine." *Solaris* 109 (1994): 20–24.

———. "Guinea Pig." Trans. Jane Brierley. In *Tesseracts³*. Ed. Candas Jane Dorsey and Gerry Truscott, 408–19. Victoria: Porcépic, 1993. Trans. of "La Petite." *imagine...* 46 (1989): 105–120.

———. "The Mother Migrator." Trans. Wendy Greene. In *Tesseracts Q*. Ed. Élisabeth Vonarburg and Jane Brierley, 64–79. Edmonton: Tesseracts/The Books Collective, 1996. Trans. of "La Migratrice." *Solaris* 63 (1985): 5–10.

———. "The Sea Below." Trans. Sheryl Curtis. In *Tesseracts⁸*. Ed. John Clute and Candas Jane Dorsey, 73–100. Edmonton: The Books Collective, 1999.

Perrot-Bishop, Annick. "Emptiness." Trans. Neil B. Bishop. *TickleAce* 21 (1991): 71–80. Trans. of "Le Grand Vide." *Mœbius* 31 (1987): 49–59.

———. "The Last Dance." Trans. Neil B. Bishop. In *Tesseracts⁵*. Ed. Robert Runté and Yves Meynard, 236–40. Edmonton: The Books Collective, 1996. Trans. of "Les Yvanelles." *Solaris* 114 (1995): 17–19.

———. "Memory's Dawn." Trans. Neil B. Bishop. *TickleAce* 17 (1989): 11–15. Trans. of "À l'aube de la mémoire." *imagine...* 23 (1984): 21–24.

———. "The Ourlandine." Trans. Neil B. Bishop. In *Tesseracts Q*. Ed. Élisabeth Vonarburg and Jane Brierley, 373–82. Edmonton: Tesseracts/The Books Collective, 1996. Trans. of "L'Ourlandine." *imagine...* 36 (1986): 11–20.

———. "Prologue: Stories from Aya." Trans. Neil B. Bishop. *TickleAce* 25 (1993): 78–83.

———. "She Who Drowned." Trans. Neil B. Bishop. *Tickle Ace* (2002): 92–97. Trans. of "La Noyée." In *Fragments de saisons*, 31–40. Hull: Vents d'Ouest, 1998.

———. "Swallowed Anger." Trans. Neil B. Bishop. *TickleAce* 20 (1990): 54–55. Trans. of "La Colère avalée." *The Pottersfield Portfolio* 12 (1990): 41.

———. "Uhla." Trans. Neil B. Bishop. In *Translit Volume 3: An Anthology of Literary

Translations. Ed. Nésida Loyer. Calgary: ATIA, 1996. Trans. of "Uhla." *Solaris* 113 (1995): 12–13.

———. "Voice and Silence." Trans. Neil B. Bishop. *Transversions* 3 (1995): 52. Trans. of "Silence et la voix." *Pottersfield Portfolio* (1992).

Pettigrew, Jean. "Snoopymen All Die Like Bengal Goats." Trans. Jane Brierley. In *Tesseracts Q*. Ed. Élisabeth Vonarburg and Jane Brierley, 143–49. Edmonton: Tesseracts/The Books Collective, 1996. Trans. of "Les Hommes-Snoopy meurent tous comme des chèvres du Bengale." *imagine...* 21 (1984): 35–42.

Prévost, Claude-Michel. "Akimento." Trans. Phyllis Aronoff. In *Tesseracts Q*. Ed. Élisabeth Vonarburg and Jane Brierley, 303–29. Edmonton: Tesseracts/The Books Collective, 1996. Trans. of "Akimento." *Solaris* 87 (1989): 56–65.

———. "Happy Days in Old Chernobyl." In *Tesseracts³*. Ed. Candas Jane Dorsey and Gerry Truscott, 183–69. Victoria: Porcépic, 1993; Rpt. in *Northern Suns: The New Anthology of Canadian Science Fiction*. Ed. David G. Hartwell and Glenn Grant, 254–62. New York: Tor, 1999. Trans. of "La Marquise de Tchernobyl." *imagine...* 41 (1987): 31–39.

———. "Tears for Érsulie Frèda: Men Without Shadow." In *Whispers from the Cotton Tree Root: Caribbean Fabulist Fiction*. Ed. Nalo Hopkinson, 83–92. Montpelier: Invisible Cities Press, 2000.

Proulx, Monique. "Am Stram Gram." Trans. Yvonne M. Klein. In *Celebrating Canadian Women*. Ed. Greta Hofmann Nemiroff, 205–11. Markham: Fitzhenry and Whiteside, 1989. Trans. of "Am stram gram." In *Sans cœur et sans reproche*, 13–23. Montréal: Québec/Amérique, 1983.

Rochon, Esther. "Canadola." Trans. John Greene. In *Tesseracts³*. Ed. Candas Jane Dorsey and Gerry Truscott, 322–26. Victoria: Porcépic, 1993. Trans. of "Canadoule." In *Le Piège à souvenirs*, 119–138. Montréal: La Pleine lune, 1991.

———. "Memory Trap." Trans. Lucille Nelson. In *Tesseracts Q*. Ed. Élisabeth Vonarburg and Jane Brierley, 99–110. Edmonton: Tesseracts/The Books Collective, 1996. Trans. of "Le piège à souvenirs." In *Dix nouvelles de science-fiction québécoise*. Ed. André Carpentier, 147–64. Montréal: Les Quinze, 1985.

———. "The Sea Star." Trans. by Alexandre Amprimoz. *Fantasy Specialist* 5 (1975): 2–7; Rpt. "The Starfish." In *Magic Realism*. Ed. Geoff Hancock, 149–54. Toronto: Aya Press, 1980. Trans. of "L'Étoile de mer." *Solaris* 47 (1982): 20–21.

———. *The Shell*. Trans. David Lobdell. Ottawa: Oberon Press, 1990. Trans. of *Coquillage*. Montréal: La Pleine Lune, 1985.

———. "Xils." In *Northern Suns: The New Anthology of Canadian Science Fiction*. Ed. David G. Hartwell and Glenn Grant, 282–85. New York: Tor, 1999. Trans. of "Nourrir tes fantômes affamés." *Pour ta belle gueule d'ahuri* 6 (1983): 31–33.

Sernine, Daniel. *Argus Steps In*. Trans. Ray Chamberlain. Windsor: Black Moss, 1990. Trans. of *Argus intervient*. Montréal: Paulines, 1983.

———. "The Friends of Mr. Soon." Trans. Jane Brierley. In *Tesseracts Q*. Ed. Élisabeth Vonarburg and Jane Brierley, 191–206. Edmonton: Tesseracts/The Books Collective, 1996. Trans. of "Les Amis de Monsieur Soon." *Solaris* 50 (1983): 33–37.

———. "Light Remembered." Trans. Sheryl Curtis. In *Tesseracts⁹*. Ed. Nalo Hopkinson and Geoff Ryman, 150–61. Calgary: Edge SF & F: 2005. Trans. of "Souvenirs de lumière." *Solaris* 138 (2001): 24–36.

———. "Only a Lifetime." Trans. Jane Brierley. In *Tesseracts³*. Ed. Candas Jane Dorsey and Gerry Truscott, 227–38. Victoria: Porcépic, 1993. Trans. of "Métal qui songe." *imagine...* 46 (1988): 9–21.

_____. *Scorpion's Treasure*. Trans. Frances Morgan. Windsor: Black Moss, 1990. Trans. of *Le Trésor du Scorpion*. Montréal: Paulines, 1980.

_____. "Stardust Boulevard." Trans. Jane Brierley. In *Tesseracts: Canadian Science Fiction*. Ed. Judith Merril, 84–100. Victoria: Press Porcépic, 1985; Rpt. in *Northern Stars: The Anthology of Canadian Science Fiction*. Ed. David G. Hartwell and Glenn Grant, 329–42. New York: Tor, 1994. Trans. of "Boulevard des étoiles." In *Le Vieil homme et l'espace*, 185–204. Longueuil: Preambule, 1985.

_____. *The Sword of Arpahal*. Trans. Frances Morgan. Windsor: Black Moss, 1990. Trans. of *L'Épée Arpahal*. Montréal: Paulines, 1981.

_____. *Those Who Watch Over the Earth*. Trans. David Homel. Windsor: Black Moss, 1990. Trans. of *Organisation Argus*. Montréal: Paulines, 1979.

_____. "The Travels of Nica Marcopol." Trans. Jean-Louis Trudel. In *Tesseracts⁵*. Ed. Robert Runté and Yves Meynard, 363–72. Edmonton: The Books Collective, 1996. Trans. of "Ailleurs." *Québec-Science* (Dec. 1994- Jan. 1995): 42–46.

_____. "Umfrey's Head." Trans. Jane Brierley. In *Tesseracts⁸*. Ed. John Clute and Candas Jane Dorsey, 21–51. Edmonton: The Books Collective, 1999. Trans. of "La Tête de Walt Umfrey." In *Espaces Imaginaires 2*, 19–51. Trois Rivières: Les Imaginoïdes, 1984.

Sévigny, Marc. "The Train." In *Tesseracts: Canadian Science Fiction*. Ed. Judith Merril, 157–71. Victoria: Press Porcépic, 1985. Trans. of "Le Train." In *Aurores boréales 1*. Ed. Norbert Spehner, 89–108. Longueil: Le Préambule, 1983.

Sormany, Pierre. "Everett's Parallel Universes or How to Make Love to Someone Without Ever Meeting." Trans. Wendy Greene. In *Tesseracts⁷*. Ed. Paula Johanson and Jean-Louis Trudel, 110–27. Edmonton: The Books Collective, 1998.

Thériault, Marie-José. *The Ceremony*. Trans. David Lobdell. Toronto: Oberon, 1980. Trans. of *La Cérémonie*. Montréal: La Presse, 1978.

_____. "The Thirty-First Bird." Trans. Luise von Flotow-Evans. In *Invisible Fictions: Contemporary Stories from Québec*. Ed. Geoff Hancock, 45–62. Toronto: Anansi, 1987. Trans. of "Le Trente et unième oiseau." In *Dix Contes et nouvelles fantastiques par dix auteurs québécois*. Ed. André Carpentier, 183–204. Montréal: Quinze, 1983.

Thériault, Yves. "Akua Nuten (The South Wind)." In *Stories from Québec*. Ed. Philip Stratford, 29–38. Toronto: Van Nostrand Reinhold, 1974. Rpt. in *Countdown to Midnight*. Ed. H. Bruce Franklin, 134–45. New York: DAW, 1984. Trans. of "Akua Nuten (Le Vent du sud)." In *Si la bombe m'etait contée*, 11–25. Montréal: Du Jour, 1962.

Tremblay, Michel. *The City in the Egg*. Trans. Michael Bullock. Vancouver: Ronsdale, 1999. Trans. of *La Cité dans l'œuf*. Montréal: Leméac, 1969.

_____. *Stories for Late Night Drinkers*. Trans. Michael Bullock. Vancouver: Intermedia, 1977. Trans. of *Contes pour buveurs attardés*. Montréal: Du Jour, 1966.

Trudel, Jean-Louis. "Contamination." Trans. Donald McGrath with Jean-Louis Trudel. In *Tesseracts Q*. Ed. Élisabeth Vonarburg and Jane Brierley, 26–46. Edmonton: Tesseracts/The Books Collective, 1996. Trans. of "Contamination." *Solaris* 108 (1994): 14–22.

_____. "The Falafel is Always Better in Ottawa." In *Ark of Ice: Canadian Futurefiction*. Ed. Lesley Choyce, 85–94. Lawrencetown Beach, N. S.: Pottersfield Press, 1992.

_____. "Holes in the Night." In *Tesseracts⁸*. Ed. Robert J. Sawyer and Carolyn Clink, 52. Edmonton: The Books Collective, 1997.

_____. "The Paradigm Machine." In *Tesseracts⁵*. Ed. Robert Runté and Yves Meynard, 93–108. Edmonton: The Books Collective, 1996.

_____. "Proscripts of Gehenna." Trans. John Greene. In *Tesseracts⁸*. Ed. John Clute and Candas Jane Dorsey, 372–91. Edmonton: The Books Collective, 1999. Trans. of "Les Proscrits de Gehenna." *Solaris* 71 (1987): 12–17.

___. "Remember, the Dead Say." In *Tesseracts⁴*. Ed. Lorna Toolis and Michael Skeet, 368–87. Victoria: Beach Holme, 1992; Rpt. in *Northern Stars: The Anthology of Canadian Science Fiction*. Eds. David G. Hartwell and Glenn Grant, 101–13. New York: Tor, 1994.

___. "Report 323: A Quebecois Infiltration Attempt." *Prairie Fire* 67 (1994): 20–26. Trans. of "Report 323." *Solaris* 101 (1992): 18–20.

___. "Stella Nova." *On Spec* 16 (1994): 30–43.

___. "Tether." In *Orbiter*. Ed. Julie Czerneda, 59–75. Toronto: Trifolium, 2002.

___. "Where Angels Fall." In *Tesseracts⁶*. Ed. Robert J. Sawyer and Carolyn Clink, 179–80. Edmonton: Tesseracts, 1997. Trans. of "Des anges sont tombés." In *Jonctions impossibles*, 9–12. Ottawa: Vermillon, 2003.

Vonarburg, Élisabeth. "Amber Rain." Trans. Kim Stanley Robinson. *Tomorrow Speculative Fiction* 14 (Apr 1995). Trans. of "Celles qui vivent au-dessus des nuages." In *Étoiles vives 2*, 138–53. Le Plessis-Brion: Orion, 1997.

___. "Band Ohne Ende." Trans Élisabeth Vonarburg. In *Slow Engines of Time*, 1–32. Edmonton: Tesseract Books, 2000. Trans. of "Band Ohne Ende." In *Janus*, 217–52. Paris: Denoël, 1984.

___. "Bird of Ashes." Trans. Jane Brierley. In *Tesseracts Q*. Ed. Élisabeth Vonarburg and Jane Brierley, 352–72. Edmonton: Tesseracts/The Books Collective, 1996. Trans. of "L'Oiseau de cendre." *Solaris* 43 (1982): 20–25.

___. "Chambered Nautilus." Trans. Jane Brierley. In *Tesseracts⁴*. Ed. Lorna Toolis and Michael Skeet, 227–62. Victoria: Beach Holme, 1992. Rpt. in *Slow Engines of Time*, 158–83. Edmonton: Tesseract Books, 2000. Trans. of "Le Jeu de coquilles de nautilus." In *Aurores boréales 2*. Ed. Jean-Marc Gouanvic, 253–90. Longueil: Le Préambule, 1985.

___. "Cogito." Trans. Jane Brierley. In *Tesseracts³*. Ed. Candas Jane Dorsey and Gerry Truscott, 62–82. Victoria: Porcépic, 1993. Trans. of "Cogito." *imagine...* 46 (1988): 154–76.

___. "Cold Bridge." Trans. Élisabeth Vonarburg and Jane Brierley. In *Invisible Fictions: Contemporary Stories from Québec*. Ed. Geoff Hancock, 267–98. Toronto: Anansi, 1987. Trans. of "Le Pont du froid." In *L'Oeil de la nuit*, 43–74. Longueil: Le Préambule, 1980.

___. *Dreams of the Sea. Tyranaël-1*. Trans. Howard Scott and Élisabeth Vonarburg. Edmonton: Tesseract Books, 2003. Trans. of *Les Rêves de la mer. Tyranaël-1*. Beauport: Alire, 1996.

___. *A Game of Perfection. Tyranaël-2*. Trans. Élisabeth Vonarburg and Howard Scott. Edge SF & F, 2006. Trans. of *Le Jeu de la perfection. Tyranaël-2*. Beauport: Alire, 1996.

___. "Gehenna." Trans. Jane Brierley. In *Per ardua ad astra 2*, 9–27. Toronto: Ad Astra Convention, 1987. Trans. of "Géhenne." In *L'Oeil de la nuit*, 107–25. Longueil: Le Préambule, 1980.

___. "High Tide." In *Twenty Houses of the Zodiac*, 64–74. Ed. Maxim Jakubowski. London: New English Library, 1979. Trans. of "Marée Haute." *Requiem* 19 (1978): 8–11.

___. "Home by the Sea." Trans. Jane Brierley. In *Tesseracts: Canadian Science Fiction*. Ed. Judith Merril, 4–20. Victoria: Press Porcépic, 1985; Rpt. in *Northern Stars: The Anthology of Canadian Science Fiction*. Eds. David G. Hartwell and Glenn Grant, 68–81. New York: Tor, 1994. Trans. of "La Maison au bord de la mer." In *Dix nouvelles de science-fiction*, 213–38. Montréal: Les Quinze, 1985.

_____. *In the Mother's Land*. Trans. Jane Brierley. New York: Bantam, 1992. Also pub. as *The Maerlande Chronicles*. Victoria, B. C: Beach Holme, 1992. Trans. of *Chroniques du Pays des Mères*. Montréal: Québec/Amérique, 1992.

_____. "In the Pit." Trans. Jane Brierley. In *Tesseracts²*. Ed. Phyllis Gotlieb and Douglas Barbour, 25–43. Victoria: Porcépic, 1987. Rpt. in *Slow Engines of Time*, 33–49. Edmonton: Tesseract Books, 2000. Trans. of "Dans la fosse." *Solaris* 15 (1983): 22–28.

_____. "Janus." Trans. Élisabeth Vonarburg. *Tomorrow Speculative Fiction* 3.6 (December 1995): 42–56. Rpt. in *Slow Engines of Time*, 50–76. Edmonton: Tesseract Books, 2000; in *Janus*, 253–85. Paris: Denoël, 1984.

_____. "The Knot." Trans. Aliosha Kondratiev and Élisabeth Vonarburg. In *Tesseracts⁷*. Ed. Paula Johanson and Jean-Louis Trudel, 129–38. Edmonton: The Books Collective, 1998. Rpt. *Amazing Stories* (February 1993): 9–13. Rpt. in *Slow Engines of Time*, 104–13. Edmonton: Tesseract Books, 2000. Trans. of "Le Nœud." In *L'Œil de la nuit*, 127–40. Longueil: Le Préambule, 1980.

_____. "Language of the Night." In *Tesseracts¹¹*. Ed. Cory Doctorow and Holly Phillips. Calgary: Edge SF & F, 2007. Trans. of "Le Langage de la nuit." In *La Nuit: Anthologie de l'exposition du Musée de la culture et de la Civilisation*. Québec: XYZ, 1995.

_____. "Paguyn and Kithulai." *Prairie Fire* 15.2 (Summer 1994): 96–104.

_____. "Readers of the Lost Art." Trans. Howard Scott. In *Tesseracts⁵*. Ed. Robert Runté and Yves Meynard, 48–62. Edmonton: The Books Collective, 1996. Rpt. in *Re: Skin*. Ed. Mary Flanagan and Austin Booth, 231–44. Cambridge: MIT Press, 2006. Trans. of "La Carte du Tendre." In *Ailleurs et au Japon*, 145–70. Montréal: Québec/Amérique, 1990.

_____. *Reluctant Voyagers*. Trans. Jane Brierley. New York: Bantam, 1995. Edmonton: Tesseract Books, 1996. Trans. of *Les Voyageurs malgré eux*. Montréal: Québec/Amérique, 1994.

_____. "See Kathryn Run." In *Tesseracts⁹*. Ed. Nalo Hopkinson and Geoff Ryman, 93–140. Calgary: Edge SF & F: 2005. Trans. of "La Course de Kathryn." In *Le Jeu des coquilles de nautilus*, 77–138. Lévis: Alire, 2003.

_____. *The Silent City*. Trans. Jane Brierley. Victoria, B. C.: Porcépic, 1988; London: The Women's Press, 1990; New York: Bantam, 1992. Trans. of *Le Silence de la cité*. Paris: Denoël, 1981.

_____. "The Sleeper in the Crystal." In *Tesseracts⁶*. Ed. Robert J. Sawyer and Carolyn Clink. Edmonton: Tesseracts, 1997. Trans. of "Le Dormeur dans le cristal." In *Ailleurs et au Japon*, 79–98. Montréal: Québec/Amérique, 1990.

_____. "The Slow Engine of Time." Trans. Howard Scott and Élisabeth Vonarburg." In *Slow Engines of Time*, 114–57. Edmonton: Tesseract Books, 2000. Trans. of "La Machine lente du temps." In *Janus*, 63–116. Paris: Denoël, 1984.

_____. *Slow Engines of Time*. Edmonton: Tesseract Books, 2000.

_____. "... Stay Thy Flight." Trans. Élisabeth Vonarburg. In *Slow Engines of Time*, 77–88. Edmonton: Tesseract Books, 2000. Trans. of "Suspends ton vol." *Solaris* 99 (1992): 21–26.

Chapter Notes

Introduction

1. While technically *imperialism* refers to the acquisition, often by force, of territory to further the creation of an empire and *colonialism* refers to the settlement of colonists on such territory, the two phenomena typically go hand in hand and may occasionally be conflated here. The argument is that empire cannot exist without colonization and colonization cannot occur without some form of imperial conquest.

2. Greg Grewell demonstrates this in "Colonizing the Universe" going so far as to challenge the accuracy of the term postcolonial itself, given the extent of neocolonialism and so called cultural imperialism in today's global economy (39–40).

3. This and subsequent translations, unless otherwise credited, are my own.

4. Since the publication of Tzvetan Todorov's *The Fantastic in Literature*, confusion between the French term *le fantastique* and the Anglo-American genre of *fantasy* has caused problems not only for theorists of these two forms, but for publishers and fans alike. The French publishing world has adopted the English term *fantasy* to describe works of what has variously been called high fantasy, heroic fantasy, even mythopoeic fantasy, while *fantastique* refers to what we now might call dark fantasy or urban fantasy: texts which operate the insertion of an unexplainable or apparently supernatural phenomenon into a mimetic contemporary or historical setting.

5. While the acronym SFQ is widely used within the community of science-fiction writers of Québec, some prefer the term *science-fiction canadienne d'expression française* or French-Canadian science fiction, which is much more inclusive and, indeed, accurate since several important writers in the "SFQ" community are not originally from the province of Québec. Since almost all of Canada's French-language science fiction is published in Québec (the current exception being a few works from Ottawa's Éditions Vermillon), and its conferences, prizes and reviews are also headquartered in Québec, the use of the term appears justified. Even Jean-Louis Trudel, a Franco-Ontarian now living in Montréal, the main proponent for a less restrictive (and perhaps more accurate) terminology admits in the *New York Review of Science Fiction* that "SFQ" for short is simply more convenient ("French" 16).

6. The title of this chapter and the desire to articulate the relationship between SF and a defined branch of literary theory is inspired by Carl Freedman's incisive contribution, *Critical Theory and Science Fiction* (2000).

7. It must be noted that any analysis such as this suggests a totalizing image of the object of study. Since postcolonial criticism rejects such a possibility, this is obviously problematic. While it would be more accurate for me to qualify what I mean every time I refer to "Québec" as "certain intellectuals in Québec," "particular elements in Québec's nationalist movement," this would quickly become cumbersome. "Québec" in this analysis has become a sign referring to an imaginary referent for a somewhat unified culture within a certain geographical boundary, which may even conflate (as does the acronym SFQ) French-Canadian elements outside the boundaries of the province with Québec proper, just as it admittedly excludes Anglo-Québécois and other ethnic instances active in the province today.

8. Allaire's figures are based on the 1997 Canadian Census (20); Statistics Canada's postings for the 2001 Census reveal very similar numbers for French as a mother tongue.

9. Essays by Hutcheon, Mishra and Hodge, Mukherjee, Slemon ("Scramble"), among others, grapple with this question. Bart Moore-Gilbert's *Postcolonial Theory* and Robert Young's *White Mythologies* provide excellent overviews of the major proponents of postcolonial criticism (Bhabha, Said, Spivak and others) and their theoretical underpinnings.

10. The term *hybrid* itself has been controversial; see critiques in essays by JanMohamed, Loomba (307–08), and Parry. Neal Baker also cites concerns raised by Puri and Shohat ("Syncretism" 229 n. 2). In addition, Kwame Anthony Appiah warns that not all syncretism results from a postcolonial sensibility ("Post-" 348).

11. Vijay Mishra and Bob Hodge's "What is Post(-)colonialism?" provides an excellent example of the critiques leveled at *The Empire Writes Back*. The present author's "Oppositional Postcolonialism and the Science Fiction of Québec" applies their definition of postcolonialism to a range of works of SFQ.

12. While some African nations' inclusion in "the postcolonial" seems uncontroversial, the case of India, as Spivak points out, is much more complex given that prior and simultaneous to British occupation of India, Hindu/Aryan peoples had occupied the territory of and subsequently oppressed (by turning them into an untouchable caste) the highly diverse indigenous groups of the Asian subcontinent (*Critique* 141). Vonarburg's depiction of the history of the planet Tyranaël, in her series analyzed in detail in later chapters, may be a reference to India's complex colonial history.

13. Indeed, several collections of essays include studies of Québécois literature without questioning its status as postcolonial or, sometimes without even referencing postcolonial theory. *Postcolonial Subjects: Francophone Women Writers* (1996), edited by Jack Yeager, includes essays which largely employ feminist (not postcolonial) theory in readings of African francophone writers along with Québec's Anne Hébert, Marie Laberge, Marie-Claire Blais and others. Similarly *Us/Them: Translation, Transcription and Identity in Post-Colonial Literary Cultures* (1992), includes translations and French-language texts by, as well as Luise von Flotow's essay rooted in feminist theory on, Nicole Brossard, Anne Dandurand and Claire Dé. Denis Salter's contribution to *(Post)Colonial Stages: Critical and Creative Views on Drama, Theatre and Performance* (1999) does use postcolonial theory to read Michel Tremblay's *Hosanna* (1974). However, its description of the playwright's desire for closure with an essentialized Québécois male subject as a "postcolonial" desire does not take into account the large number of postcolonial critics who argue that postcolonial literatures actually do just the opposite: they question any essential notion of a national identity. In the francophone world the term "postcolonial" is not widely adopted, but Jean Bessière and Jean-Marc Moura edited the acts of a seminar at the Sorbonne dealing with *Littératures postcoloniales et représentations de l'ailleurs: Afrique, Caraïbe, Canada* (1999).

14. Slemon attributes this term to Alan Lawson ("Unsettling" 104). While Canada may belong to this Second World (many would maintain, however, that as an industrialized, Western democracy it is part of the First World), Nadesan Satyendra asserts that Québec may belong to the "Fourth World" of nations without a state.

15. In Vonarburg's *Tyranaël* series this is signaled through the name of the boat meant to navigate the mysterious Sea of energy the first Earth expedition finds on the planet, as it is called *L'Entre-deux*, rendered in the English translation, *Dreams of the Sea*, as the *In-Between*. In *Le Roman mémoriel*, Régine Robin discusses the migrant and split identities of the contemporary world in a manner clearly similar to, without expressly signaling, that of postcolonial theorists. Robin speaks at length of Kafka (a postcolonial subject *avant la lettre*) and the emblematic figure of the "entre-deux" in his work (161). Kafka's clear position as a model for many writers of SFQ has to my knowledge yet to be explored.

16. My summary of Québec's history owes a great debt to several volumes used to "fact check," including the French version of Craig Brown's *Illustrated History of Canada* and the two-volume *Histoire du Québec contemporain* by Paul-André Linteau, René Durocher, Jean-Claude Robert and François Ricard. My interpretation of events is necessarily colored by the first history of the province I read, Hamelin and Provencher's *Brève histoire du Québec*. As the historical data (as well as the geopolitical figures cited earlier in this section) can be found in a wide number of sources, including Wikipedia, I have not given specific attribution for each datum. At this point it might also be well to recall for some readers the great differences between Canada's history and that of the United States. The latter established itself as a sovereign nation with two radical acts of liberation from the imperial power of Great Britain: the thirteen participating colonies' Declaration of Independence in 1776 and the

subsequent Revolutionary War. In contrast, Canada as we know it today was founded in 1867 by a negotiated piece of legislation: the British North America Act, which allowed its remaining colonies on that continent to unite as a confederation, while retaining the status of subjects of the British Empire. Complete Canadian sovereignty was not granted until 1931 with the Act of Westminster; the Canadian flag, with its distinctive maple leaf, was not adopted until 1965. To this day, however, Canada remains a member of the British Commonwealth; the British sovereign Elizabeth II appeared on Canadian currency well after Trudeau's repatriation of the Constitution in 1982, often viewed as the final cut of the apron strings. As a member of the Commonwealth, Canada and all of its provinces, including Québec, remain to some degree under the tutelage of the former British Empire, problematizing somewhat their status as truly postcolonial.

17. Publication of Angenot's essay, which purports to describe objectively the worldwide phenomenon of these "ideologies of resentment" and which clearly contains a not at all subtle subtextual critique of the conservative, ethnic nationalism still lingering in Québec, coincided with that of his scathing letter to the editor of *Le Devoir*, "Démocratie à la québécoise" (13 June 1996). A summary of the polemic sparked by this letter and a critique of Angenot's pseudo-scientific approach and possibly scary adoption of a Nietzschean stance of superiority appears in Jacques Pelletier's *Au-delà du ressentiment. Réplique à Marc Angenot* (1996). Pelletier particularly points out Angenot's conflation of all forms of nationalism in Québec with its conservative, ethnically based branch; at times, the present study may appear to do the same, although such is not my intention.

18. Remaining because after the passage of Bill 101 and other measures designed to protect the French language there occurred a notable exodus of the long-present English-speaking community, particularly from Montréal (Castonguay 43).

19. I realize that the contrast set up between the first and second halves of this sentence appears to make light of treatment of First Nations and Inuit peoples in Canadian settlement; while much has been made of "Indian Wars" in the United States, the genocide of the Beothuk peoples of Newfoundland, among other tragedies chronicled elsewhere, should be pointed out. In more recent history, conflict over native land rights and the desire to build a golf course on a sacred burial site resulted in the armed standoff between Mohawk First Nations and Québec's police force and, eventually Canada Forces in the Oka Crisis of 1990. In 2002 tensions reversed in Sept-Îles/Uashat over agreements made between the government and the Innu people residing there as members of the French community felt they had not been adequately informed or consulted (Harel 61–62).

20. Ironically, French Canadians were the original "Canadiens," memorialized in the mid-nineteenth-century novel by Philippe Aubert de Gaspé (the father of Québec's first fantastic novelist), *Les Anciens canadiens* (1864), an image maintained through the early twentieth century in works like Frenchman Louis Hémon's *Maria Chapdelaine* (1916). Then, a Québécois was someone from the city of Québec. It was only with the contemporary nationalist movement, which developed out of the Quiet Revolution (and the tandem efforts of Anglo-Canadians to construct a national "Canadian," rather than "English," identity) that the term Québécois began to signify a "native" of the province. I put scare quotes around "native" to call attention to the other problems involved in calling the French Canadians the "original" Canadians; this move reflects how they placed themselves into the position of the native to adopt the stance of colonized victim, effectively usurping a position of indigene rightly belonging to the First Nations and Inuit. This stance becomes all the more problematic as some, like Pierre Vadeboncoeur in *Un génocide en douce* (1976), have taken that position so far as to label the oppression of French Canadians as a form of genocide. The arrival of the English, of course, provides the key factor in Québec's difference from other settler colonies of the British Empire. While an objective examination of history would identify *two* instances of conquest of the territory, first the French, then the English, for many French Canadians/Québécois there is only *one* conquest, as French Canada effectively erased elements of a French conquest from its historical landscape and, with the arrival of the British, they staked out the territory of the *indigène* for themselves. While Marie Vautier, one of the few literary critics actively applying postcolonial theory to Québec's cultural productions today, argues that the blurring of boundaries between the allegorical Native American tribe of the *Clipocs* and the allegorical French settlers, the *Vieux-paysans* in François Barcelo's *La Tribu*, represents an example of the postcolonial strategy

of ambivalence/ambiguity (214), some would argue that his inclusion of the Québécois in a list with northeastern Native American tribes in his dedication of the novel to "toutes les tribus du monde qui tardent à succomber aux tentations de la liberté" ("all the tribes in the world who have been late in succumbing to the temptations of freedom"; 7) is an offensive appropriation of this status. This example highlights the stickiness of applying the term postcolonial to Québec. While Bart Moore-Gilbert reminds us that "a state like Québec ... which seems to be postcolonial from one perspective can be simultaneously (neo-)colonial in its relationship to other groups" (10), Vautier argues that Native American relations have been in the hands of the Federal government since its creation (xviii).

21. In another irony of Canadian history, while the Irish (Catholics) eventually resisted British rule on most of the territory of their home island with the creation of the Republic, Irish Canadians would be lumped in with English Canadians and would assert their own difference from French Canadians through the establishment of separate parishes.

22. Duplessis' Québec has been compared to the clerical fascism of Franco's Spain and Mussolini's Italy, with their shared emphases on the Catholic faith and an authoritarian traditionalism based on the patriarchal family.

23. One example of the reexamination of the effectiveness of the Quiet Revolution's progressive modernization of social services appears in Nicole Laurin's arguments that from an efficient, frugal, caring system of health care run by nuns, secularization of Québec's hospital system transformed these into impersonal, administration-heavy, dehumanized institutions. A satiric critique of the current state of health care in Québec, which supports Laurin's position, appears in filmmaker Denys Arcand's depiction of a protagonist's hospitalization for cancer in *Les Invasions barbares* (2003).

24. This discriminatory term, "white niggers of America," appears in political cartoons of the era which sought to point out its use by some Anglo-Canadians. The parallel being made between Canada's French Problem and America's Black Problem was then turned on its head by radical Pierre Vallières and others who appropriated the term to point out the real economic discrimination leveled at the French Canadian in Québec in order to condemn and provoke resistance to it. The Haitian-Canadian critic Max Dorsinville discusses at length what he terms "Black Québec" (*Pays natal* 117–28), asserting that while there was some factual and cultural basis for certain Québec nationalists to identify their situation with that of the decolonizing world, "[l]'image du Noir ne s'applique plus au Québec" ("the image of the Black no longer applies to Québec"; 129). Haitian-Canadian writer Gérard Étienne's later study of this phenomenon finds that while there was a clear appropriation of the discourse of *négritude*, a systematic examination of Québécois novels from 1960–1980 (46) reveals an ambivalence to race, even expressing a certain racism (174–75).

25. Bruce Sterling includes Rushdie's *Grimus* in his categorization of fiction that uses SF tropes, but which is not quite SF as "slipstream." While a large number of postcolonial texts might also fit Sterling's category, the usefulness of slipstream as either a genre or a category given its strong overlap with the more widely accepted postmodern is questionable as Pawel Frelik points out in "Against the (Slip)stream" (Unpublished paper delivered at the SFRA Conference, White Plains, NY, June 22–24, 2006).

26. Not surprisingly, given the close relationship often articulated between feminist and postcolonial criticism, Marleen Barr's application of her concept of "feminist fabulation," an SF resistant to Western, patriarchal master narratives, to texts by Doris Lessing ("Everything") and Salman Rushdie (*Lost*) serves as a precursor to more explicitly postcolonial analyses. Nigerian writer Buchi Emecheta's *The Rape of Shavi* figures in analyses by both Barr (*Lost*) and Donna Haraway, as well as in Pordzik's *The Quest for Postcolonial Utopia* (100); interestingly, it depicts an aircraft especially designed to resist nuclear fallout crashing outside the African village of Shavi in a first chapter titled "The Bird of Fire," an image that resonates with several works of SFQ discussed here.

27. Special thanks to Veronica Hollinger for calling this work, as well as the Csicsery-Ronay article discussed in this section, to my attention. A review of Hopkinson and Mehan's anthology by Brian Attebery, which includes its suggested use in the classroom, perhaps demonstrates that the concept of postcolonial science fiction has arrived. Yet, a paper delivered by Ericka Hoagland titled "Postcolonial Science Fiction: Towards a Theory of an Emerging Genre" at the Science Fiction Research Association Conference (White Plains, NY, June 22–24, 2006) still elicited little interest among members of the SF establishment: of approximately seventy-five attendees some six attended the session.

28. Elana Gomel has argued, much less convincingly, that SF is a discourse of totalitarianism; such reductive, totalizing analyses simply do not hold true when a close review of the full scope of SF literature is made. The body of feminist SF and the criticism that attended its development, along with the growing fields of African-American and queer SF fiction and criticism overwhelmingly demonstrate SF's potential to serve as a discourse that contests the dominant order. I am not the only critic replying to such arguments with texts from the corpus of SFQ; Juan Ignacio Muñoz's unpublished paper reads Jean-Pierre April's *Le Nord électrique* (1985) against Csicsery-Ronay, Jr.'s conception of SF as Empire ("Le futur du vernaculaire et le présent de la conscience planétaire," International Colloquium on Québec, territoire à occuper: la réception de la science-fiction et du fantastique du Canada francophone, Montréal, University of Concordia, May 4–6, 2006).

29. Brooks Landon identifies SF as "the literature of change" (xi), while Tom Moylan asserts its preoccupation with presenting "an 'elsewhere,' an alternative spacetime" (*Scraps* 5). I would assert with Moylan that "as with any imaginative mode, science fiction is not essentially progressive or conservative" but holds the potential for both (*Scraps* 29). Colin Greenland begins his study of the New Wave era arguing that: "Science fiction, essentially the literature of altered circumstances, is the obvious place to seek a language for the unprecedented, especially since it offers as many anxious images as utopian ones" (7). Even during the so-called Golden Age of pulp SF, an era intuitively associated with a conservative ideology of faith in Western science and values, Peter Stockwell points out that the genre's readership were the disempowered members of society: "adolescent boys, young men in office and retail jobs, and new immigrants to the United States" (99).

30. An assertion supported in Peter Stockwell's *The Poetics of Science Fiction* (2000) which points out that even in its most white-male, pro-imperialist era (the so-called Golden Age), readers of pulp-style SF were indeed marginals in the dominant Anglo-American society: "very broadly, adolescent boys, young men in office and retail jobs, and new immigrants to the United States for whom English was often a fairly poor second language. These were largely people without much social or economic power who perhaps gained some vicarious control over their environment by reading stories of blaster-wielding heroes who won out by logical thought rather than economic status" (99).

31. Although several critics (as mentioned earlier) have read mainstream novels from both Québec and Canada using postcolonial theory, observing similar (and sometimes different) themes and tendencies, a full-length comparative study of Anglo-Canadian and French-Canadian SF has yet to appear. Allan Weiss has contributed several articles to the field and David Ketterer's admirable *Canadian Science Fiction and Fantasy* includes both, but as a thorough history it has space for little in-depth analysis.

Chapter One

1. See the second paragraph of the Introduction for a translation of this citation.

2. This section owes a great debt to works by Joël Champetier ("*Solaris*," "Histoire"), Jean-Marc Gouanvic ("Réflexions"), Claude Janelle ("Au Québec"), David Ketterer (*Canadian*), Michel Lord ("Architectures"), Daniel Sernine ("Historique") and Jean-Louis Trudel ("Science," "French-Canadian").

3. At least in academic circles (both anglo- and francophone) it seems that while readers of SF and fantasy often read widely in mainstream literature and have strong literary cultures in terms of the canon, unfortunately the reverse cannot always be said.

4. Sponsored by the Centro interuniversitario di Studi Quebecchesi, the Séminaire international de L'Aquila (29–30 September, 2000) invited authors (like André Carpentier and Esther Rochon), as well as scholars (such as Roger Bozzetto and Michel Lord) to address the topic; co-organizer Novella Novelli published the acts of the conference as *Au Coeur de l'avenir* (2002).

5. Edited respectively by Ransom and Sophie Beaulé, and by Nicholas Serruys these forthcoming volumes will include essays on Québécois and French-Canadian science fiction, fantasy, horror, and other "littératures de l'imaginaire," and on utopia/dystopia from Québec and French Canada.

6. For a more thorough treatment of "proto-SFQ," see articles by Bouchard ("Généologie"), Gouanvic ("Rational"), Trudel ("Science" and "Pulps"), Saint-Gelais ("Orbites").

7. For more on "SFQ jeunesse," or children's/young adult science-fiction in French Canada see articles by LeBrun ("Science" and "Science-fiction"), Sernine ("Science"); Watson's examination of Canadian youth litera-

ture also includes references to French-Canadian works.

8. Several excellent histories of science fiction, which describe this period of transition for the genre, exist in French and in English, although some are becoming dated. These include Jacques Sadoul's *Histoire de la science-fiction moderne* (1973), Brian W. Aldiss' *Trillion Year Spree* (1986), and Donald K. Wollheim's *The Universe Makers* (1971). Colin Greenland's *The Entropy Exhibition* (1983) specifically examines the British New Wave in SF of the 1960s. More recent works include Brooks Landon's excellent introduction, *Science Fiction Since 1900* (1997) and Adam Roberts' *The History of Science Fiction* (2006).

9. Efforts at canon making appeared in the early pages of *Solaris* in the essays by Janelle and Sernine cited here. Jean-Marc Gouanvic's checklist of SFQ includes a number of texts that I would argue are only marginally SF ("A Past").

10. While Colin Greenland points out the central role of Burroughs as a model in Michael Moorcock's revisionist SF of the 1960s New Wave, Bruce Sterling's inclusion of Burroughs on the "slipstream" list seems more appropriate.

11. Janelle observes the connection between Ray's novel *Malpertuis* and Tremblay's *La Cité dans l'oeuf* ("Au Québec" 10), articulated in detail in an unpublished paper by Arnaud Huftier (delivered at "Le futur du vernaculaire et le présent de la conscience planétaire," International Colloquium on Québec, territoire à occuper: la réception de la science-fiction et du fantastique du Canada francophone, Montréal, University of Concordia, May 4–6, 2006).

12. See note 6 for proto-SFQ sources, as well as entries for Neal Baker, Sophie Beaulé, Sylvie Bérard, Jean-Marc Gouanvic, Claude Janelle, Michel Lord, Amy J. Ransom, Nicholas Serruys, Jean-Louis Trudel in the Works Cited for studies of contemporary SFQ.

13. The many social and economic reforms instituted during Québec's Quiet Revolution included an overhaul of the educational system and the creation of the "cégep" (collège d'enseignement générale et professionel), a system of public community colleges.

14. This choice of namesake, a Stanislaw Lem novel which critiques imperialism is perhaps significant; an educator like Spehner would certainly have been aware of the discourse of decolonization's impact in Québec. For a complete history of these three reviews, their generic tendencies and editorial approaches see Painchaud ("Fantastique"). For a thorough history of *Solaris* see Champetier.

15. The group reflects a true generation, since most were born in the post-war period and shared development as children and young adults during the Quiet Revolution (roughly 1960–66) and its aftermath.

16. On French terminology: *roman* denotes a novel; a collection of stories by one author is referred to as a *recueil*; several authors would contribute to a *collectif*, while an *anthologie* is edited by a third party. Shorter works are typically referred to as *nouvelles*, which can be a few pages to a hundred; the term *conte* also appears. As might be guessed, the distinction between the *conte* and the *nouvelle* has changed over time; while once synonymous, Lise Morin concludes that today, the *conte* greater freedom for development and digression, deriving from the oral act of storytelling (*conter, raconter*), while the *nouvelle* must be concise and focused on the development of a simple plot element, told with a direct, logically sequencial form (*La nouvelle fantastique québécoise de 1960 a 1985* [Montréal; Nuit blanche, 1995]: 99).

17. This typical future dystopia has at times been classified as an adolescent novel, but its style, tone, sexual content and historical references suggest an adult audience.

18. A pair of letters by the two entitled "In Dispute" in *Science-fiction Studies* 15 (1988) attests to the tension between these two founding fathers of SFQ. As Nicolas Serruys pointed out to me, Spehner and Gouanvic are both French (E-mail to the author, 26 May 2006). The fact that both of its founding fathers, as well as its mother/midwife (Vonarburg), are French adds another dimension to the issue of SFQ as a colonial/postcolonial discourse. Several historians, in particular Heinrich Weinmann, have looked at Québec's history within the framework of Freud's family romance; such a history of SFQ might prove interesting (particularly given the extent of the founding-mother metaphor in Vonarburg's work).

19. These are collections of SF or other popular genres published in Europe, which include both French authors and translations of Anglo-American works. Before the 1990s only Élisabeth Vonarburg's first novel and second short-story collection, *Le Silence de la cité* (1981) and *Janus* (1984), appeared under French Denoël's Présence du futur label. While they made efforts to include European French-speakers in their collective efforts, especially in the pages of *imagine...*, the Québécois received little reciprocity from the French publication

establishment beyond inclusion in a few anthologies. Things opened up somewhat, in part because of an active fan-exchange, as well as some interest by important French critics like Roger Bozzetto and Max Milner. In the 1990s, Jean-Pierre April succeeded in having a reedition of his *Berlin-Bangkok* published in J'ai lu's SF collection in 1993; Jean-Louis Trudel published two novels with Paris' Fleuve noir in 1994. Joël Champetier and Yves Meynard have published heroic fantasy with smaller presses in France.

20. However, exhibiting a trait that seems typical of genre lit in Québec, quite a few authors blur the lines between genres; the labeling system of Alire would provide great material of study for a genre critic.

21. *Sur le seuil/Evil Words* (2003), directed by Éric Tessier and adapted for the screen by Tessier and Senécal and *La Peau blanche/White Skin* (2004), directed by Daniel Roby and adapted for the screen by Champetier. A dubbed version of the latter has also been released as *Cannibal*. Three film projects remain in various stages of production: Senécal's scenario for *Les 7 jours du Talion* is directed by Daniel Grou for August 2009 release by Go Film. Eric Tessier directs Senécal's scenario for *5150, rue des Ormes*, due in theatres October 2009. Daniel Roby was slated to direct his script for *Aliss*, the latter two projects produced by Cirrus. A translation of Senécal's Québécois best-seller is forthcoming and one of Champetier's novel is complete, seeking a publisher.

22. Sophie Beaulé provides a thorough thematic overview of the SFQ short story ("Cauchemars").

23. This story's original title is in English, "Canadian Dream." While Howard Scott sought to reproduce the estrangement of the reader faced with a title in the *other* language, in my opinion, it simply obscures the text. While many French Canadians are bilingual, a much lower proportion of Anglo-Canadians are (Castonguay 56–58).

24. As historian Caroline-Isabelle Caron points out, the city of Québec reflects precisely this division from the seventeenth through the early twentieth centuries, with the merchant class residing in the upper city and the artisans in the lower (E-mail to the author, 27 June 2006). Today, the lower city's renovation for tourism represents what some consider a "folklorization" of Québec's history-based identity. Such place-specific codings occur frequently in SFQ; Vonarburg also uses the upper- and lower-city division in *Tyranaël*; Rochon's *L'Espace du diamant*, the final novel in the Vrénalik Cycle, may refer to Québec city's *Cap du diamant*, Diamond Head.

Chapter Two

1. See Introduction, note 1.

2. Born in the former Yugoslavia, Suvin lived in Montréal for some years and cofounded *Science-Fiction Studies* at the Université de Montréal. Québécois Marc Angenot worked with Suvin and both became internationally recognized theorists of SF. They did not, however, focus to any degree on the (as yet inexistant) corpus of contemporary SFQ, but rather on Anglo-American, Eastern European and Russian SF texts.

3. Spivak argues in *The Post-colonial Critic* that such a critic must be transparent about the socio-cultural and ideological space from which he or she writes, using the term positionality to refer to this phenomenon. Incidentally, I should signal my own position as a middle-class, feminist, political liberal, wife and mother; as a speaker and instructor of languages and cultures other than English (namely, French and Spanish) and as a member of the Academy, I can claim the ambiguous status of intellectual. While my current socio-economic status and some of my cultural and ethnic background aligns me with the white, Anglo-Saxon, protestant majority in the United States. My childhood experience, which focused on an ethnically Dutch heritage and religious denomination, which in turn placed me in the private, rather than public, educational system, afforded me a sense of my own difference from those around me. (Indeed, my grandmother's union with the son of a local "American" farming family in Western Michigan was considered a mixed marriage by her Dutch immigrant family.) That said, my interest in Québec studies and the postcolonial risks taking on elements of the very exoticism critiqued by Edward Said in *Orientalism*.

4. Sernine names the central character of *Chronoreg* Blackburn in a respectful homage to Rochon.

5. The analysis that follows relies almost exclusively on what the author labels as "la version définitive" of the group of texts that have been identified as *Le Cycle de Vrénalik* (AP "Repères bibliographiques" np). Using the following set of abbreviations: AP = *L'Aigle des profondeurs*; RC = *Le Rêveur dans la Citadelle*; AN = *L'Archipel noir*; ED = *L'Espace du diamant* and ES = *L'Épuisement du soleil*, parenthetical citations, unless otherwise noted, refer

to the tetralogy's first three volumes as revised by the author and republished by Éditions Alire from 1999 to 2002. The fourth and final volume, *L'Espace du diamant* (1990), is cited in the original, since its revision was not yet available as I wrote this study. Alire has just published it as *La Dragonne de l'aurore* (2009). To further complicate matters, another version of the first volume in the Vrénalik cycle appeared in 1986, slightly edited for a youth audience as *L'Étranger sous la ville* (The Stranger under the City). All translations of titles and passages are my own.

6. The plural noun Asven appears invariable in the Éditions Alire publications; *L'Espace du diamant*, still in the original Pleine lune edition, indicates the plural as "Asvens," hence the apparent inconsistency that may appear in citations from the various books of the Vrénalik cycle.

7. Rochon's mise-en-abîme demonstrates her skill as a writer, as well as her sense of humor. In both editions of the Vrénalik novels, she passes off *Le Rêveur dans la Citadelle*, which retells the origin of the four-hundred-year-old culture of Hatzlén, as the work of fictional character, Green. In the first edition, a pseudo-title page precedes this section of the narrative (*L'Épuisement du soleil* 115–56) while the revised edition describes Sutherland reading a rather trashy dime-novel version of Green's text whose cover is described precisely as Guy England's illustration for the Alire edition of Rochon's novel (AN28).

8. Unlike Rochon and Vonarburg, who played key roles, Brossard does not appear to have participated actively in the SFQ movement to any degree, although, on the other hand, he did not reject it either. His long interview with a team from *Solaris* (Pomerleau and Sernine) reveals his positive attitude toward SF and his pleasure at being associated with a form identified by the literary center as marginal, an attitude also reflected in an interview with mainstream literary critic Claude Grégoire.

9. The following abbreviations refer to parenthetical citations from each volume: AA = 1 *Les Années d'apprentissage*; RA = 2.A *Le Recyclage d'Adakhan*; GP = 2.B *Le Grand projet*; SQP = 2.C *Le Sauve-qui-peut*; AE = 3 *Les Années d'errance*. Again, all translations are my own.

10. It also contrasts with that of his near contemporary, sociologist and historian Denis Monière, who recently published an alternate history exploring the vicissitudes of the province's development after the victory of a "yes" vote in 1980 in *Histoire de la République du Québec* (2006). Monière makes clear, though, that his *uchronie* is not a novel; it appears more in the vein of the "counterfactual" history.

11. Michel Lord notes the similarity between *L'Oiseau de feu* and Corriveau's trilogy, the final volume of which is titled *L'Oiseau de feu* ("Feu d'artifices" 19), and Jean-Louis Trudel has also commented, although not in detail, on the similarities between *L'Oiseau de feu* and Corriveau's *Compagnon du soleil* (E-mail to the author, January 2006).

12. The "AC" of the date refers simultaneously to "l'Avant-Centrale, l'Avant-Catastrophe ou l'époque de l'Ancien Calendrier" ("before the Centrale, before the Catastrophe or the epoch of the Ancient Calendar"; RA167) a time prior to the cataclysmic nuclear war, which destroyed all else on Earth and a group of some thousand scientists, foreseeing the coming conflagration, built the Centrale under the "désert de Gobb" ("Gobb desert"; RA172) and sought refuge there, after which the 12,000 survivors remaining on the surface mobbed the entrance to the underground shelter.

13. André Belleau describes the fascination with German literature evident in Québécois literary circles during the 1960s and 1970s (39–48), an affinity shared by Brossard as he openly admits in interviews (Pomerleau and Sernine 18, Grégoire 62) and with the epigraphs from Goethe, Novalis, as well as Rilke, Hesse and Mann, peppered throughout *L'Oiseau de feu* (AAvii, AA293, RA7, RA223, AE7, AE115). His SFQ saga reveals its appurtenance not only to the *roman psychologique*, but also to the related form which developed from German Romanticism, the *Bildungsroman*, as observed by its reviewers (Filion 190, Imbert 225, Pomerleau). Like the *révolté* of Québécois literature, the Romantic hero, too, was alienated and isolated, an impotent rebel, whose life ended more often in suicide than in revolutionary glory. Adakhan shares with the Romantic hero a curiosity, a drive for knowledge, which also sets him apart from those around him who are lulled or forced into complacency through the surveillance and conditioning imposed by the Centrale.

14. Two examples come directly to mind: Senegalese writer Birago Diop's "Sarzan" (in *Contes d'Amadou Koumba*, 1947) tells how a young man recruited into the Senegalese Riflemen unit of the French Colonial Army returns to his village scornful of his people whom he now finds "uncivilized." Diop's tale, written during the colonial period, nonetheless reflects the resistant aspects typical of postcolonial dis-

course in its depiction of Sarzan's ultimate reduction to madness as his *hubris* is punished by the village's ancestral spirits. A later text, Ngugi wa Thiong'o's "A Meeting in the Dark" (1964), reflects a similar theme's effect on the next generation of colonized individuals. The son of the village preacher, inculcated by his family in Christianity and Western values, unable to deal with the conflict between his parents' expectations of his behavior and plans for his university education and his affinity with the people of the village, murders his village girlfriend when she pressures him to acknowledge the baby she is carrying and marry her.

15. Markham's translation reveals its own imbededness in a colonialist discourse in its rendering of Fanon's neutral term, *le métropole*, as "the mother country," *not* the indigene's mother country, but that of the colonizer.

16. Jeremy Bentham composed the "Panopticon" essay in 1787, which included the architectural concepts behind the creation of prisons (and other social institutions housing large numbers of inmates whose behavior was perceived as necessitating observance) which afforded full surveillance of all residents by a small number of guards, a concept which included a central observation tower. His principles were put into practice during the Victorian era and their application for imperialistic uses appears clearly in Dublin's Kilmainham Gaol, where several leaders of the 1916 Rebellion were imprisoned and executed. Michel Foucault, in *Discipline and Punish*, analyzes the panopticon, and theories of surveillance in the contemporary world figure largely in the works Baudrillard, Deleuze, Žižek and others. The volume *CTRL-SPACE: Rhetorics of Surveillance from Bentham to Big Brother*, edited by Thomas Y. Levin, Ursula Frohne and Peter Weibel provides a nice theoretical overview to this question.

17. The websites of organizations like Baby Milk Action (www.babymilkaction.org) and IBFAN (www.ibfan.org) provide links to media coverage of this issue.

18. Brossard inserts a phonetic rendering of English (and other language) expressions; these often serve as part of the system of oppression or describe the strains and ennuis of life in the Centrale. Sylvia Söderlind's linguistic/poststructuralist examinations of Québécois novels from the same period as *L'Oiseau de feu* note the significance of this type of linguistic play in postmodern/postcolonial literatures. A specific study of Brossard's linguistic strategies, many of which resemble those identified in postcolonial literatures by Ashcroft, Griffiths and Tiffin (*Empire* 28–56) has yet to be undertaken.

19. Parenthetical references to the series' five volumes will be indicated by the following abbreviations: DS = *Dreams of the Sea (Tyranaël 1)*; GP = *A Game of Perfection (Tyranaël 2)* both cited in the published translations by Howard Scott and Élisabeth Vonarburg. Translations from the subsequent volumes are my own: MF = *Mon frère l'ombre (Tyranaël 3)*; AR = *L'Autre rivage (Tyranaël 4)*; MA = *La Mer allée avec le soleil (Tyranaël 5)*.

20. These include Jean Dion's "Base de négotiation," Denis Côté's "1534," Jean-Louis Trudel's "Remember, the Dead Say" and "Report 323, A Québécois Infiltration Attempt," Jean-Pierre April's "Le Vol de la ville," among others. See analyses of these works in essays by Ransom, Weiss and Baker.

21. All of what she pieces together as what happened at this stage remains a "what might have happened," for the Ranao left Tyranaël without proof that the Dreams representing this particular future-history configuration — among the millions of possibilities — would actually occur.

22. The imagery of the ghost recurs throughout this volume not only in John Carghill's reference to his former self, Tige, but in Virginian references to the Ranao, ostensibly absent, yet eerily present on a day-to-day basis as they move into the abandoned structures.

23. Not only does "Légaré" mean "the lost one" in French, Abram Viateur recalls the wanderings of the nomadic biblical Abraham coupled with the Latin for "voyager." Dutch signals the Flying Dutchman, forced to wander the centuries in his ghost ship (although a connection to Ronald Reagan might be interesting), Constantin Apatrides, the expatriot, man without a country, Serje Peregrino, the Pilgrim, and so on. The thinly veiled reference to Robert L. Stevenson's Dr. Jekyll and the theme of the double cannot be missed.

24. In addition to other instances within *Tyranaël* (for example, Taïriel in *La Mer allée avec le soleil*) and Vonarburg's earlier novels and short stories (e.g. *The Silent City*, "*Cogito*"), a number of other SFQ works deal with this theme, such as Francine Pelletier's "Guinea Pig" and "Les Noms de l'oubli," René Beaulieu's "Inaccessible," and Claudette Charbonneau-Tissot's "Mutation."

25. Not to mention the possible reference to Baudelaire's introduction to the *Fleurs du mal*, which begins "Mon semblable, mon

frère," an interpellation to the reader to identify with the cycle's implied narrator/alienated hero, which Vonarburg would know inside and out because of her classical French education. Her other works have more transparent references to Baudelaire and other nineteenth-century poets like Rimbaud and Mallarmé.

26. To distinguish between Earth years and the much longer Virginian year, Vonarburg uses the convention of capitalizing the latter, each of which represents four Earth years, which are referred to as "seasons." Virginian characters count their age in seasons, a device obviously designed to assist Vonarburg's Terran readers.

27. This reference to Judith Merril, the Anglo-Canadian who first asked Vonarburg to have a story translated into English to appear in her *Tesseracts* anthology, does not stand alone in *Tyranaël*, as Virginian city names include references to other SF writers Roger Zelazny (Zlazny) and Clifford Simak (Simck).

28. The fact that Vonarburg uses the stereotypical Anglo-Canadian "eh" here, rather than the French rendering of hesitation "hein," again underscores the alignment of a stance of racial ignorance with that group, again supports the reading of the text as national allegory. I thank Nicholas Serruys for pointing out the use of the Canadianism here to me, a detail that I overlooked even while translating the passage.

29. This verisimilitude or "plausibility" is often argued to be one of the hallmarks of true SF as opposed to the satire or allegory. Those who assert that Orwell's *1984* is *not* SF (an argument that could be applied, actually, to a large number of overt satires and allegories found in the SFQ canon) would perforce accept the *Tyranaël* series as "true" SF.

Chapter Three

1. My thoughts on utopia and the SFQ saga developed through several conference presentations: "Utopia, Dystopia and Uchronia and the Science-Fiction Saga from Québec." Thirty-Eighth Science Fiction Research Association Convention. Kansas City, MO, July 5–8, 2007; "Utopie et dystopie dans la saga SFQ." Colloque Boréal 2007: Univers parallèles et autres non-lieux. Université Concordia 27–29 avril, 2007; "Utopian Aspects of Québec's Science-Fiction Sagas." 2007 Popular Culture Association/American Culture Association National Conference in Boston, April 4–7, 2007.

2. A note on capitalization: in this chapter I refer to several "new worlds." When speaking of the "New World Myth" form as outlined by Marie Vautier, I refer to it in capital letters. When I refer to the New World of the Americas for Renaissance and later Europeans, I use capitals. When I refer to a "new world," in the sense of any world or territory that is new to its settlers, I use lower-case letters.

3. As early as 1946, Arthur E. Morgan in *Nowhere was Somewhere* argued that More actually met a Raphael Hythloday in Antwerp and based his insular society upon a first-hand account of the Incas (Jameson, *Archaeology* 230). While that theory has not gained wide acceptance, Vespucci's accounts of his voyage were published as early as 1504, with a Latin version circulating widely in Europe by 1507 (Jameson, *Archaeology* 233).

4. This work has been occasionally appropriated as part of the SFQ canon; see also Introduction, note 20.

5. Indeed, Jean Pettigrew specifically compares Rochon's *L'Espace du diamant* to Le Guin's *The Dispossessed* (167). Rochon implements a number of elements also used by Le Guin, including the emphasis on the spiral imagery (particularly in *Always Coming Home*), details of *The Tombs of Atuan* also find strong resonances in Rochon's first Vrénalik novel, *En Hommage aux araignées*, and the rowan tree — Tàim Sutherland's totemic tree — holds especial importance for Ged in *The Wizard of Earthsea* (see note 11 below for its role in Rochon). Other similarities between the work of Le Guin and that of both Rochon and Vonarburg have yet to be analyzed in detail, in particular the American's Taoism in relation to Rochon's Buddhism and Vonarburg's exploration of Eastern thought systems.

6. A discussion at the 2007 Colloque Boréal Univers (see note 1) focused precisely on this confusion.

7. Both Samuel Butler's *Erewhon* (1872) and William Morris's *News from Nowhere* (1890) invoke this reading of the pun.

8. Indeed, some of Brossard's critics read this device not as sophisticated pastiche, but rather as ineptitude with the science-fictional form, as the label "mainstream dabbler" (Ketterer 131) reveals. The author of *L'Oiseau de feu* responds to these in the afterword to the saga (AE583-87); his credentials in SF, including his readings and influences appear in his interview with Luc Pomerleau and Daniel Sernine. Perhaps the most salient legitimation of his status as a "real" SF writer was the renaming of the Grand Prix de la science-fiction et du

fantastique québécois as the Prix Jacques Brossard in 2007.

9. These include: Pierre Filion (his editor at Leméac), Pierre Vadeboncoeur (the well-known nationalist/unionist essayist), Anne Hébert (Québec's foremost writer of mainstream literature whose works nonetheless frequently touch on the marvelous and the fantastic), Pierre Morency (poet and playwright who published in the counterculture nationalist journal *Hobo-Québec*), Pierre Turgeon (a well-known Québécois novelist), Gilles Vigneault (Québec's best known popular singer whose career developed directly during the Quiet Revolution, and whose songs and poetry participated in the development of a contemporary Québécois national identity), Roland Giguère (poet and engraver), Pierre Trottier (poet and essayist active in the Quiet Revolution review *Cité Libre*). Trottier, Morency and Turgeon all published in *Liberté* (<http://www.litterature.org/recherche/>).

10. By combing through Rochon's work, I have found a similar sentence in "Le Labyrinthe": "Certains invesstissent tant dans la quête qu'ils meurent en touchant au but" (*Le Traversier* 30 but none identical to it. Have I, too, been taken in by a false lead?

11. One wonders if at some level Rochon is parodying those who leave Québec to spend the winter in Florida as the Asven leave their frigid Archipelago for the south. The quirky humor apparent throughout her *œuvre* suggests this possibility as does Christian Morissonneau's schema of directionality for Québec.

12. Rochon's unique style has been discussed earlier. While it is not my purpose here to argue whether or not *Les Chroniques infernales* represent a *bona fide* work of science fiction, I feel it necessary to acknowledge that a large number of readers might exclude it from SF as a genre. Its overall tone and theme link this work much more closely to the realm of fantasy; yet, key SF tropes dominate the work such as the conception of human and other life forms spread out over a number of viable "worlds," the use of advanced technology including robots and portals that allow travel from one world to another to occur, the encounter by humans and their interaction with life forms that are not human, and so on. Ultimately, I accept Rochon's own designation of her writing as science fiction as an adequate guarantee of the text's participation in that generic tradition.

13. Citations from the various volumes of the *Chroniques infernales* will refer to the following abbreviations, presented in order of publication, which also corresponds to their chronological order in terms of the narrative time: L = *Lame*, A = *Aboli*, O = *Ouverture*, S = *Secrets*, Or = *Or*, So = *Sorbier*.

14. Gayatri Chakravorty Spivak ("Subaltern") and Homi K. Bhabha draw upon Antonio Gramsci's conception of the subaltern, a status devoid of autonomy, subordinate to another hegemonic group (Bhabha cites A. Showstack Sassoon, *Approaches to Gramsci* [London: Writers & Readers, 1982: 16])

15. Some readers will recall the practice of Count Dracula's supposed historical model, the fifteenth-century ruler of Wallachia Vlad Dracul (1431–1476), who gained notoriety by having his enemies impaled live upon enormous stakes pushed through the anus or vagina and on through the internal organs to exit through the mouth.

16. In the story "Devenir vivante," Rochon develops the backstory of this period in Rel's previous life and explains his name as an acronym for "Roi à l'esprit libre" (King with an Open/Free Mind).

17. Deirdre Byrne establishes a similar relationship for works by Ursula K. Le Guin.

18. The Tibetan epic *Gesar de Ling*, translated by Robin Kornman, appears credited in the "Remerciements" at the end of *Sorbier* (416).

19. As in the previous chapter, the various volumes are abbreviated as follows in the parenthetical page references: DS = *Dreams of the Sea*, GP = *A Game of Perfection* for the two volumes available in translation, with references as well to the original French edition as: RM = *Les Rêves de la mer*, JP = *Le Jeu de perfection*, MF = *Mon frère l'ombre*, AR = *L'Autre rivage* and MA = *La Mer allée avec le soleil*.

20. This term, indicating a token, folkloristic, tourist-friendly representation of indigenous/Anishnaabe cultures, was coined by Sara Sutler-Cohen, "'Spirit Guides Me': An Exploration into Neoshamanism in Northern California." University of California, Santa Cruz, (Ph.D. dissertation): June 2005.

21. Caroline-Isabelle Caron also points out the similarity to the European Game of the Goose (E-mail to author, 23 September 2008), which also takes the form of a spiral (http://en.wikipedia.org/wiki/Game_of_the_Goose), a form central to Suvin's conception of the open-ended utopia.

22. The titles of its five volumes play on names of cards and suits in an Asian tarot-deck: *La Maison d'Oubli* (The House of Forgetting; 2005), *Le Dragon de feu* (The Dragon of Fire; 2005), *Le Dragon fou* (The Mad

Dragon; 2006), *La Princesse de Vengeance* (The Princess of Vengeance; 2006), and *La Maison d'Équité* (The House of Equity; 2007).

Chapter Four

1. My understanding of this nuance comes from Denise O'Neil Green, associate vice-president for diversity at Central Michigan University.

2. Étienne's *Un ambassadeur Macoute à Montréal* appears on Jean-Marc Gouanvic's list of early SFQ. The novel mixes Haitian history and politics with those of Québec in this surreal/fantastic narrative about race relations and social justice. The Canadian government (in collaboration with the CIA) invites a Haitian diplomat (one of Papa Doc Duvalier's tonton-macoute) to clean up Montréal. The plot references Hubert Aquin's *Prochain épisode* as Alexis Accius, an illegal Haitian immigrant becomes the target of the Ambassador's forces, but with the help of Claire ("une canadienne pure-laine") and an unnamed "petit blanc," he rallies the other oppressed "petits blancs" ("little whites") of Montréal to resist and eject the Diplomat from power.

3. The Métis people formed a group distinct from both French Canadians and Amerindian bands. These descendants of French *voyageurs* and Amerindian women adopted Catholicism and a version of the French language called *Michif*. They lived (particularly in the western territories that would become Manitoba and Alberta) a hybrid lifestyle of farming supplemented with — for as long as the population sustained this — buffalo hunting (Martel). With the Inuit and the First Nations they are recognized in Canadian law as an aboriginal group.

4. The most notable exception would, of course, be Yves Thériault, whose treatment of Montagnais (*Ashini* and "Akua Nuten") and Inuit (*Agaguk*) protagonists can be read ambivalently as either sensitive efforts to understand and depict the violence of contact with the West for authochthonous peoples or, particularly when read in the context of nationalist discourse, as allegorical usurpation of their position by the Québécois.

5. Their fear may be based on/inspired by the real extinction of an indigenous group of island peoples, the Beothuk of Newfoundland (see Bernard Assiniwi's fictional account *The Beothuk Saga*, 1996, trans. Wayne Grady. New York: St. Martin's, 2002).

6. Readers of international SF will note the similarities between Vonarburg's Sea and the mysterious planet featured in Stanislaw Lem's *Solaris* (1961), clearly a touchstone work for SFQ in that the milieu's magazine chose to reference Lem's work in its title.

Appendix

1. Special thanks to René Beaulieu for supplying me with additional titles for this list; an alternate version appeared in the New York Review of Science Fiction, summer 2009.

Works Cited—Primary Sources
See Appendix for SFQ works available in English.

April, Jean-Pierre. *Berlin-Bangkok.* Autres mers, Autres mondes 5. Montréal: Logiques, 1989.
———. *La Machine à explorer la fiction.* Chroniques du futur 2. Longueil: Le Préambule, 1980.
———. *Le Nord électrique.* Chroniques du futur 10. Longueil: Le Préambule, 1985.
———. "Rêve canadien." Trans. Howard Scott. Hartwell and Grant *Suns* 299–317. Trans. of "Canadian Dream." 1982. *Chocs baroques.* Ed. Michel Lord. Montréal: FIDES, 1991. 185–214.
Aquin, Hubert. *Blackout.* Trans. Alan Brown. Toronto: Anansi, 1974. Trans. of *Trou de mémoire.* Montréal: Le Cercle du Livre de France, 1968.
———. *Prochain épisode.* 1965. Trans. Penny Williams. Toronto: McClelland and Stewart, 1972.
Atwood, Margaret. *The Handmaid's Tale.* New York: Anchor, 1986.
Aubert de Gaspé, Philippe, fils. *The Influence of A Book.* Montréal: R. Davies, 1993. Trans. of *L'Influence d'un livre.* 1837.
Aubin, Napoléon. "Mon Voyage à la lune." 1839. Rpt. (abr.) *Napoléon Aubin.* Ed. Jean-Paul Tremblay. Classiques Canadiens 43. Montréal: FIDES, 1972.
Banks, Iain M. *Consider Phlebas.* New York: St. Martin's, 1987.
Barcelo, François. *Agénor, Agénor, Agénor et Agénor.* Montréal: Quinze, 1980.
———. *La Tribu.* 1981. Montréal: Libre Expression, 1981. Rpt. Montréal: Bibliothèque québécoise, 1998.
Barthe, Ulric. *Similia Similibus ou la Guerre au Canada: essai romantique sur un sujet d'actualité.* Québec: Telegraph, 1916.
Beaulieu, Natasha. *L'Ange écarlate.* Québec: Alire, 2000.
———. *L'Eau noire.* Québec: Alire, 2003.
———. *L'Ombre pourpre.* Québec: Alire, 2006.
Beaulieu, René. "The Bluejay." Trans. Jane Brierley. Vonarburg and Brierley 247–62. Trans. of "Le geai bleu." 1980. R. Beaulieu, *Légendes* 167–86.
———. "The Energy of Slaves." Trans. Yves Meynard. *Tesseracts 8.* Ed. John Clute and Candas Jane Dorsey. Edmonton: The Books Collective, 1999. 275–90. Trans. of "L'Énergie des esclaves." 1983. *Un fantôme d'amour.* Roberval: Ashem, 1997. 33–48.
———. "Inaccessible." 1985. *Les Voyageurs de la nuit.* n. p.: l'A Venir, 1997. 65–71.
———. *Légendes de Virnie.* Chroniques du futur 3. Longueil: Le Préambule, 1981.
Bélil, Michel. *La Ville oasis: Les Chroniques de Razzlande I.* Autres mers, Autres mondes 7. Montréal: Logiques, 1990.
Benoit, Jacques. *Jos Carbone.* Montréal: du Jour, 1967.

_____. *Les Princes*. Montréal: du Jour, 1973.
Bérard, Sylvie. *Of Wind and Sand*. Trans. Sheryl Curtis. Calgary: Edge SF & F, 2009. Trans. of *Terre des autres*. Québec: Alire, 2004.
Bergeron, Alain. *Corps Machines et rêves d'anges*. Hull: Vents d'Ouest, 1997.
_____. *Un été de Jessica*. Montréal: Quinze, 1978.
_____. *Phaos*. Québec: Alire, 2003.
Bergeron, Bertrand. "The Other" Trans. Jane Brierley. Vonarburg and Brierley 330–35. Trans. of "L'Autre" in *L'Année de la science-fiction et du fantastique québécois 1987*. Montréal: Le Passeur, 1988. 239–43.
Bersianik, Louky. *The Eugelion*. Trans. Howard Scott. Montréal: Alter Ego, 1996. Trans. *L'Euguélionne*. 1976.
_____. *Le Pique-nique sur l'Acropole: Cahiers d'Ancyl*. 1979. Montréal: Typo, 1992.
Berthos, Jean. *Eutopia*. Lévis: Le Quotidien, 1946.
Bessette, Gérard. *Les Anthropoïdes*. Montréal: La Presse, 1977.
Billon, Pierre. *The Children's Wing*. Trans. Sheila Fischman. Montréal: R. Davies, 1995. Trans. of *L'Enfant du cinquième Nord*. Montréal: Québec/Amérique, 1982; Paris: Seuil, 1982.
Blais, Marie-Claire. *Mad Shadows*. Trans. Merloyd Lawrence. Toronto: McClelland and Stewart, 1996. Trans. of *La Belle bête*. 1968.
Bolduc, Claude. *Histoire d'un soir et autres épouvantes*. Gatineau: Vents d'ouest, 2006.
_____. *Les yeux troubles et autres contes de la lune noire*. Hull: Vents d'ouest, 1998.
Bonelli, André-Jean. *Loona; ou autrefois le ciel était bleu*. Kénogami: Hélios, 1974.
Bouchard, Guy. *Gélules utopiques*. Autres mers, Autres mondes 2. Montréal: Logiques, 1988.
Bouhalassa, Mehdi. "Anne de la Terre." *Solaris* 148 (2004): 38–70.
_____. "La Tentation d'Adam." *Solaris* 144 (2003): 89–113.
Bova, Ben. *Mars*. 1992. New York: Bantam. 1993.
Brossard, Jacques. *L'Accession à la souveraineté et le cas du Québec*. Montréal: PU Montréal, 1976.
_____. "Le Boulon d'Ernest." *Écrits du Canada français* 36 (1973): 123–39.
_____. "La Cloison de verre." *Écrits du Canada français* 41 (1978): 55–65.
_____. "La Clôture." *Possibles* 2.1 (Fall 1977): 103–114. Rpt. w/var. *Écrits du Canada français* 41 (1978): 76–87.
_____. *La Cour suprême et la Constitution*. Montréal: PU Montréal, 1968.
_____. "La Grande Roue." *Écrits du Canada français* 41 (1978): 33–42.
_____. *L'Immigration. Les Droits et pouvoirs du Canada et du Québec*. Montréal: PU Montréal, 1967.
_____. "Le Mal de Terre." *Écrits du Canada français* 36 (1973): 140–55.
_____. "The Metamorfalsis." Trans. Basil Kingstone. Hancock 121–48. Trans. of "Le Métamorfaux." 1974.
_____. *Le Métamorfaux*. Montréal: Hurtubise HMH, 1974. Rpt. Montréal: Bibliothèque Québécoise, 1988.
_____. *L'Oiseau de feu: 1 Les Années d'apprentissage*. Montréal: Leméac, 1989.
_____. *L'Oiseau de feu: 2.A Le Recyclage d'Adakhan*. Montréal: Leméac, 1990.
_____. *L'Oiseau feu: 2.B Le Grand projet*. Montréal: Leméac, 1993.
_____. *L'Oiseau de feu: 2.C Le Sauve-qui-peut*. Montréal: Leméac, 1995.
_____. *L'Oiseau de feu: 3 Les Années d'errance*. Montréal: Leméac, 1997.
_____. "Le Parc." *Écrits du Canada français* 41 (1978): 43–54.
_____. "Retours." *Écrits du Canada français* 36 (1973): 156–77.
_____. *Le Sang du souvenir*. Montréal: La Presse, 1976. Rpt. Montréal: Leméac, 1987.
_____. Henriette Immarigeon, Gérard V. La Forest, and Luce Patenaude. *Le Territoire québécois*. Montréal: PU Montréal, 1970.
_____, André Paty, and Elizabeth Weiser. *Les Pouvoirs extérieurs du Québec*. Montréal: PU Montréal, 1967.

Buzzati, Dino. "The Falling Girl." Trans. Lawrence Venuti. Rpt. Rubinstein and Larson 113–16. Trans. of "Ragazza che precipita." 1966.
Callenbach, Ernest. *Ecotopia: The Notebooks and Report of William Weston.* 1975. New York: Bantam, 1990.
Campanella, Tommaso. *City of the Sun. Famous Utopias.* Intr. Charles M. Andrews. New York: Tudor, 1937.
Césaire, Aimé. *Notebook of a Return to the Native Land.* Trans. Mireille Rosello with Annie Pritchard. Newcastle Upon Tyne: Bloodaxe, 1995. Trans. of *Cahier d'un retour au pays natal.* 1956.
Champetier, Joël. *The Dragon's Eye.* Trans. Jean-Louis Trudel. New York: Tor, 1999. Trans. of *La Taupe et le dragon.* Montréal: Québec/Amérique, 1991.
———. *La Mémoire du lac.* Montréal: Québec/Amérique, 1994. Rpt. Québec: Alire, 2001.
———. *Les Sources de la magie.* Québec: Alire, 2002.
———. *Le Voleur des Steppes.* Québec: Alire, 2007.
———. "The Winds of Time." Trans. Jane Brierley. Dorsey and Truscott 286–288. Trans. of "Les Vents du temps." 1987.
Charbonneau-Tissot, Claudette. "Mutation." *Contes pour hydrocéphales adultes.* Montréal: Cercle du Livre de France. 1974. 43–72.
Cocke, Emmanuel. *L'Emmanuscrit de la mère morte.* Montréal: du Jour, 1972.
———. *Va voir au ciel si j'y suis.* Montréal: du Jour, 1971.
Corriveau, Monique. *Compagnon du soleil-1. L'Oiseau de feu.* Montréal: FIDES, 1976.
———. *Compagnon du soleil-2. La Lune noire.* Montréal: FIDES, 1976.
———. *Compagnon du soleil-3. Le Temps des chats.* Montréal: FIDES, 1976.
Côté, Denis. "1534." Trans. Howard Scott. Vonarburg and Brierley 111–21. Trans. of "1534." *Dix nouvelles de science-fiction québécoise.* Ed. André Carpentier. Montréal: Les Quinze, 1985. 65–81.
Côté, Héloïse. *Les Conseillers du roi. Les Chroniques de l'Hudres-1.* Québec: Alire, 2004.
d'Agoult, Marie. *Mémoires (1833–1854).* 11th ed. Ed. Daniel Ollivier. Paris: Calmann-Lévy, 1927.
Dandurand, Anne, and Claire Dé. "Metamorphosis." Hancock 397–401.
Dante Alighieri. *The Divine Comedy.*1308–21. Trans. Carlyle-Okey-Wickstead. 1932. Intr. C.H. Grandgent. New York: Vintage, 1950.
Des Roches, Roger. "The Vertigo of Prisons." Trans. Donald McGrath. Vonarburg and Brierley 284–302. Trans. of "Le Vertige des prisons." 1989.
Desrosiers, Emmanuel. *La Fin de la terre.* Preface Jean-Jacques Lefebvre. Montréal: Action Canadienne-Française, 1931.
Devi, Mahasweta. "Pterodactyl, Puran Sahay, and Pirtha." *Imaginary Maps.* Trans. Gayatri Chakravorty Spivak. New York: Routledge, 1994. 95–196.
Dion, Jean. "Base de négociation." 1992. *Escales sur Solaris.* Eds. Joël Champetier and Yves Meynard. Hull: Vents d'Ouest, 1993. 75–105.
Diop, Birago. "Sarzan." Trans. Ellen Conroy Kennedy. Rpt. Rubinstein and Larson 202–09. Trans. "Sarzan." *Contes d'Amadou Koumba.* 1947. Paris: Présence Africaine, 1999.
Dorsey, Candas Jane, and Gerry Truscott, eds. *Tesseracts 3.* Victoria: Porcépic, 1993.
Emecheta, Buchi. *The Rape of Shavi.* London: Agwugwu Afor, 1983.
Ellison, Harlan. *Again, Dangerous Visions.* Garden City, NY: Doubleday, 1972.
———. *Dangerous Visions.* Garden City, NY: Doubleday, 1967.
Étienne, Gérard. *Un ambassadeur macoute à Montréal.* Montréal: Nouvelle Optique, 1979.
Gagnon, Maurice. *Alerte dans le pacifique.* Montréal: Lidec, 1967.
———. *Une aventure d'Ajax.* Montréal: Lidec, 1966.
———. *Opération Tanga.* Montréal: Lidec, 1966.
———. *Les Savants réfractaires.* Montréal: Lidec, 1965.
———. *Les Tours de Babylone.* Montréal: L'Actuelle, 1972.

_____. *Unipax intervient*. Montréal: Lidec, 1965.
Ghosh, Amitav. *The Calcutta Chromosome*. New York: Avon, 1995.
Gilman, Charlotte Perkins. *Herland and Selected Stories*. 1915. Ed. Barbara Solomon. New York: Signet Classics, 1992.
Grenier, Armand. *see* Plour, Guy René de and Laurin, Florent.
Grignon, Claude-Henri. *The Woman and the Miser*. Montréal: Harvest House, 1978. Trans. of *Un homme et son péché*. 1933.
Guevremont, Germaine. *The Outlander*. Trans. Eric Sutton. New York: Whittlesea House, 1950. Trans. of *Le Survenant*. 1945.
Guillet, Jean-Pierre. *La Cage de Londres*. Québec: Alire, 2003.
Guitard, Agnès. *Les Corps communicants*. Montréal: Québec/Amérique, 1981.
Hancock, Geoff, ed. *Invisible Fictions: Contemporary Stories from Québec*. Toronto: Anansi, 1987.
Hardt, Michael, and Antonio Negri. *Empire*. Cambridge: Harvard University Press, 2000.
Hartwell, David G., and Glenn Grant, eds. *Northern Stars: The Anthology of Canadian Science Fiction*. New York: Tor, 1994.
_____. *Northern Suns: The New Anthology of Canadian Science Fiction*. New York: Tor, 1999.
Hébert, Anne. *The Torrent*. Montréal: Harvest House, 1973. Trans. of *Le Torrent*. 1950.
Hébert, Louis-Philippe. *La Manufacture de machines*. Montréal: Quinze, 1976.
_____. "The Hotel." Trans. Alberto Manguel. Hancock 165–68. Trans. "L'Hôtel." 1976.
Hémon, Louis. *Maria Chapdelaine*. 1916. Trans. W.H. Blake. New York: Macmillan, 1921.
Hopkinson, Nalo. *Brown Girl in the Ring*. New York: Warner, 1998.
_____. *Midnight Robber*. New York: Warner, 2000.
_____. *The Salt Roads*. New York: Warner, 2003.
_____, and Uppinder Mehan, eds. *So Long Been Dreaming: Postcolonial Science Fiction and Fantasy*. Vancouver: Arsenal Pulp, 2004.
Huot, Alexandre. *L'Impératrice de l'Ungava*. 1927. Montréal: Imaginaire/Nord, 2006.
Huxley, Aldous. *Brave New World*. 1932. New York: Bantam, 1958.
Jasmin, Claude. *Ethel and the Terrorist*. Trans. David S. Walker. Montréal: Harvest House, 1965. Trans. of *Ethel et le terroriste*. 1964.
King, Stephen. *Firestarter*. New York: Viking, 1980.
Kogawa, Joy. *Obasan*. 1982. New York: Anchor, 1994.
Laframboise, Michèle. *Ithuriel*. Pantin: Naturellement, 2001.
_____. "Le Vol de l'abeille." *Solaris* 159 (2006): 7–28.
_____. "Women are from Mars, Men are from Venus." *Tesseracts 10*. Eds. Edo Van Belkom and Robert Charles Wilson. Calgary: Edge SF & F: 2006.
Lalonde, Michèle. "Speak White." 1970. *Défense et illustration de la langue québécoise, suivi de Prose et poèmes*. Paris: Éditions Seghers/Laffont, 1979. 37–40.
Laurin, Florent (pseud. of Armand Grenier). *Erres Boreales*. N. p.: N. p., 1944.
Le Guin, Ursula K. *Always Coming Home*. 1985. Berkely: University of California Press, 2000.
_____. *The Dispossessed*. 1974. New York: Eos/Harper Collins, 2001.
_____. *The Tombs of Atuan*. 1970. New York: Pocket Books, 2004.
_____. *A Wizard of Earthsea*. 1969. New York: Bantam, 1989.
Lessing, Doris. "Appendix." *The Four-Gated City*. 1969. London: Granada/Panther Books, 1972.
_____. *Documents Relating To The Sentimental Agents in the Volnyen Empire. Canopus in Argos: Archives V*. London: Granada, 1983.
_____. *The Making of the Representative for Planet Eight. Canopus in Argos: Archives IV*. New York: Random House/Vintage, 1982.
_____. *The Marriages Between Zones Three, Four, and Five. Canopus in Argos: Archives II*. London: Granada, 1980.

_____. *Re: Colonised Planet 5 Shikasta.... Canopus in Argos: Archives I.* 1979. New York: Vintage, 1981.
_____. *The Sirian Experiments: The Report by Ambien II. Canopus in Argos: Archives III.* New York: Random House, 1980.
Loranger, Françoise. *Mathieu.* Montréal: Cercle du Livre de France, 1949.
Martel, Suzanne. *The City Underground.* Trans. Norah Smaridge. New York: Viking, 1964. Trans. of *Quatre Montréalais en l'an 3000/Surréal 3000.* 1963.
Martin, Michel. "Geisha Blues." 1988. Trans. Howard Scott. Vonarburg and Brierley 263–83.
Meynard, Yves. *The Book of Knights.* New York: TOR, 1998.
_____. "Equinox." *Tesseracts 4.* Eds. Lorna Toolis and Michael Skeet. Victoria: Beach Holme, 1992. 89–107.
_____. "A Letter from My Mother." *Tesseracts 7.* Eds. Paula Johanson and Jean-Louis Trudel. Edmonton: Books Collective, 1998. 220–24.
_____. *Un œuf d'acier.* Hull: Éditions Vents d'Ouest, 1997.
_____. *La Rose du désert.* Québec: Le Passeur, 1995.
_____. "The Scalemen." Trans. Jane Brierley. Vonarburg and Brierley 5–25. Trans. "Les hommes-écailles." 1989.
_____. "Stolen Fires." Hartwell and Grant, *Stars* 286–95.
Michaud, Nando. *Les Montres sont molles, mais les temps sont durs.* Montréal: Pierre Tisseyre/ Le Cercle du Livre de France, 1988.
_____. *Virages dangereux et autres mauvais tournants.* Montréal: Triptyque, 2003.
Milton, John. *Paradise Lost.* 1667. New York: Norton, 1993.
Monière, Denis. *Histoire de la République du Québec; 25 ans d'indépendance.* Québec: Québécois, 2006.
Montambault, André. *Étrangers!* Autres mers, Autres mondes 10. Montréal: Logiques, 1991.
Montpetit, Charles. "Beyond the Barriers." Trans. Charles Montpetit. Hartwell and Grant, *Suns* 207–13. Trans. of "Dégénérer." 1992.
More, Sir Thomas. "Utopia." Bruce 1–133.
Morris, William. *News from Nowhere.* 1890. *Three Works by William Morris.* Intr. A.L. Morton. New York: International, 1968.
Ngugi wa Thiong'o. "A Meeting in the Dark." 1975. Rpt. Rubinstein and Larson 684–93.
Orwell, George. *1984.* 1949. New York: New American Library, 1977.
Paquin, Ubald. *La Cité dans les fers.* 1925. Montréal: Édouard Garand, 1926.
Pelletier, Francine. *Issabel de Qohosaten. Le Sable et l'acier-3.* Québec: Alire, 1999.
_____. *Les Jours de l'ombre.* Québec: Alire, 2004.
_____. "The Mother Migrator." Trans. Wendy Greene. Vonarburg and Brierley 64–79. Trans. of "La Migratrice." 1985.
_____. *Nelle de Vilvèq. Le Sable et l'acier-1.* Québec: Alire, 1997.
_____. "Les Noms de l'oubli." *Sous des soleils étrangers.* Eds. Yves Meynard and Claude J. Pelletier. Laval: Ianus, 1989. 9–31.
_____. *Samiva de Frée. Le Sable et l'acier-2.* Québec: Alire, 1998.
_____. *Le Temps des migrations.* Chroniques du futur 11. Longueil: Le Préambule, 1987.
Perrot-Bishop, Annick. *Les Maisons de cristal.* Autres mers, Autres mondes 8. Montréal: Logiques, 1990.
_____. "The Ourlandine." 1989. Trans. Neil B. Bishop. Vonarburg and Brierley 373–82.
Pettigrew, Jean. "Snoopymen All Die Like Bengal Goats." Trans. Jane Brierley. Vonarburg and Brierley 143–49. Trans. of "Les Hommes-Snoopy meurent tous comme des chèvres du Bengale." 1984. *Anthologie de la science-fiction québécoise contemporaine.* Ed. Michel Lord. Montréal: FIDES, 1988. 145–56.
Plour, Guy René de (pseud. of Armand Grenier). *Défricheur de Hammada; Misanthrope évadé de l'Amérique.* N. p.: Les Éditions Laurin, 1952/1953.

Prévost, Claude-Michel. "Cappucino Buns." *Solaris* 69 (1986): 11–13.
_____. "Happy Days in Old Chernobyl." 1987. Trans. John Greene. Dorsey and Truscott 183–196. Rpt. Hartwell and Grant, *Stars* 254–62.
Robin, Régine. *The Wanderer*. Montréal: Alter Ego, 1997. Trans. of *La Québécoite*. Montréal: Québec/Amérique, 1983.
Rochon, Esther. *Aboli: Les Chroniques infernales-2*. Québec: Alire, 1996.
_____. *L'Aigle des profondeurs*. Québec: Alire, 2002.
_____. *L'Archipel noir*. Québec: Alire, 1999.
_____. "Canadola." Trans. John Greene. Dorsey and Truscott 322–26. Trans. of "Canadoule." 1989.
_____. "Devenir vivante." *Dérives* 5. Autres mers, Autres mondes 1. Montréal: Logiques, 1988. 123–52. Rpt. *Le Piège à souvenirs*. Montréal: La Pleine lune, 1991. 61–88.
_____. *L'Épuisement du soleil*. Longueil: Le Préambule, 1985. Chroniques du futur 8.
_____. *L'Espace du diamant*. Montréal: La Pleine Lune, 1990.
_____. *L'Étranger sous la ville*. Montréal: Éditions Paulines, 1986. Jeunesse-pop 56.
_____. *En hommage aux araignées*. Montréal: L'Actuelle, 1974.
_____. *Lame*. Montréal: Québec/Amérique, 1995. Sextant 9. Rpt. Québec: Alire, 2009.
_____. "Memory Trap." Trans. Lucille Nelson. Vonarburg and Brierley 99–110. Trans. "Le piège à souvenirs." 1991.
_____. *Or: Les Chroniques infernales-5*. Québec: Alire, 1999.
_____. *Ouverture: Les Chroniques infernales-3*. Québec: Alire, 1997.
_____. *Le Piège à souvenirs*. Montréal: La Pleine Lune, 1991.
_____. *Le Rêveur dans la Citadelle*. Québec: Alire, 1998.
_____. *Secrets: Les Chroniques infernales-4*. Québec: Alire, 1998.
_____. *The Shell*. Trans. David Lobdell. OHawa: Oberon Press, 1990.
_____. *Sorbier: Les Chroniques infernales-6*. Québec: Alire, 2000.
_____. *Der Träumer in der Zitadelle*. Munich: Heyne Verlag, 1997.
_____. *Le Traversier*. Recueil. Montréal: La Pleine Lune, 1987.
_____. "Xils." 1983. Trans. John Greene. Hartwell and Grant, *Stars* 282–84.
Roy, Gabrielle. *The Tin Flute*. Trans. Alan Brown. Toronto: McClelland and Stewart, 1989. Trans. of *Bonheur d'occasion*. 1945.
Rubinstein, Roberta, and Charles R. Larson, eds. *Worlds of Fiction*. 1993. Upper Saddle River: Prentice Hall, 2002.
Rushdie, Salman. *Grimus*. 1975. New York: Modern Library, 2003.
_____. *The Ground Beneath Her Feet*. New York: Henry Holt, 1999.
Russ, Joanna. *The Female Man*. 1975. Boston: Beacon, 1986.
Senécal, Patrick. *5150, rue des Ormes*. 1994. Québec: Alire, 2001.
_____. *Sur le seuil*. Québec: Alire, 1998.
Sernine, Daniel. *Les Archipels du temps. La Suite du temps-2*. Québec: Alire, 2005.
_____. *Boulevard des étoiles*. Montréal: Ianus, 1991.
_____. *Boulevard des étoiles 2-À la Recherche de monsieur Goodtheim*. Montréal: Ianus, 1991.
_____. *Chronoreg*. Montréal: Québec/Amérique, 1992; Rpt. Québec: Alire, 1999.
_____. *Les Contes de l'ombre*. Montréal: Sélect, 1978.
_____. *Légendes du vieux manoir*. Montréal: Sélect, 1979.
_____. *Les Méandres du temps*. Chroniques du futur 6. Longueil: Le Préambule, 1983.
_____. *Les Méandres du temps. La Suite du temps-1*. Québec: Alire, 2004.
_____. *Quand vient la nuit*. Chroniques de l'au-delà 1. Longueil: Le Préambule, 1983.
Sévigny, Marc. 1983. "The Train." Trans. Frances Morgan. *Tesseracts: Canadian Science Fiction*. Ed. Judith Merril. Victoria: Press Porcépic, 1985. 157–71.
Shakespeare, William. "The Tempest." 1611. *The Norton Shakespeare*. New York: Norton, 1997. 3047–3107.

Simmons, Dan. *The Fall of Hyperion*. New York: Doubleday, 1990.
_____. *Hyperion*. New York: Doubleday, 1989.
Somain, Jean-François. *Vivre en beauté*. Autres mers, Autres mondes 6. Montréal: Logiques, 1989.
Somcynsky, Jean-François. *La Planète amoureuse*. Chroniques du futur 5. Longueil: Le Préambule, 1982.
Tardivel, Jules-Paul. *For My Country*. Trans. Sheila Fischman. Toronto: University of Toronto Press, 1975. Trans. of *Pour la Patrie, roman du XXe siècle*. 1895. Rpt. Montréal: Hurtubise HMH, 1989.
Tessier, Mario. "Du clônage considéré comme un des beaux-arts." *Solaris* 146 (2003): 9–14.
_____. "Le Regard du trilobite." *Solaris* 159 (2006): 73–102.
Tétreau, Jean. *Les Nomades*. Montréal: Éditions du Jour, 1967.
Tremblay, Michel. *The City in the Egg*. Trans. Michael Bullock. Vancouver: Ronsdale, 1999. Trans. of *La Cité dans l'oeuf*. 1969.
_____. *Hosanna, suivi de La Duchesse de Langeais*. Montréal: Leméac, 1973.
_____. *Tales for Late Night Drinkers*. Trans. Michael Bullock. Vancouver: Intermedia, 1977. Trans. of *Contes pour buveurs attardés*. 1966.
Thériault, Yves. *Ashini*. 1960. Trans. Gwendolyn Moore. Montréal: Harvest House, 1972.
_____. *La Bête à 300 têtes*. Montréal: Lidec, 1967.
_____. *Le Château des petits hommes verts*. Montréal: Lidec, 1966.
_____. *Le Dernier Rayon*. Montréal: Lidec, 1966.
_____. *La Montagne creuse: Une aventure de Volpek*. 1965. Montréal: Centre éducatif et culturel, 1980.
_____. *Les Pieuvres*. Montréal: Lidec, 1966.
_____. *Le Secret de Mufjarti: Une aventure de Volpek*. 1965. Montréal: Centre éducatif et culturel, 1981.
_____. *Si la bombe m'était conté*. Montréal: Éditions du Jour, 1962.
_____, and Anthony Mollica. *Les Dauphins de Monsieur Yu: Une aventure de Volpek*. Montréal: Centre éducatif et culturel, 1982.
Trudel, Jean-Louis. "The Falafel is Better in Ottawa." *Ark of Ice: Canadian Futurefiction*. Ed. Lesley Choyce. Lawrencetown Beach: Pottersfield, 1992. 85–94.
_____. "The Paradigm Machine." *Tesseracts 5*. Ed. Robert Runté and Yves Meynard. Edmonton: The Books Collective, 1996. 93–108.
_____. "Proscripts of Gehenna." Trans. John Greene. Dorsey and Truscott 372–91. Trans. of "Les Proscrits de Géhenne." 1988.
_____. "Remember, the Dead Say." *Tesseracts 4*. Eds. Lorna Toolis and Michael Skeet. Victoria: Beach Holme, 1992. 368–87.
_____. "Report 323: A Quebecois Infiltration Attempt." *Prairie Fire* 67 (1994): 20–26.
Vonarburg, Élisabeth. *L'Autre rivage*. Tyranaël-4. Québec: Alire, 1997.
_____. "Cogito." Trans. Jane Brierley. Dorsey and Truscott 62–82.
_____. *Dreams of the Sea*. Tyranaël-1. Trans. Howard Scott and Élisabeth Vonarburg. Edmonton: Tesseract, 2003. Trans. of *Les Rêves de la mer*. Tyranaël-1. Québec: Alire, 1996.
_____. "Eon." *L'Oeil de la nuit* 141– 202.
_____. *A Game of Perfection*. Tyranaël-2. Trans. Howard Scott and Élisabeth Vonarburg. Calgary: Edge SF & F, 2006. Trans. of *Le Jeu de la perfection*. Tyranaël-2. Québec: Alire, 1996.
_____. "High Tide." *Twenty Houses of the Zodiac*. Ed. Maxim Jakubowski. London: New English Library, 1979. Trans. of "Marée Haute." *Requiem* 19 (1978).
_____. *In the Mother's Land*. Trans. Jane Brierley. New York: Bantam Spectra, 1992. Trans. of *Chroniques du Pays des Mères*. 1992. Québec: Alire, 1999.
_____. *La Mer allée avec le soleil*. Tyranaël-5. Québec: Alire, 1997.
_____. *Mon frère l'ombre*. Tyranaël-3. Québec: Alire, 1997.

———. *L'Oeil de la nuit.* Longueil: Le Préambule, 1980. Chroniques du futur 1.
———. *Reine de Mémoire; 1— La Maison d'oubli.* Québec: Alire, 2005.
———. *Reine de Mémoire; 2 — Le Dragon de feu.* Québec: Alire, 2005.
———. *Reine de Mémoire; 3 — Le Dragon fou.* Québec: Alire, 2006.
———. *Reine de Mémoire; 4 — La Princesse de Vengeance.* Québec: Alire, 2006.
———. *Reine de Mémoire; 5 — La Maison d'Équité.* Québec: Alire, 2007.
———. *Reluctant Voyagers.* Trans. Jane Brierley. New York: Bantam, 1995. Trans. of *Les Voyageurs malgré eux.* Montréal: Québec/Amérique, 1994.
———. *The Silent City.* Trans. Jane Brierley. New York: Bantam Spectra, 1992. Trans. of *Le Silence de la cité.* Paris: Denoël, 1981.
———. *Slow Engines of Time.* Edmonton: Tesseract, 2003.
———. "Thalassa." 1982. *Janus.* Présence du futur 388. Paris: Denoël, 1984. 33–62.
———, and Jane Brierley, eds. *Tesseracts Q.* Edmonton: Tesseracts/The Books Collective, 1996.
Wiebe, Rudy. *The Scorched-Wood People.* Toronto: McClelland and Stuart, 1977.
Wittig, Monique. *Les Guérillères.* Trans. David Le May. New York: Viking, 1971. Paris: Minuit, 1969.
Zamiatin, Yevgeny. *We.* Trans. Gregory Zilboorg. New York: Dutton, 1952.

Works Cited—Secondary Sources

Aldiss, Brian W. *Trillion Year Spree: The History of Science Fiction.* New York: Atheneum, 1986.
Allaire, Gratien. *La Francophonie canadienne: Portraits.* Québec: CIDEF-AFI/Prise de parole, 2001.
Amis, Kingsley. *New Maps of Hell: A Survey of Science Fiction.* New York: Harcourt, 1960.
Amselle, Jean-Loup. *Mestizo Logics: An Anthropology of Identity in Africa and Elsewhere.* Trans. Claudia Royal. Stanford: Stanford University Press, 1998. Trans. of *Logiques métisses anthropologie de l'identité en Afrique et ailleurs.* Paris: Payot, 1990.
Ancelovici, Marcos, and Francis Dupuis-Déri, eds. *L'Archipel identitaire.* Montréal: Boréal, 1997.
Anderson, Benedict. *Imagined Communities.* Rev. ed. London: Verso, 1991.
Andersson, Theodore. "Kings' Sagas (*Koningasögur*)." *Old Norse-Icelandic Literature: A Critical Guide.* Eds. Carol J. Clover and John Lindow. Ithaca: Cornell University Press, 1985. 197–238.
Angenot, Marc. "The Absent Paradigm: An Introduction to the Semiotics of Science Fiction." *Science-Fiction Studies* 6 (1979): 9–19.
——. *Les Idéologies du ressentiment.* Montréal: XYZ, 1997.
Anzaldúa, Gloria. *Borderlands/La Frontera: The New Mestiza.* San Francisco: Spinsters/Aunt Lute, 1987.
Appiah, Kwame Anthony. "Is the Post- in Postmodernism the Post- in Postcolonial?" *Critical Inquiry* 17 (1991): 336–57.
——. "Race." *Critical Terms for Literary Study.* Eds. Frank Lentricchia and Thomas McLaughlin. Chicago: University of Chicago Press, 1990. 274–87.
Arguin, Maurice. *Le Roman québécois de 1944 à 1965: Symptômes du colonialisme et signes de libération.* 1985. Montréal: Hexagone, 1989.
Aronowitz, Stanley. "Postmodernism and Politics." *Universal Abandon.* Ed. Andrew Ross. Minneapolis: University of Minnesota Press, 1988. 46–62.
Ashcroft, Bill, Gareth Griffiths, and Helen Tiffin. *The Empire Writes Back.* London: Routledge, 1989.
——, eds. *The Post-colonial Studies Reader.* London: Routledge, 1995.
Attebery, Brian. Rev. of *So Long Been Dreaming: Postcolonial Science Fiction and Fantasy,* eds. Nalo Hopkinson and Uppinder Mehan. *Science Fiction Studies* 33 (2006): 361–64.
Atwood, Margaret. *Survival: A Thematic Guide to Canadian Literature.* Toronto: Anansi, 1972.
Auberlen, Eckhard. "Great Creating Nature and the Human Experiment in *The Golden Notebook* and *Canopus in Argos.*" *Doris Lessing Newsletter* 13.1 (1989): 12–15.
Bailey, J. O. *Pilgrims Through Space and Time.* 1947. Westport, CT: Greenwood, 1975.

Baker, Neal. "The Politics of Language in Science Fiction from Québec." *Contemporary French Civilization* 28.1 (2004): 33–53.
_____. "Syncretism: A Federalist Approach to Canadian Science Fiction." *Extrapolation* 42.3 (2001): 218–31.
Balthazar, Louis. "The Dynamics of Multi-Ethnicity in French-Speaking Quebec: Towards a New Citizenship." *Nationalism and Ethnic Politics* 1.3 (1995): 82–95.
Bammer, Angelika. *Partial Visions: Feminism and Utopianism in the 1970s.* London: Routledge, 1991.
_____. "Xenophobia, Xenophilia, and No Place to Rest." Brinker-Gabler 45–62.
Barr, Marleen S. "Everything's Coming Up Roses." *Future Females, The Next Generation.* Lanham, MD: Rowman & Littlefield, 2000. 1–9.
_____. *Lost in Space: Probing Beyond Feminist Science Fiction.* Chapel Hill: University of North Carolina Press, 1993.
Basile, Jean. "Le monde enchanté d'Adakhan à Manokhsor." *La presse* (Montréal) 26 August 1989: I3.
Batty, Nancy, and Robert Markley. "Writing Back: Speculative Fiction and the Politics of Postcolonialism, 2001." *Ariel* 33.1 (2002): 5–14.
Bauch, Hubert. "Canada Survives: Money and ethnics defeated us, Parizeau says." *The Gazette* (Montréal) 31 Oct. 1995: A1.
Beaulé, Sophie. "«Enfants du souvenir, enfants du devenir»: Facettes de l'expérience migrante dans la science-fiction québécoise." *Migrance comparée/Comparing Migration.* Ed. Marie Carrière and Catherine Khordoc. Bern: Peter Lang, 2008. 123–38.
_____. "'Il n'y a que des cauchemars et des angoisses, des délires...': Lecture de la nouvelle fantastique et de science fiction québécoise depuis 1980." *University of Toronto Quarterly: A Canadian Journal of the Humanities* 69 (2000): 871–90.
_____. "Mémoire et expérience migrante dans la science-fiction." *Habiter la distance.* Ed. Lucie Hotte and Guy Poirier. Ottawa : Le Nordir, 2008.
_____. "Regards sur le Québec dans un numéro spécial de la revue *Solaris*." *La Francophonie panaméricaine: état des lieux et enjeux.* Ed. André Fauchon. Winnipeg: Presses Universitaires de Saint-Boniface, 2000. 103–21.
_____. "L'Utilisation du mode SF chez quelques auteurs *mainstream* Québécois." *Solaris* 99 (1992): 46–54.
Beaulieu, René. "Entretien avec Esther Rochon." *Solaris* 63 (1985): 11–18.
Beiner, Ronald, and Wayne Norman, eds. *Canadian Political Philosophy: Contemporary Reflections.* Oxford, U.K.: Oxford University Press, 2001.
Bélanger, Claude. "The Negro-King Theory." 1999. 20 May 2008 <http://faculty.marianopolis.edu/c.belanger/quebechistory/events/nking.htm>
Belleau, André. *Surprendre les voix.* Montréal: Boréal, 1986.
Bérard, Sylvie. "Amazones de tir dans la SF côté femmes!" *Tessera* 15 (1994): 42–55.
_____. "Dialogue sur l'utopie, le féminisme et autres sujets connexes: Élisabeth Vonarburg interviewée." *Tessera* 26 (1999): 95–103.
_____. "Élisabeth Vonarburg." Ivison 294–308.
_____. "Fictional Arborescence and Allusive Coherence in Élisabeth Vonarburg's Universe." *Perspectives on the Canadian Fantastic: Proceedings of the 1997 Academic Conference on Canadian Science Fiction and Fantasy.* Ed. Allan Weiss. Toronto: ACCSFF, 1998. 35–45.
_____. "He Gets Just What He Deserved: Denial, Self-Appraisal, and Other Comforting Thoughts." *Foundation* 81 (2001): 48–61.
_____. "Venues, vues, vécues: Entre le sujet science-fictionnel et l'auteure science-fictive." *Dalhousie French Studies* 47 (1999): 115–32.
Berger, Carl, ed. *Conscription 1917.* Toronto: University of Toronto Press, n.d.
Bernabé, Jean, Patrick Chamoiseau, and Raphaël Confiant. *Éloge de la Créolité.* 1989. Bilingual Ed. Trans. M. B. Taleb-Khyar. Paris: Gallimard, 1993.

Bessière, Jean, and Jean-Marc Moura, eds. *Littératures postcoloniales et représentations de l'ailleurs: Afrique, Caraïbe, Canada; Conférences du séminaire de Littérature comparée de la Sorbonne Nouvelle*. Paris: Champion, 1999.
Besson, Anne. *D'Asimov à Tolkien. Cycles et séries dans la littérature de genre*. Paris: CNRS, 2004.
Bhabha, Homi K. *The Location of Culture*. London: Routledge, 1994.
Bissoondath, Neil. "A Footnote of History?" *Canada from the Outside In: New Trends in Canadian Studies/Le Canada vu d'ailleurs: Nouvelles tendances en études canadiennes*. Ed. Pierre Anctil and Zilá Bernd. New York: Peter Lang, 2006. 25–35.
Bloch, Ernst. "Alienation, Estrangement." *Literary Essays*. Trans. Andrew Joron. Stanford: Stanford University Press, 1998. 239–46.
____. *The Principle of Hope*. 1986. Trans. Neville Plaice, Stephen Plaice, and Paul Knight. Vol. 1. Cambridge: MIT Press, 1995.
____. *The Spirit of Utopia*. Trans. Anthony A. Nassar. Stanford: Stanford University Press, 2000.
____. *The Utopian Function of Art and Literature*. Trans. Jack Zipes and Frank Mecklenburg. Cambridge: MIT Press, 1988.
Bogstad, Janice Marie. "Gender, Power and Reversal in Contemporary Anglo-American and French Feminist Science Fiction." Ph. D. Diss. University of Wisconsin, 1992.
Boivin, Aurélien, Maurice Émond, and Michel Lord, eds. *Les Ailleurs imaginaires: les rapports entre le fantastique et la science-fiction*. Québec: Nuit Blanche, 1993.
Bonin, Linda. "*Coquillage* ou La spirale du désir." *Solaris* 110 (1994): 27–28.
Bouchard, Gérard, and Charles Taylor. *Fonder l'avenir: Le temps de la conciliation*. Québec: Government of Québec, 2008.
Bouchard, Guy. "The Female Utopia in Canada." *Paradis* 188–96.
____. "Féminisme, utopie, philosophie." *Ouvertures*. Ed. Lise Pelletier and Guy Bouchard. Québec: University of Laval Press, 1988.
____. "Génologie spontanée et raisonnée de la littérature québécoise en fascicules." *Imagine...* 31 (1985): 34–58.
____. "L'Inversion des rôles masculins et féminins dans *Chroniques du Pays des Mères* d'Élisabeth Vonarburg." *Solaris* 112 (Winter 1994): 29–32.
____. *Les 42,210 Univers de la science-fiction*. Montréal: Le Passeur, 1993.
____. "Les utopies féministes, le fantastique et la science-fiction." Boivin et al. *Ailleurs* 53–76.
____. "Vonarburg, Élisabeth. *Chroniques du Pays des Mères*." *L'Année de la science-fiction et du fantastique québécois 1992*. Ed. Claude Janelle. Québec: Alire, 1997.
Bozzetto, Roger. "Esther Rochon: l'émergeance d'une écrivaine de SF au Québec dans les années 80." Novelli 133–148.
Brecht, Bertolt. *Brecht on Theatre: The Development of an Aesthetic*. Trans. John Willett. New York: Hill and Wang, 1964.
Brinker-Gabler, Gisela, ed. *Encountering the Other(s): Studies in Literature, History, and Culture*. Albany: State University of New York Press, 1995.
Broderick, Damien. *Reading by Starlight: Postmodern Science Fiction*. London: Routledge, 1995.
Brown, Craig, ed. *Histoire générale du Canada*. Montréal: Boréal, 1990. Trans. of *The Illustrated History of Canada*. Toronto: Lester & Orpen Dennys, 1987.
Bruce, Susan, ed. Introduction. *Three Early Modern Utopias*. Ed. Susan Bruce. Oxford: Oxford University Press, 1996. ix–xlii.
Bukatman, Scott. *Terminal Identity: The Virtual Subject in Post-modern Science Fiction*. 1993. Durham: Duke University Press, 1994.
Butler, Andrew M. "Postmodernism and Science Fiction." James and Mendlesohn 137–148.
Byrne, Deirdre. "Truth and Story: History in Ursula K. Le Guin's Short Fiction and the South African Truth and Reconciliation Commission." Barr, *Future* 237–246.

Cabral, Amilcar. "National Liberation and Culture." Williams and Chrisman 53–65.
Canadian Multiculturalism Act. Ottawa: Department of Justice, Government of Canada. 23 September 2008 <http://laws.justice.gc.ca/en/showdoc/cs/C-18.7///en?page=1>
Carollo, Kevin. "Tiptree's Colonial Imagination: The Ambivalent Home of a Haploid Heart." *Extrapolation: A Journal of Science Fiction and Fantasy* 39.3 (1998): 219–35.
Caron, Caroline-Isabelle. "La narration généalogique en Amérique du Nord francophone. Un moteur de la construction identitaire," *Ethnologies comparées. Revue en ligne du CERCE*, 4 (Spring 2002): <alor.univ-montp3.fr/cerce/revue.html>.
Carpentier, André. "Aspects des genres littéraires appliqués à la science-fiction." Boivin et al. *Ailleurs* 15–38.
_____. "La Science-fiction comme genre prospectif." Novelli 59–86.
Castonguay, Charles. "The Fading Canadian Duality." *Language in Canada*. Ed. John R. Edwards. Cambridge: Cambridge University Press, 1998. 36–60.
Césaire, Aimé. *Discours sur le colonialisme*. Paris: Présence Africaine, 1955. Trans. Joan Pinkham. *Discourse on Colonialism*. New York: Monthly Review, 1972.
_____. *Notebook of a Return to the Native Land*. Trans. Clayton Eshleman and Annette Smith. Middletown: Wesleyan University Press, 2001. Trans. of *Cahier d'un retour au pays natal*. 1939.
Chambers, Claire. "Postcolonial Science Fiction: Amitav Ghosh's *The Calcutta Chromosome*." *Journal of Commonwealth Literature* 38.1 (2003): 57–72.
Champetier, Joël. "Une histoire des trentes premières années de *Solaris*." *Solaris* 150 (2004): 5–56.
_____. "*Solaris*: Twenty Years of Québec Science Fiction." Paradis 212–19.
Chapdelaine, Annick. "Inner and Outer Space in the Works of Esther Rochon." *International Women's Writing: New Landscapes of Identity*. Ed. Anne E. Brown et al. Westport, CT: Greenwood, 1995. 126–36.
Clareson, Thomas D. Foreword. Bailey vii–xix.
Clayton, Cherry. "White Settlers in the Heart of Empire: Visionary Power in Lessing's *The Four-Gated City*." *Spiritual Exploration in the Works of Doris Lessing*. Ed. Phyllis Sternberg Perrakis. Westport, CT: Greenwood, 1999. 55–61.
Clemente, Bill. "Tan-Tan's Exile and Odyssey in Nalo Hopkinson's *Midnight Robber*." *Foundation* 91 (2004): 10–24.
Colas-Charpentier, Hélène. "Four Québécois Dystopias, 1963–1972." *Science-Fiction Studies* 20 (1993): 383–93.
Collier, Gordon, ed. *Us/Them: Translation, Transcription and Identity in Post-Colonial Literary Cultures*. Amsterdam, the Netherlands: Rodopi, 1992.
Colombo, John Robert. "Four Hundred Years of Fantastic Literature in Canada." Paradis 28–40.
Cornwell, Grant H., and Eve Walsh Stoddard. "Introduction: National Boundaries/Transnational Identities." Cornwell and Stoddard *Global* 1–27.
_____, eds. *Global Multiculturalism: Comparative Perspectives on Ethnicity, Race, and Nation*. Lanham, MD: Rowman & Littlefield, 2001.
Cousture, Patrick. "La Nuit des longs couteaux." 20 May 2008 <http://www.republiqueli bre.org/cousture>
Cranny-Francis, Anne. *Feminist Fiction: Feminist Uses of Generic Fiction*. New York: St. Martin's, 1990.
Csicsery-Ronay, Jr., Istvan. "Science Fiction and Empire." *Science Fiction Studies* 30 (2003): 231–45.
Cunningham, Frank. "Nations and Nationalism: The Case of Canada/Quebec." *Diversity and Community: An Interdisciplinary Reader*. Ed. Philip Alperson. Malden: Blackwell, 2002. 182–208.
D'Allemagne, André. *Le Colonialisme au Québec*. Montréal: R-B, 1966.

Daye, Russell. *Political Forgiveness: Lessons from South Africa*. Maryknoll: Orbis, 2004.
DeGraw, Sharon. *The Subject of Race in American Science Fiction*. New York: Routledge, 2007.
Desroches, Vincent. "Uprooting and Uprootedness: Haitian Poetry in Quebec (1960–2002). Ireland and Proulx 203–16.
Dillon, Grace. "Totemic Human-Animal Relationships in Recent sf." *Extrapolation* 49.1 (2008): 70–96.
Dorsinville, Max. *Caliban without Prospero: Essay on Québec and Black Literature*. Erin: Porcépic, 1974.
———. *Le Pays natal: Essais sur les littératures du Tiersmonde et du Québec*. Dakar: Nouvelles Éditions Africaines, 1983.
Dorion, Gilles. "Le Roman de 1968 à 1996." Hamel 352–80.
Duchastel, Jules. *Marcel Rioux: Entre l'utopie et la raison*. Montréal: Nouvelle optique, 1981.
Dumont, Fernand. *Raisons communes*. 1995. Montréal: Boréal, 1997.
Dupont, Louis, and Nathalie Lemarchand. "Official Multiculturalism in Canada: Between Virtue and Politics." Cornwell and Stoddard 309–35.
Dupuis, Gilles. "Entretien virtuel avec Jean Pettigrew." Novelli 163–70.
Elbaz, Mikhaël, Andrée Fortin, and Guy Laforest, eds. *Les Frontières de l'identité*. Ste. Foy: Les Presses de l'Université Laval; Paris: L'Harmattan, 1996.
Elliott, Robert C. *The Shape of Utopia: Studies in a Literary Genre*. Chicago: University of Chicago Press, 1970.
Emberley, Julia. *Thresholds of Difference: Feminist Critique, Native Women's Writings, Postcolonial Theory*. Toronto: University of Toronto Press, 1993.
Encinas, Rosario. "José Vasconcelos." *Prospects* 24 (1994): 719–29.
Étienne, Gérard. *La Question raciale et raciste dans le roman québécois*. Montréal: Balzac, 1995.
Fanon, Frantz. *Black Skin, White Masks*. Trans. Charles Lam Markmann. New York: Grove, 1967. Trans. of *Peaux noires, masques blancs*. Paris: Seuil, 1952.
———. "On National Culture." Williams and Chrisman 36–52.
———. *The Wretched of the Earth*. Trans. Constance Farrington. New York: Grove, 1968. Trans. of *Les Damnées de la terre*. Paris: F. Maspero, 1961.
Fee, Margery. "Howard O'Hagan's *Tay John*: Making New World Myth." *Canadian Literature* 110 (1986): 8–27.
Fernández Retamar, Roberto. *Caliban and Other Essays*. 1974. Trans. Edward Baker. Minneapolis: University of Minnesota Press, 1989.
Ferns, Chris. *Narrating Utopia: Ideology, Gender, Form in Utopian Literature*. Liverpool: Liverpool University Press, 1999.
Filion, Pierre. "La Genèse de *l'Oiseau de feu* de J.-E. Brossard." *Possibles* 23.1 (1999): 190–97.
Fitting, Peter. "Utopian Effect/Utopian Pleasure." *Styles of Creation: Aesthetic Technique and the Creation of Fictional Worlds*. Ed. George Slusser and Eric S. Rabkin. Athens: University of Georgia Press, 1992. 153–64.
Freedman, Carl. *Critical Theory and Science Fiction*. Hanover: Wesleyan/New England University Press, 2000.
Freud, Sigmund. "The Uncanny." 1919. *Studies in Parapsychology*. New York: Macmillan, 1963. 19–62.
Fukuyama, Francis. "Comments on Nationalism and Democracy." *Nationalism, Ethnic Conflict and Democracy*. Ed. Larry Diamond and Marc F. Plattner. Baltimore: Johns Hopkins, 1994. 23–28.
Galef, David. "Tiptree and the Problem of the Other: Postcolonialism versus Sociobiology." *Science Fiction Studies* 28 (2001): 201–22.
Geaves, Ron. "Swastika." *Key Words in Hinduism*. Washington, D.C.: Georgetown University Press, 2006.

Gomel, Elana. "Aliens Among Us: Fascism and Narrativity." *JNT: Journal of Narrative Theory* 30.1 (2000): 127–62.
Goodwin, Barbara, and Keith Taylor, eds. *The Politics of Utopia.* New York: St. Martin's, 1982.
Gouanvic, Jean-Marc. "A Past A Future: Québec Science Fiction." Paradis 66–75.
_____. "Figures d'altérité et imaginaire centrifuge dans la science-fiction québécoise contemporaine." *Revue Francophone de Louisiane* 3.2 (1988): 25–31.
_____. "Rational Speculations in French Canada, 1839–1974." *Science-Fiction Studies* 44 (1988): 71–81.
_____. "Réflexions sur l'état de la SFQ à travers les années de *Requiem/Solaris*." *Solaris* 58 (1984): 5–6.
Green, Mary Jean. "Transcultural Identities: Many Ways of Being Québécois." Ireland and Proulx 11–22.
Greenland, Colin. *The Entropy Exhibition: Michael Moorcock and the British "New Wave" in Science Fiction.* London: Routledge, 1983.
Grégoire, Claude. "Une écriture de l'inconscient. Interview of Jacques Brossard." *Québec français* 76 (1990): 60–62.
_____. Rev. of *L'Oiseau feu: 2.B Le Grand projet*, by Jacques Brossard. *Québec français* 95 (1994): 19–20.
Grewell, Greg. "Colonizing the Universe: Science Fictions Then, Now, and in the (Imagined) Future." *Rocky Mountain Review of Language and Literature* 55.2 (2001): 25–27.
Hamel, Réginald. *Panorama de la littérature québécoise contemporaine.* Montréal: Guérin, 1997.
Hamelin, Jean and Jean Provencher. *Brève histoire du Québec.* Montréal: Boréal, 1987.
Hamilton, Graeme. "Harper's Motion Just the Beginning." *National Post* 24 Nov. 2006: A1.
Handler, Richard. *Nationalism and the Politics of Culture in Québec.* Madison: University of Wisconsin Press, 1988.
Hannan, Annika. "Esther Rochon." Ivison 225–36.
Haraway, Donna. *Simians, Cyborgs, and Women: The Reinvention of Nature.* New York: Routledge, 1991.
Harel, Simon. *Braconnages identitaires: Un Québec palimpseste.* Montréal: VLB, 2006.
Hartwell, David, and Kathryn Cramer, eds. *The Space Opera Renaissance.* New York: Tor, 2006.
Hoare, Dorothy M. *The Works of Morris and Yeats in Relation to Early Saga Literature.* 1937. New York: Russell and Russell, 1971.
Hollinger, Veronica. "Feminist Science Fiction." *Extrapolation* 31 (Fall 1990): 229–30.
_____. "Feminist Theory and Science Fiction." James and Mendlesohn 135–136.
_____. "Specular SF: Postmodern Allegory." *The State of the Fantastic. Eleventh International Conference on the Fantastic in the Arts, 1990.* Ed. Nicholas Ruddick. Westport, CT: Greenwood, 1992. 182–96.
Huggan, Graham. *Territorial Disputes: Maps and Mapping Strategies in Contemporary Canadian and Australian Fiction.* Toronto: University of Toronto Press, 1994.
Hutcheon, Linda. "'Circling the Downspout of Empire': Post-colonialism and Postmodernism." *Ariel* 20.4 (1989): 149–75.
Imbert, Patrick. "Utopias." Rev. of *L'Oiseau de feu: 1 Les Années d'apprentissage*, by Jacques Brossard, and *L'Écologie du réel*, by Pierre Nepveu. *Canadian Literature* 129 (1991): 225–26.
Ireland, Susan, and Patrice J. Proulx, eds. Introduction. *Textualizing the Immigrant Experience in Contemporary Quebec.* Westport, CT/London: Prager, 2004. 1–10.
Ivison, Douglas, ed. *Canadian Writers of Science Fiction and Fantasy. Dictionary of Literary Biography 251.* Westport, CT: Gale, 2002.
James, Edward, and Farah Mendlesohn, eds. *The Cambridge Companion to Science Fiction.* Cambridge: Cambridge University Press, 2003.
Jameson, Fredric. *Archaeologies of the Future: The Desire of Utopia and Other Science Fictions.* London: Verso, 2005.

_____. "'If I Find One Good City I Will Spare the Man': Realism and Utopia in Kim Stanley Robinson's Mars Trilogy." *Learning from Other Worlds: Estrangement, Cognition and the Politics of Science Fiction and Utopia.* Ed. Patrick Parrinder. Durham: Duke University Press, 2001. 208–32.
Janelle, Claude. "Brossard, Jacques. *L'Oiseau de feu-2A Le recyclage d'Adakhan.*" Janelle and Pettigrew *ASFFQ 1990.*
_____. "La Fantasy existe-t-elle au Québec?" *Solaris* 54 (1984): 22–24.
_____. "Rochon, Esther. *L'Épuisement du soleil.*" *L'Année de la science-fiction et du fantastique québécois: 1985.* Ed. Jean Pettigrew. Québec: Le Passeur, 1986.
_____. "La Science-fiction au Québec: Petit historique et perspectives d'avenir." *Solaris* 50 (1983): 6–10.
_____. "La Science-fiction québécoise au seuil du XXe siècle." *Québec français* 118 (2000): 82–85.
_____. "La Science-fiction totale." *Lettres québécoises* 73 (1994): 29–30.
_____, and Jean Pettigrew, eds. *L'Année de la science-fiction et du fantastique québécois: 1990.* Québec: Le Passeur, 1992.
_____. *L'Année de la science-fiction et du fantastique québécois 1997.* Québec: Alire, 1999.
JanMohamed, Abdul R. "The Economy of Manichean Allegory: The Function of Racial Difference in Colonialist Literature." *Critical Inquiry* 12 (1985): 59–87.
Juárez, Nicandro F. "José Vasconcelos and La Raza Cósmica." *Aztlán* 3.1 (1972): 51–82.
Karmis, Dimitrios. "Identities in Quebec: Between 'la souche' and Atomization." *Cahiers du PÉQ* June 1997: 3–27.
Kerslake, Patricia. *Science Fiction and Empire.* Liverpool: Liverpool University Press, 2007.
Ketterer, David. *Canadian Science Fiction and Fantasy.* Bloomington: Indiana University Press, 1992.
Killheffer, Robert J. Rev. of *Northern Stars* and *Alien Shores*, by David Hartwell. *Fantasy & Science Fiction* 88.4 (1995): 24.
Kivisto, Peter. *Multiculturalism in a Global Society.* Malden/London: Blackwell, 2002.
Kress, Gunther. *Linguistic Processes in Sociocultural Practice.* 1985. Oxford: Oxford University Press, 1989.
Laforest, Guy. "The True Nature of Sovereignty: Reply to my Critics Concerning *Trudeau and the End of a Canadian Dream.*" Beiner and Norman 298–310.
Landon, Brooks. *Science Fiction After 1900: From the Steam Man to the Stars.* New York: Twayne, 1997.
Laroche, Maximilien. *Le Miracle et la métamorphose. Essai sur les littératures du Québec et d'Haïti.* Montréal: Jour, 1970.
LaRue, Monique. *L'Arpenteur et le navigateur.* Montréal: Fides, 1996.
Laurin, Nicole. "Le projet nationaliste gestionnaire: De l'hôpital des religieuses au système hospitalier de l'État." Elbaz et al. 95–104.
Leane, Elizabeth. "Chromodynamics: Science and Colonialism in Kim Stanley Robinson's Mars Trilogy." *Ariel* 33.1 (2002): 83–104.
Lebeau, Hélène. "Élisabeth Vonarburg: Le futur clair et Net." *Elle: Québec* Sept. 1997: 38
LeBrun, Claire. "Planète-Québec (7)." *Imagine...* 30 (1985): 121–27.
_____. "The Science Fiction Novel for Young People in Québec From the 1960s to the 1990s." Paradis 86–96.
_____. "La Science-fiction pour la jeunesse: Les Modèles québécois." *Revue Francophone de Louisiane* 4.2 (1989): 73–80.
Lefanu, Sarah. *In the Chinks of the World Machine: Feminism and Science Fiction.* London: Women's Press, 1988. Rpt. Bloomington: Indiana University Press, 1989.
Leggatt, Judith. "Other Worlds, Other Selves: Science Fiction in Salman Rushdie's *The Ground Beneath Her Feet.*" *Ariel* 33.1 (2002): 105–25.
Leroux, Jean-François, and Camille R. La Bossière, eds. *Worlds of Wonder: Readings in Canadian Science Fiction and Fantasy Literature.* Ottawa: University of Ottawa Press, 2004.

Létourneau, Jocelyn. *Passer à l'avenir, histoire, mémoire, identité dans le Québec d'aujourd'hui*. Montréal: Boréal, 2000.
Lévesque, René. *Option Québec*. Montréal: l'Homme, 1968.
Levin, Thomas Y., and Ursula Frohne, eds. *Ctrl [space]: Rhetorics of surveillance from Bentham to Big Brother*. Karlsruhe/Cambridge: ZKM Center for the Arts/MIT Press, 2002.
Levitas, Ruth. *The Concept of Utopia*. Syracuse: Syracuse University Press, 1990.
Lewis, C. S. *Of Other Worlds*. New York: Harcourt, 1975.
L'Hérault, Pierre. "Pour une cartographie de l'hétérogène." *Fictions de l'identitaire au Québec*. Montréal: XYZ, 1991. 55–102.
Linteau, Paul André, René Durocher, Jean-Claude Robert, and François Ricard. *Histoire du Québec contemporain*. Montréal: Boréal, 1989. 2 vols.
Lionnet, Françoise. "'Logiques métisses:' Cultural Appropriation and Postcolonial Representations." Yeager 321–32.
Loomba, Ania. "Overworlding the 'Third World.'" Williams and Chrisman 305–23.
Lord, Michel. "Architectures de l'imaginaire: Le Récit fantastique et de science-fiction au Québec depuis la Révolution tranquille." Hamel 241–81.
———. "Esther Rochon: Interview." *Lettres québécoises* 40 (1985–1986): 36–39.
———. "Un feu d'artifices éblouissant." *Lettres québécoises* 55 (1989): 28–29.
———. "Un feu roulant en perpétuelles mutations: La Science-fiction québécoise." *La Licorne* 27 (1993): 155–66.
Louder, Dean R., and Eric Waddell, eds. *French America: Mobility, Identity, and Minority Experience Across the Continent*. Trans. Franklin Philip. Baton Rouge: Louisiana State University Press, 1993. Trans. of *Du continent perdu à l'archipel retrouvé: Le Québec et l'Amérique française*. Québec: PU Laval, 1983.
———, and Christian Morissonneau. Introduction. Louder and Waddell 1–14.
Lovecraft, Howard Phillips. "A Description of the Town of Quebeck." *To Québec and the Stars*. Ed. L. Sprague DeCamp. West Kingston: Donald M. Grant, 1976. 111–309.
Mailhot, Laurent. *La Littérature québécoise*. Montréal: Typo, 1997.
Major, André. "Langagement (1969–1975)." *Voix et images* 1 (1975): 120–24.
Mandal, Somdatta. "'Professor Shonku': The Science Fiction of Satyajit Ray." *Journal of Commonwealth and Postcolonial Studies* 5.1 (1997): 91–99.
Mannheim, Karl. *Ideology and Utopia: An Introduction to the Sociology of Knowledge*. 1929. Trans. Louis Wirth and Edward Shils. New York: Harcourt, 1936.
Manuel, Frank, and Fritzie Manuel. *Utopian Thought in the Western World*. Cambridge: Cambridge University Press, 1979.
Markley, Robert. "Falling Into Theory: Simluation, Terraformation, and Eco-Economics in Kim Stanley Robinson's Martian Trilogy." *MFS: Modern Fiction Studies* 43.3 (1997): 773–99.
Marin, Louis. *Utopics: Spatial Play*. Trans. Robert A. Vollrath. Atlantic Highlands: Humanities, 1984. Trans. of *Utopiques: Jeux d'espaces*. Paris: Minuit, 1973.
Martel, Gilles. "When a Majority Becomes a Minority: The French-Speaking Métis in the Canadian West." Louder and Waddell 69–99.
Mazrui, Ali A. "The 'Other' as the 'Self' under Cultural Dependency: The Impact of the Postcolonial University." Brinker-Gabler 321–32.
Memmi, Albert. *The Colonizer and the Colonized*. Trans. Howard Greenfeld. New York: Orion, 1965. Trans. of *Portrait du colonisé*. 1957. Montréal: Étincelle, 1972.
Ménard, Fabien. "Les Pièges de l'utopie." Rev. of *L'Espace du Diamant*, by Esther Rochon. *Solaris* 95 (1991): 26–27.
Merril, Judith. Foreword and Afterword: "We Have Met the Alien (And It Is Us)." *Tesseracts*. Ed. Judith Merril. Victoria: Press Porcépic, 1985. 1–3 and 274–84.
Michaels, Walter Benn. "The Shape of the Signifier." *Critical Inquiry* 27.2 (2001): 266–83.
Midal, Fabrice. *Chögyam Trungpa: His Life and Vision*. Boston: Shambhala, 2004.

Mishra, Vijay, and Bob Hodge. "What is Post(-)colonialism?" Williams and Chrisman 276–90.
Monière, Denis. *Ideologies in Quebec: The Historical Development*. Trans. Richard Howard. Toronto: Toronto University Press, 1981. Trans. of *Le Développement des idéologies au Québec*. Montréal: Québec/Amérique, 1977.
Moore-Gilbert, Bart. *Postcolonial Theory: Contexts, Practices, Politics*. London: Verso, 1997.
Morgan, Ceri. "*Le Nord électrique*, Travel Book." Leroux and Lebossière 155–66.
Morissonneau, Christian. "The 'Ungovernable' People: French-Canadian Mobility and Identity." Louder and Waddell 15–32.
Morton, A. L. *The English Utopia*. London: Lawrence and Wishart, 1952.
Moylan, Tom. "Bloch against Bloch." Moylan and Daniel 96–121.
―――. *Demand the Impossible: Science Fiction and the Utopian Imagination*. London: Methuen, 1986.
―――. *Scraps of the Untainted Sky: Science Fiction, Utopia, Dystopia*. Boulder: Westview, 2000.
―――, and Raffaella Baccolini, eds. *Dark Horizons: Science Fiction and the Dystopian Imagination*. New York: Routledge, 2003.
―――, and Jamie Owen Daniel, eds. *Not Yet: Reconsidering Ernst Bloch*. London: Verso, 1997.
Mukherjee, Arun. "Whose Post-colonialism and Whose Post-modernism?" *World Literature Written in English* 20.3 (1990): 1–9.
Negley, Glenn. *Utopian Literature: A Bibliography*. Lawrence: Regents Press of Kansas, 1977.
Negley, Glenn, and J. Max Patrick, eds. *The Quest for Utopia: An Anthology of Imaginary Societies*. New York: H. Schulman, 1952.
Nelson, Diane M. "A Social Science Fiction of Fevers, Delirium and Discovery: *The Calcutta Chromosome*, the Colonial Laboratory, and the Postcolonial New Human." *Science Fiction Studies* 30 (2003): 246–66.
Nepveu, Pierre. *L'Écologie du réel*. Montréal: Boréal, 1988.
Novelli, Novella, ed. *Au Coeur de l'avenir: Littérature d'anticipation dans les textes et à l'écran. Actes du Séminaire international de l'Aquila (29–30 septembre 2000)*. L'Aquila: Angelus Novus, 2002.
Painchaud, Rita. "Le Fantastique et la science-fiction dans les périodiques québécois spécialisés (1974–1984)." Boivin et al. *Ailleurs* 121–35.
―――. "Rochon, Esther." *Sorbier. L'Année de la science-fiction et du fantastique québécois 2000*. Québec: Alire, 2005.
Palmer, Christopher. "Galactic Empires and the Contemporary Extravaganza: Dan Simmons and Iain M. Banks." *Science Fiction Studies* 26 (1999): 73–90.
Paradis, Andrea. *Out of this World: Canadian Science Fiction & Fantasy Literature*. Ottawa: Quarry Press/National Library of Canada, 1995. Trans. *Visions d'autres mondes: La littérature fantastique et de science-fiction canadienne*. 1995.
Parfitt, Tudor, dir. *The Lost Tribes of Israel*. Documentary Film for *Nova*. Aired February 22, 2000. <pbs.org/wgbh/nova/transcripts/2706israel.htm>
Parry, Benita. "Problems in Current Theories of Colonial Discourse." Ashcroft et al. *Postcolonial* 36–44.
Pascal, Gabrielle. "Esther Rochon: merveilleux et transgression." in *Le Roman québécois au féminin*. Ed. Gabrielle Pascal. Montréal: Triptyque, 1995. 47–56.
Péan, Stanley. "Rêver un impossible rêve." *Ici* (Jan. 1–8, 1998).
Pelletier, Denise. "Élisabeth Vonarburg donne une forme écrite au rêve qu'elle fait depuis 30 ans." *Progrès-Dimanche* [Chicoutimi] 1 Dec. 1996: B1.
Pelletier, Jacques. *Au-delà du ressentiment: Réplique à Marc Angenot*. Montréal: XYZ, 1996.
―――. "October 1970 et la transformation des rapports littérature/société depuis la Révolution tranquille." *Québec Studies* 11 (1990–1991): 45–62.
Pettigrew, Jean. "Rochon, Esther. *L'Espace du diamant*." Janelle and Pettigrew *ASFFQ 1990*.
Poliquin, Daniel. *Le Roman colonial*. Montréal: Boréal, 2000.

Pomerleau, Luc. "La Géométrie de la quête de l'identité." *Solaris* 88 (1989): 21.
_____. "De science et d'absence: Notes sur la science dans la science-fiction." *Solaris* 84 (1989): 45–49.
_____, and Daniel Sernine. "Entrevue: Jacques Brossard." *Solaris* 90 (1990): 17–20, 22–23.
Pordzik, Ralph. *The Quest for Postcolonial Utopia: A Comparative Introduction to the Utopian Novel in the New English Literatures.* New York: Peter Lang, 2001.
Provencher, Jean. *La Grande Peur d'octobre '70.* Montréal: Aurore, 1974.
Puri, Shalini. "Canonized Hybridities, Resistant Hybridities: Chutney Soca, Carnival, and the Politics of Nationalism." *Caribbean Romances: The Politics of Regional Representation.* Ed. Belinda J. Edmondson. Charlottesville: University Press of Virginia, 1999. 12–28.
Ramraj, Ruby. "Power Relationships and Femininity in Nalo Hopkinson's *The Salt Roads.*" *Foundation* 91 (2004): 25–35.
Ransom, Amy J. "Critical Reception and Postmodern Violation of Genre Conventions in Jacques Brossard's *Oiseau de feu:* Un Monument aux marges." *Studies in Canadian Literature* 33.1 (2008): 229–56.
_____. "A Distant Mirror: Ideology & Identity in Québec's Science Fiction by Women." Leroux and Labossière 167–80.
_____. "The Imagined Communities of Québec's Science Fiction and Esther Rochon's *Cycle de Vrénalik.*" *West Virginia Philological Papers* 53 (2006 [2007]): 92–101.
_____. "New Maps of Hell." Unpublished manuscript in preparation for submission.
_____. "Oppositional Postcolonialism and the Science Fiction of Québec." *Science Fiction Studies* 33 (2006): 291–312.
_____. "(Un)common Ground: National Sovereignty and Individual Identity in Contemporary Science Fiction from Québec." *Science Fiction Studies* 27 (2000): 439–60.
Reid, Malcolm. *The Shouting Sign Painters: A Literary and Political Account of Quebec Revolutionary Nationalism.* New York: MR, 1972.
Resnick, Philip. "Civic and Ethnic Nationalism: Lessons from the Canadian Case." Beiner and Norman 282–97.
Richter, Payton. *Utopias: Communal Ideals and Social Experiments.* Boston: Holbrook, 1971.
Rieder, John. *Colonialism and the Emergence of Science Fiction.* Middletown: Wesleyan University Press, 2008.
Robert, Lucie. "Les Revues." Hamel 141–85.
Roberts, Adam. *The History of Science Fiction.* Basingstoke: Palgrave, 2006.
Robin, Régine. *Le Roman mémoriel: de l'histoire à l'écriture du hors-lieu.* Longueuil: Le Préambule, 1989.
Rochon, Esther. "Esther Rochon." *Littérature et la vie au collégial.* Mont-Royal: Modulo, 1991. 88–93.
_____. "Présentation subjective des *Chroniques infernales.*" 2002. Novelli 19–58.
Sadoul, Jacques. *Histoire de la science-fiction moderne (1911–1975).* Rev. ed. Paris: Albin Michel, 1973. 2 vols.
Said, Edward. *Culture and Imperialism.* 1993. New York: Vintage, 1994.
_____. *Orientalism.* New York: Vintage, 1979.
Saint-Gelais, Richard. "Orbites elliptiques de la proto-science-fiction québécoise: Napoléon Aubin et Louis-Joseph Doucet dans les parages de Cyrano de Bergerac et de Jules Verne." *Voix et images* 27 (2002): 493–503.
_____. "La Science-fiction diagonale: Signes d'altérité en science-fiction québécoise contemporaine." Novelli 113–31.
Salter, Denis. "Performing Sovereignty: Michel Tremblay's *Hosanna.*" *(Post)Colonial Stages: Critical and Creative Views on Drama, Theatre and Performance.* Ed. Helen Gilbert. London: Dangaroo, 1999. 64–77.
Santoro, Miléna. "L'Autre Millénaire d'Esther Rochon." *Women in French Studies* 5 (1997): 97–105.

Sargent, Lyman Tower. "The Three Faces of Utopianism." *Minnesota Review* 7.3 (1967): 222–30.
_____. "The Three Faces of Utopianism Revisited." *Utopian Studies* 5.1 (1994): 1–37.
Sargisson, Lucy. *Contemporary Feminist Utopianism*. London/New York: Routledge, 1996.
_____. "The Curious Relationship Between Politics and Utopia." *Utopia Method Vision: The Use Value of Social Dreaming*. Ed. Tom Moylan and Raffaella Baccolini. Bern: Peter Lang, 2007. 25–46.
Sarra-Bournet, Michel, and Pierre Gendron, eds. *Le Pays de tous les Québécois*. Montréal: VLB, 1998.
Satyendra, Nadesan. "Fourth World — Nations Without a State." 12 September 2008. <http://www.tamilnation.org/selfdetermination/fourthworld/index.htm>.
Sauble-Otto, Lorie. "Writing in Subversive Space: Language and the Body in Feminist Science Fiction in French and English." Ph. D. Diss. University of Arizona, 2001.
Scholes, Robert. *Structural Fabulation*. Notre Dame/: University of Notre Dame Press, 1975.
Sernine, Daniel. "Historique de la SFQ." *Solaris* 79 (1988): 41–47.
_____. "Science Fiction and Fantasy for the Young: An Overview of the Planet." *Paradis* 96–104.
Serruys, Nicholas. "Véhicules (é)garés: du mouvement et de la stase dans le(s) territoire(s) québécois science-fictionnel(s)." *Poétique(s) de l'espace dans les oeuvres fantastiques et de science-fiction*. Ed. Françoise Dupeyron-Lafay and Arnaud Huftier. Paris: Michel Houdiard, 2007. 76–94.
_____. "Xénototalité : l'utopie, l'uchronie et l'anticipation canadiennes-françaises et québécoises dans l'optique de l'allégorie nationale." *Voix plurielles*.
Shohat, Ella. "Notes on the Post-colonial." *Social Text* 10. 2–3 (1992): 99–113.
Siebers, Tobin. "What Does Postmodernism Want?" *Heterotopia: Postmodernism, Utopia and the Body Politic*. Ed. Tobin Siebers. Ann Arbor: University of Minnesota Press, 1994. 1–39.
Simon, Sherry. *Hybridité culturelle*. Montréal: Île de la tortue/Les Élementaires-Une Encyclopédie vivante, 1999.
_____. *Translating Montreal: Episodes in the Life of a Divided City*. Montreal: McGill/Queen's University Press, 2006.
Slemon, Stephen. "Magic Realism as Postcolonial Discourse." *Magical Realism: Theory, History Commentary*. Ed. Lois Parkinson Zamora and Wendy B. Faris. Durham: Duke University Press, 1995. 407–26.
_____. "Modernism's Last Post." *Ariel* 20.4 (1989): 3–17.
_____. "The Scramble for Post-colonialism." Ashcroft et al. *Postcolonial* 45–53.
_____. "Unsettling the Empire: Resistance Theory for the Second World." Ashcroft et al. *Postcolonial* 104–10.
Söderlind, Sylvia. *Margin/Alias: Language and Colonization in Canadian and Québécois Fiction*. Toronto: University of Toronto Press, 1991.
Somay, Bülent. "Towards and Open-Ended Utopia." *Science-Fiction Studies* 11 (1984): 25–38.
Soyinka, Wole. *Myth, Literature and the African World*. 1976. Cambrdige: Cambridge University Press, 1978.
Spehner, Norbert, and Jean-Marc Gouanvic. "In Dispute." *Science-Fiction Studies* 15 (1988): 254–56.
Spivak, Gayatri Chakravorty. "Can the Subaltern Speak?" Williams and Chrisman 66–111.
_____. *A Critique of Postcolonial Reason*. Cambridge: Harvard University Press, 1999.
_____. *In Other Worlds: Essays in Cultural Politics*. London: Routledge, 1987.
_____. *The Post-colonial Critic*. Ed. Sarah Harasym. London/New York: Routledge, 1990.

_____. "Subaltern Studies: Deconstructing Historiography." *The Spivak Reader*. Ed. Donna Landry and Gerald Maclean. London: Routledge, 1996. 204–35.

Statistics Canada. "Mother Tongue, 2001 Counts for Both Sexes, for Canada, Provinces and Territories." 12 September 2008 <http://www12.statcan.ca/english/census01/products/highlight/Language Composition>

Sterling, Bruce. "Slipstream." *Catscan* 5 (1989). September 20, 2007 <http://www.eff.org/Misc/Publications/Bruce_Sterling/Catscan_columns/catscan.05>

Stockwell, Peter. *The Poetics of Science Fiction*. Harlow: Longman/Pearson, 2000.

Suvin, Darko. "Defining the Literary Genre of Utopia: Some Historical Semantics, Some Genology (sic), a Proposal and a Plea." *Studies in the Literary Imagination* 6 (1973): 121–45.

_____. "Locus, Horizon, and Orientation: The Concept of Possible Worlds as a Key to Utopian Studies." Moylan and Daniel 122–37.

_____. *Metamorphoses of Science Fiction*. New Haven/London: Yale University Press, 1979.

_____. "Science Fiction and Utopian Fiction: Degrees of Kinship. 1974. *Positions and Presuppositions in SF*. Kent: Kent State University Press: 1988. 33–43.

_____. "The SF Novel as Epic Narration." 1982. *Positions and Presuppositions in SF*. Kent: Kent State University Press: 1988. 74–85.

_____. "The State of the Art in Science Fiction Theory: Determining and Delimiting the Genre." *Science-Fiction Studies* 6 (1979): 32–45.

_____. "Theses on Utopia." Moylan and Baccolini 187–201.

Taylor, Charles. Interview. Ancelovici and Dupuis-Déri 23–35.

_____. "The Politics of Recognition." *Multiculturalism: Examining the Politics of Recognition*. Ed. Amy Gutman. Princeton: Princeton University Press, 1994. 25–73.

Taylor, Sharon. "Dystopies et eutopies féminines: L. Bersianik, E. Vonarburg, E. Rochon." Ph. D. Diss. McGill University, 2002.

Tiffin, Helen. "Post-colonial Literatures and Counter-discourse." Ashcroft et al. *Postcolonial* 97–98.

Touraine, Alain. *The May Movement: Revolt and Reform*. Trans. Leonard F. X. Mayhew. New York: Random House, 1971.

Trudel, Jean-Louis. "French-Canadian Science Fiction & *Fantastique*." *French Science-Fiction, Fantasy, Horror and Pulp Fiction*. Ed. Jean-Marc Lofficier and Randy Lofficier. Jefferson, NC: McFarland, 2000.

_____. "French SF and SF in French: A Primer." *New York Review of Science Fiction* 8.4 (88; Dec 1995): 12–17.

_____. Rev. of *L'Oiseau de feu: 1 Les Années d'apprentissage*, and *2.A Le Recyclage d'Adakhan*, by Jacques Brossard. *New York Review of Science Fiction* 43 (1992): 13–14.

_____. "Science Fiction in Francophone Canada (1839–1989)" Paradis 51–65.

_____. "La Science-fiction dans les *pulps* québécois." *Solaris* 131 (1999): 33–40.

Trungpa, Chögyam. Commentary. *The Tibetan Book of the Dead [Bardo Thodol]. The Great Liberation Through Hearing in the Bardo*. Trans. Francesca Fremantle. Berkely & London: Shambhala, 1975. 1–29.

Vadeboncoeur, Pierre. *Un génocide en douce*. Montréal: Héxagone/Parti pris, 1976.

Vallières, Pierre. *White Niggers of America*. Trans. Joan Pinkham, 1971. Trans. of *Nègres blancs d'Amérique*. Montréal: Parti pris, 1969.

Van Belkom, Edo. "Élisabeth Vonarburg." *Northern Dreamers: Interviews with Famous Science Fiction, Fantasy, and Horror Writers*. Kingston: Quarry, 1998): 211–34.

Vasconcelos, José. 1925. *La Raza cósmica: Misión de la raza iberoamericana. Argentina y Brasil*. 4th ed. Mexico: Espasa-Calpe Mexicana, 1948. 1976.

Vautier, Marie. *New World Myth: Postmodernism and Postcolonialism in Canadian Fiction*. Montréal: McGill-Queen's University Press, 1998.

_____. "La Révision postcoloniale de l'histoire et l'exemple réaliste magique de François

Barcelo." *Studies in Canadian Literature/Études en Littérature Canadienne.* 16.2 (1991): 39–53.
Vial, Éric. Préface. *L'Histoire revisité: panorama de l'uchronie sous toutes ses formes.* Éric Henriet. Amiens: Encrage, 1999. 7–12.
Vierne, Simone. "Le Jeu du coquillage et la quête: La science-fiction québécoise au féminin." *Solaris* 99 (1992): 27–31.
von Flotow, Luise. "Women's Desiring Voices from Québec: Nicole Brossard, Anne Dandurand and Claire Dé." Collier 101–19.
Vonarburg, Élisabeth. "Cities of the Future." *Paradoxa* 2.1 (1996): 73–80.
_____. Interview. "Elisabeth Vonarburg: A World Apart." *Locus* Sept. 1991: 5, 77.
_____. "Notes sur Esther Rochon." *Solaris* 63 (1985): 19–23.
_____. Rev. of *L'Aigle des profondeurs*, by Esther Rochon. *Solaris* 144 (Winter 2003): 126–29.
_____. "L'Utopie ambigüe: Erotisme et pouvoir dans quelques utopies féminines récentes." *Transformations of Utopia: Changing Views of the Perfect Society.* Ed. George W. Slusser, et al. New York: AMS, 1999. 291–303.
Wallerstein, Immanuel. "Africa in a Capitalist World." 1973. *The Essential Wallerstein.* New York: New Press, 2000. 39–68.
Watson, Greer. "Young Adult Science Fiction in Canada." *Young Adult Science Fiction.* Ed. C. W. Sullivan. Westport, CT: Greenwood, 1999. 37–53.
Weber, Eugen. "The Anti-Utopia of the Twentieth Century." *Utopia.* Ed. George Kateb. New York: Atherton, 1971. 81–89.
Wegner, Philip E. *Imaginary Communities: Utopia, the Nation, and the Spatial Histories of Modernity.* Berkeley: University of California Press, 2002.
Weinmann, Heinz. *Du Canada au Québec: Généalogie d'une histoire.* Montréal: Hexagone, 1987.
Weiss, Allan. "The Canadian Apocalypse." Leroux and LaBossière 35–46.
_____. "Separations and Unities: Approaches to Québec Separatism in English- and French-Canadian Fantastic Literature." *Science-Fiction Studies* 25 (1998): 53–60.
Wiemer, Annegret. "Utopia and Science Fiction." *Canadian Review of Comparative Literature* 19.1–2 (1992): 171–200.
Williams, Patrick, and Laura Chrisman, eds. *Colonial Discourse and Post-colonial Theory: A Reader.* New York: Columbia University Press, 1994.
Wilson, Richard A. *The Politics of Truth and Reconciliation in South Africa: Legitimizing the Post-Apartheid State.* Cambridge: Cambridge University Press, 2001.
Wollheim, Donald A. *Universe Makers: Science Fiction Today.* New York: Harper & Row, 1971.
Wolmark, Jenny. *Aliens and Others: Science Fiction, Feminism and Postmodernism.* Iowa City: University of Iowa Press, 1994.
Yeager, Jack, Ed. *Postcolonial Subjects: Francophone Women Writers.* Minneapolis: University of Minnesota Press, 1996.
Young, Robert J. C. *Colonial Desire: Hybridity in Theory, Culture, and Race.* London & New York: Routledge, 1995.
_____. *White Mythologies.* London: Routledge, 1990.
Zipes, Jack. "Toward a Realization of Anticipatory Illumination." Bloch *Utopian Function* xi–xliii.

Index

Acadian(s) 6, 9, 17, 145
Act of Union (1840) 17
Action française 18
Adisa, Opal Palmer 27
Affirmative action 184
Africa(n) 19, 25, 90, 100, 134, 193, 194, 224n12
ailleurs 7, 135, 177
Alaska 9
Aldiss, Brian W. 5, 24, 228n8
Algeria 2, 20–21, 83
alienation 2, 3, 22, 30, 31, 49–54, 59, 60–64, 65, 70, 75–77, 80, 81, 82, 85–87, 90, 97, 99, 102–08, 115, 125, 138, 162, 166, 174, 175, 193, 198, 210
Alire, Éditions 4, 6, 33, 41, 42, 44, 50, 69, 229n20, 229n5, 230n6–7
Allaire, Gratien 9, 223n8
allegory: biblical 129–36; national 27, 53–54, 56, 73–74, 77–79, 83, 84–86, 96–98, 144, 154–60, 159, 232n28
Amazing Stories 27
Amberstone, Celu 27
Amis, Kingsley 5
Amselle, Jean-Loup 188–89, 196
Ancelovici, Marcos 186
Les Anciens Canadiens 225n20
Anctil, Pierre 188
Anderson, Benedict 148
Andersson, Theodore 61
Angenot, Marc 7, 16, 80, 97
Anglo-American 47, 55, 118, 140, 171–72, 210, 211, 228n19, 229n2; fantasy 223n4; literary theory 23; literary utopia 118, 140; science fiction 6, 7, 25–26, 33, 35, 45, 210–11, 228n19; society 78, 227n30
Anglo-Canadian 15, 18, 19, 41, 78, 98, 156, 225n20, 226n21, 226n24, 229n23; literature 129; science fiction 45, 182, 227n31, 232n27
Anglo-Saxon 6, 48, 100, 110, 198, 229n3
Anishinaabe 27, 184, 198
L'Année de la science-fiction et du fantastique québécois 39, 47
Antilles 2, 64, 90

anti-utopia 56, 123, 125, 135, 175, 232n6; *see also* dystopia
Anzaldúa, Gloria 161, 177, 188, 193
Appiah, Kwame Anthony 114
April, Jean-Pierre 38, 39, 40, 46, 47, 51, 52, 54, 227n28, 229n19, 231n20
Aquin, Hubert 65, 161, 234n2
Arcand, Denys 226n23
Arctic 9
Arguin, Maurice 64–66, 69, 70–72, 74, 76, 78, 79, 81, 85–90, 94, 96, 97, 100–02
Ariel 24, 29
Aronowitz, Stanley 150
Ashcroft 10
Ashcroft, Bill 6, 7, 10, 11, 13, 14, 62, 131, 231n18
Ashem 41
Asimov, Isaac 26, 28, 41, 137
assimilation 17, 27, 57, 90, 97, 134, 156, 184, 188, 193, 195
Assiniwi, Bernard 234n5
Astounding Science Fiction 27
Attebery, Brian 226n27
Atwood, Margaret 53, 54, 170
Auberlen, Ekhard 26
Aubert de Gaspé, Philippe (*fils*) 34, 225n20
Aubert de Gaspé, Philippe (*père*) 225n20
Aubin, Napoléon 34
Aude *see* Charbonneau-Tissot, Claudette
Audet, Noël 142
Australia 10, 14, 186
Autres mers, autres mondes 39, 50, 52
Aztlán 193

Baccolini, Raffaella 119, 123, 169, 175, 180
Bailey, J. O. 24
Baker, Neal 4, 22, 27, 57, 182–83, 195, 211, 224n10, 228n12, 231n20
Ballard, J. G. 60
Balthazar, Louis 186
Bammer, Angelika 31, 122, 152
Banks, Iaian M. 28
Barbarella 36
Barcelo, François 40, 46, 83, 120, 142, 225–26n20

Bardo Thödol 162, 199
Barr, Marleen S. 31, 226n26
Barthe, Ulric 34
Basile, Jean 85
Batty, Nancy 24, 29
Bauch, Hubert 113, 148, 185
Baudelaire, Charles 169, 198, 232n25
Beaulé, Sophie 4, 27, 37, 49, 101, 142, 146, 154, 171, 173, 183, 194–95, 211, 227n5, 228n12, 229n22
Beaulieu 74, 138
Beaulieu, Natasha 44
Beaulieu, René 4, 38, 51, 52, 67, 69, 231n24
Begamudré, Ven 27
Bélanger, Claude 19
Bélil, Michel 38, 39, 46, 53
Bellamy, Edward 120
Belleau, André 21–22, 23, 48, 60, 230n13
Benoit, Jacques 36
Bentham, Jeremy 231n16
Beothuk 215, 224
Bérard, Sylvie 45, 54, 59, 99, 100, 171–72, 203, 210, 228n12
Berger, Carl 18
Bergeron, Alain 38, 43
Bergeron, Bertrand 50
Bernabé, Jean 188, 190, 193–94, 203
Bernardo, Susan 211
Bernier, Thomas (Alfred) *see* Berthos, Jean
Bersianik, Louky 55, 138
Berthos, Jean 35, 132
Bessette, Gérard 69, 131
Bessière, Jean 224n13
Besson, Anne 61
Bhabha, Homi K. 1, 6–7, 11, 13, 62, 63, 182, 188, 208, 224n9, 233n14
Bildungsroman 81, 87, 128, 134, 136, 230n13
Bilingualism-Biculturalism, Canadian policy 183–84
Bill 101 187, 225n18
Bill 22 187
Billon, Pierre 40
Bissoondath, Neil 185
Black Skin, White Masks 2, 62, 90, 156
Blais, Marie-Claire 65, 224n13
Bloch, Ernst 63, 121, 126–27, 136, 140, 143, 162, 172, 179–80
Boer War 18
Bogstad, Janice M. 100, 171
Boivin, Aurélien 39
Bolduc, Claude 44
Bonelli, André-Jean 38, 52
Bonin, Linda 149
Borduas, Paul 19
Bouchard, Gérard 16, 186, 196
Bouchard, Guy 39, 52, 54, 100, 122, 142, 171, 227n6
Bouhalassa, Mehdi 45, 210
Bourassa, Henri 18
Bourassa, Robert 160
Bourque, Gilles 142, 146

Bova, Ben 25, 28
Bozzetto, Roger 68, 227n4, 229n19
Brecht, Bertolt 7, 62, 63, 62–63, 63
Breton, André 36
British North America Act (1867) 17; *see also* Confederation, Act of
Broderick, Damien 31
Brossard, Jacques 3, 36, 39, 41–42, 47, 56, 61, 66, 81–99, 101, 103, 108, 115, 117, 118–119, 120, 121, 122, 124–38, 141, 143, 160, 168, 169, 170, 171, 172, 178, 180, 183, 187, 189–95, 199, 202, 203, 207, 208, 210, 230n8–9, 230n11, 231n18, 232–33n8; *Les Années d'apprentissage* 84–89, 97, 124–25, 135, 190, 194, 210n9; *Les Années d'errance* 89, 124, 129–35, 136, 192, 208, 230n9; *Le Grand projet* 89, 93–95, 97, 124–126, 133, 230n9; *L'Oiseau de feu* 3, 36, 41–42, 61, 81–99, 111, 118, 124–38, 141, 145, 160, 169, 170, 178, 180, 189–95, 199, 202, 206, 230n9, 230n11–13, 231n18, 232n8; *Le Recyclage d'Adakhan* 86, 89–94, 97, 124, 125, 126, 191, 230n9; *Le Sauve-qui-peut* 89, 95, 98, 124, 135, 230n9
Brossard, Nicole 224n13
Brown, Craig 18, 224n16
Bruce, Susan 121
Bucknell, Tobias S. 27
Bukatman, Scott 31
Burma 178
Burroughs, William S. 36
Butler, Andrew M. 31
Buzzati, Dino 83
Byrne, Deirdre 233n17

Cabet, Étienne 120
Cabral, Amilcar 83
Les Cahiers de la décolonisation 20
Callenbach, Ernest 127
Cameroon 51
Campanella, Tommaso 127
Canada 1, 3, 6, 8, 9, 10, 14, 15, 17–24, 27, 33, 34, 35, 39, 40, 42, 47, 51, 53, 54, 56, 57, 60, 61, 78–80, 85, 98, 99, 100, 101, 112, 116, 123, 134, 156, 164, 184–86, 210, 224–25n16, 226n21, 227n31
Canadiens 17, 159–60, 225n20
"Canadola" 56, 79
Canopus in Argos 26, 164
Cantin, Serge 95
Caribbean 19, 26, 27, 169, 188, 193
Carollo, Kevin 25
Caron, Caroline-Isabelle 4, 201, 229n24, 233n21
Carpentier, André 47, 48–49, 227n4
Cartier, George-Étienne 17, 184
Cartier, Jacques 4, 51
Castonguay, Charles 225n18, 229n23
Catholic Church: depiction in proto-SFQ 34, 35, 50, 54, 97; doctrine 166; role in French-Canadian history 9, 17–19, 132, 211, 226n21–23

Index 259

Césaire, Aimé 20, 62, 96, 155, 157, 188
Chambers, Claire 26, 68
Chamoiseau, Patrick 188, 190, 193–94, 195, 203
Champetier, Joël 4, 27, 33, 38, 41, 43, 44, 45, 50, 182, 227n2, 228n14, 229n21
Chapdelaine, Annick 68
Charbonneau-Tissot, Claudette 231n24
Chen, Ying 187
Chicoutimi (Qc) 38
Chile 163
Chklovski, Viktor 62
Chrisman, Laura 8
Chroniques du futur 38, 50, 52
Cité libre 19
Clareson, Thomas D. 24
Clayton, Cherry 26
Clemente, Bill 27
Cocke, Emmanuel 36
Colas-Charpentier, Hélène 55
Cold War 36
Colombo, John Robert 34
Commonwealth, British 49, 225n16
Confederation, Act of (1867) 17, 159, 184
Confiant, Raphaël 188, 190, 193–94, 195, 203
Congrès Boréal 4, 38, 49
Conquest of 1760 17, 23, 65, 71, 73, 86, 134, 159, 165, 184, 225n20
Cornwell, Grant H. 183, 188
Corriveau, Monique 41, 52, 84, 230n11
Côté, Denis 38, 50
Côté, Héloise 45
Cousture, Patrick 22
Cramer, Kathryn 28
Cranny-Francis, Anne 12, 210
Cree 73
Cross, James 21
Csicsery-Ronay, Istvan, Jr. 8, 24, 28–30, 128, 226n27, 227n28
Cunningham, Frank 187, 199

d'Agoult, Marie 182, 199
Dahrendorf, Ralf 126
d'Allemagne, André 20
Dandurand, Anne 56, 224n13
Dante Alighieri 149, 168
Daye, Russell 163
Dé, Claire 56, 214
deconstruction 5, 12
DeGraw, Sharon 210
Delany, Samuel R. 171
Des Roches, Roger 56
Desroches, Vincent 188
Desrosiers, Emmanuel 35
Devi, Mahasweta 2, 26
Dick, Philip K. 26, 36
Dillon, Grace 27, 211
Dion, Jean 27, 38, 50, 110, 231n20
Diop, Birago 220
disalienation 156, 193, 210
The Divine Comedy 149, 168
Dr. Strangelove 36

Dorion, Gilles 19, 84
Dorsinville, Max 13, 20, 64, 169, 226n24
Duchastel, Jules 127
Dumont, Fernand 16, 186
Duplessis, Maurice 19, 50, 53, 78, 226n22
Dupont, Louis 184–85, 186, 195
Dupuis, Gilles 6, 44
Dupuis-Deri, Francis 186
Durand, Lucile *see* Bersianik, Louky
Durham, Lord 17
dystopia 3, 27, 54–56, 119, 124–25, 134, 137, 148–52, 171, 172, 175–76, 227n5, 228n17; definition of 122–23; versus anti-utopia 123, 232n6

Elizabeth I 175
Elliott, Robert 126
Ellison, Harlan 36
Emberley, Julia 13, 15, 189
Emecheta, Buchi 216
Émond, Maurice 39
The Empire Writes Back 6, 7, 11, 14, 62, 224n11
Encinas, Rosario 192
Engels, Friedrich 121
estrangement 7, 30, 50, 154, 180, 229n23; definition of 62–63; in utopia 118–19
Étienne, Gérard 188, 226n24, 234n2
Europe 6

Fan Chen 162
Fanon, Frantz 1–2, 13, 20, 62, 83, 90, 97, 154, 156, 231n15
le fantastique 223n4
fantasy 4, 6, 27, 39, 41, 42, 49, 54, 61, 67, 119, 148, 154, 158, 180, 188, 189, 197, 211, 223n4; colonial 66, 98, 133–34, 137, 189; heroic 44–45, 46, 53; historical 178
Fee, Margery 120
Fernández Retamar, Roberto 169
Ferns, Chris 126, 142
Filion, Pierre 4, 84, 85, 230n13, 233n9
First Nations 15, 27, 184, 185, 198, 225n19, 234n3
First World 27, 156, 214
Fitting, Peter 126
Fleuve Noir 41
FLQ (Front de Libération Québécois) 21
Foucault, Michel 231n16
Fourier, Charles 121
France 8, 9, 15, 17, 18, 20, 23, 24, 29, 40, 43, 45, 48, 64, 97, 100, 101, 121, 128, 156, 159, 167, 179, 229n19
Franco, Francisco 226n22
Franco-Ontarian 6, 16, 49, 57–58, 223n5
Frankenstein 2, 30
Franks 82
Franz-Ferdinand, Archduke 34
Freedman, Carl 223n6
Frelik, Pawel 226n25
French Canada 55, 97, 123, 130, 159, 168; history of 15–19, 144, 156, 225n20

French-Canadian 16, 73–74, 132; literature 15, 23, 35, 36, 49, 61, 64–66, 70, 78–79, 86, 88, 94, 96, 130, 137, 168, 187, 191, 225n20; nationalism/self-determination 55, 84; science fiction 8, 34–59, 83, 227n5–6, 228n12; society 2, 85, 95, 130, 158; society's depiction in literature 70, 73, 78, 97, 102
French Canadians 19, 54, 62, 69, 73, 74, 82, 97–98, 134, 165, 226n21, 226n24
French-speaking 1, 6, 8, 9, 46, 47, 49, 60, 73, 101, 184, 186
Freud, Sigmund 7, 63, 228n18
Frohne, Ursula 231n16
Fukuyama, Francis 187

Gagnon, Maurice 35, 52, 55
Gaiman, Neil 189
Galactic Empire 28, 29, 30, 114
Galef, David 25
Gauls 82
Geaves, Ron 197
Gendron, Pierre 16, 186
George III 184
Gernsback, Hugo 27, 128
Ghandi, Leela 25
Ghosh, Amitav 26, 68
Giguère, Roland 233n9
Gilman, Charlotte Perkins 141
The Globe and Mail 19
Golden Age of Science Fiction 27, 34, 128, 210, 226n29, 227n29–30
Gomel, Elana 227n28
Goodwin, Barbara 121
Gouanvic, Jean-Marc 7, 34, 36, 37, 39, 40, 49, 52, 131, 227n2, 227n6, 228n9, 228n12, 228n18, 234n2
Gramsci, Antonio 233n14
Le Grand Dérangement 17, 18, 116, 145
Grand Prix de la science-fiction et du fantastique québécois 4, 39, 233n8
La Grande Noirceur 19, 53
Grant, Glenn 40
Great Britain 7, 8, 9, 15, 17, 18, 25, 36, 97, 224n16
Green, Mary Jean 189, 200
Green, Renée 208
Green Peace 56
Greenland, Colin 60, 227n29, 228n8
Grégoire, Claude 83, 124, 141, 230n13
Grenier, Armand 55; *see also* Plour, Guy René de; Laurin, Florent
Grewell, Greg 213
Griffiths, Gareth 6, 7, 10, 11, 14, 231n18
Grignon, Claude-Henri 36
GRILFIQ (Groupe de recherche interdisciplinaire sur les littératures fantastiques dans l'imaginaire québécois) 39
Groulx, Lionel 16, 18
Guadeloupe 64
Guevremont, Germaine 130
Guillet, Jean-Pierre 53

Guitard, Agnès 38
Gurik, Robert 55

Hairston, Andrea 27
Hamel, Réginald 138
Hamelin, Jean 224n16
Hamilton, Graeme 22, 187
Hamou, Sion 27
Handler, Richard 8, 17
Hannan, Annika 69, 138, 139, 148
Hantsch, Ingrid 126
Haraway, Donna 57, 226n26
Hardt, Michael 29
Harel, Simon 183, 189, 208, 225n19
Harper, Stephen 22, 187
Hartwell, David 28, 40
Hébert, Anne 65, 224n13, 233n9
Hébert, Louis-Philippe 39, 56
Heinlein, Robert A. 26, 36
Hélios, Éditions 38
Hémon, Louis 130, 168, 225n20
Herbert, Frank 41
Herland 141
Hitler, Adolf 22, 112, 126, 191
Hoagland, Ericka 226n27
Hoare, Dorothy M. 61
Hodge, Bob 13, 224n11
Hollinger, Veronica 4, 31
Homel, David 187
Hopkinson, Nalo 27, 182, 226n27
horror literature 41, 44, 227n5
Hudson's Bay 9
Huggan, Graham 14
Hugo, Victor 169
Huot, Alexandre 54
Hutcheon, Linda 13, 98, 224n9
Huxley, Aldous 123
hybrid/hybridity 12, 23, 56, 57–59, 81, 100, 107, 141, 182–83, 189, 210, 224n10, 234n3; definition 192–93; hybrid characters in SFQ 153, 157, 179, 192–93, 198, 204–05, 208; SFQ as 46, 124, 148, 180
Hydro-Québec 10

imagine... 37, 43, 229n19
Imbert, Patrick 124, 230n13
India 14
Indochina 99, 100
Innu 225n19
Inuit 15, 73, 78, 101, 184, 185, 225n20, 234n3–4
Ireland 15, 110, 231n16
Ireland, Susan 23, 185, 187

J'ai lu 41, 229n19
Jameson, Fredric 25, 31, 122, 141, 181, 232n3
Janelle, Claude 4, 36, 37, 38, 39, 38–40, 44, 45, 78, 81, 124, 148, 227n2, 228n11–12
JanMohamed, Abdul R. 188, 2224n10
Jasmin, Claude 65, 88

Johnson, Daniel 160
Juárez, Nicandro F. 193

Kafka, Franz 56, 84, 224n15
Karmis, Dmitrios 186
Kay, Guy Gavriel 41
Kerslake, Patricia 7, 25–26, 128, 189, 210–11
Ketterer, David 227n2, 232n8
Killheffer, Robert J. 47
Kilpatrick, Nancy 41
King, Stephen 40, 44
Kivisto, Peter 184
Kobayashi, Tamai 27
Kogawa, Joy 120
Kokis, Sergio 187
Kornman, Robin 233n18
Kress, Gunther 12, 210
Kubrick, Stanley 36

Laberge, Marie 224n13
Labrador 9
Laforest, Guy 182
Laframboise, Michèle 45
Lalonde, Michèle 20, 209
Lamontagne, Michel 38
Landon, Brooks 227n29, 228n8
Laroche, Maximilien 20, 64
LaRue, Monique 156, 166, 187
Laurier, Wilfrid 18
Laurin, Florent 35; see also Grenier, Armand
Laurin, Nicole 226n23
Lawson, Alan 224n14
Leane, Elizabeth 25
Lebeau, Hélène 99
Le Brun, Claire 74, 78, 138, 227n7
Lefanu, Sarah 31
Leggatt, Judith 26
Le Guin, Ursula K. 26, 42, 121, 122, 172, 211, 232n5, 233n17
Lem, Stanislaw 209, 228n14
Lemarchand, Nathalie 184–85, 186, 195
Lemba 114
Leméac 4, 41, 233n9
Lemelin, Roger 65
Lesage, Jean 19, 160
Lessing, Doris 26, 164, 226n26
Létourneau, Jocelyn 15–16, 17, 95, 98
Let's Build Québec Together 16
Lévesque, René 20, 21, 22
Levin, Thomas Y. 221
Levitas, Ruth 121, 125, 135, 136, 162
Lewis, C. S. 5
L'Hérault, Pierre 64
Liberal Party 19, 160
La Ligue nationaliste canadienne 18
Linteau, Paul 158, 224n16
Lionnet, Françoise 13, 188, 189
Liszt, Franz 199
littérature migrante 23, 187, 191
Longueil (Qc) 37
Loomba, Ania 224n10

Loranger, Françoise 65
Lord, Michel 39, 43, 46, 69, 70, 81, 227n2, 227n4, 228n12, 230n11
Lortie, Alain see Sernine, Daniel
Louder, Dean R. 9
Louis XV 17
Lovecraft, H. P. 37, 144, 198
Loyalists 15

MacLeod, Ken 28, 189
magic realism 7, 83
Mailhot, Laurent 47
Major, André 143
Mallarmé, Stéphane 232n25
Mandal, Somdatta 27
Manitoba 18, 144, 184, 234n3
Mannheim, Karl 121, 162
Manuel, Frank 129, 170, 175
Manuel, Fritzie 129, 170, 175
Maria Chapdelaine 130, 137, 168, 225n20
Marin, Louis 136
Maritime Provinces 9, 21
Markley, Robert 24, 25, 29
Martel, Gilles 234n3
Martel, Julie 45
Martel, Suzanne 35, 41, 55
Martin, Michel 50
Martinique 64, 188, 193, 194
Marx, Karl 64, 121
Marxism 138
Marxist theory 7, 20, 28, 62, 121–22, 125, 154
Mazrui, Ali A. 156, 157
McAllister, Laurent 43, 45
Médiaspaul 35, 45
Mehan, Uppinder 27, 226n27
Memmi, Albert 64, 90, 97, 161
Ménard, Fabien 138, 139
Merril, Judith 11, 31, 39, 232n27
Metamorphoses of Science Fiction 7, 30, 62–63
mestizo/mestizaje 188, 192, 196
Métis 18, 101, 144, 189, 198, 234n3
métissage 57, 73, 177, 188, 189, 194, 203, 208
Meynard, Yves 33, 38, 41, 43, 45, 51, 53, 58, 229n19
Michaels, Walter Benn 25
Michaud, Nando 40
Midal, Fabrice 141, 144, 162, 163, 167
migrant literature see littérature migrante
Milton, John 168
Milner, Max 229n19
Miron, Gaston 21, 69
Mishra, Vijay 13, 224n11
Mohawk 82, 225n19
Monière, Denis 18, 230n10
Montambault, André 39, 53
Montcalm 17, 166
Montpetit, Charles 27, 57
Montréal 9, 21, 22, 23, 34, 35, 45, 51, 84, 100, 148, 151–53, 161–65, 167, 184–86, 188, 196, 197–98, 200, 223n5, 225n18, 227n28, 228n11, 229n2, 234n2

262 Index

Montréal, Université de 82
Moorcock, Michael 36, 228n10
Moore-Gilbert, Bart 12, 224n9, 226n20
More, Sir Thomas 118, 119, 120, 126, 136
Morency, Pierre 233n9
Morgan, Arthur E. 232n3
Morgan, Ceri 54
Morissonneau, Christian 73, 130, 233n11
Morris, William 121, 232n7
Morton, A. L. 119, 121, 140
Mount Royal 55
Moylan, Tom 118, 119, 121, 123, 127, 135, 147, 148, 153, 169, 175, 180, 227n29
Mukherjee, Arun 10, 224n9
multiculturalism 3, 35, 57–59; Canadian policy 22, 184–87
Murphy, Graham 211
Mussolini, Benito 226n22

Nauvoo 120
Negley, Glenn 123
Nègres blancs d'Amérique *see* White Niggers of America
Negri, Antonio 29
négritude 20, 188, 193, 226n24
Nelson, Diane M. 26, 68
Nepveu, Pierre 23, 49, 68, 124
New Brunswick 9
New England 9, 120
New France 23
New Wave 36, 227n29, 228n10
New York Review of Science Fiction 223n5
Newfoundland 9, 225n19, 234n5
Ngugi wa Thiong'o 231n14
Nigeria 14
1984 (also *Nineteen Eighty-Four*) 39, 50, 56, 57, 120, 123, 136, 175, 232n29
North Africa 58, 90
North America 6, 9, 18, 21, 34, 35, 46, 58, 60, 63, 67, 73, 98, 100, 132, 153, 187
Nova Scotia 9
Novelli, Novella 68, 227n4
novum 63
Nunavut 9

October Crisis (1970) 21, 34, 78
Ollivier, Émile 188
Ontario 58
Orientalism 1, 62, 219
Orwell, George 50, 56, 123, 222
the Other 2, 8, 13, 17, 25, 50, 63, 67, 71–80, 88, 90, 97–98, 109, 134, 138, 156, 177, 186, 195, 198–99, 206–08
Ottawa 9, 34, 51, 58, 213
Ouellette, Fernand 69
Ouellette-Michalska, Madeleine 142

Painchaud, Rita 46, 149, 228n14
Palmer, Christopher 28
Paquin, Ubald 34
Paradise Lost 168

paraliterature 10
Parfitt, Tudor 114
Paris 9, 38, 219; Treaty of (1763) 17, 134
Parizeau, Jacques 16, 113, 148, 185, 186
Parry, Benita 224n10
Parti pris 19, 20, 85
Parti Québécois 16, 20, 21, 22, 53, 82, 113
Pascal, Gabrielle 68
Patrick, J. Max 123
Patriots' Rebellion 17, 165
Péan, Stanley 38, 42, 57, 188
Pelletier, Denise 101
Pelletier, Francine 4, 38, 39, 41, 42, 51, 52, 53, 58–59, 119, 231n24
Pelletier, Jacques 225n17
Perrot-Bishop, Annick 39, 57
Pettigrew, Jean 4, 6, 8, 33, 38, 39, 43–44, 45, 47, 50, 53, 68, 78, 138, 232n5
Pinochet, Augusto 88
Pisan, Christine de 152
Plains of Abraham, Battle of (1759) 17, 73, 166
Plour, Guy René de 35; *see also* Grenier, Armand
Poliquin, Daniel 16, 97
Pomerleau, Luc 47, 85, 127, 137, 230n13, 232n8
Popper, Karl 126
Pordzik, Ralph 3, 7, 29–30, 119, 122, 124, 137, 152, 226n26
postcolonial discourse 59, 66, 74, 76, 78, 81, 98, 116, 134, 137, 153, 180, 228n18, 231n14
postcolonial science fiction 1, 8, 27, 57, 200, 211, 226n27
postcolonial sensibility: Rochon 67–70; Vonarburg 99–100, 133, 171; 224n10
postcolonial utopia 119, 122, 124–25, 133, 137–38, 148, 152, 180
postmodernism 26, 28, 31, 40, 46, 51, 78, 82, 83, 120, 122, 137, 161, 226n25, 231n18
post-structuralism 12
Poulin, Jacques 142
Pour ta belle gueule d'ahuri 37
Le Préambule 38, 39, 52
Prévost, Claude-Michel 38, 56, 57, 188
Prix Jacques Brossard *see* Grand Prix de la science-fiction et du fantastique québécois
Proto-SFQ 34–35, 55, 118, 223n5, 227n31, 227n5
Proulx, Patrice J. 23, 185, 187
Provencher, Jean 10, 21, 224n16
Provencher, Marc 38
Puri, Shalini 224n10

Québec 1–4, 10–11, 14, 60–61, 63–68, 70, 73, 77, 78, 79, 81–86, 94, 97, 98, 99, 100, 101, 102, 110, 112, 116, 118, 121, 122, 123, 127, 132, 134, 137, 138, 142, 143, 144, 148, 153, 154, 155, 156, 158, 159, 160, 161, 164–66, 168, 170, 171, 180–89, 195, 196, 197, 200, 201, 202, 209, 210–11, 223n7, 224n14, 225n17, 225n19, 225–26n20, 226n23–24, 228n13–14, 229n3, 230n10, 233n11, 234n2; geography 9; history

of 9–10, 14–22, 224–25n16, 226n22; literature 3, 23, 36, 48, 49, 61, 87, 191, 224n13, 227n31, 233n9; science fiction *see* SFQ; society 24, 84, 164; writers 6–8, 83
Québec Act (1774) 17, 184
Québec City 225n20, 229n24
québécitude 20, 124, 188
Québécois 6, 15, 16, 19, 20, 22, 23, 30, 31, 39, 44, 47, 48, 53, 57, 59, 61, 62, 64, 67, 69, 73, 77, 79, 83, 85, 89, 97, 98, 100, 102, 108, 115, 129, 138, 142, 148, 156, 165, 169, 170, 185–88, 192, 200, 204, 223n7, 225–26n20, 224n13, 225n20, 226n20, 226n24, 229n2, 233n9, 234n4; de souche 82, 166, 185, 187, 191–92; identity 23, 69, 82, 225n20
Quiet Revolution 9, 16, 19, 20, 34, 53, 55, 69, 78, 84, 95, 97, 121, 156, 160, 161, 164, 168, 187, 211, 225n21, 226n23, 228n13, 228n15, 233n9

Radio-Canada 97
Ramraj, Ruby 27
Ransom, Amy J. 42, 57, 59, 81, 148, 152, 227n5, 228n12, 231n20
Ray, Jean 37, 227n3, 228n36
Ray, Satyajit 27
Referendum *see* sovereignty
Refus global 19
Reid, Malcolm 16
Requiem 37
Resnick, Philip 186
revanche des berceaux 18, 103, 132, 158, 202, 207
Richter, Payton 120
Rieder, John 211
Riel, Louis 18, 144
Rimbaud, Jean-Arthur 232n25
RIN (Rassemblement pour l'Indépendance Nationale) 20
Ringuet 65
Robert, Lucie 20
Roberts, Adam 218
Roberval 144
Robin, Régine 23, 161–62, 189, 200, 224n15
Robinson, Eden 27
Robinson, Kim Stanley 25, 26, 42, 133, 211
Roby, Daniel 229n21
Rochon, Esther 3, 31, 37, 38, 39, 41, 42, 45, 46, 47, 56, 61, 66–81, 84, 86, 96, 97, 99, 100, 101, 108, 115, 117, 118, 119, 120, 121, 122, 124, 125, 137, 138–70, 171, 175, 177, 180, 183, 187, 195, 196, 197, 199, 208, 210, 227n5, 229n24, 229n4, 230n7–8, 232n5, 233n10–12, 233n16; *Aboli* 150–51, 153, 159–60, 233n13; *L'Aigle des profondeurs* 69–73, 80, 196, 229n5; *L'Archipel Noir* 69, 71, 73, 74–78, 146, 196, 229n5; *Les Chroniques infernales* 3, 42, 46, 67, 119, 124, 139, 148–70, 180, 195, 197–99, 233n12–13; *Coquillage* 46, 68, 137; *Le Cycle de Vrénalik* 3, 42, 46, 61, 66–81, 86, 97, 99, 118–19, 124, 138–48, 153–54, 157, 159, 160, 169, 187, 195–98, 229–30n5; *L'Dragonne de l'aurore* 230n5; *L'Épuisement du soleil* 39, 69, 138, 230n5, 230n7; *L'Espace du diamant* 74, 138–48, 170, 196–97, 229n4, 230n5–6, 232n5; *Lame* 148, 150, 159–60, 162–63, 233n13; *Or* 152–53, 157, 160, 164–68, 233n13; *Ouverture* 163, 168, 233n13; *Le Rêveur dans la Citadelle* 69, 79, 81, 140, 229n5, 230n7; *Secrets* 150, 155, 157, 160, 163, 180, 233n13; *Sorbier* 150, 160, 163, 169, 198, 233n13
roman de contestation 65, 88
roman mémoriel 162
roman de mœurs urbaines 65, 70–71, 76, 78, 79, 88, 98, 108
roman du terroir 18, 35, 65
roman psychologique 65, 86–89, 230n13
Roy, Gabrielle 36, 65
Rushdie, Salman 26, 216
Russ, Joanna 54

Sadoul, Jacques 218
Saga: Icelandic 61, 122; SFQ 61, 63, 64, 66, 69, 79, 80, 81, 85, 86, 96, 98, 99, 114, 115, 117, 119–25, 135–36, 141, 148–49, 157, 165, 169, 172–73, 175, 176, 177, 178, 180–81, 183, 189, 190–91, 194–95, 196–97, 199–200, 202, 204, 207, 230n13, 232n1
Said, Edward 1, 2, 7, 13, 25, 62, 83, 224n9, 229n3
Saint Lawrence 9, 50
Saint-Gelais, Richard 47, 227n6
Saint-Jean Baptiste, Société de 18
Salter, Denis 214
Sand, George 36
Santoro, Milena 138, 143, 147, 195
Sargent, Lyman Tower 121, 126, 147
Sargisson, Lucy 122, 126, 153, 154, 180
Sarra-Bournet, Michel 16, 186
Satyendra, Nadesan 224n14
Sauble-Otto, Lorie 56, 100, 171
Sauvé, Clodomir 37
Scholes, Robert 46
science fiction (SF) 1–2, 5–8, 10, 42, 47, 60–64, 67, 74, 93, 115, 139, 148, 154, 159, 171, 197, 209; Anglo-American 6, 33–34, 35–36, 39, 45, 47, 140, 171–72, 189; Anglo-Canadian 31, 39, 45, 182; and the postcolonial 24–31, 62–64, 200; theory 7, 61–62; utopia and 120, 136, 139; *see also* SFQ
Science Fiction Research Association 226n25, 226n27, 232n1
Second World 14, 214
Second-Cup Café bombing 22
semiotics 12
Senécal, Patrick 4, 41, 44, 229n21
Senegal 20, 230n14
Senghor, Léopold Sédar 20
Sernine, Daniel 27, 36, 37, 38, 40, 41, 42, 43, 52, 53, 85, 118, 119, 137, 182, 227n2, 227n7, 228n9, 229n4, 230n8, 230n13, 232n8

Index

Serruys, Nicholas 4, 27, 54–55, 195, 211, 227n5, 228n12, 228n18, 232n28
Sévigny, Marc 50, 51, 54
SFQ (science fiction from Québec) 1–4, 6–8, 10–11, 15, 18, 22, 27, 31, 33–59, 60–66, 69, 77, 81, 84, 99, 100–01, 106, 118, 131, 138, 140, 158–59, 182, 188, 194, 195, 208, 210–11, 223n5, 224n11, 216, 227n28, 227n5, 228n11, 228n18, 229n20, 230n8, 231n24, 232n29, 232n4, 234n2
Shakespeare, William 168–69, 179, 207
Shelley, Mary W. 2, 30
Shohat, Ella 224n10
Shonku, Professor 27
Siebers, Tobin 122
Simmons, Dan 28
Simon, Sherry 143, 160, 182, 187, 188, 198
Singh, Vandana 27
Sirois, Guy 50
Six Brumes 41
Skinner, B. F. 121
Slemon, Stephen 7, 13, 14, 224n9, 224n14
slipstream 226n25, 228n10
Sloan, Thomas 19
Smith, M. G. 183
Söderlind, Sylvia 14, 23, 119, 142, 161, 162, 231n18
Solaris (Québec) 4, 37, 38, 44, 45, 85, 137, 228n14, 230n8; *see also* Lem, Stanislaw
Somain, Jean-François 38, 39; *see also* Somcynsky, Jean-François
Somay, Bülent 119, 120, 121
Somcynsky, Jean-François 38, 39; *see also* Somain, Jean-François
South Africa 163
sovereignty, Canada 15, 19, 22, 225n16
sovereignty, Québec 16, 39, 47, 82, 121, 143, 159, 185, 187; 1980 Referendum on sovereignty-association 9, 20, 21, 78, 160, 187; 1995 Referendum on 29, 2, 113, 118, 148, 185
Soyinka, Wole 13, 60
"Speak White" 20, 209
Spehner, Norbert 37, 38, 39, 52, 228n18
Spivak, Gayatri Chakravorty 1–3, 13, 62, 64, 82, 224n9, 229n3, 233n14
Stephenson, Robert Louis 231n23
Sterling, Bruce 226n25, 228n10
Stern, Daniel *see* Marie d'Agoult
Stockwell, Peter 227n30
Stoddard, Eve Walsh 183, 188
subaltern 149, 154, 156, 157, 233n14
Suleri, Sara 25
Suvin, Darko 7, 30, 62–63, 119–22, 125–26, 129, 135–36, 139, 141, 147, 150, 169–72, 174, 178, 229n2, 233n22
Swift, Jonathan 30
syncretism 27, 57, 147, 195, 196, 204

Tagore, Rabindranath 83
Tardivel, Jules-Paul 34, 54
Taylor, Charles 16, 183, 186, 196, 201
Taylor, Keith 121
Taylor, Sharon 55, 100, 138, 139, 145, 147, 160, 171
The Tempest 168–69, 179
Tepes, Vlad 149
terraforming 7, 159
Tesseracts 31, 39, 49, 56, 232n27
Tessier, Éric 229n21
Tessier, Mario 45
Tétreau, Jean 37
Texas 9, 120
Thériault, Yves 35, 37, 65, 88, 234n4
Third Reich 58, 126
Third World 1, 10, 12, 14, 15, 24, 25, 30, 92
Thomas, Sheree R. 27
Tiffin, Helen 6, 7, 10, 11, 13, 14, 231n18
Todorov, Tzvetan 223n4
Touraine, Alain 121
transculturalism 185, 186, 199
Tremblay, Michel 36–37, 43, 224n13, 228n11
Trinidad 183, 184
Trottier, Pierre 223
Trudeau, Pierre Elliot 9, 15, 21, 22, 184, 225n16
Trudel, Jean-Louis 4, 27, 33, 34, 35, 38, 43, 45, 49, 51, 54, 57, 58, 81, 223n5, 227n2, 227n6, 228n12, 229n19, 230n11, 231n20
Trungpa, Chögyam 162, 197
Truth and Reconciliation Commissions 163
Turgeon, Pierre 223
2001: A Space Odyssey 36
Tyranaël 3, 42, 55, 61, 84, 99–117, 118, 124, 133, 167, 169, 170–77, 178, 179, 180, 190, 199, 200, 201, 202, 205, 206, 207, 208, 224n15, 229n24, 231n19, 231n21–24, 232n26–29, 233n19

The Uncanny 7, 63
unhomely 7, 63
United Kingdom 1, 7, 42; *see also* Great Britain
United States 1, 6, 7, 8, 9, 10, 14, 15, 19, 25, 27, 28, 29, 33, 34, 36, 39, 40, 42, 73, 78, 79, 97, 112, 166, 183, 184, 185, 193, 224n16, 225n19, 227n29–30
utopia 3, 25, 27, 30, 54–56, 61, 67, 118–81, 197, 227n5, 232n1, 233n21

Vadeboncoeur, Pierre 225n20, 233n9
Vadim, Roger 36
Vallières, Pierre 2, 20, 118, 127, 226n24
van Belkom, Edo 100, 101
Vasconcelos, José 190, 192, 193, 194, 205
Vautier, Marie 10, 14, 23, 83, 119, 120, 125, 129, 131, 136, 142, 149, 159, 160, 165, 168, 172, 225–26n20, 232n2
Vents d'Ouest 41
Verfremdungseffekt 7, 62–63
Vial, Éric 178
Vierne, Simone 100
Vigneault, Gilles 233n9
von Flotow, Luise 224n13
Vonarburg, Élisabeth 3, 4, 33, 38, 41, 42, 45,

46, 47, 52, 53, 54, 55, 61, 66, 68, 69, 70, 81, 84, 99–117, 118–19, 120, 121, 122, 124, 125, 133, 138, 167, 169, 170–80, 183, 190, 199–209, 210, 224n12, 224n15, 228n18, 229n24, 230n8, 231n19, 232n26–28, 234n6; *L'Autre rivage* 104, 107–08, 116, 173–74, 177, 203, 206, 231n19, 233n19; *Chroniques du pays des Mères* see *In the Mother's Land*, below; *Dreams of the Sea* 42, 55–56, 102–04, 108, 118, 172–75, 200, 224n15, 231n19, 231n21, 233n19; *A Game of Perfection* 42, 56, 104–05, 109, 110–11, 116, 175–76, 201, 202, 204, 231n19, 233n19; *In the Mother's Land* 42, 53, 55, 100, 138, 171, 207; *Jeu de la perfection* see *A Game of Perfection*, above; *La Mer allée avec le soleil* 104, 177, 200, 204, 206–07, 231n19, 231n24, 233n19; *Reine de Mémoire* 3, 42, 100, 119, 124, 170, 171, 172, 177–80; *Reluctant Voyagers* 42, 100–01, 171, 178; *The Silent City* 42, 55, 100, 138, 171, 231n24; *Voyageurs malgré eux* see *Reluctant Voyagers*, above
Vor-Schein 172–73
Vrénalik Cycle 69

Wallerstein, Immanuel 15
Watson, Greer 35, 227–28n7
Weber, Eugen 123

Wegner, Philip E. 126, 180
Weibel, Peter 231n16
Weinmann, Heinz 228n18
Wells, H. G. 26, 53
White Niggers of America 2, 19–20, 21, 60, 118
Wiebe, Rudy 120
Wiemer, Annegret 126
Willett, John 62
Williams, Patrick 8
Wilson, Richard A. 163
Wittig, Monique 55
Wolfe 17, 45, 166
Wollheim, Donald A. 27–28, 228n8
World Science Fiction Convention 34
World War I 18, 34, 123
World War II 27, 35, 64, 83
Wyndham, John 26

Yeager, Jack 224n13
Young, Robert J. C. 188, 207, 224n9
young adult literature 35

Zamiatin, Yevgeny 123
Zimbabwe 26
Zipes, Jack 143

www.ingramcontent.com/pod-product-compliance
Lightning Source LLC
Chambersburg PA
CBHW051213300426
44116CB00006B/557